My God, you did not look at my past, you did not stop before my weakness; in one hand you placed the rosary, in the other a pen, and you said to me: "Write, they will listen to you, for it is I who will place in your heart the word of life."

~ Blessed Bartolo Longo

Rev. Andrew J. Middleton—Carl
August 12, 2011

CHAMPIONS
OF THE ROSARY

The History and Heroes of a Spiritual Weapon

Donald H. Calloway, MIC

Available from:
Marian Helpers Center
Stockbridge, MA 01263

Prayerline: 1-800-804-3823
Orderline: 1-800-462-7426
Websites: fathercalloway.com
marian.org

Publication Date:
August 8, 2016. Memorial of St. Dominic.
In Honor of the 800th Anniversary of the Founding of the Dominicans (1216–2016)

Imprimi Potest:
Very Rev. Kazimierz Chwalek, MIC
Provincial Superior
The Blessed Virgin Mary, Mother of Mercy Province
May 31, 2016

Nihil Obstat:
Dr. Robert A. Stackpole, STD
Censor Deputatis
May 31, 2016

Library of Congress Catalog Number: 2016907907
ISBN: 978-1-59614-343-2

Cover Image: The shield insignia is a modified version of a design created by
Fr. Richard Heilman for the Holy League organization. With the permission of
Fr. Heilman, Fr. Calloway commissioned Jordan Barry of JB Guardian Graphics, LLC
to modify the shield insignia for *Champions of the Rosary*.
www.JPGuardianGraphics.com

Cover design and inside pages layout by Kathy Szpak

Editing and Proofreading: Michelle Buckman, Chris Sparks, Robert Stackpole, STD,
Joan Lamar, Andy Leeco

Acknowledgments: Marian Fathers of the Immaculate Conception,
Mr. and Mrs. Donald & LaChita Calloway, Matthew T. Calloway,
Ileana E. Salazar, Teresa de Jesus Macias, Milanka Lachman, Bethany Price

Printed in the United States of America

MARIAN PRESS
STOCKBRIDGE MA 01263
PRO CHRISTO ET ECCLESIA

Dedicated to:

Ileana E. Salazar
Daughter of God, Champion of the Rosary, Dearest Friend.
I am forever grateful to Jesus, Mary,
St. Joseph, and St. Philomena for the gift of your friendship.

Faithful friends are a sturdy shelter:
he who finds one has found a treasure.
Faithful friends are beyond price;
no amount can balance their worth.
Faithful friends are life-saving remedies;
and those who fear the Lord will find them.

~ Sirach 6:14-16

The Mother of God, the Virgin most powerful, who in times past co-operated in charity that the faithful might be born in the Church, is now the intermediary, the Mediatrix of our salvation. May she shatter and strike off the multiple heads of the wicked hydra.

~ Pope Leo XIII

Let victory be thine, O Mother. Thou wilt conquer. Yes, thou hast the power to overcome all heresies, errors, and vice. And, I, confident in your powerful protection, will engage in the battle, not only against flesh and blood, but against the prince of darkness, as the Apostle [Paul] says, grasping the shield of the holy rosary and armed with the double-edged sword of the divine word.

~ St. Anthony Mary Claret

ENDORSEMENTS FROM DOMINICANS

What a joy to read these pages where the Dominican Order is so present! As Dominicans around the world celebrate the 800th anniversary of our foundation (1216–2016), the Order of Preachers and all members of the Dominican family are ardently striving to renew and intensify our tradition of promoting the rosary. It is my hope that *Champions of the Rosary* will strengthen our resolve and also awaken everywhere fervent and enthusiastic apostles of the rosary for our times.

Very Rev. Bruno Cadoré, OP
Master General of the Order of Preachers
Rome, Italy

Champions of the Rosary is an encyclopedic and inspiring work on the rosary, the spiritual weapon that has been given to the Church. In a remarkable way, it presents the fascinating saga of the birth and development of the devotion so linked to the Dominican Order! This is a wonderful tool for better understanding the rosary, promoting its use, and championing it in our troubled world. I am certain that these pages will inspire us all to take up our rosary!

Fr. Louis-Marie Ariño-Durand, OP
Promotor Generalis pro Rosario
Rome, Italy

Champions of the Rosary is an extremely insightful, pious, and scholarly work on the rosary. Father Calloway's insights and contributions into the history and heroes of the rosary will not go unnoticed or unappreciated.

His Eminence Christoph Maria Cardinal Schönborn, OP, STD
Archbishop of Vienna, Austria

In *Champions of the Rosary*, Fr. Calloway has written what is probably the most comprehensive book ever written on the rosary. The author deftly negotiates the complexities of the story of the rosary, weaving the historical, theological, and devotional strands into a veritable masterpiece of scholarship and piety. This book should turn every one of its readers into a champion of the rosary.

Most Rev. J. Augustine Di Noia, OP, PhD
Assistant Secretary of the Congregation for the Doctrine of the Faith
Vatican City

With his *Champions of the Rosary*, Fr. Calloway has done the world a great service. This book is a Mariological *tour de force*, containing an extensive history of the rosary, accounts of the lives and writings of 26 champions of the rosary, and tips on why and how the rosary should be prayed. Would that every family would obtain and read this remarkable book and then pray the rosary every day. The rosary is indeed the spiritual sword so needed in our time.

Most Rev. Anthony C. Fisher, OP, DD, DPhil
Archbishop of Sydney, Australia

Champions of the Rosary is the fruit of much prayer, extensive historical research, and solid theology. Father Calloway's writing is inspiring, easy to read, and gives great glory to God. This book is a masterpiece of Mariology!

Most Rev. Socrates B. Villegas, OP, DD
Archbishop of Lingayen-Dagupan, Philippines,
and President of the Catholic Bishops' Conference of the Philippines

The rosary is a rich part of the Dominican heritage, and as a Dominican bishop, I welcome this work of Fr. Calloway. *Champions of the Rosary* is historical, inspiring, well-researched, and provides its readers with a profound understanding of the rosary. Today, we need prayer warriors on the spiritual battlefield, armed with the powerful spiritual weapon of the rosary!

Most Rev. Robert Rivas, OP, DD
Archbishop of Castries, St. Lucia

It is with great joy that I endorse this beautiful book by Fr. Calloway, published during the 800th anniversary of the founding of the Order of Preachers. May these pages help us more deeply appreciate the rosary as a means of prayer, contemplation, and preaching. Whether in the United States, Italy, Mexico, the Philippines, Vietnam, Nigeria, Argentina, or any other country in the world, may the rosary be championed!

Most Rev. Carlos Alfonso Azpiroz Costa, OP, JCD
Archbishop Coadjutor of Bahía Blanca, Argentina,
and former Master General of the Order of Preachers

Father Calloway has written a book on the rosary whose profundity and scholarship is unquestionable. *Champions of the Rosary* not only offers a clear presentation of the history of the rosary, but also a clarion call for everyone to enlist as a soldier in the army of the Queen of the Rosary. We are in a new and most dangerous spiritual battle, making the Lepanto of old appear elementary. To fight the Lepanto of our times, we need to once again be reminded that the rosary is a spiritual weapon. Only then will we be able to conquer and banish the culture of death, the modern attacks against the Church and her teachings, and the diabolical agents who raise their weapons against Christ and his Cross. This book has been put into our hands so that we might understand the spiritual power of the sword of Mary. All that is left for us is to wield it!

Most Rev. Ayo-Maria Atoyebi, OP, DD
Bishop of Ilorin, Nigeria

In *Champions of the Rosary*, Fr. Calloway provides us with a splendid historical and theological background to the beautiful prayer of the rosary. May this work help those who read it to increase their love for our Blessed Mother.

Most Rev. Vincent Darius, OP, DD
Bishop of St. George, Grenada

As a Dominican missionary and bishop in the Solomon Islands, I can enthusiastically state that the rosary has been one of the main tools used in my evangelization efforts. Our youth, in particular, have fully embraced the rosary and are diligently praying it. They understand it to be their "mobile phone" that connects them to heaven. *Champions of the Rosary* is a wonderful and blessed book that will most certainly encourage millions to draw closer to Jesus and Mary through the rosary!

Most Rev. Christopher M. Cardone, OP, DD
Bishop of Auki, Solomon Islands

For those who desire to learn what the rosary is and where it originated, *Champions of the Rosary* will greatly enlighten them. The wisdom of the saints and popes presented in these pages is tremendous, and I admire the research and prayer that went into producing this fascinating work.

Most Rev. George A. Frendo, OP, DD
Auxiliary Bishop of Tiranë-Durrës, Albania

In the lives of individuals and communities, periods of growth, stagnation, and decline are always present. In Slovakia, during the socialist era, religion was persecuted and its public expressions were repressed. Yet it was during that difficult time that the people turned to the rosary as a mainstay of the faith. *Champions of the Rosary* tells the story of the rosary in many such instances, offering its readers the complete history of the rosary's glory, seeming oblivion, ongoing developments, and championing heroes. This book teaches us that the rosary is a permanent support of the Church's faith and is here to stay!

Very Rev. Reginald Adrián Slavkovský, OP, PhD
Prior Provincial of the Slovakian Province
Zvolen, Slovakia

Champions of the Rosary is a masterpiece and an immense treasure for the Church. It will be difficult for one to go through these pages without falling in love with the sublime devotion of the rosary. This exhaustive presentation is a gift for generations to come!

Very Rev. Charles E. Ukwe, OP, JCD
Prior Provincial of the Province of St. Joseph the Worker
Nigeria and Ghana, Africa

Champions in the Rosary provides an excellent history of the rosary and is a great resource for encouraging greater devotion to Our Lady and her spiritual weapon. May we all imitate the heroes presented in this book by championing this beautiful devotion!

Very Rev. Mark C. Padrez, OP
Prior Provincial of the Province of the Most Holy Name of Jesus
Oakland, California

In *Champions of the Rosary*, Fr. Calloway has written a most complete history of the rosary. For Dominicans, who have been so connected with the origin of the rosary, the publication of this book perfectly coincides with the celebration of the 800th anniversary of the foundation of the Order. This book will serve to renew our devotion to the rosary!

Very Rev. Kevin Saunders, OP
Prior Provincial of the Province of the Assumption of the Blessed Virgin Mary
Camberwell, Australia

In this magnum opus, Fr. Calloway joins the ranks of the great preachers and promoters of the Psalter of the Blessed Virgin, the rosary. He stands with the giants, especially Alan de la Roche and Louis-Marie Grignion de Montfort, in this beautiful historical and spiritual treatise. *Champions of the Rosary* is probably the greatest book written on the rosary in centuries. This book is worthy of every Dominican library and is a tool which reminds the Dominican Family of its marvelous heritage and the treasure of the rosary entrusted to our father Dominic. The Order of Preachers is in debt to Fr. Calloway, and I encourage all Rosarians of the Rosary Confraternity, as well as all the faithful, to drink deeply of this work, for it breathes forth the truth of Christ Jesus contemplated through the eyes of Mary.

Very Rev. John H. Walsh, OP
Prior and Promoter of the Rosary Apostolate and Confraternity
Dundalk, Ireland

Champions of the Rosary is the most carefully researched book on the rosary I have ever encountered. It is remarkably accessible and the content in these pages will help all of us become champions of the rosary.

Very Rev. Reginald Martin, OP
Prior of St. Albert Priory and Director of the Rosary Center
Oakland, California

Champions of the Rosary is incredible and I loved it! It clearly explains how the rosary was fashioned to be a weapon and why Mary's intercession is so important in overcoming evil. It provides many examples from history of how Our Lady and her biblically based prayer have been instrumental in obtaining graces from her divine Son. An excellent read!

Very Rev. Jordan Turano, OP
Prior of St. Vincent Ferrer Priory
New York, New York

This is a monumental and inspiring work that greatly enriches the landscape of the rosary. It is a scholarly work that betokens much research and loving attention to detail. Yet it is an eminently readable book that keeps the reader turning the pages to reveal the next thrilling episode in the long saga of the rosary. *Champions of the Rosary* is a treasure trove of information and is no doubt destined to become a classic. I believe that generations to come will give thanks that so much treasure of the past has been collected and handed on to those who love the rosary.

Fr. Gabriel Harty, OP
The Rosary Priest of Ireland

Champions of the Rosary is so comprehensive, attractive, and readable that one cannot help but love the rosary more. The passion and labor that one perceives in this book is a testament to the piety of the author. It is a work that is carefully documented and spiritually infectious. The Dominican Family will take great delight in it, and every Catholic home should have a copy!

Fr. Oluyemi E. Taiwo, OP
Promoter of Lay Dominicans and the Dominican Family
Ibadan, Nigeria

Without a doubt, *Champions of the Rosary* is the most profound work ever written on the rosary. It presents the history of the rosary in its entirety, from the original preached form employed by St. Dominic to the method prayed throughout the world today. I commend Fr. Calloway for this beautiful presentation.

Fr. José Filipe da Costa Rodrigues, OP
President – International Liturgical Commission of the Order of Preachers
Lisbon, Portugal

Champions of the Rosary is a wonderful and comprehensive *summa* of the rosary of the Mother of God. I am sure that it will help everyone, from newcomer to those already devoted to the rosary, to secure the graces unleashed by this powerful devotion.

Fr. Nicanor Pier Giorgio Austriaco, OP, PhD, STD
Associate Professor of Biology
Providence College, Rhode Island

A comprehensive and enthralling historical survey of the origins and development of the rosary, *Champions of the Rosary* provides in a single accessible work a panoramic sweep of the history of the spiritual weapon that is the rosary. In this book, Marian piety and solid historical analyses are delicately intertwined and this work will, like the rosary, stand the test of time!

Fr. Thomas Azzi OP
Promoter of Vocations, Province of the Assumption of the Blessed Virgin Mary
Sydney, Australia

It is widely known that those who pray the rosary are close to Jesus and Mary. As the promoter of Dominican vocations in Bolivia, the rosary makes up an essential part of my ministry. I highly recommend *Champions of the Rosary* because it will help people draw closer to Jesus and Mary.

Fr. Aldo Torrez Roca, OP
Vice Province Vocation Director
Santa Cruz de la Sierra, Bolivia

Champions of the Rosary is an historical and theological compendium of the rosary for the people of the 21st century. This book will inspire many to take up that wondrous sword of faith that is the rosary of Our Lady.

Fr. Augustine Agwulonu, OP, PhD
Dominican Institute
Ibadan, Nigeria

A masterful blend of scholarly erudition and popular appeal, *Champions of the Rosary* is a veritable *Summa* on the rosary. As a Dominican, I commend Fr. Calloway for affirming St. Dominic's role in founding and propagating the rosary. If the rosary is a "compendium of the Gospel," then this book is a compendium of everything there is to know about the rosary.

Br. Marwil N. Llasos, OP, JD
Author, *Defending Mary, Our Mother*
Manila, Philippines

Like the rosary which it champions, *Champions of the Rosary* is both "a weapon and a rose," ably confronting common objections while honoring God's providential and merciful love for his own. Readers will encounter this love as they see the life of the rosary unfold, from its origin in the mind of God through the weak but willing hands of its champions. It is evident that Fr. Calloway has written this book not merely about, but through the power of the rosary.

Sr. Anna Wray, OP
Dominican Sisters of St. Cecilia
Nashville, Tennessee

Champions of the Rosary is like the rosary itself: simple yet profound, sharp as a sword but also as gentle as our spiritual mother. It is filled with hope and reminds us that our security lies in the rosary of Our Lady. Dominicans have been waiting for a book like this for a very long time!

Sr. Barbara Bagudić, OP
Dominican Sisters of the Guardian Angels
Dubrovnik, Croatia

CHAMPIONS OF THE ROSARY

The History and Heroes of a Spiritual Weapon

INTRODUCTION

Dear reader, I promise you that if you practice this devotion [the rosary] and help to spread it you will learn more from the rosary than from any spiritual book. And what is more, you will have the happiness of being rewarded by Our Lady in accordance with the promises that she made to Saint Dominic, to Blessed Alan de la Roche and to all those who practice and encourage this devotion which is so dear to her. For the holy rosary teaches people about the virtues of Jesus and Mary, and leads them to mental prayer and to imitate Our Lord and Savior Jesus Christ. It teaches them to approach the Sacraments often, to genuinely strive after Christian virtues and to do all kinds of good works, as well as interesting them in the many wonderful indulgences which can be gained through the rosary.[1]

The words above are not mine. They are taken from the greatest book ever written on the rosary, *The Secret of the Rosary* by St. Louis de Montfort. Written in the early 18th century, it has been the single most influential book on the rosary ever published. "Then why write another book on the rosary?" you might ask.

Here's the reason: In his day, St. Louis de Montfort wrote *The Secret of the Rosary* to teach people about the history and power of the rosary. As an itinerant preacher and Third Order Dominican, he loved the rosary and used it as a spiritual sword to combat the many theological errors in circulation in his time. The rosary was his sword, catechetical tool, and secret for re-evangelizing fallen away Catholics. It had — and still has — the power to bring souls back to Christ and his Church. Today, we find ourselves confronting a similar situation. The world is fraught with immorality and darkness, and in need of being re-evangelized. The story of the rosary needs to be told again in all its wonder for the people of our times. People today need to know about the weapon capable of combating and conquering immorality and evil. I have written *Champions of the Rosary* to recap and pick up where St. Louis de Montfort left off. Three centuries have gone by since St. Louis de Montfort penned his monumental work, and many things have taken place. Many miracles, victories, conversions, developments, discoveries, and champions of the rosary need to be added to the story of the sword for the people of our times. Trust me: I know firsthand how the rosary can help a soul convert. Allow me to explain what the rosary did for me years ago.

When I first encountered the rosary, I was a sick man — sick in my heart and sick in my soul. I had been living a very immoral life, to the point where I had to drop out of high school. I was worldly, hedonistic, and without hope of ever changing. My life was so out of control that at the age of 15, I was forcibly removed from the country of Japan due to my criminal activity. (My step-father was a naval officer at the time). After being deported from Japan, my life of crime and sin continued. I did two stints in drug rehabilitation centers in Pennsylvania and was thrown in jail in Louisiana as soon as I turned 18. By the age of 20, I was completely lost and at the point of taking my own life. I was about as far away from God as a person can get. In fact, I hated anything religious, especially anything to do with Jesus and the Catholic Church.

But one night in 1992, I picked up a book that my parents, who had recently converted to Catholicism, had purchased and left on their bookshelf. The book was about a beautiful woman named Mary. It alleged that she was coming from a place called heaven with a message of love, mercy, and conversion. I had no idea who Mary was or what a Marian apparition was, but the message intrigued me, and I stayed up all night reading it. The contents of that book hit my foul soul like a divine two-by-four, so I went to a Catholic church the very next day to find a priest and get some answers. That visit was the first time I had ever been inside a Catholic Church. It was also the first time I encountered the rosary.

I remember creeping into the small military chapel of Our Lady of Victory on Norfolk Naval Base in Norfolk, Virginia. I entered with fear and trembling, fully aware that I was no friend of God. I intentionally sank down as low as I could in the last pew in order to avoid eye contact with the only other people in the chapel: the five Filipino women up front. Then I witnessed something bizarre. Each of the ladies pulled something out of their purse resembling a necklace. I had no idea what it was or what they were going to do with it, but within a few seconds they were using it and saying words I had never heard before. Due to their thick Filipino accents, I couldn't entirely make out what they were saying, but it went something like this: "Hail Mary, something, something ... Jesus," followed by "Holy Mary, something, something ... death. Amen."

Next, and to my total surprise, the apparent leader turned around and looked at me, the longhaired hippie sitting in the back. She jingled her necklace at me and asked me to pray the next decade. "What? A decade! Are you kidding me?" I thought to myself. For me, a *decade* meant one thing – 10 years! I was clueless and confused, and, seeing the bewildered expression on my face, the kind Filipino lady offered a clarification. "The Second Sorrowful Mystery," she said. My reaction to her was complete silence. The clarification didn't help me understand what she was trying to communicate to me. I had absolutely no idea what this woman was up to by jingling her necklace at me and asking me to pray for 10 years. Needless to say, they carried on without me.

Though I didn't join them that day, it didn't take long for me to be told what they were doing. The priest I talked to told me the ladies prayed the rosary before Mass every day. I remembered a diagram of something called the rosary in that book about Mary, but I hadn't known what it was at the time. Well, within a matter of days, the Filipino women took me under their care and taught me how to pray it. I was completely fascinated. Before long, I had all the prayers and mysteries memorized and was leading it, turning to others and inviting them to pray the next decade. I began to carry those little beads in my pocket wherever I went. That little 20-minute prayer helped me fall madly in love with Jesus and Catholicism. The rosary helped me turn from a life of sin to a life of freedom. It gave me the courage to surrender my heart, mind, and soul completely to Jesus and his Church. The Virgin Mary and her rosary saved my life.

Skip forward many years, and now I'm a Catholic priest. I continue to pray the rosary every day. It's my daily companion and is *always* in my pocket. I don't go anywhere without it. After all these years, I'm still intrigued by the fact that I first encountered the rosary and was conquered by it in a naval chapel dedicated to Our Lady of Victory. Those facts might seem insignificant to most people, but once a person knows the history of the rosary, their significance truly stands out. At the time, I was completely unaware that the greatest triumph of the rosary occurred at a naval battle, and that the title given to Mary to commemorate that rosary triumph was Our Lady of Victory.

The above explains why I have such a passion for the rosary. I simply love it. I love it so much that for years I begged Our Lady to give me insights into the mystery of the rosary so that through my preaching I could touch hearts and help people fall in love with Jesus and his Church. I specifically asked her to reveal to me what makes the rosary so powerful and how its origins are to be understood. After much prayer, many novenas, and countless hours before the Blessed Sacrament, I believe the Queen of Heaven has led me to the three "keys" necessary for unlocking the history and power of the rosary.

The first key is to understand the rosary as a *spiritual sword* made by God, the Divine Craftsman. This key unlocks the mystery of what the rosary is, why it has so much power, and why the devil constantly seeks to destroy it. Satan does not have a sword of equal power, and because he is jealous of the rosary, he ceaselessly attempts to strip it out of the hands of God's children. As history will prove, the ancient serpent will entice people to neglect the rosary, cause entire nations to forbid it, and repeatedly get historians and theologians to deny its heavenly origins. Lucifer knows that the sword of the rosary has the power to slay him, and he hates it. Nevertheless, as you will read in these pages, the sword of the rosary can be neglected, forbidden, forgotten, insulted, belittled, and even buried, but it can never be destroyed! It was made by God!

The second key is to respect and defend what is called the *pious tradition*. The pious tradition is the papal belief that the rosary and its Confraternity were founded by St. Dominic in the 13th century. This tradition has been affirmed by dozens of popes in official documents and, in a certain sense, is not only considered a pious tradition but also a papal tradition and teaching. This key unlocks the mystery of the divine origins of the sword. While it is true that popes are only infallible in matters of faith and morals and not in matters of history, the fact that so many popes have affirmed the pious tradition gives the tradition great weight. To date, no pope has ever taught a history of the rosary that has gone against the pious tradition.

The third key is to appreciate the *antecedents and developments* that have occurred in the history of the rosary. This key unlocks the mystery of the human origins of the sword, revealing the Divine Craftsman worked through the Church in putting the sword together and that the rosary is capable of further development. The blade will always need to be re-sharpened throughout history.

The format and content of *Champions of the Rosary* is very simple. The book is divided into three parts. The first part presents an in-depth and thoroughly researched history of the rosary. This aspect of the book took years to write and is the fruit of intense historical study. However, in an attempt to present a smooth and hopefully edifying read, I omitted academic citations that could potentially clutter the text. When citations and endnotes are required, they are provided. If you are not interested in the detailed history of the rosary, feel free to skip to the second part of the book.

The second part of the book presents 26 champions of the rosary. Although countless numbers of men and women have championed the rosary throughout history, I limited the text to 26 because I discovered that these particular champions wrote about the rosary or made beautiful statements about it, thereby providing "rosary gems" for our edification. Trust me: When I was putting this section together, it was hard to stop at only 26 champions. Even St. John Paul II once remarked: "It would be impossible to name all the many saints who discovered in the rosary a genuine path to growth in holiness."[2] Personally, I find it inspiring that many of the champions have been popes.

Finally, in the third part of the book, I present information on praying the rosary. It would be a mistake to assume that everyone reading this book already knows how to pray the rosary or is familiar with many of the things associated with it. Therefore, in this section, I provide reasons for praying the rosary, a diagram of how to pray the rosary, a list of all the mysteries, practical ways on how to become a champion of the rosary, the 15 promises made by Our Lady to those who pray the rosary, and a section describing the indulgences attached to the rosary. Concluding the book are two appendices that present beautiful artwork on the rosary, as well as a lengthy statement that Our Lady made to Blessed Alan de la Roche on the rosary.

My greatest desire is that those who read this book will be inspired to want to pray the rosary daily and further the cause of Jesus Christ and his saving mysteries. Our world needs the rosary today more than ever. Every person who reads this book is capable of wielding this sword and becoming a champion of the rosary.

Very Rev. Donald H. Calloway, MIC, STL
Vicar Provincial — Marian Fathers of the Immaculate Conception
The Blessed Virgin Mary, Mother of Mercy Province

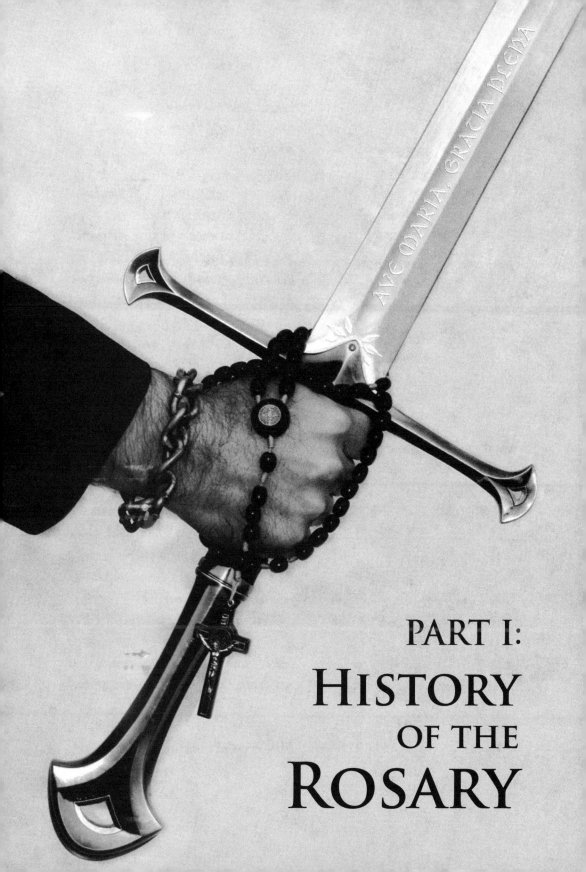

PART I:
HISTORY
OF THE
ROSARY

The rosary is a spiritual weapon, a heavenly sword, fashioned by the hands of a Divine Craftsman. All swords take time and skill to make, but this heavenly sword required the greatest of efforts — centuries — to produce. It is a weapon unlike any other. It has the power to slay dragons, convert sinners, and conquer hearts. The blade of this sword was forged in the fire of the living Word of God, shaped by the hammer of divine inspiration, and entrusted to the Queen of Heaven and her chosen servants.

When the weapon was finally battle-ready and the time set for the Divine Craftsman to unsheathe its power, the Queen of Heaven, the Blessed Virgin Mary, revealed it to the world and chose a zealous preacher to be its founder. She knighted him with the divine weapon and commissioned him to preach it far and wide.

From this holy man an Order of Preachers would be formed to champion the weapon with its mysteries and hand on the sword to all who desire to wield it. These chosen souls are known throughout history as champions of the rosary.

Here begins the story of the making of the rosary and its champions ...

FROM THE
ANGELIC SALUTATION
TO THE 12TH CENTURY:
The Antecedents of the Rosary

God has established that the bookends of history involve a woman and her offspring conquering and crushing a serpent dragon (see Gen 3:15; Rev 12). The woman is the Blessed Virgin Mary. Her offspring is Jesus Christ, the Savior of the world. The serpent dragon is Lucifer.

As in any battle, victory comes through a weapon. The weapon through which this battle is won and the serpent dragon defeated is the Paschal Mystery of the God-Man, Jesus Christ. The sacred mysteries of his life, death, and resurrection have the power to conquer evil and set souls free. They are spiritual weapons through which death is conquered, Lucifer vanquished, and trusting souls given eternal life in the kingdom of heaven.

Without the Virgin Mary, we would not have these mysteries. In God's kingdom, Mary is not only the mother of the Savior but also the new Eve and mother of all the living. As such, she is the Queen Mother who reigns at the side of her divine Son. She is the spiritual mother of all his adopted brothers and sisters. Her only desire is to serve the King and help her spiritual children be fully conformed to the likeness of her first-born Son.

Satan knows all of this and hates it. The serpent abhors the Queen Mother and her spiritual children. Throughout history, he has nipped at her heels and prowled the earth like a roaring lion searching for her children in order to devour them (see Rev 12:17; 1 Pt 5:8).

Foreseeing this, God, working as the Divine Craftsman, began to forge a weapon for the woman and her children. It would take centuries to make the weapon, but, once completed, it would have the power to slay the malicious dragon since it would be equipped with the only thing capable of defeating him — the saving mysteries of the God-Man. The dragon would hate the weapon and, envious of those who possess it, earnestly strive to destroy it through a variety of means, but most especially by undermining our memory of its origins. The evil one's most pernicious assault would take the form of an attack against the very founder of the weapon and his association with it. Satan would hate any acknowledgment of such an association. Working deceptively down the centuries, he would burn documentary evidence and instill doubts in the hearts of men regarding the sword and its association with St. Dominic. At times, even scholars and historians would deny the pious tradition that recognizes St. Dominic as the founder of the weapon, but God would inspire books to be written that would defend the tradition and assert that it is both reliable and true.

The weapon can never be destroyed. It is the rosary-sword of the Queen!

As our story unfolds, it is important to remember that swords can be made in several ways. For example, bronze swords are cast from molds while steel swords are forged from iron. For the making of the spiritual sword, the Divine Craftsman used a combination of both techniques. Though this sword is spiritual in nature and not made of metal, the process employed for its construction involved both a mold and a forging method. The mold for the spiritual sword is the indestructible and inerrant Word of God. The two main elements to be poured into the mold were the Hail Mary and the Our Father. Once the mold was set, the Divine Craftsman forged the weapon so that men, women, and children could hold it in their hands and wield it against the enemy.

The various elements that were gathered by the Divine Craftsman for the construction of the sword are referred to as *antecedents of the rosary*. Most of the antecedents took centuries to develop. The Divine Craftsman brought them all together when he saw that the time was right for the construction of the sword. He infused the saving mysteries of his Son into the sword and entrusted the weapon to the Queen of Heaven. She, in turn, chose a man to be its founder. The chronological order of the antecedents is as follows:

1) The Hail Mary
2) The Our Father
3) Prayer Beads
4) The Marian Psalter

The Hail Mary

God always intended his weapon to be a Marian sword since he knew the woman and her children would be under attack. It was fitting, then, that the first element to be poured into the mold was the sweet *Ave: "Hail, full of grace, the Lord is with you!"* (Lk 1:28). This divinely inspired announcement, uttered first by the Archangel Gabriel, is known as the Angelic Salutation. It is the beginning of the life-saving mysteries of the God-Man and the first element required in the making of the sword. All future mysteries will follow it, for without the Virgin Mary, neither the God-Man nor his saving mysteries would exist. Salvation came into the world *through* Mary.

The Catholic Church is the workshop that the Divine Craftsman used to assemble the sword. As God Almighty, he could have constructed the sword in one act. However, since the construction of the sword was to occur in time, he allowed for the gathering of the elements in his workshop to take centuries. For example, it was not until the sixth century that the Catholic Church combined the *Angelic Salutation* with the *Evangelical Salutation*. The Evangelical

Salutation is the inspired greeting of St. Elizabeth to Mary: "*Blessed are you among women, and blessed is the fruit of your womb!*" (Lk 1:42). Forged together in the sixth-century Offertory Prayer for the Mass of the last Sunday of Advent, they became the first part of the shaft of the sword. The words are inspired and everlasting: "*Hail, full of grace, the Lord is with you! Blessed are you among women, and blessed is the fruit of your womb!*"

Taken directly from the Word of God, the melded Evangelical Salutation and Angelic Salutation formed the first half of what would become known as the *Ave Maria* or Hail Mary. Centuries later, St. Louis de Montfort would note the following: "The Hail Mary is a sharp and flaming shaft which, joined to the Word of God, gives the preacher the strength to pierce, move and convert the most hardened hearts."[1]

Up to the 11ᵗʰ century, the Hail Mary prayer consisted only of the combination of the Angelic Salutation and the Evangelical Salutation. The Divine Craftsman wanted an intercessory dimension to be given to the flaming shaft, and he waited patiently for his Church to help participate in this development. Until that time, the Hail Mary was understood by the Church to be a prayer of praise in which Mary was honored. It was seen as a way of greeting her, especially when turning to her in prayer and petition. Though the Hail Mary did not yet have an explicit intercessory dimension, it was viewed as a preparatory prayer said before formally petitioning the Virgin for a particular grace. All Christians understood that if they greeted Mary with such a lovely salutation, she would not be so impolite as to fail to return the greeting and bring with her the Holy Spirit and an abundance of grace.

The Our Father

Unlike the Hail Mary, which took centuries to compose, the greatest and most powerful prayer in the sword came fully intact. It was a prayer uttered by the God-Man himself. It is the Lord's Prayer, also referred to as the Our Father or the *Paternoster* (see Mt 6:9-13; Lk 11:2-4). The Our Father has been dear to the hearts of Christians since the days when our Lord walked this earth and taught the prayer to his disciples. It is a prayer that exemplifies how a follower of Christ ought to pray. In the words of Pope Leo XIII: "There is no language so fit to lead us to the majesty of God as the language of the Lord's Prayer."[2]

Prior to the 13ᵗʰ century, the Divine Craftsman had allowed the Hail Mary and the Our Father to exist side-by-side in his workshop. On occasion, they would intermingle in the lives of the pious, but they had never been joined together in a devotional formula. It was only in the 13ᵗʰ century, in anticipation of many future battles with evil, that the Divine Craftsman began to forge these elements together. Although it would be a spiritual blade "sharper than any two-edged sword, able to pierce between soul and spirit, joints and marrow, and discerning the thoughts and intentions of hearts" (Heb 4:12), it was destined to have a material component. After all, all swords are made to be held in a person's hand. Looking through his workshop, the Divine Craftsman found exactly what he needed to give the spiritual sword its material form.

Prayer Beads

For centuries, a cord of prayer beads had been used in the Divine Craftsman's workshop. It was his plan to wind the Hail Mary and the Our Father around this string of beads so that the spiritual sword could take shape and be manifested to the world. All three of the antecedent elements of the sword (Hail Mary, Our Father, prayer beads) had been in use for centuries, but they had never been joined together until the 13th century.

The Holy Spirit inspired the Christian use of prayer beads long before the 13th century. In Christian practice, prayer beads began to be used as early as the third century. The use of beads, or even small pebbles, was a practical method used by Christians for keeping track of how many prayers they had said. Sometimes they were used to fulfill a prescribed penance or prayer commitment. In the fourth century, for example, an Egyptian hermit named Paul of Thebes was accustomed to praying 300 penitential prayers a day. He used small pebbles to help him remember how many he had prayed. However, carrying around 300 pebbles, no matter how small they were, proved to be a rather cumbersome practice, a form of penance in itself. It is easy to understand, then, how Christians eventually transitioned from using pebbles to count their prayers to using prayer beads. A string of beads was much easier to carry and allowed this form of prayer to be offered anywhere and by anyone. Even the great biblical scholar St. Jerome (347–420) used prayer beads.

Prior to the 13th century, the prayer that was most commonly said on prayer beads was the Our Father. The universal name given to these types of prayer beads was *Paternoster* beads. Throughout most of the Middle Ages (the fifth through the 15th centuries) there existed the pious practice of successively praying *Paternosters* as a form of penance and devotion. In many eighth-century penitential books, the prescribed penance for certain sins consisted of reciting up to 50 *Paternosters*. In 1096, the monks of Cluny were in the habit of praying 50 *Paternosters* upon the death of a fellow monk. In 1128, the Knights Templar were required to pray 57 *Paternosters* if they were unable to attend common prayers; they were also required to pray 150 *Paternosters* every day for a week upon the death of one of their brethren.

In addition to monks and priests, there were also famous lay people who fervently used *Paternoster* beads. Some of these individuals treasured their beads so much that they expressed a desire to have their beads buried with them or bequeathed them to someone upon their death. The most famous of these devotees was Lady Godiva of Coventry. Made famous by Alfred, Lord Tennyson, the naked lady who rode on horseback in protest against the taxation of the poor was also a devout practitioner of using prayer beads. Upon her death in 1075, her will disclosed that she had made her own set of prayer beads and requested that, when she died, they be placed on a statue of the Blessed Virgin Mary. Some historians have speculated that Lady Godiva may have even prayed the existing form of the Hail Mary on her *Paternoster* beads.

Another famous person who used prayer beads was St. Rosalia (d. 1160). A relative of the Emperor Charlemagne, St. Rosalia possessed a set of beads that had a large cross at the end. She treasured her beads and requested that they be buried with her upon her death. Prayer beads were also found in the tombs of the Abbess Gertrude of Nivelles (the daughter of Pippin I; d. 659) and St. Norbert (12th century).

Of particular historical interest is the fact that in many paintings of the Middle Ages, especially those depicting the first Crusade (1096–1099), monks and priests were shown wearing prayer beads as part of their religious attire. Obviously, these were *Paternoster* beads, not rosary beads, since the rosary did not yet exist. However, the wearing of prayer beads on the belt served as an antecedent and a preparation for understanding the rosary as a sword that could be worn on the belt. During the 12th century, even those who were not involved in the Crusades began to wear *Paternoster* beads on their belt. It was a popular practice for monks and laity alike.

With these historical facts in mind, it goes without saying that the Divine Craftsman was at work and on the verge of bringing all the pieces of the sword together. He had found the material component of the sword in the prayer beads. All that was left was to transform the *Paternoster* beads into Marian beads. This transition would transform the prayer into a Marian sword. The perfect time to do this came in the late 12th and early 13th centuries, when medieval piety developed something known as the Marian Psalter.

The Marian Psalter

From ancient times, the faithful have prayed a beautiful liturgical prayer known as the Breviary. (Today, it is most frequently referred to as the Liturgy of the Hours.) This form of prayer has its roots in the many monastic traditions of Catholicism which required monks to participate in praying the 150 psalms of the Old Testament in common. In ancient monasteries, this practice required the monks to have the ability to read and understand Latin. The reality, however, was that in those days, many of the monks were uneducated, illiterate, and therefore unable to participate in the daily prayers. For this reason, as early as the ninth century, particularly in Ireland, both brothers (men who are monks but not priests) and lay people who could not read were allowed to substitute the chanting of the 150 psalms with the recitation of 150 *Paternosters*. In the 11th century, this practice spread beyond the shores of Ireland and became common for anyone who wanted to participate in the Breviary but was unable to read.

The use of *Paternoster* beads really began to flourish after the 11th century. It was also during this era that the practice of praying 150 *Paternosters* increased in popularity as well. The many monks and members of the laity who were praying 150 *Paternosters* as a substitute for the 150 psalms naturally gravitated toward owning a set of *Paternoster* beads. This version of the *Paternoster* beads became known as the "poor man's breviary." Since it was a portable means of prayer and many people wanted to wear it from their belt, people soon realized that it was much easier to wear a set of 50 beads rather than 150 beads. This led to the practice of praying the 50-beaded *Paternoster* three times so that all 150 *Paternosters* were said. *Paternoster* beads became so popular in the 12th century that there was a street named Paternoster Row in London, where skilled crafts-men worked as professional bead-makers. In the year 1268, there existed four guilds in Paris that specialized in the making of *Paternoster* beads. Some types were set on a cord that was open at both ends, while other types were circular. Both were accepted and commonly used.

At the same time that the *Paternoster* cord grew in popularity in the 12th century, the Hail Mary prayer also became more widely used in devotions. In fact, it was around this time that the word "chaplet" (meaning "crown") began to be used to designate a set of 50 prayers. There are many reasons why the Hail Mary prayer gained greater popularity during this time. One of the main reasons was the renewal in Marian devotion brought about in the 12th century by several monastic reform movements. Men like St. Bernard of Clairvaux (1090–1153) and Blessed Isaac of Stella (1100–1170), both Cistercian monks, began to interpret much of the wisdom literature of the Old Testament in a Marian way, which had a profound effect upon Marian devotion in general. Because Mary was understood to be the dove of beauty from the Song of Songs and the seat of wisdom from the Book of Proverbs, the 150 psalms began to take on a Marian dimension as well. From this monastic piety, a new form of Marian devotion emerged that took the poor man's breviary as its foundation. There is even a story from this era of a hermit named Albert (d. 1140) who recited 150 Hail Marys in imitation of the 150 psalms. He observed this practice as a form of corporal penance. For the first hundred Hail Marys he genuflected, and for the last 50 he prostrated himself. Imitating such examples as this, and wanting to further express a devotion to the Mother of God, monks began to develop a Psalter dedicated to honoring Mary that paralleled the poor man's breviary. It consisted of using the same *Paternoster* beads, but instead of praying 150 Our Fathers, they prayed 150 Hail Marys. Within a short period of time, 15 Our Fathers were added to break up the 150 Hail Marys into sets of 10. These sets of 10 became known as "decades."

The Cistercians deserve credit for being the originators of the Marian Psal-ter. However, they were not the only ones emphasizing a renewed devotion to Mary. Another monastic order that influenced the development of the Marian Psalter was the Carthusian Order. Founded in 1084 by St. Bruno of Cologne (1030–1101), the Carthusians were (and still are) one of the most strict and ere-mitic religious orders in the Church. Both of these great monastic communities were at the heart of the medieval development of the Marian Psalter since they both had their own versions. The Marian Psalters these orders developed, however, consisted only of praying Hail Marys interspersed with antiphons. Neither of their Marian Psalters contained any mysteries from the life of Christ to meditate on while praying the Hail Marys. As such, their Marian Psalters were generally not intended for public recitation, but for individual recitation by monks. Also, since both orders are monastic in nature, their Marian Psalters did not have any apostolic or missionary dimension. For the Cistercians and the Carthusians, praying the Marian Psalter was the Marian parallel to the *Paternoster* devotion and nothing more. Neither of these orders used the Marian Psalter as a method for preaching or as a weapon for conquering heresy. They most certainly did not understand it as a spiritual weapon.

The Divine Craftsman was very pleased with their love and praise of Mary, and used their Marian Psalter as a prototype for the creation of a completely new type of Marian Psalter — the preached and meditated version. The new Marian Psalter was infused with the saving mysteries of the life of Christ and made into a spiritual sword to be used against evil, falsehood, and sin. Unlike its monastic predecessor, the new Marian Psalter was intended as a spiritual weapon and an evangelical tool to conquer heresy and the devil. Such a weapon would be much needed at the beginning of the 13th century. The Holy Spirit was already at work in the Church preparing zealous men to become founders of mendicant religious orders. These orders would be apostolic in nature, sent out to do combat with the forces of darkness. The Divine Craftsman would not send them out without a weapon.

After all of the pieces had been brought together in the 12th century — the Hail Mary, the Our Father, prayer beads, and the Marian Psalter — the sword was ready to be assembled and entrusted to a man who would be forever known as its founder. Since the rosary was to be Mary's sword, God granted her the privilege of selecting a man to be its founder. The chosen man would be the first person to wield the sword and test its ability in spiritual combat. The Queen of Heaven had just the man in mind.

THE 13TH CENTURY:
St. Dominic and
the Birth of the Rosary

At the beginning of the 13th century, the Church was experiencing violent opposition from a group known as the Albigensians, a heretical sect named after the town of Albi in southern France where it originated. This pernicious and radically puritanical sect had many adherents and was spreading rapidly. Its main teaching was that only spiritual realities were good and everything material was evil. According to their doctrine, each person's soul is imprisoned in an evil body. If a person wants to experience "salvation," they need to be freed from the material prison of their flesh. This belief system was a direct attack against Christian morality and the saving mysteries of the God-Man, especially the Incarnation, the Passion, and the Resurrection. The Christian teaching that God took on flesh in order to save us was unthinkable to the Albigensians, and they violently opposed the incarnational Christian religion. At one point, they even became violent and murdered a papal legate who had been sent to dialogue with them.

It was during this time that the Divine Craftsman chose to turn the Marian Psalter into the spiritual sword of the rosary. Into the sword he would infuse sacred mysteries, the very same mysteries that the Albigensians were attacking. The sword was going to be unsheathed and used against the enemies of Christianity.

St. Dominic

During the spread of the Albigensian heresy, a Spaniard named Dominic Guzman established himself as a dynamic orator against their errors. A member of the Canons Regular — priests who live according to a particular rule of life — he had become increasingly concerned about the spread of Albigensianism and the threat it posed to Catholics. His response was to set out on a preaching campaign, walking from town to town proclaiming the truths of Christianity. Divine Providence had, in fact, chosen him for this mission.

In 1170, when Dominic was born, his mother, Blessed Juana de Aza, experienced a prophetic dream about her son. In her dream, she saw a dog leaping from her womb with a flaming torch in its mouth. The dog went all throughout the world setting the world on fire with the torch. Unbeknownst to her at the time, her son would end up founding a religious order that would be called the Order of Preachers (the Dominicans). The mission of the Dominicans would be to set the world on fire with a love for Jesus through zealous preaching on the sacred mysteries of Christianity. In time, the Order would even be referred to as the *Domini canes*, that is, the "dogs of God." Fulfilling his mother's prophetic dream, Dominic's dogs of God traverse the highways and byways of the world, "sniffing" out heresy and eradicating it from the hearts and minds of the wayward. But before all of this came to fruition, Dominic had to learn an important lesson. As the one chosen to be the founder of a band of itinerant preachers and a new form of evangelical preaching, he needed to learn that all his power would come through the sweet *Ave Maria*.

Our Lady Entrusts the Weapon to St. Dominic

Preparing for his efforts to correct the errors of the Albigensians, Dominic had reasoned that since he was gifted with great oratorical ability and theological acumen, he would be able to win souls back to Christ rather easily. However, after having spent several years ardently preaching in town after town, he realized that his methods were not as effective as he had hoped and came to the conclusion that he needed something more. He knew he was up against a formidable spiritual power and needed something strong enough to overcome the enemy.

In 1208, he retreated into the silence of the Prouille forest near the town of Toulouse, France, to pray, begging heaven to come to his aid and give him what he needed to overcome the Albigensians. After three days of intense prayer, fasting, and penitential acts, the Queen of Heaven came to his assistance. According to ancient accounts, on the third day, a ball of fire and three holy angels appeared in the sky, after which the Virgin Mary spoke to St. Dominic. She informed him that his efforts in preaching had been noble, but it was the *Ave Maria* that would give his preaching power. The Queen of Heaven informed him: "Wonder not that until now you [St. Dominic] have obtained so little fruit by your labors; you have spent them on a barren soil, not yet watered with the dew of divine grace. When God willed to renew the face of the earth, he began by sending down on it the fertilizing rain of the Angelic Salutation. Therefore, preach my Psalter."[1] This was the founding moment of the holy rosary of Mary. It was the moment the sword was unsheathed.

It is important to remember that the Marian Psalter was already being recited by several groups when Our Lady instructed St. Dominic to use it. What made the exhortation of Mary to St. Dominic unique was that she explicitly instructed him to *preach* her Psalter. She did not intend for St. Dominic to simply make others aware of the existing Marian Psalter by preaching *about* it; she intended for him to spread it by *using* it as a preaching tool. He was to combine the fertilizing rain of the *Ave Maria* with his preaching on the saving mysteries of Christ. The combination of the *Ave Maria* and preaching on the mysteries of Christ would then lead to meditation and conversion. This method would be a spiritual sword in his hands, giving him the ability to win hearts back to Christ and overcome the enemy.

Saint Dominic was not the founder of the monastic Marian Psalter; that already existed before his vision. Rather, he was chosen to be the founder and the father of a new way of praying the Marian Psalter, an evangelical way infused with meditation on the sacred mysteries. Before St. Dominic, the Marian Psalter had only been prayed as a way of honoring Mary. Through St. Dominic, the Marian Psalter took on an apostolic and meditative dimension. The Church has always stated that when Mary exhorted St. Dominic to preach her Psalter, she also revealed to him specific mysteries that were to be associated with it. These mysteries would serve for all future generations as a meditative battering ram against theological error.

Accordingly, when she gave him the mysteries, the Queen of Heaven instructed St. Dominic to divide the 150 Hail Marys of the Marian Psalter into 10 Hail Marys, with each decade attached to a particular mystery. The faithful were to meditate on the mysteries while praying the 10 Hail Marys. The mysteries Mary provided directly answered the errors being promoted by the Albigensians. They focused on the Incarnation, Passion, and glorious triumph of her divine Son.

The fact that the rosary was born in France and given to St. Dominic in the manner noted above was affirmed by Pope Leo XIII during the dedication of the 15 altars of the rosary at the Rosary Basilica in Lourdes, France, in 1901. At that celebration, Pope Leo XIII stated the following:

> We avail ourselves of this occasion with the greatest pleasure because of its connection with those regions in France which have had lustre shed on them by so many and such great favors of the Blessed Virgin, which are famous because of the presence within them at one time of the Patriarch and Legislator, St. Dominic, and in which is to be found the cradle of the rosary. Every Christian knows that St. Dominic, after journeying from Spain into France, was the invincible opponent of the Albigensian heresy which at that time was spreading like an evil pestilence through almost the whole of southern France to the foot of the Pyrenees. By his explaining and preaching on the wonderful and sacred mysteries of God's gifts, the light of truth burned brightly in the very places that had been overshadowed by the darkness of error. For this is what each series of the rosary mysteries, which we so highly esteem, does for us.[2]

After having been knighted by the Virgin with the spiritual sword, St. Dominic continued his preaching campaign with renewed fervor and won countless souls back to Christ and the Church. The preaching of the Marian Psalter proved extremely effective, just as Our Lady had promised. Father Reginald Garrigou-LaGrange, one of the greatest Dominican theologians of the 20th century, explained the marvel of St. Dominic's preaching method in the following way:

Our Blessed Lady made known to St. Dominic a kind of preaching till then unknown, which she said would be one of the most powerful weapons against future errors and in future difficulties. Under her inspiration, St Dominic went into the villages of the Albigensians, gathered the people, and preached to them the mysteries of salvation — the Incarnation, the redemption, eternal life. As Mary had taught him to do, he distinguished the different kinds of mysteries, and after each short instruction, he had ten Hail Marys recited — somewhat as might happen even today at a Holy Hour. And what the word of the preacher was unable to do, the sweet prayer of the Hail Mary did for hearts. As Mary promised, it proved to be a most fruitful form of preaching.[3]

As the first champion of the rosary, St. Dominic quickly became the most fruitful preacher of his age, unparalleled in his ability to articulate truth and win back hearts. The spiritual sword of the rosary had proven itself to be very powerful! Pope Leo XIII would later praise the success of St. Dominic in these words: "Thanks to this new method of prayer — when adopted and properly carried out as instituted by the Holy Father St. Dominic — piety, faith, and union began to return [to France]; and the projects and devices of the heretics to fall to pieces."[4] Saint Dominic was known to be so bold in his preaching that early accounts of his life recount how he often challenged the Albigensians to a test of fire. The challenge was intended to detect whose books contained theological error, and required that both he and his opponents throw their books into a fire. It was mutually understood by both parties that, if their books burned, it was a sign that their books contained errors and were displeasing to God. The Albigensians accepted his challenge, and every time they threw their books into the fire they were destroyed, but when St. Dominic threw his books into the fire, they were never touched by the flames. His mother's dream proved to be a prophecy in more ways than one. Saint Dominic had been born to set the world and theological error on fire.

Meditation on the Sacred Mysteries of Christ

It cannot be emphasized enough that the characteristic that distinguished the Marian Psalter of St. Dominic from the pre-existing Marian Psalter was his meditative method of preaching on the sacred mysteries of the life of Christ. Though St. Dominic had a God-given ability to preach, it was his preached-and-prayed Marian Psalter that gave his ministry its extraordinary evangelical power. Were this not the case, St. Dominic could have simply preached about the existing Marian Psalter and brought about the same effect, but because that method would have lacked the mysteries of Christ and meditation, it would not have been fruitful. The Marian Psalter used by the Cistercians and Carthusians was not intended to be an evangelical prayer used to convert heretics, while the Marian Psalter of St. Dominic forged just that, something entirely new and exactly what the times needed. In essence, Our Lady had instructed St. Dominic to take the Marian Psalter out of the monasteries, infuse it with sacred mysteries and meditation, and take it into the streets to become a weapon of mass conversion. This ingenious method even became a vital tool of the mendicant order he founded. In fact, it was so effective that all the other mendicant orders that were founded in the 13th century (and there were many) adopted his method of prayer and used it in their own apostolic endeavors. The Marian Psalter of St. Dominic became an apostolic and evangelical weapon used by all the spiritual knights of the late medieval Church.

Meditation on the mysteries became the very soul of the new Marian Psalter. Prayerful meditation on the mysteries gave the Marian Psalter the power to change people's hearts. Prior to this, there existed no such method of evangelization, which is the reason why the Church has never ascribed to anyone other than St. Dominic the title of "founder of the rosary." Though the Cistercians and the Carthusians were responsible for inventing the Marian Psalter, their respective Marian Psalters were only precursors and antecedents to the Marian Psalter of St. Dominic — the rosary. Neither the Cistercians nor the Carthusians are to be understood as the inventors or the founders of the rosary because they never associated any mysteries with the prayers or used the Marian Psalter as a meditative and evangelical prayer.

The Name "Rosary"

During the life of St. Dominic, and for many centuries after his death, the method of prayer he had been exhorted to preach by Our Lady continued to be called the Marian Psalter. Since the material component of the devotion (the beads) that Our Lady gave him did not differ in appearance from the preexisting Marian Psalter prayed on *Paternoster* beads, his Marian Psalter went practically unnoticed by his contemporaries. Also, since he never boasted of his many mystical experiences, the rosary remained somewhat hidden during its initial years. This should not be taken to mean, however, that his form of prayer wasn't called the rosary during his lifetime. It was. Nevertheless, it took centuries for the prayer to transition from being known as the Marian Psalter to being universally known and acclaimed as the rosary.

Historically, the word "rosary" was in use even before the time of St. Dominic. Prior to the 13th century, the Latin word *rosarium* was used to describe a rose garden or a grouping of roses in a wreath or a bouquet. Yet it was only during the lifetime of St. Dominic that the word came to be associated with the Marian Psalter. In fact, it was only in the 13th century that May devotions in honor of Mary began to be practiced in the Church. Because St. Dominic was a

Spaniard and universally acclaimed as a great Marian preacher, King Alfonso X of Spain paid him homage by imitating him and crowning images of Mary during the month of May, the month of roses.

Evidence that the Marian Psalter of St. Dominic was described as a rosary during the 13th century can be seen in Abbot Engelbert of Admont's book, *The Psalter of the Blessed Virgin Mary*. In his book, he presented 150 prayers to Mary that all started with the phrase "Ave, rose." The blending together of the Marian Psalter, the *Ave Maria*, and the rose was his way of explaining how each Hail Mary of the Marian Psalter was akin to giving Mary a rose.

Also of significance in this century is the fact that after St. Dominic founded the Dominican rosary, the Seven Founders of the Order of the Servants of Mary (Servites) formulated a type of rosary based on the Seven Sorrows of Mary. They claimed to have had visions and revelations from Our Lady that led them to promote the Seven Sorrows of Mary rosary as a Marian Psalter particular to their order. Interestingly, the Dominican martyr St. Peter of Verona (1206–1252) served as the director of the Servites and is often considered a second founder of their order since he helped the order receive papal approval.

Centuries later, St. Maximilian Kolbe shared the following story with his friars about how the devotion referred to as the Marian Psalter came to be universally called the "rosary":

> Originally the rosary was called the Psalter of Mary, because as the Davidic Psalter is composed of 150 psalms, so also in the rosary we find 150 Hail Marys. The following circumstance, according to its application, contributed to the name change: A pious young man [a Franciscan novice, in the year 1422] had a habit of frequently adorning an image of the Blessed Virgin Mary with roses. He later joined a monastery. Within the walls of the monastery, he no longer had the opportunity to bring flowers to Mary; this grieved him very much. While he was afflicted in this way, the Blessed Virgin Mary appeared to him and said: "Recite devoutly my psalter, and adorn me with the most beautiful flowers." He began therefore to pray the rosary, and immediately he saw how for each Hail Mary the Blessed Virgin Mary took forth from his mouth a rose of wondrous beauty and weaved with those roses a garland for herself. At the Our Father she wove into the garland a resplendent lily. This was the origin of the name "Rosary."[5]

Besides the images and message of the roses and lilies imparted during the prayers, this 1422 Marian apparition also imparted to the Franciscan novice a specifically Franciscan type of rosary, which became known as the Franciscan Crown Rosary. Despite these revelations to a Franciscan, St. Maximilian remained firm in his belief that St. Dominic was the founder of the rosary. He simply, and quite rightly, understood the Marian Psalter prayed by St. Dominic to be the exact same prayer that would later become universally acclaimed as the rosary.

This 1422 apparition was the pivotal moment after which *all* Marian Psalters began to be referred to as rosaries because the revelation of the Franciscan Crown Rosary emphasized that all rosaries are ways of *crowning* Mary with spiritual roses. Thus, ironically, though St. Dominic was the founder of *the* rosary, God used the Franciscans to help the Marian Psalter of St. Dominic become universally known as *the first rosary*. The pontiff to write most prolifically on the rosary, Pope Leo XIII, was aware that the Dominican rosary had gone by various names during the first few centuries of its existence. He once made the following pertinent comment:

> This practice of devotion to Mary which St. Dominic, under God's inspiration and by his help, was the first to think of, introducing in turn the mysteries of the Redemption, has justly been called the rosary. For as often as we greet Mary with the Angelic Salutation, "full of grace," we present to the Blessed Virgin, in the repetition of our words of praise, roses which emit the most delightful perfume.[6]

A weapon and a rose — that's what the Dominican rosary has always been. It is what the Divine Craftsman intended from the beginning, even though it took centuries for the prayer to be universally known as the rosary. The rose and the weapon had even been linked together at the first rosary victory during the lifetime of St. Dominic. There the rosary proved itself to be both a powerful spiritual weapon and a crown of roses for the Queen of Heaven.

The Battle of Muret

The first rosary victory was won at the Battle of Muret on September 12, 1213. A small town in southern France near the city of Toulouse, Muret was a stronghold for the Albigensians as they sought to expand and take over France. The pope at the time, Pope Innocent III, was deeply concerned about their expansion and sought to organize a Crusader army that would rid France of their heretical influence once and for all. With the pope's blessing, a Catholic force was assembled in southern France by Count Simon de Montfort. Unfortunately, the army only consisted of 1,500 men. Count Simon had hoped for reinforcements from northern France, but they never arrived. The Albigensian forces, on the other hand, had more than 30,000 men and were led by Raymond of Toulouse and Pedro II of Aragon. Theirs was a voracious group of warmongers with one goal in mind: Wipe out the puny Catholic militia. Confident in their greater numbers, the Albigensian army was convinced that they would crush the opposing Catholic force.

Believing they were invincible, the Albigensian army spent the night before the battle in drunkenness and debauchery — an error that would prove to be their downfall. In contrast, the entire Catholic army, under the joint command of Count Simon de Montfort and St. Dominic, spent the night before the battle praying the rosary. In the early hours of the morning, Holy Mass was celebrated for the Catholic militia, and many men went to confession. Saint Dominic retreated to the Church of Saint-Jacques in Muret to pray for victory. Sure enough, in the time it took him to pray a rosary, Simon de Montfort and his men were able to rush upon the hung-over and disorganized Albigensians and completely rout them. The Albigensian army never saw it coming. Chroniclers and historians who recorded the events of the battle described the routing of the Albigensian militia as the felling of many trees under the axes of an army of lumberjacks. With the complete triumph of the Catholic forces, the territorial expansion of the Albigensian heresy ended. The sect itself would continue to exist and Dominicans would continue to preach against it, but after the Battle of Muret, it never exceeded its previous numbers.

After the battle, every Catholic in the area attributed the victory to the rosary. Simon de Montfort and the local people even constructed a chapel dedicated to the rosary in the Church of St. Jacques where St. Dominic had been praying during the battle — the first chapel ever to be dedicated to the rosary. A painting that depicted the Blessed Virgin giving the rosary to St. Dominic was enshrined in the chapel. In the image, St. Dominic stood to the side of Our Lady holding a crucifix in one hand and receiving the rosary from Our Lady with the other. On the other side of Our Lady knelt Simon de Montfort and Bishop Fulk of Toulouse. Unfortunately, this image was destroyed during the French Revolution, but there is written testimony that verifies that it did exist.[7]

In addition to this painting, there were other contemporary witnesses that made mention of the importance of the rosary at the Battle of Muret. In early 1214, less than one year after the battle, a notary of Languedoc — formerly a small province in southern France — wrote a poem describing how St. Dominic brought roses to the battle, offered them repeatedly, and made a wreath out of them. This, of course, was a poetic reference to the successive praying of Hail Marys by St. Dominic during the battle. The poem is significant because it combines two images: The rosary is to be understood both as a spiritual weapon and a crown of roses for the Queen of Heaven. Though the original manuscript of the poem no longer exists, a copy was discovered in a book published in 1693. Long before the re-discovery of this poem, however, the Dominicans themselves had affirmed the role of St. Dominic at the Battle of Muret. The 14th century English Dominican historian Nicholas Trivet noted: "St. Dominic warred by prayer, de Montfort by arms!"[8]

After the Battle of Muret, many of the followers of St. Dominic continued to give heroic witness to the power of the preached Marian Psalter in their ongoing battles with the Albigensians and other heretics. Saint Peter of Verona, the Dominican who helped the Servites form their religious order, was even assassinated by the Albigensians. He became a martyr for the faith when the Albigensians cut off the top half of his head.

Artistic depictions often present St. Peter of Verona as an early Dominican witness to the rosary. For example, he is depicted in Caravaggio's *Madonna of the*

Rosary (see page 361). He is the Dominican standing on the right and pointing to the Virgin and Child. On his forehead can be seen the wound that led him to be raised to the honors of the altar.

The Confraternity of the Rosary

According to ancient tradition, St. Dominic also founded an association of prayer to further promote the rosary. This association of prayer was intended to be a way of passing on the spiritual weapon to future generations. Interestingly, its history has a great deal in common with the history of the rosary. Just as the word "rosary" grew in popularity over time, so too did the association of prayer started by St. Dominic also take time to become universally described as the "Confraternity of the Rosary." In fact, during the first few centuries of its existence, it went by many names. At various times it was described as the Confraternity of Prayer, the Confraternity of the Rosary, the Sodality of the Rosary, or even the Society of the Rosary. Eventually, the most popular title became the Confraternity of the Rosary. Yet, regardless of what title it was known by, St. Dominic was always credited as its founder. Numerous popes have affirmed this lineage. The earliest known papal affirmation is found in a 1495 document by Pope Alexander VI. In all likelihood, he was not the first pope to affirm that St. Dominic had founded the Confraternity, but his reference is the oldest existing papal affirmation. In 1897, Pope Leo XIII offered the following concise explanation of the antiquity of the association of prayer founded by St. Dominic: "If we regard its [the Confraternity of the Rosary's] origin, we find it distinguished by its antiquity, for St. Dominic himself is said to have been its founder."[9]

There is historical proof that St. Dominic founded at least one confraternity during his lifetime; the last will and testament of a man named Anthony Sers. Sers' will was drafted in 1221, the same year that St. Dominic died. The will states that Sers had been a member of a confraternity founded by Dominic Guzman in Palencia, Spain. No year when the confraternity was founded is provided in the will, but the will clearly states that, upon his death, it was Sers' desire that the brethren of the Palencia confraternity gather together to pray for his soul. In return for their kindness, and to offer them some form of payment for the wax to be used for the candles lit during the prayers, Sers bequeathed to the members of the confraternity three measures of wheat, as well as certain other food items to be distributed among them equally. Based on the fact that St. Dominic was in Palencia, Spain, in 1218, it seems likely that he founded a confraternity there that same year. There are strong suggestions, however, that this confraternity in Spain may not have been the first confraternity St. Dominic founded.

According to many historians and popes, St. Dominic founded a confraternity in Rome before he founded the one in Spain in 1218. In an apostolic letter of Pope Clement VIII that dates from 1601, the pope made mention of the presence of St. Dominic in the Church of St. Sixtus in Rome and explicitly noted the following: "Afterwards, in the Church of the same monastery [St. Sixtus],

St. Dominic instituted and promulgated the Rosary of the Blessed Virgin, in the year of our Lord 1216."[10] Saint Dominic's promulgation of the rosary in Rome was possibly the founding of the first confraternity of the rosary. After all, what could be a better place to initiate an association of prayer than in Rome?

Though it may never be known exactly how many confraternities St. Dominic established during his lifetime, it is certain that the confraternities began to spread all over Europe after his death. For example, in Lille, France, in the collegiate Church of St. Peter, there is preserved an ancient confraternity document on parchment bearing the date 1231. This document contains the registry of names for a confraternity called the *Trielle*. Within the registry are inscribed the names of several pious ladies who offered "Psalters of Our Lady" in lieu of money or candles. Dominican tradition also affirms that something called Confraternities of the Virgin Mary (most likely confraternities of the rosary) were founded in Dominican convents in Mantua in 1255, in Perugia and Pavia in 1258, and in Lucca in 1272. In addition, in 1288, in the beautiful city of Orvieto, a confraternity titled "Congregation-Society of the Blessed Virgin Mary and St. Dominic" also came into existence. All of these confraternities were most likely confraternities of the rosary.

Though writing in the late 16th century, Pope Sixtus V affirmed that the 13th and 14th century pontiffs Urban IV (pope from 1261–1264) and John XXII (pope from 1316–1334) granted indulgences to rosary confraternities. It's an incredible affirmation that the Confraternity of the Rosary was in existence during the century of St. Dominic. Pope Sixtus V wrote:

> Remembering, then, how great a help to our religion has been the institution of the most holy Psalter, called the Rosary of the glorious and ever Virgin Mary the Holy Mother of God, which was devised by the Founder of the Order of Friars-Preachers, Blessed Dominic, by the inspiration, as it is believed, of the Holy Ghost; remembering, too, what great benefit has thence accrued, and daily accrues, to the world, and mindful that in consequence, confraternities of the Faithful of both sexes have been canonically erected under the invocation of the Rosary of the same Blessed Virgin Mary in divers churches, chapels, and altars of the world, and that their Brethren and Sisters deservedly obtained not only confirmation and growth of these Confraternities, but also Indulgences and privileges, and especially of happy memory from Urban IV and John XXII ... .[11]

The historical value of the above statement cannot be underestimated since it explicitly affirms that a pope who lived in the same century as St. Dominic granted indulgences to the members of the Confraternity of the Rosary. In the same document, Pope Sixtus V also named 13 other popes who had granted indulgences to the Confraternity of the Rosary prior to his pontificate. In addition, the document of Pope Sixtus V affirms, as we will see in the next section, that even when the Confraternity suffered neglect and was almost forgotten during the 14ᵗʰ and 15ᵗʰ centuries, it continued to be endorsed and given indulgences by popes.

Early Dominicans

When Pope Honorius III approved the founding of the Order of Preachers in 1216, he stated that the spiritual sons of St. Dominic would be the future champions of the faith and the true lights of the world. This proved to be a prophetic statement. After the death of St. Dominic in 1221, the Dominicans championed the rosary and spread it throughout the Church. It was the torch they used to illuminate the darkness and bring many souls back to Christ. For example, according to Dominican tradition, Blessed Jordan of Saxony (1190–1237), the second Master General of the Dominicans, was known to offer a meditation while praying the Hail Marys with his brethren. During his life, he taught and encouraged others to employ this same method of prayer.[12] There really can be no doubt that he was teaching others the rosary. It is also well known that the very learned Dominican priest and Doctor of the Church St. Albert the Great (1193–1280) authored a theological work on the Virgin Mary titled *De Laudibus B. Maria* (*On the Praise of Blessed Mary*). In this work, he compared the Virgin Mary to the rose of Jericho, each blossoming with 150 petals. It is almost impossible not to recognize an allusion to the Marian Psalter of Our Lady in such a statement. This same saint, along with his pupil and fellow Doctor of the Church St. Thomas Aquinas (1225–1274), used the Hail Mary prayer as the basis for many sermons. Many Franciscan saints of the 13ᵗʰ century, such as St. Bonaventure (1221–1274; also a Doctor of the Church), did the same.

The Dominican tradition also points to the fifth Master General of the Dominican Order, Humbert de Romanis, as a witness to the rosary. De Romanis, who died 40 years after St. Dominic, was known to impress upon the Dominican novices the superiority of meditation over vocal prayer. As part of his teaching, he encouraged the novices to meditate on the mysteries of the Incarnation, the Nativity, and the Passion of Our Lord while praying the Our Father and the Hail Mary.[13] What could this form of prayer coupled with meditation have been if not the rosary? These examples affirm that the rosary has always been at the heart of the Dominican Order. At times throughout history, the Dominicans would even be referred to as the "Order of the Rosary."

Several of the early developments of the rosary after the death of St. Dominic have been attributed to the influence of the sons of St. Dominic. Historians have noted that because the early Dominicans who prayed the rosary sought to closely imitate the Liturgy of the Hours (Breviary), the Glory Be and the *Salve Regina* prayer became attached to the rosary. Since the Glory Be prayer was included after each Psalm when praying the Breviary, they deemed it appropriate to include a Glory Be at the end of each decade of the Marian Psalter. Historically, the Glory Be prayer had been in liturgical use since the early sixth century and was approved for common usage at the Third Council of Vaison in 529.

The *Salve Regina* prayer, originating in the 12th century and traditionally attributed to St. Bernard of Clairvaux, was used by Cistercian monks as a conclusion for Compline (Night Prayer). When the Dominicans were founded in the 13th century, they imitated the Cistercians in this practice and concluded Night Prayer with the chanting of the *Salve Regina*. Then, as the custodians of the rosary and desiring it to parallel approved liturgical norms, the Dominicans began to pray the *Salve Regina* prayer at the end of the Marian Psalter.[14] The practice quickly caught on and became the normative way of concluding the rosary.

Other examples also show the popularity of the Marian Psalter among the Dominicans of the 13th century. In 1243, the Dominican chronicler Br. John de Mailly drew up a collection of the lives of the saints in which he made mention that it was the custom of many holy women of his day to pray the Angelic Salutation 150 times. He explicitly referred to this devotion as the "Psalter of the Blessed Virgin." The Dominican hagiographer Bartholomew of Trent also wrote about this same practice and related the story of a nun named Sister Eulalia. This nun was very devoted to the Blessed Virgin Mary and prayed 150 Angelic Salutations every day in her honor. Bartholomew of Trent stated that Our Lady had once appeared to Sr. Eulalia and informed her how pleasing this practice was to her, especially when the words *Dominus tecum* ("the Lord is with you") were pronounced slowly and devoutly. What Our Lady seemed to be asking of Sr. Eulalia was that she meditate as she prayed the Hail Marys and not rush through them too quickly.[15]

The Dominican nun Blessed Emilia Bicchieri (1238–1314) was so devoted to the rosary that she gave 15 loaves of bread to the poor every day in honor of the 15 mysteries of the rosary. The Dominican priest Blessed Romee of Livia (d.1261), a direct disciple of St. Dominic, is said to have died while squeezing in his hands the knotted cord on which he prayed his Hail Marys. Throughout his life as a Dominican, he was known to meditate using his knotted cord and even instructed his friars in this particular form of devotion.[16]

The rosary had become so popular during this century that, just as a street in London was named Paternoster Row in the 12th century, so too was there a street in London that became known as Ave Maria Lane in the 13th century. It was on that street that craftsmen made rosaries.

Although the rosary did not become an *official* part of the Dominican habit until centuries later, learned Dominican historians have often asserted that it may have been an unofficial part of the habit from the beginning. In fact, many renditions of early Dominicans in art show them wearing rosaries. All historians know that the wearing of *Paternoster* beads was a common practice of the crusading military religious orders during the 11th and 12th centuries. These groups wore *Paternoster* beads as a type of spiritual weapon when they went off to fight the battles of the Lord. The normative practice was to wear the beads on the left side of the belt, in imitation of a knight who carried his sword on his left side for easy access. It is possible that St. Dominic had his men imitate this practice and wear their spiritual sword on the left side of their habit.

Whether or not the practice of wearing the rosary on the side of the habit was done by St. Dominic or the early Dominicans, we may never know, but there is a fascinating fact about another saint who was present at the Battle of Muret that may offer some insight into its likelihood. According to the *Acta Sanctorum* (*Lives of the Saints*), there was a man at the Battle of Muret named St. Peter Nolasco (1189–1256). Like St. Dominic, St. Peter was the founder of a religious order in the 13ᵗʰ century. His order was called the Order of the Blessed Virgin Mary of Mercy, commonly known as the Mercedarians. This military order had been founded to help with the ransom of captives, not just with prayer, but with literal swords! When the Mercedarians were founded, they wore a religious habit that was practically identical to the Dominican habit, but with one exception: The Mercedarian habit came fully equipped with a sword of steel! One cannot help but wonder if St. Dominic and St. Peter knew each other. Since the Crusader army only consisted of 1,500 men and St. Dominic was its spiritual captain, it is very possible that St. Peter Nolasco and St. Dominic knew each other and were brothers-in-arms at the Battle of Muret. While St. Peter was fighting by the side of Simon de Montfort with his sword of steel, St. Dominic was warring by prayer with the spiritual sword of the rosary. Was St. Dominic inspired by the sword-carrying habit of St. Peter to do something similar in his order with the rosary? It was, after all, a time of knights and swords. To this day, the Mercedarian and Dominican habits remain almost identical in appearance (especially now that the Mercedarian habit no longer comes equipped with a sword of steel!).

The Beguines of Ghent

In 1236, 15 years after the death of St. Dominic, Dominican priests were serving as the directors of a religious community known as the Beguines of Ghent. A religious community of women, the Beguines were required by their rule to pray three sets of 50 Hail Marys on a daily basis. Before each Our Father, the leader was to read aloud a mystery from the life of Jesus so that everyone could meditate on the mystery while praying the Hail Marys. The fact that the Beguines were performing this practice under the direction of the Dominicans has made many historians posit that the religious women were praying all the mysteries of the rosary — Joyful, Sorrowful, and Glorious — every day.

The specific term that the Beguines used to designate their method of dividing up the rosary into three sets of five mysteries was "chaplet," which means "small crown." Today, we usually understand praying the rosary to mean only praying five decades, but during the time of St. Dominic and shortly after his death, the terminology of chaplet/small crown came into existence to differentiate a five decade chaplet from the full rosary. The Beguines were not alone in this practice, either. The 13th century Dominican nuns of Toes, Switzerland, were also in the habit of praying chaplets of mysteries throughout the day. They recited three chaplets of 50 Hail Marys per day and called it the Psalter of the Blessed Virgin. They, too, counted the Hail Marys by using a string of beads held in their hand.[17]

The Silent Witness

Many historians have been perplexed by so little having been written on the rosary during the first few centuries of its existence. From what has been presented in this chapter, it should be clear to the reader that there was not a total silence on the rosary during the century in which it was founded. As has been emphasized, it would take centuries for the evangelical Marian Psalter of St. Dominic to become universally referred to as the rosary. This fact alone should put to rest the worries of historians who are unable to find sufficient mention of the word "rosary" in the early period of its history. Add to this the fact that many ancient documents have been lost and/or burned and destroyed during times of persecution, and it makes perfect sense why few ancient documents can be found. But there may be another reason why few ancient sources exist today: What if the wide-spread silence on the origins of the rosary during the first few centuries of its existence was intentional on the part of the Divine Craftsman?

Perhaps the Divine Craftsman may have intended the initial silence on the rosary as a way of protecting it. Observing silence can be a very prudent and effective method for keeping a secret weapon away from an enemy. If the enemy were to find out about the weapon, he might try to destroy it, confiscate it, or cause confusion, suspicion, and doubt regarding its effectiveness. Under such circumstances, the owner of the weapon might seek to cloak the weapon under a different name for a while. The "secret" would not have to be kept forever, but only for a time. God has been known to use the tactic of silence to conceal things from the enemy in other instances. Saint Ignatius of Antioch once noted the following about the silence God initially observed regarding the very foundations of Christianity. He wrote: "Mary's virginity and her giving birth escaped the notice of the prince of this world, as did the Lord's death — those three secrets crying to be told, but wrought in God's silence."[18] In light of this, the initial silence on the rosary may have been planned from the beginning as a way of protecting the rosary from the enemy.

Unfortunately, as we will see in later centuries, no answer seems to satisfy the critics of the rosary tradition. They continue to remain disturbed by the silence. In the 18th century, the critics will argue that because of the silence on the rosary in the early biographies of St. Dominic, St. Dominic should not be considered the founder of the rosary. Nevertheless, even outside of the notion that the silence about the rosary may have been intentional on God's part, there are legitimate historical reasons that can help us understand the silence.

First of all, the earliest biographical sketches on the life of St. Dominic really do not deserve to be classified as biographies at all. While it is true that the rosary is not mentioned in any of these accounts, the reason it is not mentioned is because these accounts are extremely short and in no way present a complete biography of St. Dominic. Take, for example, the earliest and best-known "biography" of St. Dominic written by Blessed Jordan of Saxony. When a person looks at Bl. Jordan's account, they are often surprised to find that it is not a bulky tome presenting a detailed life of the saint, but rather a tiny little pamphlet. The reality is that Bl. Jordan only met St. Dominic twice during his life, and one of those times was before Bl. Jordan was even a Dominican. As a matter of fact, many Dominican historians who have studied the early biographies of St. Dominic have noted that very important historical facts about the life of St. Dominic were left out of the biographies.[19] Almost none of the early accounts mention that St. Dominic founded a Third Order, preached against the Albigensians, or performed many miracles. It was due to this severe deficiency in the early accounts of their founder that the General Chapter of the Dominicans held in Cologne, Germany, in 1245, ordered its members to gather more information and present a more detailed historical account of the life of their founder at the next General Chapter. Unfortunately, this request by the Chapter was neglected and not fulfilled till much later. As time went by, the living witnesses died. Many important memories of the life of St. Dominic were lost to history and are now shrouded in silence. But silence does not mean absence.

Another argument that is put forth by the critics is that since the rosary was not mentioned in any of the depositions in the canonization process of St. Dominic, the rosary cannot be said to have originated with him. Once again, there are reasons for the silence in the depositions. Almost all of the depositions consisted only of brief affirmations of the truthfulness of statements already formulated and put together by the commission investigating the heroic virtue of St. Dominic. These pre-written statements did not focus on the private revelations and mystical experiences of St. Dominic, but rather on whether or not he was a virtuous and holy man. Those called forth to give sworn depositions were not allowed to supply their own statements or give testimony about the particulars of his life and apostolate. They were simply called forward to acknowledge and affirm what the commission had investigated and written down regarding St. Dominic's virtues and holiness. In other words, the witnesses did not speak on their own behalf about St. Dominic.

Then there is the silence on the part of St. Dominic himself. Why didn't St. Dominic write anything about the rosary? Perhaps he did, but the reality is that today there does not exist *anything* written *on any topic* by the hand of St. Dominic. All has been lost to history. Should we conclude from this that St. Dominic never wrote or spoke about anything? Of course not. Further, all Dominican historians affirm that St. Dominic was known to keep secrets, especially those regarding his visions and mystical experiences. Take, for example, the origins of the white outer garment of the Dominican habit, also called the Dominican scapular. The Dominican scapular originated from a vision given to the Dominican Blessed Reginald of Orleans as he lay sick and suffering in Rome in the year 1218. Blessed Reginald was a dear friend of St. Dominic and had joined the Dominican Order as one of its first members. After he received an apparition from Mary, Bl. Reginald informed St. Dominic of the contents of the mystical experience, which St. Dominic accepted as a sign that Mary wanted the white outer scapular to be part of the Dominican habit. To the surprise of everyone, however, St. Dominic kept the vision of Bl. Reginald, along with the knowledge of the origin of the white Dominican scapular, a secret until Bl. Reginald's death in 1220. Why did he remain silent? In all likelihood, he didn't want to open the door to controversy over an aspect of the Dominican habit stemming from its origins in private revelation. He may very well have done the same thing regarding the rosary. Saint Dominic was an intelligent, prayerful, and prudent man. He may have had the foresight to know that not speaking or writing anything about the rosary would keep the weapon away from the watchful eye of the enemy. Also, according to Dominican tradition, Mary never requested that St. Dominic write down his experience for others to read. In many private revelations given to saints over the centuries, the visionary is asked by Jesus or Mary to compose a diary or a journal recounting aspects of their mystical experiences, such as messages or new forms of devotion. Since Mary never asked St. Dominic to do this, he may have considered it an act of disobedience if he put into writing something Mary never requested him to write down. In other words, he himself did not want to break the silence. He trusted in heaven's plan.

As it was for St. Dominic, it is sufficient for us also to trust. Where there is mystery and silence regarding the origins of the rosary, God speaks through his Church, and the Church has spoken on this matter many times. The official statements of numerous popes over the last 800 years have made it quite clear that St. Dominic is to be understood as the founder of the rosary. This papal tradition is not a position born out of ignorance and blind piety, either. Many of the papal statements not only affirm that St. Dominic is the founder of the rosary, but also acknowledge and affirm the antecedents and ongoing developments that have occurred in the history of the rosary. Their important pronouncements teach us that there is no contradiction in affirming the antecedents, the ongoing developments, and the pious tradition all at the same time.

Only a few decades after the death of St. Dominic, Pope Urban IV (pope from 1261–1264) broke the silence and praised the power of the spiritual weapon when he declared: "Every day the rosary obtains fresh boon for Christianity."[20]

"So then, brethren, stand firm and hold to the traditions which you were taught by us, either by word of mouth or by letter."

— 2 Thess 2:15

THE 14TH CENTURY:
Plagues and Schism:
The Rosary is (Almost) Forgotten

The sword of the rosary was forged, unsheathed, and entrusted to St. Dominic during the 13th century. It was used as a weapon against the Albigensian heresy — and it worked. It was used to crown Mary's head with spiritual roses, and a chapel was built in its honor. At the beginning of the 14th century, the "dogs of God" continued to journey all throughout Europe, defending the truths of Catholicism by their dynamic preaching on the sacred mysteries of Christ. Yet the century would be fraught with many challenges.

As glorious as the 13th century was for Catholicism, the 14th century turned out to be one of the most difficult, plagued by disease, theological controversy, and endless political and ecclesiastical drama. In France, from 1315 to 1322, there were so many consecutive years of bad weather that unprecedented famines and starvation struck the country, resulting in a 10 percent mortality rate in some areas. Southern France was hit the hardest and experienced an even higher mortality rate, with famines lasting well into the middle of the century. It was a time of great distress and anxiety. As badly as it was needed, the rosary suffered severe neglect to the point of almost being forgotten. And this was only the beginning.

The Black Plague

Beginning in 1347 and lasting until 1351, the Black Plague (also known as the Black Death) swept through all of Europe at a rate that affected and devastated every city and town. Nothing like it had ever been experienced before. It impacted everyone, from peasants to priests, from saints to princes. It is estimated that during those four years, one third of the population of Europe contracted the plague and died. To put this in perspective, about 25 million people died. These figures do not include the millions of people who died in Asia and parts of the world unknown at that time.

The Black Death caused the very foundations of civilization to be rattled. People feared for their lives and, in many cases, lost hope. Many priests and sisters abandoned their people and fled the larger cities for fear of contracting the plague themselves. This abandonment by clergy and religious led to a loss of morale among the laity, giving them little confidence in their spiritual leaders. There were, of course, heroic examples of men and women who did not abandon their people, and instances of saints who stayed with the afflicted to aid them and ease their suffering as they prepared for death. Often, these saints contracted the plague themselves and died in the service of their fellow man.

During the time of the plague, a bizarre sect known as the Flagellants emerged. The Flagellants believed that the plague was a chastisement from God, and in order to show their contrition for their sins, they paraded through the streets of the cities flagellating (flogging) themselves in violent displays of penance. Sometimes they nearly bled to death because of their floggings. Oddly, the sect attracted many followers and became widespread. Not only did this sect promote extreme practices of penance and self-abuse, but it also taught major theological errors, errors that were in opposition to Christian teaching. For example, they believed that the shedding of their blood was sacred and had the power to cleanse people from their sins. As they paraded through the streets violently whipping themselves, they announced that their blood was comparable to Christ's and had the power to save sinners. Although Pope Clement VI condemned the sect in 1349, it continued to function and drew many followers.

The death, chaos, confusion, and turmoil of the era had a devastating effect upon the practice of the rosary. Although God may have intended for the rosary to be shrouded in silence as a way of protecting it, he never intended for it to be forgotten and abandoned by his people, which is precisely what began to happen during this century. Love dwindled for the rosary as more and more people became preoccupied with surviving the disastrous plague. The lack of interest in the rosary also meant that the keeping of any records or historical information related to it became less and less of a concern. Vast amounts of historical documents were lost during the time of the Black Death since many areas and buildings were burned to prevent further spread of the plague. These facts are important to keep in mind regarding the history of the rosary. Masie Ward, the 20th century author of the popular book *The Splendor of the Rosary,* made this very point when she noted the following: "Discussions of what happened [to the practice of the rosary] in the Middle Ages are apt to be obscured by the fact that so many documents have been lost, especially during the ravages of the Black Death."[1]

Ironically, even as the rosary was experiencing a severe decline, the Divine Craftsman was at work in his Church grafting onto the existing Hail Mary a new development, which came about as a result of the dire circumstances of the times — an addition to the Hail Mary that emanated from the hearts of God's afflicted people and gave the Hail Mary prayer the added dimension of urgent petition and supplication.

The Second Half of the Hail Mary

Until the 14th century, the rosary was prayed using the existing form of the Hail Mary: the combination of the Angelic Salutation and the Evangelical Salutation. This form of the Hail Mary contained an *implicit* prayer of petition, since it was an invocation to the mediating Mother of Jesus Christ. When the Black Death hit Europe, the Divine Craftsman inspired his people to formulate an *explicit* and urgent prayer of petition that he grafted onto the existing Hail Mary. By forging the intercessory prayer of his people into the flaming shaft of the sword, the Divine Craftsman gave the rosary the added bonus of being a prayer against death itself. After all, millions of people were dying. Everyone, at all levels of society, lived with the imminent fear of death. The Venerable Fulton J. Sheen articulated this point quite well:

> This [the second half of the Hail Mary] was not introduced until the latter part of the Middle Ages. Since it seizes upon the two decisive moments of life: "now" and "at the hour of our death," it suggests the spontaneous outcry of people in a great calamity. The Black Death, which ravaged all Europe and wiped out one-third of its population, prompted the faithful to cry out to the Mother of Our Lord to protect them at a time when the present moment and death were almost one.[2]

After the Black Death, the second half of the Hail Mary began to appear in the breviaries of religious communities, especially those of the Mercedarians, Camaldolese, and Franciscans. Its insertion into various breviaries also resulted in the full Hail Mary beginning to be used in the Dominican rosary. Like many things involving the rosary, however, it took a few centuries for this development to become universal practice. It wasn't until the prayers of the rosary were officially codified by the Church in the 16ᵗʰ century that inclusion of the second half of the Hail Mary became the norm.

The people of the 14ᵗʰ century greatly needed the "hope-filled" dimension of the second half of the Hail Mary prayer. They not only needed to know that Mary would pray for them "at the hour of their death," but also that she would pray for them "now" in their current, dire situation. In addition to the plague, the people found themselves in another challenging situation: the confusion of the Avignon Papacy. As if the Black Death were not enough, the politically motivated ordeal of the Avignon Papacy lasted from 1305–1377 and caused great anxiety, confusion, and concern among the faithful. Even after the crisis ended in 1377, it was soon followed by the Hundred Years War between France and England. The people of the 14ᵗʰ century endured non-stop stress and anxiety. For those who had survived the Black Death and the many other anxieties of the first half of the century, the latter part of the century offered them a new crisis in the form of the Great Western Schism. At times there were as many as three different individuals claiming to be the true pope. Even various saints were at odds over which pope was the real one, arguing with each other over the matter and defending the person they believed to be the authentic Vicar of Christ. This crisis began in 1378 and lasted until the early 15ᵗʰ century. The Great Western Schism was a theological nightmare, causing further division and confusion among the clergy and the laity. In the medieval mind, there was no doubt that they needed Mary's intercession "now" and at the "hour of death."

Dominicans

In general, the rosary suffered the same neglect among the Dominicans as it did from everyone else during the 14th century. Along with everyone else, the Dominicans were preoccupied with surviving the Black Death and matters related to the various crises of the day. This is not to say that the rosary was entirely abandoned by the Dominicans. It wasn't. Tidbits of historical information bear witness to the reality that many Dominicans continued to practice and promote it during those troubled times.

The renowned preacher Blessed Henry Suso (1300–1366) continued to promote the crowning of Mary with roses during the month of May. He was even known to weave together crowns for Mary himself. He also wrote brief, one-line meditations for use while praying the Our Father and Hail Marys. He specifically noted that these meditations were to be used while praying sets of 10 Hail Marys (decades).[3]

The Dominican mystic St. Vincent Ferrer (1350–1419) also kept the Dominican tradition alive by praying Hail Marys and preaching on the mysteries of Christ's life, especially the Nativity, the Passion, and the Resurrection of Jesus — and he preached on them in that exact order. To this day, one of the rosaries used by this great Dominican mystic remains on display in the Carmelite convent in Nantes, France.[4] Blessed Marcolino of Forli (1317–1397), also a famous Dominic preacher, always had a string of beads in his hand on which he prayed his Our Fathers and Hail Marys. Blessed Clara Gambacorta (1362–1419), prioress of the Dominican convent near Pisa, Italy, was a devout practitioner of the rosary all throughout her life. She encouraged others to pray it, too.

Further evidence can be seen in the Church of Santa Maria in Florence which contains the tombstone of the Dominican tertiary Monna Tessa (d. 1327). The tombstone clearly shows a rosary with distinct decades. There are many such examples of effigies on 14th century Dominican tombstones that depict rosaries. In Soissons, France, a poem is preserved, addressed to Our Lady by an unknown Dominican. The poem recounts how St. Dominic had been given a mission from heaven to evangelize the world by a form of preaching that employed the Hail Mary and meditation on the sacred mysteries of Christ. The poem dates from the early 14th century. Also, a Dominican convent in Tortosa, Spain, was dedicated using the title of the rosary in this century. So, even though the Dominicans in general neglected the rosary and its promotion, it was not altogether abandoned by the sons of St. Dominic. Nor did the rosary completely disappear from the hands of the laity and members of other religious communities.

Laity and Religious

An example of how members of the laity valued the rosary during the 14th century can be seen in a document dating from 1332. The document recounts how a devout woman who loved her rosary beads once touched them to the deceased body of a holy Franciscan priest, Blessed Francis Fabriano (1251–1322), as a sign of reverence for his renowned sanctity. The pious woman considered his body to be a relic and desired to sanctify her beads by touching them to his holy remains.

Another example can be seen in the Church of St. James in Paris, where there is a tombstone adorned with the effigies of the Lord of Villepierre, his wife, and his mother. In the mother's hand, in particular, there is a rosary composed of 15 decades, each separated by a larger bead that represents the Our Father. In the same church, there also once existed a magnificent monument of brass bearing the date 1355. It was erected over the remains of Humbert, Dauphin of Viennois. Humbert had given up his power, wealth, and title to enter the Dominicans. Around the effigy of Humbert were figures of Dominicans holding five-decade rosaries in their hands. Unfortunately, both the effigies of the family of the Lord of Villepierre and of Humbert were destroyed during the French Revolution in the 18th century. However, before they were destroyed, exact descriptions of both were written down by the 18th century Dominican historian Thomas Maria Mamachi.[5]

Another powerful witness of the rosary was St. Nuno Álvares Pereira (1360–1431). To this day in his native Portugal, he is revered and known as the "Precursor of Fatima" because during the 14th and 15th centuries he ardently promoted the rosary and the brown scapular. Saint Nuno was a medieval knight who defended the Church and his native Portugal from the threat of outside invasion. He always carried a sword on his person and was never known to back down from a fight, especially when it involved the Church. He loved the Virgin Mary and would fast three days a week in her honor. He was so devoted to the Queen of Heaven that he even consecrated his sword to her and named it "Maria." After many years of doing battle for the Church and Portugal he retired to his castle, which was situated above a little unknown village called Fatima. In 1423, inspired by his love for prayer and contemplation, he became a lay brother in the Carmelites. As a Carmelite, he continued to carry Maria under his long outer Carmelite scapular. Once, when a messenger was sent to inform him that there were new threats being made against Portugal, he pulled back his Carmelite scapular and displayed Maria to the eyes of the messenger. When the messenger caught sight of Maria, St. Nuno instructed the messenger to tell those making the threats that it would be unwise to attack Portugal because Maria would be unsheathed!

England (The Dowry of Mary)

In the same year that St. Dominic died (1221), the first Dominican priests arrived on the shores of England. From the earliest time of their presence in England, the Dominicans were known as the Blackfriars. This was due to the black outer cape they wore over their white habit. The Dominicans are called Blackfriars in England to this day. The Blackfriars clearly brought the rosary with them to England; it was during the 13th century that Ave Maria Lane in London, where large quantities of rosaries were produced, came into existence. In fact, Edmund Wateron's book *Pietas Mariana Britannica: A History of English Devotion to the Most Blessed Virgin Mary*, published in 1879, provided an inventory of a jeweler's shop dating from 1381, which included four sets of *Paternoster* beads made of coral and six sets of Hail Mary beads covered in silver and gold.

Many historians know that in the 14th century, England became known as the "Dowry of Mary." There are many reasons given for the origins of this title. Most pertinent for our purposes is the fact that, unlike many places in Europe where the rosary had been neglected and abandoned, England greatly promoted the rosary in the 14th century. As the Dowry of Mary, England had been given to the Queen of Heaven during the chaos of the 14th century so that devotion both to her and to her rosary could find a place of refuge amidst the confusion, chaos, and death that were wreaking havoc on mainland Europe. The refuge of England would ensure that the rosary was not completely lost. Centuries later, on April 14, 1895, Pope Leo XIII reaffirmed England's 14th century title of the Dowry of Mary in an allocution to the bishops of England.

England had not been entirely exempt from the ravages of the Black Death, but there, unlike in mainland Europe, the use of the rosary did not diminish. Evidence of this can be seen in the many references to rosary beads in the wills of English dukes and earls during this century. The rosary was in such common usage that, in 1362, as part of the statutes of Canterbury Hall, Archbishop Islip ordered those who were unable to attend Mass to pray 50 Hail Marys with the Our Father and the Apostles' Creed. In England, praying the Apostles' Creed as part of the rosary became the general custom. Many historians have noted that the Apostles' Creed became associated with the rosary in England because it was a practice taught to the English people by the Dominicans after they had arrived on their shores in the previous century.

Not only did the pious people of England keep the practice of the rosary alive during the 14th century, but they also introduced the rosary into art. During this century many of the stained glass windows and statues in English churches depicted the rosary. This practice began in the 14th century and carried over into the 15th century, often through artwork whose theme was "St. Michael and the Scales." This specific motif (see page 354) depicted St. Michael the Archangel holding weighing scales. In many of these pieces, the Virgin Mary was included off to one side of the scales. One of St. Michael's scale pans always held a soul;

the other scale pan held devils or ugly figures that represented the person's sins. The understanding was that St. Michael was responsible for weighing each side of the scale to find out which of the two was heavier. The artwork intended to show how a soul is judged, and whether or not a person would be sent to heaven or to hell. In these paintings and sculptures, Mary was frequently depicted placing a set of rosary beads in the scale pan of the soul. Mary's rosary would tip the scale in favor of the soul so that the person would go to heaven and not hell. The people of England knew that the rosary had heavenly weight! They knew it was an instrument that could be used to help them escape the fires of hell.

Of course, it is sometimes difficult to tell from the historical record whether what is referenced in medieval writings or depicted in sacred art is merely another form of the Marian Psalter or whether it's the Dominican rosary specifically. Still, even on strictly historical grounds, there is evidence of early forms of the rosary proper in the life of St. Dominic himself; in the lives of 13th century Dominicans and the Beguines of Ghent; and, as will be shown, in the "*Rosarius*" text (ca. 1300) and the preaching and writings of early Dominicans — all of which antedate the great proponent of the rosary, Blessed Alan de la Roche. (Some historians falsely claim Bl. Alan "invented" the Dominican rosary and began pious legends to promote it. More on him later.)

Observant Reform Movement

As the 14th century was coming to a close, a reform movement began to emerge in the Dominican Order. The difficult times of the 13th and 14th centuries caused the observance of religious discipline and piety to wane in many religious orders. Nevertheless, in the early part of the 14th century, certain religious communities were experiencing a renewal and returned to their original fervor. This renewal became known as the Observant Reform Movement. In general, the movement fulfilled a desire to return to a more intense prayer life and a communal life lived in accord with the original charism of the founder of the respective religious institute. The Franciscans appear to have been the first to initiate this renewal around the year 1330. Members of the Augustinians and Dominicans initiated their own renewal movement around the year 1380. When Blessed Raymond of Capua (1330–1399), St. Catherine of Siena's spiritual director, became the Master General of the Dominicans in 1380, he helped lead the reform movement among the sons of St. Dominic. He was zealous in his efforts to bring back a more strict observance and ordered that at least one house in each province (geographical region) of the Dominicans have a strict cloister for those members who wanted to return to the early practices and ideals of their founder, St. Dominic.

With the advent of the Observant Reform Movement in the Dominicans, the Queen of Heaven set the stage for the rosary's leap back across the English Channel and its full-force return to mainland Europe. For a time, it had been kept offshore for safekeeping, but it would soon be greatly needed to combat the many threats headed toward the Church. There were many battles on the horizon, and the spiritual blade of the rosary needed to be re-introduced and re-presented to a new generation of Catholics. In fact, certain movements were already afoot in mainland Europe that prompted the emergence of other types of Psalters and rosaries. Founders of religious communities, in particular, were being given visions from heaven that offered their respective religious communities variations of Marian Psalters and rosaries specific to their particular charism. For example, the great spiritual writer, foundress of a religious congregation, and mystic St. Bridget of Sweden (1303–1373) received visions from Jesus and Mary and was entrusted with a particular type of rosary known as the Brigittine rosary. Carthusian monks also began to formulate a contemplative form of the rosary during this time.

With the Observant Reform Movement sweeping across Europe and new versions of the rosary being promoted by religious communities, the "dogs of God" also began to be inspired to return to the original charism of their founder. The time was ripe for the rediscovery and renewal of the Dominican rosary.

THE 15TH CENTURY:
Blessed Alan de la Roche and the Revival of the Confraternity of the Rosary

A s the Observant Reform Movement gained momentum in the early 15th century, efforts were already being made by various groups and individuals to promote the Dominican rosary and its variations. One such person was St. Nicholas of Flüe (1417–1487). Saint Nicholas, a captain in the army in his native Switzerland, was a deeply religious man. As a defender of the Church and the Dominicans, he was known to carry a sword in one hand and a rosary in the other. He helped bring about peace in Switzerland by assisting in preventing a civil war. On one occasion, he also defended a Dominican monastery against Swiss confederates. In the middle of the century, the Franciscan mystic St. Catherine of Bologna (1413–1463) wrote a lengthy poem titled *Rosarium (The Rosary)* that dealt explicitly with the 15 mysteries of the rosary. Also, Carthusian monks were promoting a version of the rosary that was very similar to the Dominican rosary, and popes were making attempts to promote the rosary in the East. By the end of the century, a complete renewal of the Dominican rosary and its ancient Confraternity would be realized.

Popes

The most notable pope in the first half of the 15th century to promote the Dominican rosary was Pope Eugene IV (pope from 1431–1447). Though the document he promulgated to promote the rosary is most likely buried in a Vatican archive somewhere, it is certain that he wrote such a letter since it was referenced in the 1895 rosary encyclical *Adiutricem* of Pope Leo XIII: "Knowing what power Our Lady's rosary possesses, not a few of our predecessors [previous popes] took special care to spread the devotion throughout the countries of the East — in particular [Pope] Eugene IV in the Constitution *Advesperascente* issued in 1439."[1] The historical value of this statement cannot be underestimated, especially in light of the fact that the only type of rosary ever mentioned in any of the encyclicals of Pope Leo XIII is the Dominican rosary. How exactly Pope Eugene IV sought to spread the Dominican rosary in the East is uncertain, but Pope Leo XIII definitively affirms that the Dominican rosary was already in existence and being promoted by a pope before the rosary was revitalized by the Dominicans at the end of the century. Based on the combined weight of this written historical evidence and the many pieces of evidence we've discussed previously, it should be clear that the rosary did not originate with the Dominicans of the late 15th century.

Dominicans

Before the famous efforts to renew the rosary by the Dominicans in the late 15th century occurred, a handful of Dominicans were already attempting to bring about a renewal. While their efforts did not lead to a universal renewal or the reinstitution of the ancient Confraternity of the Rosary, their efforts are noteworthy. We have already mentioned Bl. Clara Gambacorta as one example. At the age of 12, she frequently gathered her friends together and had them kneel down so she could teach them how to pray the rosary. Another example can be found in the life of Blessed Giovanni Licci (1400–1511). This saintly Dominican lived to be 111 years old and had many miracles attributed to his intercession. He founded a Dominican convent in Sicily and had a marble image of Our Lady of the Rosary placed there.

One of the most intriguing Dominicans associated with the rosary during this time was Blessed Anthony Neyrot (1425–1460). The life of this Dominican provides a most interesting witness to the Dominican rosary. Shortly after being ordained a Dominican priest, Bl. Anthony was on a sea voyage to Naples when his ship was overtaken by Moors (Muslims). Everyone on board, including Neyrot, was taken captive and brought to northern Africa. As a captive, he disdained his imprisonment and his deplorable living conditions. To better his situation, he decided to deny his faith and volunteered to translate the Koran for the Muslims. As a reward for his renunciation of the Christian faith, he was adopted by a Muslim king and allowed to marry a Turkish noblewoman. Some time later, however, he had a dream of his former Dominican teacher, St. Antoninus of Florence (1389–1459). The dream led him to a radical change of heart and his re-conversion to Christianity. Neyrot denounced Islam, went to Confession, made a public announcement of his reversion to Christianity, and expressed his desire to return to the Dominicans. He even began to wear his old Dominican habit again in full view of the Muslims. These actions resulted in him being stoned to death by an angry mob of Moors. Dominican tradition asserts that while Bl. Anthony was being stoned to death, he held in his hands a crucifix and a rosary. Lastly, a Dominican bishop from the 15th century, Jean de Monte of Trèves (d. 1442), gave witness to the validity of the Dominican rosary tradition when he frequently noted in his homilies how St. Dominic had been a most ardent and zealous preacher of the Marian Psalter.[2]

England

The people of England continued to remain as devoted to the rosary in the 15th century as they had been during the 14th century. King Henry VI, in particular, seems to have been a great advocate of the rosary during this time. When a New Year's celebration was held in his honor in 1437, it was expected that all the guests in attendance would confer upon the king gifts befitting his royalty. Chroniclers have noted that one of the guests presented the king with a set of rosary beads as a New Year's gift; it was graciously accepted and considered a fitting gift for a king. Also, when King Henry VI founded Eton College in 1440, he put into the statutes of the college that every student was required to recite daily the complete Psalter of the Virgin Mary (the rosary), which at that time consisted of praying the Apostles' Creed, 150 Hail Marys, and 15 Our Fathers. A similar practice was implemented by Bishop William Waynflete of Winchester when he founded Magdalen College in Oxford in 1458. He not only required the students to daily pray 50 Hail Marys with each group of 10 Hail Marys separated by an Our Father, but also required the president of the college to do the same. Both the students and the president were to do this on their knees! The rosary was not just promoted at academic institutions in England, though. In many churches throughout England, it was customary to place rosaries at the entrance of the church in a basket so that those who did not possess their own set of beads could use the ones available. This practice was so edifying that news of it reached mainland Europe. A Dominican named Bl. Alan de la Roche made reference to it when he revived the rosary later in the century.

For one of the most frequently misunderstood aspects of the adaptation of the Dominican rosary during the 15th century, we must turn our attention to several Carthusian monks on the mainland.

Henry of Kalkar

Henry of Kalkar (1328–1408) was a devout Carthusian priest from Germany who was known to favor the reform movements of the time. As a member of one of the strictest religious orders in the Church, Kalkar thought the Carthusians could also benefit from this movement by introducing various elements of reform into the Order. He had come to this conclusion because he had once been the official visitator of the Carthusian houses in Germany. He himself was a very pious monk and wanted his brother monks to live a more devoted life in line with the ideals of their founder, St. Bruno.

According to the chronicles of the Carthusians of Cologne, Kalkar is said to have had a vision of Mary at some point during his monastic life in which she taught him a contemplative method of praying at least 150 Hail Marys. Similar to St. Bridget of Sweden and the Seven Founders of the Order of Servites, Henry Kalkar received a vision in which he was given a unique type of rosary. Like the other new forms of the rosary introduced in visions, his version was intended for use by his own religious order. Historians have noted that his Carthusian version of the Marian Psalter offered his brother monks a more contemplative method of praying the Marian Psalter than the one they'd been using for centuries. The new version consisted of 150 clauses dedicated to honoring Mary. It was prayed by first saying an Our Father, followed by 10 Hail Marys repeated 15 times or more, all while meditating on the designated clause.

The Carthusian-style rosary was different from the Dominican rosary. The Dominican rosary was intended for both individual and communal recitation, while the Carthusian rosary was only intended for individual recitation; a monk was free to pray as many Hail Marys as he wanted until he felt ready to move on to the next meditation. For this reason, the number of beads on a Carthusian rosary also differed from the Dominican rosary. The Dominican rosary had a set number of either 50 or 150 beads while the Carthusian rosary only consisted of 15 beads because it required that *at least* 15 Hail Marys be said. If a monk wanted to say more, he was free to do so and would just keep gliding his fingers over the same 15 beads. Interestingly, there is no record that Kalkar ever wrote down his 150 clauses for meditation. Most likely his version of the rosary was never intended to be prayed in common, which left every monk free to create his own personal set of clauses since there was no established norm.

The method of praying the Marian Psalter devised by Kalkar is a very honorable contemplative method. It allowed a monk to deeply reflect on a particular aspect of the lives of Jesus and Mary. Though it was never the intention of Kalkar to change or replace the Dominican rosary with his more monastic version, it did open up the possibility for confusion. Unlike the Brigittine rosary and the Servite Rosary of the Seven Sorrows, the Carthusian version closely resembled the Dominican rosary. However, it was through the emergence of the other types of rosaries that the Dominican rosary itself began to experience a renewal and was given pride of place among all the other versions. In fact, it would soon be revealed that, from the one great sword of the Dominican rosary, the Divine Craftsman had allowed other smaller swords to come into existence. The emergence of other versions of the rosary would gain for the Dominican rosary the honor of being known as "the rosary," rather than needing a qualifier to describe it, as was the case with the Brigittine rosary, the Servite rosary, and the Carthusian rosary.

In order to teach his people that all variations of the rosary trace their roots back to the Marian Psalter of St. Dominic, the Divine Craftsman used another religious order: the Franciscans. In the year 1422, a Franciscan novice received a vision of Mary in which she gave him what is known as the Franciscan Corona (Crown) rosary. This apparition proved to be extremely important, causing all versions of the Marian Psalter to be called rosaries.

As mentioned in a previous section (see page 40), Mary appeared to the Franciscan novice because he was saddened that, as a friar, he was no longer able to make a crown of flowers for Mary's statue, as had been his custom before entering the monastery. As part of his vision, Mary gave him a Franciscan version of the Marian Psalter and revealed to him that each time the Hail Mary was prayed, a rose was placed upon her head. As news of this vision spread, the word "rosary" began to emerge as the normative name for any method of praying a meditative Marian Psalter, whether Dominican, Brigittine, Servite, Carthusian, or Franciscan.

At that time, since everyone knew that the Dominican rosary had pre-existed all the other rosaries, it alone began to be referred to as *the* rosary. In addition, even though the other religious orders discussed above prayed a version of the rosary particular to their order, the members of those various orders continued to pray the original version of the rosary, as well. All variations of the rosary trace their roots back to the Dominican rosary. The Dominican rosary is the father of them all.

Dominic of Prussia

The first Carthusian monk to ever write down specific mysteries associated with the Carthusian rosary was another Dominic — Dominic of Prussia (1381–1461). Born in the city that is known today as Gdansk, Poland, Dominic later moved to the southern Polish city of Krakow. It was there that he spent his youth and received his education. According to his own testimony, the most influential teacher during his time in Krakow was a learned Dominican priest. In all likelihood, it was from this Dominican priest that he first learned of the rosary. Since the Observant Reform Movement was occurring in the Dominican Order during this time, Polish Dominicans would have also been experiencing a renewal of the rosary.

After Dominic of Prussia finished his studies in Krakow, he spent several years being something of a vagabond as he struggled to find his place in life. At some point, Dominic experienced a desire to give himself completely to Jesus Christ and follow him more closely, which led Dominic to become a Carthusian monk. Upon his entrance into the Carthusians, he became aware of the contemplative version of the rosary that had been promoted by Henry Kalkar. He liked this contemplative version very much, and during his novitiate in 1409, set out to modify it so as to make it simpler.

To simplify Kalkar's method, Dominic reduced the 150 clauses to 50 clauses. He also decided to write the clauses down. (Remember, Henry of Kalkar never wrote the clauses down.) Dominic also noted that the clauses were to be inserted after the first half of the Hail Mary. A Hail Mary in the Carthusian rosary was prayed like this: "Hail Mary, full of grace, the Lord is with thee. Blessed art thou among women and blessed is the fruit of thy womb, Jesus, conceived at the Annunciation."[3] Dominic claimed to be the first person to ever write down 50 clauses associated with the rosary and record them in a book. In time, his contemplative version of the rosary became known as the "Life of Christ rosary."

There is no reason to doubt that Dominic of Prussia was the first person to write down the 50 clauses *of the Carthusian rosary*. After all, 50 clauses needed to be written down because no one could be expected to remember 50 items. For this reason, Dominic of Prussia rightly deserves credit for having adapted and simplified the Marian Psalter of Henry of Kalkar. As was the case with Henry of Kalkar, however, Dominic of Prussia never claimed to be the inventor or originator of the rosary itself. His only claim to originality was that he was the first to write down 50 clauses on the life of Christ to be meditated on while praying the Hail Marys *according to the Carthusian method*.

To confirm this, the greatest chronicler and historian of the Carthusian Order up until the 17th century, Dom Le Couteulx, adamantly stated that neither Henry Kalkar nor Dominic of Prussia were to be understood as the founders of the rosary. Le Couteulx affirmed that it was St. Dominic, founder of the Dominicans, who was the founder of the rosary and not a Carthusian. Dominic of Prussia himself even noted in his book that he had added something to the already existing rosary. The exact word he used to describe what he did was "decorated"; he had "decorated" the rosary. By "decorating" it, he meant that he had given it many more meditations and made it more contemplative.

In contrast to the "decorated" rosary, the genius of the Dominican rosary was the mysteries did not need to be written down since there were only 15. It is easy to remember 15 mysteries; it is not easy to remember 50. The Dominican rosary had been given from heaven as an evangelical tool for a mendicant order. It was intended to be simple and mobile, not carried around in a book. The Dominican rosary had even been founded with a weekly cycle for the 15 mysteries that could be easily memorized. Furthermore, the confraternity of prayer associated with the Dominican rosary showed that it was intended for public recitation. The Carthusian rosary, on the other hand, had none of these dimensions.

As time went on, the Carthusian rosary never really caught on, even among Carthusians. To date, there does not exist a widespread practice of praying the Carthusian rosary anywhere in the world. It remains almost unknown outside of a few Carthusian circles. Perhaps this is because it has never received any indulgences from popes and was never intended for public recitation, but rather for individual prayer by contemplative monks. Nonetheless, the Life of Christ Rosary of the Carthusians is a very noble method of praying the rosary. Holy men such as St. Louis de Montfort, Blessed Pope Paul VI, and St. John Paul II have recommended it.

What all the above shows is that a rosary renaissance was occurring. The contemporary fervor for promoting various rosaries provides the spiritual context for understanding the re-birth of the Dominican rosary and the confraternity of prayer associated with it. If Mary was appearing to many religious priests and nuns during this era to give them rosaries particular to their orders, why would she not also appear to a son of St. Dominic and instruct him to revive the father of all rosaries?

The Dominican rosary had been kept alive in England. In the late 15th century, it was time for it to return to the mainland. The perfect place to re-introduce it would be a Dominican house located in mainland Europe, but geographically close to England. If there were a Dominican at that house who was involved in the Observant Reform Movement, God could use him to revive the Dominican rosary. Providentially, there was such a man.

Blessed Alan de la Roche, OP

In the mid-15ᵗʰ century, there was a Dominican priest involved in the Observant Reform Movement who lived very near to the English Channel at a Dominican house in Douai, France. The priest's name was Bl. Alan de la Roche (1428–1475). He had been born in Brittany and, during his youth, had wandered from a life of virtue. However, after experiencing a conversion, he joined the Dominicans and quickly advanced in virtue and wisdom. He gained a reputation as an eloquent preacher and a skilled theologian and teacher. At one point during his priesthood, the Dominican tradition states that Our Lady appeared to him and informed him that she had been the one responsible for obtaining the grace of his conversion. She then told him that she had a specific mission for him to accomplish: reviving and renewing the ancient Dominican rosary. To help him understand all that this mission entailed, she began to appear to him frequently and instruct him in what to do. In many of these visions, Jesus and St. Dominic also appeared to him and provided him with further instructions. Unfortunately, Bl. Alan seems to have been a little slow in doing what heaven was asking of him. In one of the apparitions, Jesus chastised him for not preaching the rosary, saying: "You [Bl. Alan] have all the learning and understanding that you need to preach my mother's rosary, and you are not doing so."[4] Our Lord then said to him, "The world is full of devouring wolves, and you, unfaithful dog, know not how to bark."[5] As a Dominican, Bl. Alan was a "dog of God," and the words of Jesus were a wake-up call that he should have been preaching the rosary. After this apparition, Bl. Alan became completely consumed with reviving the rosary and making it known.

The first order of business for Bl. Alan was to author a book that presented a clear history of the origins of the Dominican rosary. This book would serve as the manual for the renewal of the rosary. As a Dominican, he was familiar with the tradition regarding the rosary's origins and how it was prayed. He had even witnessed it being prayed in common when he had once visited the Beguine convent in Ghent. Thus, one of the first things he wrote about was how he was renewing the rosary and not founding or re-founding it. He made it very clear that the founder of the rosary was St. Dominic. Interestingly, he even noted that St. Dominic could also be considered a restorer of the rosary since the essence of the rosary — the Our Father, the Hail Mary, and the sacred mysteries of the life of Jesus — had been in existence from the beginning of the Church. In his mind, St. Dominic had simply been instructed by Our Lady to give ancient Christian truths a new devotional form. At any rate, to distinguish the Dominican rosary from all the others in vogue at the time, he noted that the Dominican rosary was founded to be a weapon against heresy and a mobile form of prayer for itinerant preachers. Although there were other Marian Psalters before St. Dominic's, Bl. Alan insisted that the Marian Psalter used by St. Dominic was the first of its kind to include mysteries and meditations.

He also stressed that the Dominican rosary's 15 mysteries made it simpler to pray than the 50 clauses of the Carthusian rosary. In his writings, he also noted that the 15 mysteries together made for a total of 150 Hail Marys, which imitated the 150 psalms of the Old Testament. Blessed Alan was aware that the vision given to the Franciscan novice in 1422 had helped cause all Marian Psalters to be referred to as rosaries, but he wanted the Dominican rosary to be referred to as the Marian Psalter in order to retain the original title and keep it closely associated with the 150 psalms.

It may seem odd that the Dominican responsible for renewing the Dominican rosary did not want it to be called a rosary, but he had several reasons for wanting to return to the ancient title. For one, the word "rosary" had taken on a vulgar connotation in popular culture during the late 15th century. "Rosary" was now being used in secular circles to refer to the flower of Aphrodite, as well as the symbol for the cult of Venus. It had become a symbol for people desirous of engaging in lustful pursuits, especially those desiring to have illicit rendezvous and sexual encounters behind rosebushes. In the late 15th century, the phrase "picking a rose" had the same connotation that the expression "deflower" has in English today. Therefore, to avoid any scandal or association with such things, Bl. Alan desired to return to the practice of referring to the prayer as the Marian Psalter. His other reason for the change in name was to establish a firm connection between the Dominican rosary and the 150 psalms. He reasoned that since Our Lady had originally revealed this form of prayer as "her Psalter," it should retain its name and be associated with the 150 psalms.

Despite Bl. Alan's noble intentions, heaven had not revealed to him that he was to revert to calling the Dominican rosary the Marian Psalter. Heaven's acceptance of the name "rosary" signaled an extremely important development in the history of the rosary: It meant that the Divine Craftsman intended to further develop the Dominican rosary by making it less dependent on its association with the 150 psalms of the Old Testament. This opened up the possibility of future developments and additional mysteries. Limiting the rosary to an association with the 150 psalms would have forever precluded such developments. The Divine Craftsman knew that additional mysteries might be needed in different circumstances to combat and confront future heresies. The rosary would always have its roots in the Marian Psalter and the 150 psalms, but heaven desired the prayer to be known henceforth as the rosary. As it turns out, Bl. Alan's intention to return to the original name was misinterpreted; some groups began to refer to it as "Alan's Psalter." When word of this reached Bl. Alan, he was not pleased and insisted that it never be called Alan's Psalter. In the end, as we will soon see, God used another Dominican of that era to ensure that the Church promoted the prayer under the title of the rosary.

Blessed Alan also mentioned in his book a fascinating practice of the Dominicans ("Blackfriars") in England. The Blackfriars observed an "old" custom by vesting each newly professed friar with a rosary, which was to be hung from his belt. Blessed Alan greatly admired this old custom and sought to make it part of his revival efforts among the Dominicans in mainland Europe.

All in all, Bl. Alan's efforts to restore the rosary were very successful. Indeed, the revival of the rosary proved to be an essential element of the further reform of the Dominican Order. In towns in which there was a reformed house of Dominicans, the members almost always prayed the rosary in common. On the other hand, where there was a Dominican house that was resistant to the reform movement, it was almost certain that they did not pray the rosary together. Love for the rosary became a telling sign of the spirit at work in a particular Dominican house. Later Dominicans would stress this reality and acknowledge that the fruitfulness of the order depended upon their love for the rosary. One such Dominican was the 17th century Master General Fr. Antoninus de Monroy. He said, "The rosary is the most beautiful flower of the [Dominican] Order. When that flower begins to fade, the charm and splendor of our Institute likewise disappears ... but when it revives it draws down upon us the plenteous dew of heaven."[6]

Renewal of the Confraternity of the Rosary

The primary means by which Bl. Alan sought to bring about the re-birth of the Dominican rosary was the re-establishment of the ancient Confraternity of the Rosary. He was aware that St. Dominic had established an association of prayer to accompany the rosary, and knew that when the Confraternity of the Rosary diminished in the 14th century, the neglect of the rosary soon followed. Saint Louis de Montfort would phrase it this way: "All things, even the holiest, are subject to change, especially when they are dependent on man's free will. It is hardly to be wondered at, then, that the Confraternity of the Holy Rosary only retained its first fervor for one century after it was instituted by Saint Dominic. After this, it was like a thing buried and forgotten."[7] Buried and forgotten, indeed, but Bl. Alan's mission was to bring it to life again.

In many ways, Bl. Alan understood the renewal of the Confraternity of the Rosary to be an extension of the Observant Reform Movement for the Dominican Order. He realized that promoting the Confraternity of the Rosary would be a way of promoting the Dominicans and, in turn, re-igniting his brothers with the torch of truth to set the world on fire. With this in mind, in the year 1470 in the town of Douai, France, he initiated the renewal of the Confraternity of the Rosary, and established the first confraternity associated with the renewal of the Dominican rosary.

In order to boost the Confraternity, Bl. Alan wrote an instruction booklet, titled *Book and Ordinance*, which was very well received. It became the first manual for the renewed Confraternity and was widely promoted. In his book he referenced another work on the rosary that had been written in 1275 — *How*

Our Lady's Psalter Was First Founded. He thereby confirmed to the members of the confraternity that, just as he was not the founder of the rosary, he was also not the founder of the Confraternity. Further, he repudiated the practice of referring to the rosary as "Alan's Psalter."

In his writings, he also referenced the official document of Pope John XXII (see page 44) from the early 14th century in which the Vicar of Christ promoted the rosary and attached indulgences to the Confraternity. He testified that he had seen the original papal document in the Dominican Convent in Avignon. Unfortunately, neither the original manuscripts of the 1275 rosary book, nor of the rosary document of Pope John XXII, exist today.

Part of the genius of Bl. Alan's revival of interest in the rosary was that he chose to include in his book miraculous stories about how the rosary had converted people back to the faith, delivering them from demons and lives of sin. This would become the method used to promote the rosary in almost all subsequent Confraternity books because reading the documentation of miracles instilled in people a desire to participate in such a powerful prayer. He also promoted many popular rosary songs to further embed the rosary in the thoughts of the faithful. These simple songs were easy to remember and greatly aided his renewal efforts.

Blessed Alan also provided many reasons for people to join the Confraternity. He insisted that the promotion of the Confraternity of the Rosary would greatly strengthen parish life and turn Catholic homes into domestic churches. Indeed, Catholic families began to gather in the evenings to pray the rosary. Many homes erected tiny chapels where the rosary was prayed.

Since the rosary could be prayed in a person's native language, Bl. Alan's preaching on the rosary helped to bring it to the common man. In contrast to many pious associations of the time, the Confraternity admitted anyone. Men, women, clergy, the poor, and even lepers could become members. There were no dues, either. A member was not required to be literate or educated.

Some of the most appealing aspects of being a Confraternity member were the "after death" benefits. When a member of a particular confraternity died, the surviving members of the confraternity promised to continue to pray for the deceased member. Thus, being a member of the Confraternity was a great help for getting out of purgatory and into heaven sooner. A person could even enroll another person in the Confraternity without that person's knowledge. This dimension of the Confraternity was particularly appealing to those who lived with difficult spouses and/or children and were worried about the fate of their souls.

In the Confraternity handbook, Bl. Alan also advocated the wearing and carrying of the rosary by the members to publicly remind others of eternal realities. When Bl. Alan sought to revive the "old" Dominican custom of wearing the rosary as part of their habit, he also sought to instill the habit of doing something similar in the members of the Confraternity. His idea for the laity was that the rosary should be worn over the shoulder, like one wears a sling for a quiver, or from the belt, as a knight wears a sword. This style of wearing the rosary helped reinforce the idea that the rosary is a spiritual weapon. Blessed Alan made it an honor to be a member of the Confraternity, and members began to be referred to as "Rosarians." There can be no doubt that Bl. Alan was one of the greatest champions of the rosary to ever live.

Fr. Jacob Sprenger, OP

After Bl. Alan renewed the confraternity in Douai in 1470, another Dominican priest — Fr. Jacob Sprenger — initiated a confraternity in Cologne, Germany, in 1475. He, too, was involved in the Observant Reform Movement. Father Sprenger was honored by having his renewed confraternity become the first to be officially recognized by the Church, even before Bl. Alan's. This was due to a request sent to the pope by a very prominent member of the Cologne confraternity — the Holy Roman Emperor, Frederick III. The Emperor was so impressed with the Confraternity that he personally sent a request to the pope asking for the confraternity in Cologne to be officially recognized by the Church. His request was quickly granted, and the Cologne confraternity received ecclesiastical approval on September 8, 1475, the Feast of the Birth of Mary. It was on that same day that Bl. Alan died in Zwolle, Holland.

When Sprenger renewed the confraternity in Cologne, he imitated what Bl. Alan had done for the Douai confraternity, authoring a manual and preaching about the rosary everywhere he went. Sprenger also imitated Bl. Alan by acknowledging that he had not founded the rosary or the confraternity. Quite the contrary; he explicitly wrote:

> To the honor of the esteemed mother and unblemished Virgin Mary,
> I, Brother Jakob Sprenger, Doctor of the Holy Scriptures and prior
> of the great Dominican convent of Cologne, have in the year 1475,
> on the day of Our Lady's birth, revived and reestablished the tradi-
> tional, old prayer of the rosary of Our Lady.[8]

Since Sprenger's confraternity was the first renewed Confraternity to be officially recognized by the Church, it received major support. During the first seven years of its existence, it enrolled more than 100,000 members! Sprenger had become a true champion of the rosary.[9]

In addition to his successful renewal of the rosary and the confraternity in Germany, Fr. Sprenger is also rightly credited for maintaining that the ancient prayer of St. Dominic would no longer be primarily referred to as a Marian Psalter, but would go by the name "rosary." Sprenger was aware of the mundane and immoral connotation that had become attached to the word "rosary" in his day and understood why Bl. Alan wanted to avoid the term, but still insisted that the devotion should be primarily referred to as the rosary. A development had taken place, and even though he knew that the Dominican Marian Psalter and the rosary were the same thing, he rightly discerned that heaven desired it to be called the rosary. Clearly, the Divine Craftsman approved of his efforts. In the official letter written by the papal legate giving official recognition to the Cologne confraternity, the word "rosary" was used to describe the devotion. This document helped to solidify for all future ages that this form of prayer was to be forever known as the rosary.

Confraternity Indulgences

In 1476, one year after the Church officially recognized Sprenger's confraternity, the papal legate Alexander of Forli granted indulgences to the Cologne confraternity and stated the following: "The Confraternity of the Rosary of the Blessed Virgin has recently been most salutarily established by the Dominicans in Cologne; rather, restored and renewed; since, in various histories it is read that it was preached by Blessed Dominic, but had fallen into disuse and almost into oblivion."[10] This declaration was followed by official papal documents from Pope Sixtus IV in 1478 and 1479 that confirmed the indulgences given to the confraternity. The 1479 document was titled *Ea Que* and made reference to the rosary being prayed since "ancient times."

What also greatly aided the spread of the Confraternity and its membership was an action of Pope Sixtus IV in 1476. In a papal document, he declared that all indulgences could be used for the souls in purgatory, rather than only for the person who had actually performed the indulgenced act. This proved to be a major incentive for people to become Rosarians. Members were now able to apply the indulgences gained from being members of the Confraternity to their deceased family members and friends.

The Church's decision to grant the Confraternity various indulgences resulted in the rapid growth of confraternities in other cities and towns across Europe. In 1478, one was established in Lisbon, Portugal. This was followed by the rapid establishment of confraternities in Schleswig, Germany, in 1481; Ulm, Germany, in 1483; and Frankfurt, Germany, in 1486. On February 26, 1491, as more confraternities continued to be erected all over Europe, Pope Innocent VIII issued a document titled *Splendor Paternae Gloriae*. The document referred to the restored Dominican tradition as "a most devout confraternity" and granted even more indulgences to it.[11] This document was soon followed in 1495 by the document *Illius qui* by Pope Alexander VI, in which he confirmed the Dominicans in their apostolate of promoting the Confraternity, affirmed all the previous indulgences granted by his papal predecessors, and officially validated what has become known as the pious tradition of the rosary.

The Pious Tradition

The pious tradition is the papal belief that the rosary and the Confraternity of the Rosary were both founded by St. Dominic. *Illius qui*, the 1495 document of Pope Alexander VI on the Confraternity of the Rosary, is generally understood to be the official starting point of this tradition. It is almost certain that popes believed the pious tradition before 1495, but *Illius qui* is the beginning of the *written* evidence for the tradition in the writings of the popes.

The statement by Pope Alexander VI was included within the context of his praise for the Dominican Confraternity of the Rosary and the benefits and indulgences granted to it. It is a simple statement that reads: "Through the merits of the Virgin Mary herself and the intercession of Saint Dominic, [who was] once the excellent preacher of this Confraternity of the Rosary, this entire world was preserved."[12] This simple statement traces the origin of the Confraternity back to St. Dominic. It implies that since the Dominican rosary and the Dominican Confraternity of the Rosary did not preexist the founder of the Dominican Order, St. Dominic not only founded the Confraternity of the Rosary, but also the rosary itself. After 1495, the pious tradition clearly became a papal tradition and began to be affirmed in official documents of the Church.

Picture Books, Woodcuts, Altarpieces

In their renewed enthusiasm for the rosary, the Dominicans began to produce edition after edition of rosary picture books, woodcuts, and altarpieces. All of these were a way of encouraging people to meditate on the sacred mysteries and resulted in confraternities beginning to also commission similar artwork, woodcuts, and altarpieces. Many of these works became known as "picture rosaries," since many people were unable to read but were able to see the images and understand the mysteries associated with them.

One of the earliest examples was a booklet called *Our Dear Lady's Psalter*, created by an anonymous Dominican friar in 1483 and supposedly drawn directly from the writings of Bl. Alan de la Roche himself. This booklet of images included the Joyful, Sorrowful, and Glorious Mysteries, as well as a diagram showing the entire structure of the rosary and how it should be prayed, much as is done today in pamphlets on the rosary (see page 441). The 1483 booklet underwent seven editions before 1503.

An early example of a rosary woodcut was produced by the Dominican priest Francisco Domenech in 1488. It bears witness to the long-standing rosary tradition within the Dominican Order. He fashioned this particular woodcut, appropriately titled *"Rosarius,"* for the Monastery of St. Catherine in Barcelona, Spain. The woodcut depicted the 15 Joyful, Sorrowful, and Glorious Mysteries. This *"Rosarius"* woodcut also featured an image of St. Dominic holding a rosary in his hand.

By the end of the 15th century, the revival of the rosary was in full swing. Leonardus Mansueti, the Master General of the Dominicans during the time that the rosary confraternity was revived, had offered to everyone who prayed the rosary a share in the merits and graces available through the good works and prayers of the Dominican Order. Such promotion of the rosary led to many members of the diocesan clergy expressing concern over the rapid spread of the confraternities. The Dominican confraternities had gained so many members that pastors were concerned that their churches would soon be empty, since so many people were enrolling in the confraternity and attending Mass at Dominican chapels.

Johannes Gutenberg's invention of the printing press during the mid-15th century also greatly helped to promote the rosary and its Confraternity. Prior to the 15th century, it made little sense to write about the rosary and its mysteries if only 5 percent of the population could read. This 95 percent illiteracy rate helps to explain why the mysteries were not written down in previous centuries, but rather "told" and passed down from one generation to the next via oral tradition. It also helps us to understand why the praying of the rosary in ancient times was often referred to as "telling the beads."

All of this changed, however, with the invention of the printing press. The rosary and the Confraternity were set to spread to the four corners of the globe during the 16th century.

	12th century	1208	13th century	14th century	14th century	15th century	1422	1470
	Cistercians/ Carthusians	St. Dominic	Order of Servites of Mary	St. Bridgit	Henry of Kalkar	Dominic of Prussia	Franciscan Novice Roche	Bl. Alan de la Roche
	Marian Psalter	Preached Marian Psalter (The Rosary); Confraternity of the Rosary	Seven Sorrows Rosary	Brigittine Rosary	Meditated Carthusian Marian Psalter	Life of Christ Rosary (Corona)	Franciscan Crown	Renewal of the Dominican Rosary and Confraternity of the Rosary
	No mysteries/ meditations	15 mysteries/ meditations on Jesus and Mary	7 mysteries/ meditations on Mary	18 mysteries/ meditations on Jesus and Mary	150 clauses/ meditations on Jesus and Mary	50 clauses/ meditations on Jesus and Mary	7 mysteries/ meditations on Mary	15 mysteries/ meditations on Jesus and Mary
	Individual Prayer	Individual and Communal Prayer	Individual and Communal Prayer	Individual and Communal Prayer	Individual Prayer	Individual Prayer, rarely Communal Prayer	Individual and Communal Prayer	Individual and Communal Prayer
	Monastic	Mendicant	Mendicant	Cloistered	Monastic	Monastic	Mendicant	Mendicant

THE 16TH CENTURY:
The Rosary in Battle:
Lepanto and Our Lady of Victory

At the beginning of the 16th century, Europe was experiencing the peak of the Renaissance. This re-birth was not only cultural, but also spiritual, and the confraternities played a major role in reviving piety and devotion. The practice of bowing the head and striking the breast as a form of penance during the *Salve Regina* became common during this time. Membership in the confraternities increased on a daily basis, and they continued to spread everywhere. After Italian translations of two of Bl. Alan's books appeared in 1505, there was hardly a church in Italy that did not have a confraternity of the rosary. In 1521, a book on the rosary by the Dominican priest Alberto da Castello became wildly popular and was one of the most referenced works on the rosary of that century. Yet even as piety and devotion were spreading, the 16th century witnessed the land of England turn against the rosary, a fallen-away German priest initiate a rebellion against the Church, and the followers of Islam threaten to conquer the heart of Christendom. Ultimately, rosary victories were won, feast days associated with the rosary were established, and great missionaries took the rosary with them to all their foreign destinations.

Flourishing of the Confraternities

One way that the confraternities contributed to the cultural renaissance of the 16th century was by commissioning well-known artists to paint images for their chapels. These images always reflected the pious tradition of the rosary's origins and history. Paintings depicting the rosary had been around since the Battle of Muret in 1213, but as part of the re-birth of this particular form of Marian piety, confraternities desired to have their own image on display in the altarpiece for their regional chapel. One famous painter by the name of Giuseppe Cesari was commissioned by the confraternity in Cesena, Italy, to paint such an image during this time. His painting was given the title "La Madonna del Rosario." It is a masterpiece of rosary art. However, one of Cesari's pupils, Caravaggio, painted the most famous rosary image of this century, the "Madonna of the Rosary." Historians agree that Caravaggio's rosary masterpiece was commissioned by the confraternity in Dubrovnik, Croatia, for the Dominican Church in the city. As in all the rosary altarpieces, it depicted the Queen of Heaven entrusting the rosary to St. Dominic.

Even the famous "Last Judgment" by Michelangelo, painted on the wall of the Sistine Chapel between the years 1534–1541, paid homage to the rosary. In the center of the "Last Judgment," there is a figure who, while ascending into heaven, is also pulling souls up by means of the rosary. It's a powerful image and was intentionally included in the painting to teach the viewer that the rosary has the power to snatch souls from the flames of hell.

The confraternities were so highly regarded during this era that many popes became members of the Confraternity themselves. One such pope was Pope Leo X. He was greatly devoted to the rosary and in 1520, in an official document titled *Pastoris Aeterni,* he offered a concise history of the Confraternity, its downfall, and its renewal. He wrote:

> A petition presented by our beloved sons, the prior and preaching brethren of Cologne [Dominicans], stated that of old, as is read in history, a confraternity of the faithful of both sexes, and called the rosary of the Holy Virgin Mary, was instituted by St. Dominic in honor of the Hail Mary, and had been widely preached with signs that followed. With the passage of time this confraternity became neglected and forgotten. In 1475, when the city and diocese of Cologne were oppressed by war, the same confraternity ... was renewed and reinstituted. This form of prayer is commonly called the Psalter or rosary of the Holy Virgin.[1]

Immediately after Pope Leo X, Pope Adrian VI declared that "the rosary is the scourge of the devil,"[2] and Pope Julius III hailed the rosary as the "glory of the Roman Church."[3] Toward the end of the century, Pope Sixtus V, also a devout member of the Confraternity, reaffirmed that the rosary and its Confraternity were founded by St. Dominic. And the greatest pope of the 16ᵗʰ century, St. Pope Pius V, declared in 1569 that it was by means of the Confraternity of the Rosary that "Christians began suddenly to be transformed into other men, the darkness of heresy to be dispelled, and the light of Catholic faith to shine forth."[4] The strong papal statements on the greatness of the rosary and the Confraternity were being made for a particular purpose by these popes. Unlike the 14ᵗʰ century when the rosary had been severely neglected and almost forgotten, the 16ᵗʰ century was experiencing an all-out attack on the rosary from a disgruntled and fallen-away German priest.

The Protestant Rebellion

The main leader of the Protestant rebellion was a disgruntled Catholic priest named Martin Luther (1483–1546). Many others followed his example and turned on the Catholic Church and her teachings during this era. Luther disdained the authority of the pope, many of the teachings of the Church, and was inimical toward many of the pious devotions practiced by Catholics. He especially hated the rosary.

Due to their close association with indulgences and prayer for the souls in purgatory, the rosary and its Confraternity came under direct fire from Luther and the other rebels. Luther and his followers believed the rosary to be a forbidden repetitious prayer (see Mt 6:7), a "work" performed to somehow "earn" salvation, and therefore useless and unnecessary. As they sought to change many of the teachings of Catholicism, they saw no reason to pray the rosary since they taught that indulgences were an invention of the pope. Also, since they did not believe in purgatory's existence, a rosary indulgence was obtained for no one. In their minds, the rosary was superstitious and offensive to Christ, and they attacked it as a false devotion of the Catholic Church.

Martin Luther deserves the title of first historical-critic of the rosary and its Confraternity. Evidence of this is clearly seen in Martin Luther's copy of Marcus von Weida's rosary handbook. This book still exists today in the holdings of the library of the University of Jena, in Germany. The historian Anne Winston-Allen offers an overview of the outright hatred Martin Luther had for the rosary, specifically noting the comments he made in von Weida's rosary handbook. She wrote:

> The comments that Luther jotted in the margins of the book mock the authenticity, the antiquity, and the efficacy of the rosary. At one point Luther exclaims, "Where the devil do so many and various lies come from?" In the margin next to a story about a wayward youth who is reformed by praying the rosary, Luther comments, "And thus through a stupid work he merited justification." Later, reacting to the tale of a nobleman saved from condemnation through the rosary-psalter and Mary's intercession, Luther writes, "not through Christ, but by works."[5]

For all the hatred that Martin Luther had for the rosary, when he himself translated the Song of Songs into German, he changed all of the lilies mentioned in the Vulgate version to roses! It is also rather odd that the man who desired to approach Christianity from a *sola scriptura* ("Scripture alone") method failed to comprehend that the rosary itself is primarily a scriptural prayer and a spiritual sword forged from the very Word of God to combat the dragon-serpent. How he posited that a meditation rooted in Scripture was offensive to the Savior is beyond logical comprehension. In his arrogance, he also failed to realize that when a person mocks the biblical sword of the rosary, they are also mocking the maker of the sword. The rosary wasn't made by man; it was made by God.

As inimical as the Protestant rebels were toward the rosary, they could not stop the renewal of the rosary from taking place. In fact, the Protestant rebellion only helped fan the flames of the rosary renaissance. Devout Catholics reacted to the rebels by becoming even more zealous in founding confraternities and praying the rosary. The rosary became a sign of a true Catholic and a devoted son of the Church. As when Our Lady had given it to St. Dominic, the rosary once again became an evangelical tool, a badge of orthodoxy, and a weapon against heretics. The Protestants tried everything to destroy it, but didn't succeed. Tragically, in one of their attempts to destroy the rosary, they burned the archives of the Beguines of Ghent in 1566. This futile attempt to rid the world of the indestructible sword by burning the Beguine archives destroyed invaluable documents related to the history of the rosary. Had they only had the humility to take the sword into their own hands, they could have become champions and heroes themselves, witnesses to the power of the rosary later in the century, when the rosary-sword saved Western Civilization — and Christianity itself — from the threat of Islamic conquest.

For all their attempts to rid the world of the rosary, Protestants ended up doing more to promote it than to destroy it. For example, the Protestant rejection of purgatory was not very consoling to a continent that only a few centuries earlier had lost one third of its population during the Black Plague. Even during the 16ᵗʰ century, people continued to die from plagues. From 1575–1577, almost 47,000 people died in Venice from a plague. Such events caused many people to cling to the rosary all the more as a chain of mercy. In the end, as history affirms, the very things that Protestants rebelled against during the 16ᵗʰ century — the papacy, the Holy Sacrifice of the Mass, Confession, priests, the intercession of the Virgin Mary, the rosary, and confraternities — were the very things that saved Christianity and Western Civilization from being overtaken by the spiritual plague of Islam. By throwing these things away, the Protestants lost their chance of becoming canonized saints.

The Sodality of Our Lady

During the Protestant rebellion, the confraternities were thriving, so much so that there arose a sister movement known as the Sodality of Our Lady. Shortly after the founding of the Society of Jesus (Jesuits) by St. Ignatius of Loyola in 1534, a devout Jesuit priest named Fr. John Leunis initiated the first sodality at the Jesuit Roman College in 1563. As devout associations of the faithful, the sodalities of Our Lady had a structure and purpose similar to those of the confraternities, and the members of both Sodality and Confraternity were known to be valiant defenders of Mary against the theological errors of the Protestants. The ultimate goal of the Sodality was to transform society through Marian devotion and the practice of the works of mercy. The Sodality offered people a method for undergoing a deeper personal conversion while also making a positive impact on the culture. The rosary was a prominent feature of the Marian devotion of the Sodality.

Since the Sodality had been founded by the Jesuits, the meditative style of prayer found in the *Spiritual Exercises* of St. Ignatius of Loyola blended very well with the members' daily meditation on the mysteries of the rosary. Many historians have even noted that St. Ignatius himself most likely developed his method of "composition of place," or imaginative meditation, through his familiarity with the meditative style of praying the rosary. In fact, all early Jesuits had a profound love of the rosary. One example is found in the life of St. Alphonsus Rodriguez (1532–1617). This devout Jesuit brother not only prayed the rosary every day, but was also known to pray endless Hail Marys throughout his day in order to sanctify all his activities.

When the founder of the sodalities, Fr. Leunis, died in 1584, the sodalities did not cease to exist, but continued to flourish. In fact, 16 days after Fr. Leunis' death, Pope Gregory XIII issued an apostolic constitution on the sodalities called *Omnipotentis Dei*. In this document, he gave the Sodality of Our Lady full canonical status and enriched it with many indulgences and privileges. In 1587, Pope Sixtus V authorized the Superior General of the Jesuits to establish more sodalities throughout the world. Jesuits began to erect them everywhere they went. They grew so rapidly that, by 1658, the original sodality at the Roman College had 1,459 other sodalities affiliated with it. Unlike the confraternities, which both men and women could join, these sodalities were limited to male members only. It would not be until the beginning of the 18th century that groups of women were slowly introduced into the sodalities. In 1751, Pope Benedict XIV granted the Superior General of the Jesuits the authority to fully admit women to the sodalities. By the mid-20th century, there were more than 80,000 sodalities worldwide. Through the Jesuits' promotion of the sodalities and the Dominicans' promotion of the confraternities, these two great religious communities used the rosary to help transform the culture and bring many souls and hearts to Jesus through Mary.

Saints

As the ancient confraternities and the new sodalities drew people's attention to the truths of Catholicism by meditation on the sacred mysteries of the life of Christ, a proliferation of saints became devoted to the rosary. Saint Philip Neri (1515–1595), known as the "Apostle of Rome," wandered the streets of the Eternal City inviting fallen-away Catholics to join him at his oratory, where he would entertain them, instruct them in the faith, and teach them how to pray the rosary. He also revived the practice of honoring Mary during the month of May, especially through the rosary. By his example and love for the rosary, many people re-discovered Catholicism.

Another great rosary saint of this era was St. Francis Borgia (1510–1572). A great defender of the faith and a prolific theologian, he added rosary meditations to his important writings on Christian theology. Saint Peter Canisius (1521–1597), a zealous Jesuit who wrote the first major work on Mary after the Protestant rebellion, greatly emphasized the rosary and taught that praying the Hail Mary and the rosary was an honorable way of making reparation to God for the errors of the Protestants. It was largely due to his Mariological writings that the second half of the Hail Mary was officially recognized by the Church and promoted during the papacy of St. Pope Pius V. Saint Peter Canisius also helped clear up the confusion, lingering since the previous century, over what mystery is actually the last Glorious Mystery. He adamantly stated that the last mystery was the Coronation of Mary, not the Final Judgment, as some had suggested.

There were also great orators during this time who extolled the wonders of the rosary. Saint Camillus de Lellis (1550–1614) zealously preached about the rosary everywhere he went and handed out rosaries to people he met in the streets. Defenders of the faith like St. Robert Bellarmine (1542–1621) and St. Francis de Sales (1567–1622) also preached about the rosary. Saint Francis de Sales, in particular, was a faithful member of a sodality and wrote the short work titled *How to Say Our Lady's Rosary Devoutly*. When he was appointed to the position of bishop of Geneva, he spent an hour a day praying the rosary and wore the rosary on his belt. He instilled in his people a great love for the rosary by his monthly participation in a rosary procession.

Saint Charles Borromeo (1538–1584), also a member of a sodality, was another great defender of the faith and promoter of the rosary. Like St. Philip Neri, he, too, emphasized that May is a month particularly dedicated to Mary and her rosary. As the cardinal archbishop of Milan, he sought to transform the cultural "rites of spring" — bouts of drunkenness and orgies that occurred every May in Milan. He fought the despotism of vice by teaching the rosary to the people of his archdiocese. In 1579, speaking from his cathedral, he ordered that devotions to Our Lady be conducted during the month of May in order to correct the sins of the people and focus their attention on the beauty of Our Lady. He even wrote a directive that recommended the rosary of St. Dominic to everyone. He was so devoted to the rosary that he often gave personal instruction to others on how to pray it and frequently gave away books on the rosary, including his favorite, *Introduction and Guide to the Meditation on the Mysteries of the Most Blessed Virgin and Mother,* which he gave to St. Aloysius Gonzaga (1568–1591). The book, written by the devout Jesuit priest Fr. Gaspard Loarte, was very popular at that time.

Missionaries

The great missionary endeavors of the Church during the 16ᵗʰ century helped spread the rosary to new Catholics around the world. During the era in which Protestant rebels were causing Catholics in Europe to abandon the one true Church, zealous Catholic missionaries were taking the rosary to foreign lands and offering its sacred mysteries to others. When the Dominicans, Jesuits, Franciscans, and many other religious communities set out from Europe to preach the truths of Catholicism to the four corners of the globe, it was common practice for them to carry a rosary on their person. The missionaries did not carry many books or cumbersome liturgical items with them when they traveled. Rather, they carried the Gospel of Jesus Christ on a string of beads. Most of the missionaries even wore it as part of their missionary attire. The flexibility and ease of carrying the Gospel in this fashion made the rosary a global evangelical tool. Protestantism tried to rid Christianity of the spiritual sword of the rosary, but the Divine Craftsman multiplied those who wielded it and sent them out as warrior-apostles.

The great Jesuit missionary St. Francis Xavier (1506–1552) brought his rosary to India and the regions of the Far East. He prayed it every day and taught others to do the same. As the Jesuits established missions in the Far East, the

Dominicans also reached parts of Asia in the 16th century. The sons of St. Dominic brought the rosary with them as well. In the Philippines, the Dominicans were responsible for instilling in the Filipino people a tremendous love for Our Lady and her rosary, especially through promoting devotion to Our Lady under the title "*Nuestra Señora del Santissimo Rosario*" ("Our Lady of the Most Holy Rosary"). To this day, one of the most popular statues dedicated to Mary in the Philippines is a miraculous ivory image of Our Lady of the Rosary known as "*La Naval de Manila*" (loosely translated, "the Navy of Manila") that is credited with saving the city of Manila and the Filipino people on numerous occasions during times of war. In their zeal for Mama Mary, the Filipino people are second to none in expressing their love for her rosary. Every year, they have grand processions and festivities in honor of La Naval on the second Sunday of October.

The Dominicans also arrived in Mexico in the year 1525. Though the Franciscans had arrived there first, it was the Dominicans who instilled into Mexican culture a tender love for the rosary. In fact, the Dominicans established the Confraternity of the Rosary in Mexico in 1538. The first rosary shrine ever to exist in Mexico was housed within the first Dominican church in Mexico in 1576, and aptly named the Church of Santo Domingo. Unfortunately, the shrine was destroyed by the anti-Catholic movement in Mexico in the early 20th century. The new rosary shrine present inside the church today dates from 1946, and the Church of Santo Domingo continues to be the headquarters for the Confraternity of the Rosary in Mexico. Inside this beautiful church, there is also a shrine dedicated to Our Lady of Covadonga. This shrine recounts the story of how a Spaniard named Pelayo, with the miraculous assistance of Our Lady, protected northwest Spain from an invasion of Muslims in the early eighth century.

For the Mexican people, Our Lady is understood to be "*La Conquistadora*" ("the Conqueress"). They themselves had welcomed her to their land during the 16th century when she had conquered the false gods of the Aztec nation. Through the miraculous image of Our Lady of Guadalupe, the Mexican people were made aware that the sacred mysteries of Jesus were *within* Mary. Also, when St. Juan Diego opened his *tilma* for the bishop, roses dropped to the floor like an unstrung rosary. Our Lady put an end to the Aztecs' human sacrifices and converted 10 million people to Catholicism in less than eight years. After her great conquest in Mexico, La Conquistadora returned to Europe with the same image and overcame the false prophets of the religion of Islam. Unbeknownst to many, when the miraculous image of Our Lady of Guadalupe was given to St. Juan Diego in 1531, several copies were made. One of these copies ended up onboard one of the Christian vessels that defeated the Muslim Turks at the Battle of Lepanto!

When the Dominicans began arriving in Central and South America in the 16th century, miraculous events involving the rosary began to occur. One of the most famous of these was the miracle of the restored image of Our Lady of the

Rosary of Chiquinquirá in Colombia. In the year 1562, the Spanish colonist Antonio de Santana had requested that a Dominican priest, Fr. Andres Jadaque, find an artist to paint an image of Our Lady of the Rosary for his personal use. Father Jadaque found a skilled artist named Alonso de Narváez and assigned the task to him. The image was painted using soil and juice from local flowers, and was done on a homespun piece of cotton that had been woven by Indians. When the painting was finished, it was placed in a small chapel. Unfortunately, the chapel only had a straw roof. After several years of hanging in the chapel, the image had been so exposed to the sun and the rain that it was completely unrecognizable and deteriorated. In 1577, it was taken down, brought to the town of Chiquinquirá, and thrown in an abandoned room that had once served as a private oratory. Eight years later, a woman named Maria Ramos found the old piece of dilapidated cloth while cleaning the former oratory and was informed by others that it had once been a beautiful image of Our Lady of the Rosary. Out of reverence, she hung up the unrecognizable painting and often prayed in front of it as she cleaned, even though she could not make anything out in the image. Then, on December 26, 1586, before her very eyes, Maria Ramos witnessed the image be miraculously restored to its former glory. All the brightness of the color came back, the figures appeared clearly and beautifully, and all the many tears and holes in the cloth were instantly gone. News of the restored image spread quickly all over South America, and people began to make pilgrimages to see the image. Similar to the woven cactus fibers of the miraculous *tilma* of Our Lady of Guadalupe, the simple cloth of the Chiquinquirá image should have deteriorated centuries ago, but it remains intact even to this day. The South American people have given the image the nickname "La Chinita" and have continued to honor her throughout the centuries. In 1829, Pope Pius VII declared her the patroness of Colombia. In 1927, the sanctuary was declared a basilica, and in 1986, St. John Paul II made an apostolic visit to the location.

Dominican priests were doing much to spread the rosary in various parts of South America during the 16th century. The Dominican mystic and miracle worker St. Louis Bertrand (1526–1581), known as the "Apostle of South America" (he baptized over 30,000 people), had a tender love for Our Lady and was very devoted to her rosary from his youth. As a priest, he always had the rosary in his hand, even in the midst of a very active ministry. His biographers have noted that he brought a girl back to life by touching her body with his rosary! Once, when asked why the rosary had so much power, he answered, "What makes you ask such a question? God does what a blacksmith would do when making an iron tool. He has made many suitable pieces of material and selects the one he pleases."[6] This great saint has been declared the patron saint of Dominican missionaries.

The Dominicans also sent fervent apostles of the rosary to engage in apostolic works in and around Lima, Peru, during this time. Saint Martin de Porres (1579–1639) was an indefatigable champion of the rosary, as was St.

Rose of Lima (1586–1617). Saint Rose prayed 15 decades of the rosary every day and used the rosary as a major tool in her apostolic work by encouraging others to pray it with her daily. Like St. Martin de Porres, she wore the rosary around her neck as a visible sign of belonging completely to Our Lady. During this time, the man who would become known as the Dominican patron for the Holy Souls in Purgatory also championed the rosary. His name was St. Juan Macias (1585–1645), a Dominican lay brother who prayed the rosary multiple times throughout the day during his daily works of mercy for the poor. He was gifted with a special devotion to the Holy Souls in Purgatory. These souls would frequently appear to him and beg his powerful intercession to speed their quick release. To help ease their suffering, he never ceased to offer his rosaries for the Holy Souls.

Popes

With so much zeal for the rosary arising across the world, it is no wonder that the rosary received major papal praise during the 16th century. In 1568, when the Dominican pontiff St. Pope Pius V issued a new edition of the Roman Breviary, he mandated that the complete Hail Mary prayer, which had been in use since the 14th century, be inserted into it. The complete Hail Mary — Angelic Salutation, Evangelical Salutation, and the intercessory second half — had been in use among the faithful long before St. Pope Pius V inserted it into the Roman Breviary. The reason this can be asserted with certainty is because the Breviaries of the Mercedarians and Camaldolese monks in use in 1514 already contained the complete version of the Hail Mary. What St. Pope Pius V did was to standardize and officially sanction the complete Hail Mary for the universal Church.

One year after St. Pope Pius V standardized the Hail Mary prayer by inserting it into the Roman Breviary, he wrote an official document on the rosary titled *Consueverunt Romani Pontifices*. In this incredible document, the Dominican pope officially granted a plenary indulgence to anyone who joined the Confraternity of the Rosary. This action gave people another powerful incentive for becoming a Rosarian. As many popes had done before him, St. Pius V also affirmed that St. Dominic was the founder of the rosary and offered a succinct history of the spiritual weapon. He wrote:

> Following the pious belief, inspired by the Holy Spirit, St. Dominic, the founder of the Friars Preachers, in an era similar to our own, when France was infested with the Albigensian heresy that had blinded so many followers of this world that they attacked the priests of the Lord, raised his eyes to heaven and to the glorious Mother of God who had crushed the head of the ancient serpent with her heel, destroyed all heresies, and with the blessed fruit of her womb saved the world condemned by the fall of our first father. Searching for an easy and accessible way for all people to be pious and pray to God so that they

could strike against a rock and produce waters of grace, he [St. Dominic] invented the so-called rosary or Psalter of the Holy Virgin Mary.

By means of this prayer the Holy Virgin is venerated with the repetition of the Angelic Salutation 150 times as in the number of the Davidic Psalter. The Lord's Prayer is inserted into each decade while specific meditations display the entire life of Our Lord Jesus Christ. After inventing this prayer he propagated it throughout the entire Holy Roman Church. Afterwards the prayer was spread by the followers of St. Dominic, the Dominicans, and was accepted by many. Set aflame by these meditations the faithful began to be transformed into other men, were liberated from the darkness of heresy, and began to open themselves to the light of the Catholic faith. The Dominicans, obedient to their superiors, began to create in various places confraternities dedicated to this form of prayer and enroll many members.[7]

Saint Pope Pius V issued this incredible document four years before the famous Battle of Lepanto.

England

As the rosary was receiving high praise and support from the Vicar of Christ, many of the people in England, the great Dowry of Mary, began to turn against it. As a result of the Protestant rebellion, Jolly Olde England had taken a turn for the worse. Various English kings, queens, and many political leaders began to wage an all-out war against Catholicism. For more than three centuries, Catholicism and Marian devotion had thrived in the land chosen to safeguard the rosary, but in 1570, when St. Pope Pius V excommunicated Queen Elizabeth I, there began an intense and relentless persecution against Catholics throughout the realm. Priests were hunted and killed; monasteries and churches were confiscated and destroyed; and Catholic services were forbidden. Those who defied the royal orders banning Catholic practice were punished, imprisoned, and even put to death. In 1571, the persecution became so intense that it became illegal to even own a crucifix or a rosary. If a person was caught bringing rosaries into the country, they were sentenced to lengthy prison terms and faced possible execution.

For faithful Catholics, attending Mass was almost impossible. In its place, the rosary became the people's spiritual lifeline to the sacred mysteries of Christ. A person could be imprisoned for owning Catholic books, but the rosary was easy to hide; many wore it under their outer garments. The prayer of the rosary became the prayer of the persecuted. Many secret confraternities were founded during that period and helped keep the faith alive. Some souls dared to defy the system by praying their rosaries in public, only to be detained and sentenced to lengthy prison terms. Heroic examples of piety and devotion to the rosary abounded in the Dowry of Mary.

One such example was the Jesuit priest Fr. Henry Garnet. Father Garnet had volunteered to go to England to minister to Catholics during the persecution. His desire was to secretly celebrate the Sacraments and clandestinely promote the rosary. Before his departure for England, he had been in Rome, where he had experienced firsthand the great fervor of the pope in promoting the rosary and witnessed the many devout confraternities thriving there. He was so inspired by their zealous faith that before leaving for his mission to England in 1587, he sought and received permission from the Master General of the Dominicans to establish confraternities in persecuted England. He was even granted a special dispensation at his specific request: None of the members of the persecuted confraternities in England would be required to inscribe their names in an official book. Signing such a book would most surely lead to their imprisonment if the authorities ever obtained it. In 1593, Fr. Garnet even wrote a confraternity handbook for use among the persecuted Catholics of England. When his Jesuit confrere St. Robert Southwell was executed at the scaffold, Fr. Garnet obtained the rosary St. Robert had thrown to the crowd moments before his heroic martyrdom. Garnet carried this martyr's rosary on his person and considered it to be a relic from a saint. Garnet himself would suffer the same fate as Southwell when, in 1606, he was captured and executed by being hanged, drawn, and quartered.

Another Jesuit priest promoting the rosary during the persecution was Fr. John Gerard. He made use of whatever materials he had available to make a rosary. In his famous *Autobiography of a Hunted Priest,* he related that during his imprisonment in the infamous Tower of London, he made rosaries by stringing orange peels together!

Another man who greatly aided the persecuted Catholics of England by means of the rosary was the Trinitarian priest St. Simón de Rojas (1552–1624). Though this Spanish priest never set foot on the shores of England, he was so devoted to the rosary that he would ship large packages of handmade rosaries to England in order to help in the evangelization efforts. He founded a religious community called the Congregation of the Slaves of Mary and became known as "Father Hail Mary," due to his constant recitation of the *Ave Maria* prayer. Today, he is known as the "Apostle of the *Ave Maria.*"

St. Pope Pius V and the Battle of Lepanto

As a result of the Protestant rebellion, Christianity in the 16th century was divided. Men who worshipped the same God began to fight against one another, and entire nations turned their backs on the Vicar of Christ and the one true Church founded by Jesus Christ. While this was happening, there was another religion in the world that sought to take advantage of the division: Islam. Its intention was to conquer Christianity by means of the powerful Turkish Ottoman Empire.

By 1453, Muslims had already taken over Constantinople, which had been the center of Christianity in the east for centuries. When the Muslims captured the city, they renamed it "Istanbul" and turned its greatest Byzantine church, Hagia Sophia, into a mosque. Today, this impressive edifice is neither a church nor a mosque, but a museum. After the sacrilegious conquest of Constantinople, the Muslims continued their exploits throughout the Mediterranean region. They subdued much of the territory of the Balkans, Hungary, and Romania. In 1529, they threatened Vienna, and in 1539, they would have easily taken the city of Kotor (a town in today's Montenegro) had it not been for a Third Order Dominican mystic named Blessed Ozana of Kotor (1493–1565). As a young girl, Bl. Ozana had converted from Eastern Orthodox Christianity to Roman Catholicism and become a Third Order Dominican. In 1539, when the Turkish Admiral Hayreddin Barbarossa was waging an assault on the city of Kotor with an army of 30,000 Muslims, Bl. Ozana exhorted the people of the city to pray the rosary as a weapon against the Muslims. The people did as she instructed, and the city was spared. It was a victory for the rosary. Their defeat infuriated the Muslims and made them refocus their attention on a prize greater than Vienna or Kotor. The ultimate goal of the Muslims was to conquer Rome.

When Suleiman the Magnificent became the leader of the Muslims in the middle of the 16ᵗʰ century, he expressed an outright hatred for Christianity. His grandfather had once made a vow that he would not rest until he had stabled his horses beneath the dome of St. Peter's and wound the head of the pope with a turban. Suleiman desired to carry out the dream of his grandfather and envisioned the Vatican as a red apple ready to be plucked and plundered for Allah. The center of Christianity was under real threat from the Muslim invaders. Indeed, the very fate of Western Civilization was at risk.

In 1565, the powerful Ottoman Empire inched closer to Rome and attempted to capture the strategic island of Malta. This event is known as the Great Siege of Malta. In this siege, the Muslim armada consisted of more than 40,000 men, while the Catholic army consisted of only about 6,000 men. Miraculously, under the leadership of Jean Parisot de Valette, the Grand Master of the Sovereign Military Order of St. John (Knights of Malta), the Catholic army was able to defend the island and expel the Muslims. While the Catholic army suffered many casualties, the Muslim army suffered the loss of more than 30,000 men.

One fascinating aspect about the Great Siege of Malta involves the sword used by Jean Parisot de Valette during the battle. In preparation for the confrontation with the Muslims, de Valette commissioned that a special sword be made for him. He requested that a rosary be engraved on the blade of his sword! After the battle, de Valette made a pilgrimage to the famous icon of Our Lady of Damascus in Birgu (also known as Vittoriosa), Malta, and laid his cap and sword at the feet of Our Lady's image. The sword, as well as the cap, remain on display to this day in the small museum attached to the Catholic Church of Our Lady of Damascus in Birgu.

Providentially, Suleiman the Magnificent died before he was able to carry out his demonic plans. However, when Suleiman's successor, Selim II, became the Sultan in 1566, he reinforced the Islamic threat against Christianity. He took the island of Cypress in 1570, raided the Venetian islands in the Adriatic in early 1571, and inched closer and closer toward Rome and the fulfillment of his great-grandfather's desires. On March 7 of that same year, the Dominican pontiff St. Pope Pius V, aware of the Ottomans' evil plots, called for the assembly of an army, a Holy League, to defeat the followers of the false prophet Mohammed. In the words of G.K. Chesterton in his epic poem *Lepanto*, "The Pope [St. Pius V] cast his arms abroad for agony and loss, and called the kings of Christendom for swords about the Cross."[8]

The Vicar of Christ was indeed calling for swords about the Cross. Unlike the politically correct leaders of our times, St. Pope Pius V knew that the long-standing tension between Christianity and Islam involved a very real spiritual battle and a clash of creeds. In order to defeat the Islamic threat, he desired two kinds of swords to defend the Cross: the sword of steel and the spiritual sword of the rosary. As a devout Dominican, he called on all Christians to wield the sword of the rosary while he gathered an army that would wield the sword of steel. Saint Pope Pius V had already dealt with the heresies of Protestantism and protected the one true church by promulgating the documents of the Council of Trent. He had even issued a new Roman Catechism and brought about a reform in the clergy. Now he had to take his focus off of the interior struggles within Christendom and focus his attention on the threat coming from the enemies of the Cross, a threat waged against the very heart of Christianity itself.

Initially, St. Pius V's pleas to form a Holy League fell on deaf ears. Germany, England, and France, countries all caught up in the errors of Protestantism, offered no help and ignored the pope. These countries, along with most other countries in Europe, contributed almost nothing in the fight to save Christian Europe from Islamic takeover. Many of these countries were not interested in defending Catholicism against Islam because they themselves were attacking it. England, for example, was not only uninterested in fighting against the Muslims since they were too far away geographically but also because they themselves had already destroyed the Church's monasteries and killed many of her priests. There were, however, a few countries that came to the aid of the Church. Earning eternal honor, Spain and Venice eventually agreed to take up the cause of St. Pius V. King Philip II of Spain agreed to send ships, troops, and his half-brother Don Juan of Austria (the illegitimate son of Emperor Charles V) to command the fleet. Venice promised to supply the majority of the war galleys needed for the battle.

Don Juan, chosen to be the commander of the Christian fleet, had not so much been sent by King Philip as he had been handpicked by St. Pope Pius V, not because Don Juan was handsome, a skilled dancer, and only 24 years old, but rather because he had already distinguished himself as a defender of Christendom against the Moors in southern Spain. The Dominican pope also wanted Don Juan to command the fleet because he was a devout Catholic and had a chivalric love for the Queen of Heaven. It was well known that he wielded (prayed) the rosary. Many historians consider Don Juan the last true knight of Europe. Saint Pope Pius V knew he had the right man in Don Juan. Looking ahead to the forthcoming battle with Islam, the pope even compared Don Juan to the forerunner of Christ, St. John the Baptist, by stating, "There was a man sent from God, whose name was John" (see Jn 1:6).

Indeed, Don Juan had been sent from God. The young captain knew that he was about to engage in a holy war with Islam. Prior to sailing off to war, he gave orders that all blasphemy was forbidden on his ships and required that all of his men fast for three days. He forbade women from entering his vessels, lest any of his men fall into the sin of lust and mar their souls before battle. He ensured that his vessels would have Jesuits, Dominicans, Franciscans, and other priests available to hear confessions and grant absolution. He also distributed a rosary to every man in his armada. Then, on the eve of battle, leading by example, he required that all of his men take the spiritual sword of the rosary into their hands and pray it — and they did.

On the morning of the battle, after Mass was celebrated on each vessel, Don Juan raised the banner of the Cross on his flagship and addressed his men with the following words: "You have come to fight the battle of the Cross — to conquer or to die. But whether you die or conquer, do your duty this day, and you will secure a glorious immortality!"[9] His words were bold. He had a tremendous reason to be so courageous: Both he and his men knew that St. Pope Pius V had granted a plenary indulgence to all the men of the Holy League fleet. Don Juan reminded them of that privilege and encouraged his men to fear nothing as they charged against the enemies of true religion.

As Don Juan was stirring up ardor in his men, St. Pope Pius V was assembling a spiritual army of prayer warriors throughout Rome and the surrounding regions. He prescribed that public devotions were to be conducted in honor of Our Lady and her rosary. In response to his plea, confraternity after confraternity assembled and began to pray rosaries for the intentions of the pope. On the evening of October 6, 1571, the day before the decisive battle, St. Pius V himself led the rosary at the Dominican convent of Santa Maria Sopra Minerva in Rome. He knew that if Europe were to be saved, it would only be through the intercession of the Virgin Mary. With tears in his eyes and a rosary in his hand, he entrusted the Christian cause to the Queen of Heaven.

On the morning of October 7, 1571, the Christian fleet set sail in search of the Muslim fleet to meet them head-on. Don Juan and his men had no idea that they were sailing toward an advanced and highly trained Muslim fleet of more than 300 vessels and 100,000 men. Though the Christian fleet had close to 285 vessels, they only had 70,000 men, many of whom were unskilled in naval combat. The two forces caught sight of each other for the first time in the large bay just south of the town of Lepanto (now Naupaktos), Greece. Once they saw each other, they formed their battle lines. The battle formation of the Christian fleet was in the shape of a cross, while the formation of the Muslim fleet was in the shape of a crescent. At the blast of a trumpet, the Christian fleet dropped to their knees in prayer as a crucifix was raised on each vessel. The battle was on. It was the cross versus the crescent.

But there was a major problem. The Christian fleet was sailing into a brisk headwind blowing against them, and the area in the bay where the Christian fleet had first spotted the Muslim ships quickly became engulfed in a thick fog. The Christian armada could no longer see the deadly Muslim fleet. This turn of events gave the Muslims tremendous confidence. With the wind in their sails, they quickly sped toward the Christian ships in full battle array. Heaven had something else in mind, however. At the exact same time that the Muslims were speeding toward the Christian fleet, the confraternities in Rome were praying their rosaries and begging heaven for victory. Incredibly, and to everyone's surprise, the wind on the bay suddenly shifted and began to favor the Christians, which caught both fleets completely off guard. Now, with the wind in their favor and the fog serving as a cloak, the Christian fleet headed full speed toward the enemy.

The battle lasted for five bloody hours. At one point Don Juan steered his vessel toward the vessel from which Ali Pasha commanded the Islamic forces. Before the two flagships collided and their crews could engage in hand-to-hand combat, Don Juan, filled with the spirit of God, danced with abandon on the deck of his ship. This act enraged Ali Pasha, but he was unable to take his revenge because he was immediately killed by a musket ball to the forehead. One of the armed prisoners who had been freed from the Muslim ship cut off what was left of Ali Pasha's head and hoisted it on a pike. The banner of Allah was taken down and ripped apart, and the banner of St. Pope Pius V was raised in its place. The battle was a complete massacre for the Muslims. The Turkish fleet lost more than 30,000 men. Thirty-four Muslim admirals and 120 galley captains were among the dead. The Muslim fleet also lost the majority of its vessels. The Christian fleet suffered losses, too, but they were as nothing compared to the losses of the Muslim fleet; the Christian fleet lost 7,000 men and 12 vessels. The Christian fleet was also able to set free nearly 15,000 Christian galley slaves that had been aboard the Muslim vessels. It was a complete and total victory for Christianity.

What is not well known is that Our Lady of Guadalupe was at the Battle of Lepanto. In the battle formation of the Christian fleet, there was a decorated admiral named Giovanni Andrea Doria who was in charge of the right wing of the fleet ships. Aboard his galley ship, he carried a most precious gift, given to him by King Philip of Spain. As history attests, after the apparitions of Our Lady of Guadalupe occurred in Mexico in 1531, Archbishop Montufor of Mexico City had five copies of the miraculous image made. Each was touched to the original image. One of these images was given to the king of Spain in 1570. King Philip, in turn, gave his copy to Admiral Doria, who brought the image with him on his ship to the Battle of Lepanto.

It is well known that, on the evening of the day that the Christians defeated the Muslims, St. Pope Pius V was in Rome in a meeting and received a vision of the victory. While in the middle of discussions in the Vatican, he suddenly broke away from his companions and stared out the window in complete ecstasy as if he were seeing something tremendous, then turned back toward his companions with a radiant face to jubilantly exclaim, "Victory! Victory!" He explained that a great victory had been won that day by the Holy League. This vision occurred more than two weeks before the official courier from Venice arrived in Rome with the news. Western Civilization had been saved from the Muslims, and St. Pope Pius V attributed the victory to the rosary.

Actually, everyone knew it was a rosary victory. In Venice, the Venetian senate commissioned the construction of a chapel dedicated to Our Lady of the Rosary. The walls of the chapel were lined with records of the battle. Reflecting their gratitude to the rosary, one inscription read: "NEITHER VALOR, NOR ARMS, NOR ARMIES, BUT OUR LADY OF THE ROSARY GAVE US VICTORY!" Later, Miguel Cervantes, one of the many valiant men who had come to the defense of Christianity and been severely wounded at the Battle of Lepanto, penned Spain's greatest novel, *Don Quixote*, and noted the following about the battle that saved the west: "Ages gone by have seen nothing like unto the Battle of Lepanto, nor has our age witnessed anything to compare with it, and in all probability ages to come will never record a more beautiful or glorious triumph for the Church."[10]

Our Lady of Victory and Rosary Sunday

For the people of that time, there was absolutely no doubt that the victory at Lepanto had been the direct result of the intercession of the Blessed Virgin and her rosary. Saint Pope Pius V was so convinced that Our Lady's intercession had brought victory that he wanted the victory to be liturgically celebrated throughout the Catholic world every year. In March of 1572, he instituted the annual Feast of Our Lady of Victory, directing that it be celebrated every year on October 7, the date of the actual Battle of Lepanto. He didn't stop there, though. In a document titled *Salvatoris Domini*, he granted a plenary indulgence to all those who, in addition to celebrating the feast on October 7, also commemorated the great victory of Lepanto on the first Sunday of October, the day of the month that the Battle of Lepanto had taken place. This annual commemoration became known as "Rosary Sunday." Like so many things associated with the rosary, the plenary indulgence attached to Rosary Sunday was known by many names. Religious communities tended to refer to it as the "Dominican Portiuncula," in imitation of the "Franciscan Portiuncula" indulgence of August 2. Theologians and scholars tended to refer to it as the *Toties Quoties*, which literally means "as often as," deriving from the number of plenary indulgences that could be gained on that day "as often as" a person fulfilled the conditions. However, the most common title used for the indulgence was to call it the

"Great Pardon of the Rosary." For centuries, this indulgence was one of the most ample indulgences ever offered by the Church.

Initially, the plenary indulgence for Rosary Sunday was only granted to members of the Confraternity of the Rosary, but it was later extended to all the faithful. The indulgence was praised and confirmed by many subsequent popes in official documents, including Pope Innocent XI in *Nuper pro parte* (July 31, 1679) and Blessed Pope Pius IX in an audience granted to the cardinal prefect of the Sacred Congregation of Indulgences on April 5, 1869. The condition for gaining the indulgence consisted of the following: A Catholic had to visit a Dominican church with a rosary altar anytime from 2 p.m. on the Saturday preceding the feast until sundown on Rosary Sunday; pray for the intentions of the Holy Father during each visit; and go to Confession and receive Holy Communion.

Pope Gregory XIII and Our Lady of the Rosary

One year after St. Pope Pius V established the Feast of Our Lady of Victory on October 7 and Rosary Sunday on the first Sunday of October, the Dominicans requested that there be a feast specifically titled "Our Lady of the Rosary." Pope Gregory XIII granted their request in 1573, in a document titled *Monet Apostolus*. In that document, which acknowledged that it was St. Dominic who founded the rosary, the pope transferred the Feast of Our Lady of Victory from October 7 to the first Sunday of October and gave the new feast the title "Our Lady of the Rosary." By doing this, Rosary Sunday and the liturgical commemoration of Our Lady of the Rosary became one day (not October 7 *and* the first Sunday of October, as St. Pope Pius V had done). However, Pope Gregory XIII restricted the annual celebration to churches that had a rosary altar. Later, in 1671, Pope Clement X extended the feast to every church in Spain, and in 1716, Pope Clement XI extended the feast to the entire Church.

Needless to say, the rosary experienced both love and hate during the 16th century. It was attacked in certain countries, but taken to others by missionaries. It was ridiculed by the Protestants, but ended up saving Christendom. It gained its own feast, had a plenary indulgence attached to it, and witnessed the worldwide growth of its confraternities. After the victory of Lepanto, the General Chapter of the Dominicans in 1574 urged its members to preach the rosary with renewed fervor, resulting in the confraternity in Rome gaining 30,000 additional members in the year 1575 alone. Liturgically, once the rosary had its own proper Mass, the Opening Prayer from that Mass began to be used by everyone as a prayer to conclude the rosary:

> O, God, whose only-begotten Son, by his life, death and resurrection, has purchased for us the rewards of eternal life; grant, we beseech thee, that, meditating upon these mysteries of the most holy rosary of the Blessed Virgin Mary, we may imitate what they contain and obtain what they promise, through the same Christ Our Lord. Amen.[11]

THE 17TH CENTURY:
Witnesses of the Rosary

As a result of the triumph of the rosary in the 16th century, countless witnesses to the rosary arose in the 17th century. Dominicans, martyrs, popes, mystics, kings, and even artwork all bore testimony to the power of the spiritual sword. During this century, the famed Dominican priest Fr. Timothy Ricci (d. 1643) founded the "Perpetual Rosary." In this movement, the members of the Confraternity collaborated with other members to ensure that the rosary was being prayed nonstop. Father Niccolò Ridolfi, the Master General of the Dominican Order at the time, wrote a circular letter to his confreres about this organization and described Fr. Timothy Ricci as "a second blessed Alanus."[1] Another dedicated champion of the rosary during this time was St. Rose Venerini (1656–1728). Saint Rose had been formed by the Dominicans and, for a short time, even discerned her vocation in a Dominican convent. She had true zeal for educating young women and helping them to overcome the temptations of the world. Among her many works of mercy, she welcomed them into her home and formed rosary prayer groups with them. She eventually founded a religious community and opened schools for women, as well. The rosary was greatly loved by many during this time, a love demonstrated by men like St. Francis de Sales, who stated, "If I did not have the obligation of the Divine Office, I would say no other prayer than the rosary."[2] Even the great promoter of devotion to the Immaculate Heart of Mary, St. John Eudes (1601–1680), devised a new type of rosary he titled the "Rosary of the Admirable Heart of Mary."[3]

Martyrs in England and Scotland

In the 17th century, Catholics in England and Scotland continued to be persecuted, and the rosary remained their most visible expression of Catholic identity. As clandestine confraternities continued to spread in Great Britain, their members received a great blessing at the beginning of the century when Pope Paul V granted them special indulgences. For Catholics of this era, the rosary was a badge of honor. Many carried this badge to the gallows. One such man was Blessed Thomas Atkinson (1546–1616), a 70-year-old priest who secretly traveled around England administering the Sacraments and encouraging people to join the Confraternity of the Rosary. When he was eventually captured, he was found to have on his person both a rosary and a piece of paper containing a list of indulgences for the rosary. As a penalty for possessing the prohibited items, he was sentenced to be hanged, drawn, and quartered at York. According to those who were with him during his imprisonment, he was the recipient of frequent visits from Our Lady. He became a martyr of the rosary in 1616.

Another witness to the rosary was the Jesuit priest St. John Ogilvie (1579–1615). He was born in Scotland, educated in mainland Europe, and returned to his native country to preach the Gospel during the persecution. In 1614, St. John was arrested in Glasgow and sent to jail in Paisley. He suffered terrible tortures during his imprisonment, including being kept awake for eight days and nights in an attempt to make him divulge the identities of other Catholics. Saint John was eventually convicted of high treason for refusing to accept the king's spiritual jurisdiction. He was sentenced to be hanged and disemboweled; he was only 36. On the final day of his life, as he was being paraded through the streets of Glasgow, St. John clutched a rosary in his hand. His rosary had always been his lifeline to heaven; now he would hand that lifeline on to others. As he mounted the gallows in preparation for death, he threw his rosary to bystanders. The rosary struck the chest of a young nobleman named Baron John ab Eckersdorff. The baron was traveling through the town of Paisley on that day, and it was Eckersdorff's chest that was blessed with the touch of the martyr's beads. The event was so life-changing that Eckersdorff later wrote it down in the following account:

> I was on my travels through England and Scotland — as is the custom of our nobility — being a mere stripling, and not having the faith. I happened to be in Glasgow the day Father Ogilvie was led forth to the gallows, and it is impossible for me to describe his lofty bearing in meeting death. His farewell to the Catholics was his casting into their midst from the scaffold, his rosary beads just before he met his fate. That rosary, thrown haphazard, struck me on the breast in such wise that I could have caught it in the palm of my hand; but there was such a rush and crush of the Catholics to get hold of it, that unless I wished to run the risk of being trodden down, I had to cast it from me. Religion was the last thing I was then thinking about: it was not in my mind at all; yet from that moment I had no rest. Those rosary beads had left a wound in my soul; go where I would, I had no peace of mind. Conscience was disturbed, and the thought would haunt me: why did the martyr's rosary strike me, and not another? For years I asked myself this question — it followed me about everywhere. At last conscience won the day. I became a Catholic; I abandoned Calvinism; and this happy change I attribute to the martyr's beads, and to no other cause — those beads which, if I had them now, gold could not tempt me to part with; and if gold could purchase them, I should not spare it.[4]

Martyrs in Ireland

Ireland, too, had its share of martyrs. The persecution of Catholics in Ireland had already begun in the 16ᵗʰ century, but escalated and increased in severity at the beginning of the 17ᵗʰ century. As it had for so many others, the rosary became a tangible source of courage for Irish Catholics during their time of persecution. The rosary had been dear to the hearts of the Irish people for centuries already. In Jerpoint, for example, a sculpture dating from 1400 depicts a figure holding a rosary. In the 16ᵗʰ century, the rosary was so popular in Ireland that it was frequently prayed in Catholic homes in the evening. This practice became known as the "family rosary." In the 17ᵗʰ century, the Dominicans in Ireland were known as the "Rosary Fathers" or the "Friars of Mary." The Irish people's love for the rosary would be greatly needed in the days ahead because a major persecution of Catholics was about to begin.

In 1639, the Wars of the Three Kingdoms began. This conflict was between England, Ireland, and Scotland, and led to a parliamentary order that all statues of the Virgin Mary in Ireland were to be destroyed. There were many who risked their lives by defying the order. Two such men were the Carmelites Fr. Thomas Aquinas of Jesus and Br. Angelus of St. Joseph. Arrested for their non-compliance with the decree, they were both mercilessly beaten and executed in 1642. As they were beaten and murdered, they each held a rosary. There were also other Carmelites, as well as Franciscans, Jesuits, Augustinians, diocesan priests, and lay people, who were martyred in Ireland for their faith during this time.

Many of these holy people clung to the rosary in the final hours of their lives. The archbishop of Armagh, St. Oliver Plunkett (1625–1681), devoutly prayed the rosary in prison as he waited for his execution. He was martyred in 1681. There were also Dominican martyrs who witnessed through their beloved prayer beads. The Dominican priest Fr. Laurence O'Farrell was one such man. He was captured by the authorities in 1651 and sentenced to be hanged for his promotion of Catholicism. As a preacher of truth and a champion of the rosary, Fr. Laurence continued to preach the truths of Catholicism up to the moment he climbed the ladder to his place of execution. He was able to retain his rosary and his crucifix at the time of his execution. In the last few minutes of his life, Fr. Laurence placed the rosary around his neck and held his crucifix under the long white scapular of his Dominican habit. When the ladder was pulled away from underneath him, he was miraculously able to raise the crucifix from underneath his scapular and display it as a sign of victory over death.

One telling account of the tremendous love that the Irish people had for the rosary during this time of persecution was written by the hand of the man who was sent to persecute and kill Catholics in Ireland: Oliver Cromwell. Cromwell was an English military leader bearing the title "Lord Protector of the Commonwealth of England, Scotland, and Ireland." During his military campaign in Ireland, he sought to rid the country of Catholics and made the following report back to his superiors in England:

All is not well with Ireland yet. You gave us the money, you gave us the guns. But let me tell you that every house in Ireland is a house of prayer, and when I bring these fanatical Irish before the muzzles of my guns, they hold up in their hands a string of beads, and they never surrender.[5]

Incredibly, to this day in the town of Clonmel, in County Tipperary — an area of Ireland where the Dominicans have not had a house since medieval times — the following prayer is said by the faithful during the recitation of the rosary:

Glorious St. Dominic,
intercede with Mary Immaculate
to crush the serpent,
and let peace reign in the whole world.
You are the founder of the most holy rosary.
Do not permit the enemy
to penetrate into these places
where the rosary is recited.
Amen.[6]

Asia and the Far East

There were also many persons outside of England, Scotland, and Ireland that bore a great love for the rosary and witnessed to its power during this time. As the Dominicans were establishing the practice of the Perpetual Rosary in Italy, other holy Dominican martyrs and members of the Confraternity were pouring out their blood for the faith in Asia and the Far East. Some of these heroic figures became the first Catholic martyrs in those parts of the world. One such man was St. Lorenzo Ruiz (1600–1637). Though he was not a Dominican priest or brother, he had received his education from the Dominicans in his native Philippines. He was a devout member of the Confraternity and always remained closely associated with the Dominicans and their apostolic works. When, in 1626, he was falsely accused of murder, he sought asylum on a ship headed to Japan with three Dominican priests aboard. Once in Japan, the Dominican missionaries and St. Lorenzo were captured by anti-Catholic authorities and imprisoned. During their captivity, St. Lorenzo prayed the rosary in preparation for what would be a very cruel and torturous death. As his captors attempted to get their prisoners to renounce the faith, he was tortured by the Japanese authorities. They used a method known as *tsurushi* (reverse hanging), in which St. Lorenzo was hung upside down and lowered into a narrow hole in the ground. It was a horrible way to die, but St. Lorenzo never renounced the faith. In fact, he told his torturers he would undergo it a thousand times out of love for Christ. Saint Lorenzo is the first Filipino saint and the proto-martyr, or first Christian martyr, of the Filipino people.

There were many others who, like St. Lorenzo Ruiz, were members of the Confraternity of the Rosary and suffered torturous deaths and martyrdom in Japan during the 17ᵗʰ century. One of the most famous martyrs was the Dominican priest Blessed Alphonsus Navarette (1571–1617). This Spanish Dominican had served for many years in the missions in the Philippines. After returning to Europe to recruit others for the missions, he made his way to Japan to serve as a missionary. After some time, he was captured by the Japanese authorities, tortured, and beaten violently before being murdered for his faith. As he was being martyred, he held a rosary in one hand and a cross in the other. He is one of the 205 Martyrs of Japan beatified by Bl. Pope Pius IX on July 7, 1867. Of these 205 martyrs, a great number were Dominican priests, and many of the others were members of the Confraternity of the Rosary.

Another champion of the rosary during this time was St. Francisco Fernández de Capillas (1607–1648). He was a Spanish Dominican priest who had gone to China as a missionary. After he arrived in China in 1643, he spent several years conducting a very fruitful apostolate and even established a community of Third Order Dominicans in China. However, in 1647, he was taken prisoner by Manchurian forces hostile to Catholicism. During his imprisonment, his ankles were crushed and he was scourged repeatedly nearly to the point of death. Finally, in 1648, he and his fellow prisoners were sentenced to death by decapitation. Before his execution, he fervently prayed the Sorrowful Mysteries of the rosary with the other prisoners about to die. Saint Francisco was the first of the prisoners to be executed and has been declared the proto-martyr of China.

In Sri Lanka, as well, there were witnesses to the rosary. The first canonized saint of Sri Lanka was St. Joseph Vaz (1651–1711). He received his education at the hands of Jesuits and Dominicans, and was greatly devoted to the rosary. A devout Catholic, he was persecuted for his beliefs by the many strict Calvinists on the island and constantly ridiculed and mocked because of his great love for Our Lady and her rosary. He remained steadfast in his devotion, regardless of the insults thrown at him, and continued to preach about Mary everywhere he went. In fact, he is responsible for bringing about a renewed interest in the dilapidated Shrine of Our Lady of Madhu. In his zeal to bring all peoples to Jesus through Mary, he walked around the island with a rosary around his neck, inviting Catholics, Protestants, Hindus, and Buddhists to venerate the Virgin Mary at the Shrine of Our Lady of Madhu.

Mystics

Martyrs were not the only ones witnessing to the rosary during this century. There were also mystics. One of the greatest mystics of this time was Venerable Mary of Ágreda (1602–1665). This holy woman was a Franciscan nun from Spain who received many heavenly visions and had many mystical experiences throughout her life. Her greatest work is a lengthy account of the life of the Virgin Mary called the *Mystical City of God*. One of the most fascinating aspects of her life was her ability to mystically bilocate to the area of the American Southwest known today as New Mexico and western Texas. These bilocations occurred between the years 1620–1623. During these bilocations, she instructed the Jumano Indians in the truths of Christianity. She informed them that Catholic priests would soon arrive in their area and bring the Sacraments to them. Incredibly, in 1629, Franciscan priests arrived in that exact region. When the Franciscan priests arrived, they were shocked to discover this tribe of Indians who were already familiar with the Catholic faith, asking to be baptized and receive the Sacraments. The Indians even had rosaries! Wondering how they had acquired knowledge of Catholicism and obtained rosaries, the Franciscans were informed by the tribe that, for several years, a "Lady in Blue" had visited them, instructed them, and given them rosaries. The missionaries initially thought the Indians had been blessed with apparitions of the Virgin Mary. However, when the Franciscans showed the Indians an image of the Virgin Mary, the tribe said it was not Our Lady who had visited them, but another woman dressed in blue. After sharing this information with their superiors back in Spain, the friars were able to ascertain and verify that the woman who had been appearing in the American Southwest was none other than the famed Spanish mystic Mary of Ágreda! During an investigation into these remarkable events, Mary of Ágreda confirmed her bilocations to the Jumano tribe. She also noted that during her frequent bilocations, she took piles of rosaries from her room and distributed them to the Indians.

Another mystic who was very devoted to the rosary during this time was Venerable Benoîte Rencurel (1647–1718). Beginning in 1664 and lasting until her death in 1718, she received apparitions and messages from the Blessed Virgin Mary in Saint-Étienne-le-Laus, France. In these apparitions, Our Lady revealed herself under the title of Our Lady of Laus, Refuge of Sinners. This series of apparitions is one of the longest-lasting approved Marian apparitions in the history of the Church. When Our Lady first appeared to Venerable Benoîte, the visionary was a young shepherdess praying her rosary. In almost every subsequent apparition, Benoîte prayed the rosary in preparation for Mary's visit. Benoîte was so devoted to the rosary that she later became a Third Order Dominican. Incredibly, the apparitions of Our Lady of Laus only received ecclesiastical approval in 2008, and Pope Benedict XVI declared Benoîte a Venerable in 2009.

Kings, Governors, Popes

Kings, governors and popes also had recourse to the rosary during the 17th century. Many of these leaders turned to the rosary in the face of anti-Catholic uprisings, Protestant revolts, and continued threats from Muslim forces. The first king to unsheathe the spiritual sword in the 17th century was King Louis XIII of France. During the early part of the century, France was torn apart by religious wars. In 1627, the Protestant Huguenots waged an all-out rebellion against the Catholic Church in the city of La Rochelle. The Huguenots wanted nothing to do with Catholicism and sought to defend the entirely Protestant city of La Rochelle against Catholic political leaders' attempts to take it back. The Huguenots even made an alliance with the Protestant rulers of England in an attempt to strengthen their forces in preparation for an inevitable battle for the city. As the situation got worse, King Louis XIII became intent on putting an end to the Protestant uprising. The king ordered that the rosary should be prayed publicly all throughout France for victory over the Huguenots at La Rochelle. The Catholic siege against the city lasted for eight months; the king himself was present for many of the battles. Dominican priests often accompanied the king on the battlefield, preaching and handing out rosaries to the soldiers. In total, more than 15,000 rosaries were handed out at the request of the king, and the soldiers were instructed to pray them at set times throughout the day. The rosary was used in battle again.

The Huguenots, much to their dismay, never received any aid from England. Near the end of October in 1628, the city of La Rochelle unconditionally surrendered to the Catholic king. On November 1, the French Catholic forces entered the city, led by Dominican priests singing the Litany of Loreto and carrying a large banner with the image of Our Lady of the Rosary. After the victorious entrance, the Dominicans distributed more than 1,500 rosaries to the Protestant survivors and brought many back to the practice of Catholicism. In gratitude for the victory of the rosary over the Huguenots, King Louis XIII financed the construction of the Shrine of Notre Dame des Victoires in Paris.

The next rosary victory came in 1646 when the Spanish governor of the Philippines, Diego Fajardo Chacón, began a campaign against an armada of Dutch Protestant ships that were threatening to take control of the Philippines. During the 16ᵗʰ century, the war between the Dutch and the Spanish in Europe made its way to the other side of the world. Through brute force and piracy, the Protestant Dutch had seized all Portuguese possessions in Southeast Asia. Now, in the 17ᵗʰ century, the Dutch Protestants desired to take control of the most distant outpost of the Spanish Empire: the Philippines. The Philippines was in no position to defend itself from this threat because the country had been experiencing major disasters since the beginning of the century.

In the 1630s, the Philippines experienced major volcanic eruptions that led to major food shortages, crippling Manila. In 1645, an earthquake hit the city and destroyed hundreds of important structures. Recent wrecks and tragedies from storms had reduced the entire Spanish-Filipino fleet to only two old ships, the *Encarnación* and the *Rosario*. This situation put the Philippines in a very precarious situation, since the Dutch invaders had an armada of 18 warships. In spite of the long odds, when the Dutch were on the verge of attacking the islands, Governor Fajardo deployed the two old ships to confront the Dutch forces. The situation seemed hopeless.

Aboard the two dilapidated Filipino vessels were four Dominican priests. They heard confessions, celebrated Mass, and prayed the rosary with the men.

The Dominicans had spread devotion to Our Lady of the Rosary (La Naval) in the Philippines during the 16th century, and the men aboard the ships made a vow to make a pilgrimage to the shrine of Our Lady of the Rosary, La Naval, if they were able to defeat the large Dutch navy.

The confrontation between the two forces lasted for six months. All in all, five battles took place. Miraculously, the severely overwhelmed ships were able to fight back the Dutch every time. Every day aboard their two ships, the Filipinos prayed the rosary on bended knee, begging Our Lady for a victory. At one point during a battle, the flagship of the tiny Filipino navy was completely surrounded by Dutch ships. Inflamed with zeal and confidence in Our Lady and her rosary, a cannoneer was observed lighting cannon after cannon with a torch in one hand and a rosary in the other, yelling at full voice: "*Viva La Virgen! Viva La Virgin!*"

To everyone's surprise, the Dutch were never able to take the islands and suffered a terrible defeat. They lost 500 soldiers, two large vessels, and almost all of their ships had major damage. The Spanish and Filipinos only suffered the loss of 15 men. Upon their return to Manila, the soldiers fulfilled their vow and went on pilgrimage to the Shrine of Our Lady of the Rosary (La Naval) barefoot. To this day, every year on the Feast of Our Lady of the Rosary, a procession is held in thanksgiving for the miraculous victory given by Our Lady and her rosary.

Another victory of the rosary occurred in 1683, reminiscent of the rosary triumph at Lepanto in the previous century. In the 17th century, the Ottoman Turks (Muslims) were once again on a rampage in Eastern Europe, besieging town after town in their efforts to spread Islam. In 1683, they made their way toward the key city of Vienna. They had tried to take the city before and failed, but now, with an army of more than 150,000 soldiers (some of whom were Protestant), they sought to conquer Vienna in the name of Allah. In imitation of what St. Pope Pius V had done in the previous century, Blessed Pope Innocent XI formed a Holy League and entrusted the defense of Vienna to the Blessed Virgin Mary. His Holy League was comprised of armies from Poland, Germany, and France. The military commander of the army was King Jan Sobieski of Poland. The fact that the military commander of the Holy League was the king of Poland was appropriate since it had been another Polish king, Jan Casimir II, who only a few decades earlier had written a letter to the Master General of the Dominicans requesting their presence and their rosary for his beloved Poland. He wrote, "I venerate your habit, and I kiss your hands, as I beg of you to send me preachers of the rosary to reform my people."[7] The request of the Polish king was granted, and the Polish nation fell deeply in love with the rosary. Now, for the glory of God and the defense of Catholicism, another Polish king would make use of the rosary in the battle against the Turks at Vienna.[8]

Although the city of Vienna was already under siege by the Muslims when Jan Sobieski set out from Warsaw with his 40,000 troops on the 435-mile march to the battlefront, Sobieski's forces marched with determination and resolve, entrusting their mission to Jesus and Mary. In fact, before they began their journey, Jan Sobieski made a detour and brought his entire army before the famous image of Our Lady of Czestochowa, entrusting their cause to the Mother of God. The long march of the army turned into a tremendous rosary procession through fields and towns across Europe. Men prayed it every day, sometimes individually, and other times in large groups. By the time Sobieski's rosary army finally arrived at Vienna, the Muslims had been attacking the city for two months. The Christian forces inside the city were in desperate need of assistance. Other, smaller armies of the Holy League had been fighting against the Muslims in and around the city, but their efforts had not met with much success. The Muslims had caused major damage to the city and were now very close to breaching the city walls.

Providentially, when the army of Jan Sobieski arrived at the scene, the soldiers found themselves in an elevated position above the Muslim tents. At the beginning of the siege, the Muslims had held the high ground on the hills surrounding the city, but as their attacks succeeded, they had moved from the hills to the lower regions near the city walls. Though Sobieski's army was late to the battle, Divine Providence had timed their arrival perfectly. Sobieski's men were able to take the high ground and look down upon the tired and battle-worn Muslim army.

On the morning of September 12, 1683 (the Feast of the Holy Name of Mary), Jan Sobieski attended Mass, entrusted his army to the hands of the Virgin Mary, and began his assault against the Muslims. As Sobieski's soldiers ran with abandon down the hill toward the Muslim army, they shouted aloud, "Jesus and Mary, save us!" And Jesus and Mary did save them, as well as the city of Vienna. The Muslims were defeated in a matter of hours. Our Lady of the Rosary had been victorious again! After the battle, King Jan Sobieski related the events of the victory to Pope Innocent XI, describing to the pontiff exactly what had happened that day. He said, "I came, I saw, God conquered!"[9] Upon his return to Poland, Jan Sobieski went immediately to the shrine of Our Lady of Czestochowa on a pilgrimage of thanksgiving and laid the banners captured from the defeated Muslim army before the miraculous image.

Blessed Pope Innocent XI was not the only pontiff who promoted the rosary during this century. At the very beginning of the century, in 1601, Pope Clement VIII had restored the Church of St. Sixtus in Rome to the Dominicans. Afterwards, the Vicar of Christ not only declared that St. Dominic had erected the Confraternity of the Rosary in the Church of St. Sixtus, but also affirmed the validity of the pious tradition. He succinctly stated, "St. Dominic instituted and promulgated the rosary of the Blessed Virgin."[10]

Later in the century, the country of Spain made a formal request to the reigning pontiff that the Feast of Our Lady of the Rosary be extended to all the churches in Spain. The request was approved by Pope Clement X in 1671. Toward the end of the century, the practice of praying an Our Father, three Hail Marys, and a Glory Be at the start of the rosary for the Holy Father's intention became common. This practice was introduced as an easy way of gaining the indulgences given by the Church since the usual conditions for the indulgences included offering prayers for the pope and his intentions. This method incorporated the prayers required to receive the rosary indulgences into the rosary itself. An additional development of the rosary occurred in 1685, when a book by Fr. Henry Bödeker recommended that the rosary could also begin with three Hail Marys asking for an increase of faith, hope, and love. This method may have already been in use, but Bödeker's popular book on the rosary helped spread the practice. Whether one prayed the initial Our Father and three Hail Marys for the pope or for an increase in virtue, both practices developed during this century.

Art

Art historians agree that the 17th century witnessed an explosion of artwork about the rosary. These pieces gave testimony to both the attractiveness of the rosary and to the pious tradition. Almost all of these pieces depicted the Virgin Mary giving the rosary to St. Dominic. Catholic art has always been used as a teaching tool, a vehicle for catechesis, which is exactly the purpose the rosary art served in this century. In fact, it was during this century that the Church condemned several new paintings of Our Lady of the Rosary because they went against the pious tradition. For example, in 1663, there appeared a painting depicting the rosary being given to St. Francis and St. Clare. This painting was condemned by the Church as a false depiction of the origins of the rosary. In 1683, a painting depicting the rosary being given to two Jesuits was also condemned. In both cases, these art pieces were condemned because they depicted the *Dominican* rosary being entrusted to someone other than St. Dominic. Had a different form of the rosary been in the paintings, they most likely would not have been condemned. The condemnation of these paintings was the Church's way of ensuring that whenever the *Dominican* rosary is represented, the pious tradition is respected. This explains why other Dominican saints were allowed to appear in the approved rosary paintings along with St. Dominic. For example, it became very popular to include St. Catherine of Siena in many of these paintings, although she lived a century after St. Dominic. The understanding was that the Dominican rosary had been given to St. Dominic and his spiritual sons and daughters, and St. Catherine of Siena was a Third Order Dominican. In time, the Church allowed non-Dominican saints to appear in such paintings, but only if the rosary was shown being given directly to St. Dominic.[11]

Some of the most famous paintings about the rosary from this period are "The Virgin of the Rosary" and the "Madonna of the Rosary" by Bartolomé Esteban Murillo (1617–1682); "Virgin of the Rosary" by Francisco de Zurbarán (1598–1664); "St. Dominic Receiving the Rosary from the Virgin Mary" by Leone Ghezzi (1674–1755); and "The Virgin Offering the Rosary to St. Dominic" by Gaspard de Crayer (1584–1669). (See Appendix A for images of the rosary in art.)

THE 18TH CENTURY:
St. Louis de Montfort
and *The Secret of the Rosary*

The rosary experienced the best of times and the worst of times during the 18th century. The greatest book ever written on the rosary was penned during this time, but, due to the anti-Catholic movements in France, it would lie hidden in a field, undiscovered until the following century. While great victories were won against the Muslims through the rosary and a pope elevated the liturgical feast in honor of Our Lady of the Rosary to a universal feast for the entire Church, the century was also plagued by rationalism and a so-called Enlightenment that saw the practice of the rosary once again diminished. The rosary was ridiculed by theologians, scholars questioned its heavenly origins, and priests mocked it from their pulpits. The response of the Divine Craftsman, however, was to give the world the miraculous image of Our Lady of Las Lajas in Colombia in 1754 and elevate another saintly son of St. Dominic to the See of Peter. This Dominican pope would answer the historical critics and assign his best scholar to investigate the evidence for the pious tradition. The fruit of the investigation would be a firm papal affirmation of the divine origins of the rosary and the insertion of a new reading into the Liturgy of the Hours that reflected the pious tradition and praised the role that Bl. Alan de la Roche had played in reviving the rosary.

St. Louis de Montfort

At the beginning of the 18th century, the Age of Enlightenment hit and rationalism ran rampant throughout France. Minds were turning against the Church and her teachings, and many scholars tried to debunk the doctrines, dogmas, and devotions of Catholicism. What the world and the enemies of the Church did not know was that, in June of 1700, a man had been ordained to the priesthood who would soon become one of the greatest Marian saints of all time. His name was St. Louis Marie de Montfort (1673–1716), and he was on fire with love for Jesus Christ. After his ordination, he had hoped to go to Canada to serve as a missionary priest. Divine Providence had other plans, though. In light of the need for a new evangelization in France, his bishop sent him to travel throughout France and preach against the errors of Jansenism. Often called the heretical stepchild of Calvinism, Jansenism denied the role of free will in salvation and stated that only a limited number of souls had been predestined by Christ for salvation. Strict Jansenism offered a harsh understanding of the role of grace and was at odds with the Church's understanding of the Sacraments of mercy and Catholic devotions. As a result of the spread of this heresy, many people experienced a lessening of interest in religious matters, especially devotions like the rosary. Even many clergymen had fallen prey to Jansenism and begun to speak against the rosary from the pulpit.

Saint Louis's natural ability to preach greatly aided his efforts in evangelization. His approach to winning back souls was two-fold: Preach both the wisdom of the Cross and true devotion to Mary. In his preaching on true devotion to Mary, he focused on total consecration to Mary and praying the rosary. With these weapons at his side, he set out on a walking tour throughout France as an itinerant preacher. As he traveled from town to town, he was known to preach with the cross in one hand and the rosary in the other. He was so zealous that in 1705, he even founded a religious community called the Missionaries of the Company of Mary (Montfort Fathers). Unfortunately, due to that era's lack of interest in religion, his religious community did not grow in great numbers during his lifetime. When he died in 1716, the community only had two priests and a few brothers. Later in the century, the architects of the French Revolution made it almost impossible for new members to join the community. The Montfort Fathers would only come back to life after the French Revolution and the rediscovery of the lost works of St. Louis.

During his itinerant preaching campaign, St. Louis de Montfort visited the Dominican monastery in Dinan, Brittany, in September of 1706, where his brother, Fr. Joseph-Pierre, OP, was serving as a chaplain. It was at the Dominican monastery in Dinan that the famed Dominican priest, Bl. Alan de la Roche, had once lived and helped revive the rosary in the 15th century. There was even an altar there dedicated to Bl. Alan, so during his visit, St. Louis took advantage of the opportunity to celebrate Holy Mass there on two occasions. After this visit, St. Louis set out with a renewed zeal to make the rosary a greater part of his apostolate. He had already been preaching about the rosary as a way of overcoming the errors of Jansenism, but after his visit to the Dominicans in Dinan, something new began to stir in his heart. His visit to Dinan had given him a deeper insight into how he could be more effective in bringing souls to the truth through the rosary. He realized it was a secret weapon that the world needed to come to know.

Preaching consecration to Mary had proven very fruitful in his apostolate, but he was an itinerant preacher who was constantly on the move. There was the possibility that, after he left, people would lose their initial fervor if they did not have something "in hand" to remind them of their consecration on a daily basis. The rosary would be the ongoing means to help people remain consecrated to Mary after he had left town.

After several years of making greater use of the rosary in his preaching, he fully realized that he had to find a way of getting even more people interested in the secret of the rosary. As a result, he began to develop a closer association with the Dominicans. Then, after much prayer, he decided to become a Third Order Dominican and receive the blessing of the Order of Preachers for his ministry of spreading the rosary. His petition to become a Third Order Dominican was unanimously accepted by the Order of Preachers, and he became a spiritual son of St. Dominic in 1710 at the Dominican priory in Nantes, France. In 1712, he wrote to the Master General of the Dominicans to ask permission to preach the rosary everywhere he went and to be given the privilege of enrolling people in the Confraternity of the Rosary. (At that time, the ability to enroll people into the confraternity was a right reserved to Dominican priests.) Occasionally there were exceptions to the rule, but they were rare. Knowing the zeal of St. Louis de Montfort for preaching the rosary and the fact that he was now a Third Order Dominican, the Master General happily granted his request. Shortly thereafter, St. Louis composed two of the greatest Marian books ever written: *True Devotion to the Blessed Virgin* and *The Secret of the Rosary*.

According to the historical records of the Montfort Fathers, St. Louis composed *True Devotion to the Blessed Virgin* in the year 1713, in the city of La Rochelle, the city that King Louis XIII had taken back from the Protestant Huguenots in 1628 with the aid of the rosary. Due to the lack of interest in Marian devotion during his lifetime, St. Louis' manuscript for *True Devotion* was never published. However, Divine Providence was at work and prevented the manuscript from being destroyed. In all likelihood, had St. Louis published *True Devotion* during his lifetime, it would have been burned by those inimical to its teachings. In light of the fact that he was often heckled during his sermons on Marian devotion and even ridiculed by his brother priests for his pietistic approach to evangelization, there can be no doubt that, during the French Revolution, his books would have been thrown into the flames and lost forever. To prevent this from happening, the Divine Craftsman allowed St. Louis' writings to remain hidden from the world. They would only come to light during another critical era.

Prophetically, St. Louis de Montfort had anticipated demonic hatred for his treatise on true devotion to Mary. Before his death, he wrote: "I clearly foresee that raging beasts will come in fury to tear to pieces with their diabolical teeth this little book and the one the Holy Spirit made use of to write it, or they will cause it at least to lie hidden in the darkness and silence of a chest and so prevent it from seeing the light of day."[1] The prophecy proved true. During the French Revolution, the manuscript for *True Devotion* was buried in a chest and hidden in a field. It was only discovered again on April 29, 1842, in a field in Saint-Laurent-sur-Sèvre, France. Satan took great delight in the fact that the book was buried and unknown to souls, but God had anticipated its burial, allowed it, and planned for it. As in the days of old, the Divine Craftsman allowed the spiritual weapon to be kept secret lest it be destroyed. It would be resurrected and given new life when the time was right. The same thing can be said to have happened to St. Louis de Montfort's other Marian masterpiece, *The Secret of the Rosary*.

The Secret of the Rosary

Historical records do not provide the exact date when St. Louis de Montfort penned his masterpiece on the rosary, but in 1842, when the chest containing *True Devotion* was discovered, it contained many other books and manuscripts by St. Louis, as well. Most Montfortian scholars agree that the manuscript for his book on the rosary was also discovered at that time, since it had never been published before and was completely unknown. Once again, in a prophetic manner, St. Louis had named his book on the rosary *The Secret of the Rosary*.

Along with his preaching and teaching on total consecration, St. Louis' enthusiasm for the rosary had not been well received by the clergy of his day. The Jansenistic mindset of the 18th century had crept into the hearts of many priests who were then hostile to his Marian approach. It was for this reason that St. Louis specifically noted in the manuscript for *The Secret of the Rosary* that it was primarily dedicated to priests. His hope was that if priests took up the rosary again, the laity would do the same. Unfortunately, it didn't happen during his lifetime. The secret would have to remain hidden until after the ravages of the French Revolution. It wasn't published until 1911.

The Secret of the Rosary has been lauded as the greatest book ever written on the rosary. First and foremost, this special book contains the most detailed and complete history of the origins of the rosary available from a saint and member of the Dominican Order. It is truly a masterpiece. It is well-written, well-researched, and piously presented. In the book, he affirms what he himself learned from the Dominicans about the Dominican rosary's history — namely, that St. Dominic had founded it. He also affirms that St. Dominic founded the Confraternity of the Rosary. The book covers the vision given to St. Dominic by Our Lady in which she gave him the rosary, the division of the 15 mysteries, the importance of meditation, the power of the communal rosary, the greatness of the Confraternity, the indulgences attached to it, the victories won by it, the popes and saints who have promoted it, and the visions given to Bl. Alan de la Roche. *The Secret of the Rosary* also provides page after page of powerful stories recounting the effectiveness of the rosary in overcoming heresy, evil, and sin.

The many stories in the book about the power of the rosary over evil are extremely inspiring. In one story, he recounts how a heretic who prevented people from praying the rosary by publicly ridiculing the 15 mysteries had 15,000 demons enter his body. The possessed man's parents took their son to St. Dominic, who used the rosary to perform an exorcism on the man. With every Hail Mary prayed by St. Dominic, 100 devils left the man's body until they were all expelled. Another story recounts how a woman who had given her soul to the devil and signed a contract in her own blood to that effect was delivered from Satan's bondage by the power of the rosary. There are many other stories in the book that present the rosary as a weapon to be used against the powers of darkness. Saint Louis strongly emphasized that where the rosary is present and devoutly prayed, demons flee in shrieks of terror and souls are saved.

Since there was much resistance to the rosary from the priests in his day, St. Louis also included many stories of the rosary for his brother priests. In one story, he recounts how an intellectually arrogant priest had become inimical toward the rosary and wanted to belittle it in front of his congregation by preaching a homily against it. Just before the priest was about to deliver the homily, he was found dead in his room! Another priest, a friend of the deceased clergyman, not convinced that his confrere had died because of his hatred for the rosary, decided to deliver the sermon himself. As he began to preach the anti-rosary sermon, he was immediately struck with paralysis and became unable to speak. He begged Our Lady to help him, was healed, and thereafter became an ardent promoter of the rosary. There are many other stories in the book that are intended to show priests that the rosary is a gift from heaven and a spiritual sword to be used in their fight against the serpent dragon.

Saint Louis also provides examples and stories from the lives of great saints who loved and prayed the rosary. He specifically mentions St. Charles Borromeo, St. Pope Pius V, St. Thomas of Villanova, St. Ignatius of Loyola, St. Francis Xavier, St. Francis Borgia, St. Teresa of Avila, St. Philip Neri, and many others. He even noted that the underlying reason for the Black Death, the Great Western Schism, and the Flagellant heresy in the 14th century was the devil's attempt to rid the world of the rosary.

The devil knows the power of the rosary and he desperately wants to destroy it and turn people against it.

From St. Louis' book, we also learn about many of the developments that have taken place in the rosary over the centuries. For example, he mentions Dominic of Prussia and his style of praying the rosary, but always affirms that it was St. Dominic who founded the rosary and Bl. Alan de la Roche who revived it. Saint Louis himself offered a more contemplative version of the rosary and informs his readers that he is the one responsible for attaching a "fruit" or virtue to each mystery as a method for asking heaven to help a soul grow in virtue. He even wrote a companion book to *The Secret of the Rosary*, titled *Methods for Saying the Rosary,* in which he instructs the reader that other mysteries from the life of Christ can be used for meditation. He specifically recommended the following: the Baptism of the Lord, the Announcement of the Kingdom, the Transfiguration, and the Institution of the Eucharist.

The Battles of Peterwardein, Temesvar, and Corfu

In 1716, the year that St. Louis de Montfort died, the Austro-Turkish war began. The conflict was due to the humiliation the Muslim Turks still felt after their defeat at the hands of King Jan Sobieski in Vienna in 1683. When they were defeated in Vienna, the Muslims had reluctantly signed a peace treaty (the Treaty of Karlowitz, 1699) in which they ceded Slavonia, Croatia, and parts of

Hungary to the Hapsburgs. The treaty never sat well with the Turks, who really had no plans for lasting peace. In fact, they wanted revenge, and, for quite some time, had been amassing an army to attack Christianity again.

In early August 1716, a Turkish army of 160,000 soldiers began an invasion into Hapsburg territory. The Christian response was to organize an army under the leadership of Prince Eugene of Savoy. This army consisted of 91,000 Austrians, Serbians, Croats, and Hungarians. When the two sides clashed in battle at Peterwardein, Hungary, Prince Eugene's Christian army was greatly outnumbered. Miraculously, however, he was able to outflank the Muslim attackers with a circle of cavalry. Realizing their great advantage, the Christian army unleashed everything they had and slaughtered the Muslims. More than 110,000 Muslim soldiers were killed. This victory over the Muslims was won on August 5, the feast day of Our Lady of the Snows.

After this victory, Prince Eugene marched east and made a series of sweeping conquests in Muslim territory, especially in the Turkish-occupied province of Temesvar, Hungary. In October of 1716, the same month that rosary celebrations were being held all throughout Christendom, the Muslim fortress of Temesvar fell to the Christian army, and Hungary was liberated from Muslim control. This defeat further infuriated the Muslims, who tried to lay siege to the bastion of Western Civilization, the Greek island of Corfu on the Ionian Sea. The Turks amassed more than 33,000 men to attack the island. The Christian army consisted of approximately 8,000 men. Incredibly, the Muslim army was unable to breach the city's defenses, and the Christians were victorious yet again. All Christendom attributed the successive victories at Temesvar and Corfu to the power of the rosary.

Pope Clement XI and the Universal Feast of the Rosary

To fully understand why the battles of Temesvar and Corfu are considered rosary victories, it is important to emphasize what Pope Clement XI did after the victory at the Battle of Peterwardein. The Christian victory against the Muslim Turks at Peterwardein occurred on a Marian feast day (August 5 — Our Lady of the Snows) and reminded all of Christendom of the great rosary victory over the Muslims at Lepanto. As a result, Pope Clement XI established the Feast of Our Lady of the Rosary as a universal feast day for the entire Church. Remember that, up to that point, the Feast of Our Lady of the Rosary was only allowed to be celebrated in churches that had a rosary altar, with the one exception of Spain, where it could be celebrated in any church. The October following the August victory of Peterwardein was the first time that all of Christendom celebrated the Feast of Our Lady of the Rosary in their respective churches. Providentially, in October of 1716, at the exact same time the new universal celebrations in honor of Our Lady of the Rosary were taking place throughout Christendom, the Battles of Temesvar and Corfu were also taking place. For this reason, and because people all over the world were praying the rosary, the Battles of Temesvar and Corfu were declared rosary victories.

In the 19th century, Pope Leo XIII affirmed these facts and offered his own commentary on the matter in two separate encyclicals. In 1883, in the rosary encyclical *Supremi Apostolatus Officio,* he wrote, "Important successes were in the last century gained over the Turks at Temesvar, in Pannonia [Hungary], and at Corfu; and in both cases these engagements coincided with feasts of the Blessed Virgin and with the conclusion of public devotions of the rosary."[2] In 1897, in the encyclical *Augustissimae Virginis Mariae,* he wrote, "The history of the Church bears testimony to the power and efficacy of this form of prayer [the rosary], recording as it does the rout of the Turkish forces at the naval Battle of Lepanto, and the victories gained over the same in the last century at Temesvar in Hungary and in the island of Corfu."[3]

With the establishment of the universal rosary feast, Christians everywhere rejoiced in the power of the rosary over the Muslims and all enemies of Christianity. If St. Louis de Montfort had not died earlier in the year (on April 28, 1716), he, too, would have rejoiced in the establishment of the universal Feast of Our Lady of the Rosary. He had spent more than a decade walking throughout Europe preaching the rosary and urging people to pray it, and now it was honored everywhere. Unfortunately, however, not everyone was enthused about the universal feast.

The Bollandists

In the 17ᵗʰ century, a group of Belgian Jesuit scholars formed. Known as the Bollandists, after the Jesuit priest Fr. Jean Bolland (1596–1665), their purpose was to use the best methods of scholarship available to research and publish the *Acta Sanctorum* (*Lives of the Saints*) on behalf of the Church. From the very beginning of their work, they began to question the historical origins of the rosary. The problem with their critical scholarship, well intentioned though it may have been, was that it challenged the pious tradition. Initially, there were some who thought that the questioning of the pious tradition by the Jesuits might have been nothing more than an expression of fraternal rivalry between the Jesuits and Dominicans, since these two religious communities were known to have their differences. Whether this was the case or not, the Jesuits had no definitive arguments to disprove the pious tradition, which had been firmly established by a number of popes since the 15ᵗʰ century and undisputed within the Catholic Church. Therefore, since the Jesuits had a strong tradition of obedience to the pope (arising in part from their unique fourth vow of obedience to the Holy Father), the Jesuit Bollandists humbly surrendered their criticism and deferred to the authority of the Vicar of Christ on the matter. During the 18ᵗʰ century, however, at the time of the Age of Reason and the Enlightenment's exaltation of the historical critical method of research, the Bollandists raised the issue again.

When Pope Clement XI established the universal rosary feast, he also inserted into the Roman Breviary a second set of readings since the celebration occurred on a Sunday (Rosary Sunday); Sundays always have two readings. The readings he included did not contain any mention of the history of the rosary, so no one, including the Bollandists, had an issue with them. However, when a group of diocesan priests petitioned the Holy See in 1724 to replace the second reading for Rosary Sunday in the Roman Breviary with the second reading used for the feast in the Dominican Breviary, the Bollandists once again criticized the pious tradition because the second reading from the Dominican Breviary affirmed that St. Dominic was the founder of the rosary and Bl. Alan de la Roche, the Dominican who revived the devotion. What further concerned the Jesuit Bollandists was that the reigning pope was himself a Dominican: the Servant of God Pope Benedict XIII. The Bollandists feared that a Dominican pope would be biased in favor of the petition and grant it without conducting an independent "scientific" investigation.

To counteract the petition of the diocesan priests, a Jesuit Bollandist named Fr. Guillaume Cuypers (1686–1741) wrote an extensive critique of the pious tradition and sent it to the Holy See. However, Fr. Cuypers offered no positive proof that St. Dominic was not the founder of the rosary. He tried to prove a negative, asserting that because there was scant written evidence proving St. Dominic was the founder of the rosary, any other position was just as valid.

For this reason, he offered two entirely different positions on the origins of the rosary with one goal: to eliminate St. Dominic from the equation. He first posited that the rosary had existed before the time of St. Dominic; therefore, St. Dominic could not have been its founder. His second proposal was that the rosary had come into existence after the life of St. Dominic, sometime in the 14th or 15th century. Even though his positions contradicted each other, were entirely based on negative arguments, and he offered no positive proof, the Holy See received his letter graciously. In the eyes of many, Fr. Cuypers' critique was a desperate attempt by the Jesuits to halt a Dominican pope from giving permission for a reading affirming the pious tradition to be placed in the universal Roman Breviary.

Pope Benedict XIII, Cardinal Lambertini, and the Roman Breviary

Pope Benedict XIII was a highly educated and prudent man. As a Dominican, he was aware that if he simply approved the petition of the diocesan priests without an investigation, it might be interpreted as the fruit of a bias in favor of the pious tradition. To avoid such a public perception, he assigned the Promoter of the Faith for the Sacred Congregation of Rites, Cardinal Prospero Lambertini, to thoroughly study the issue so that an academic response could be given to the Bollandists and a fully informed decision made about the petition of the diocesan priests. A brilliant theologian, Cardinal Lambertini was selected due to his position as top historian at the Vatican, respected by everyone for his ability to conduct objective historical research. In fact, Lambertini was *the* leading Vatican expert in matters of historical research involving the saints (a discipline called "hagiography") at that time. No one had more access to and familiarity with the historical documents and archives contained in the Vatican than Cardinal Lambertini.

Before being sent to Rome to work at the Sacred Congregation of Rites, Cardinal Lambertini had been the archbishop of Bologna, the city where the remains of St. Dominic are preserved. Though not a Dominican himself, Lambertini was known to have a great devotion to St. Dominic. Every week, he would go to St. Dominic's tomb and pray. As a theologian and historian, Lambertini was not ignorant of the oral tradition of the Dominicans regarding the rosary. He had even written a letter as the archbishop of Bologna in which he made the following remarks to the people of his diocese:

> The popes in their decrees, to which assent is to be given, rightly designated St. Dominic as the author and institutor of the rosary. St. Dominic had given a crushing blow to the dreaded errors of the Albigensians by means of this divine safeguard of the rosary.[4]

As the archbishop of Bologna, his rationale for adhering to the pious tradition was that, since it was the teaching of the popes to which assent is to be given, he accepted it as an obedient servant of the Church. As a member of the Roman Curia, he found himself appointed by the pope with the task of researching the issue more fully, with the complete Vatican library and archives at his disposal. Imitating the caution of Pope Benedict XIII, he organized a team of historians and theologians to help him study the issue in order to avoid all appearances of bias toward the pious tradition.

After a year of thorough research, Cardinal Lambertini and his team were convinced that the pious tradition was valid and informed the pope that granting the petition of the diocesan clergy would in no way be harmful to the Church. On March 26, 1726, satisfied with the thorough research of the Sacred Congregation of Rites, Pope Benedict XIII inserted into the Roman Breviary the second reading for Rosary Sunday contained in the Dominican Breviary. The Holy See also issued a response to the Jesuit Bollandists regarding the document by Fr. Cuypers. However, as a good shepherd and a Dominican, Pope Benedict XIII did not want the response to come from himself personally, since he was a son of St. Dominic. Therefore, he authorized the very man he had assigned to conduct the investigation — Cardinal Lambertini — to reply to the Bollandists. Cardinal Lambertini wrote the following to Fr. Cuypers and his colleagues:

> You [Bollandists] ask whether St. Dominic was the first institutor of the rosary, and show that you yourselves are bewildered and

entangled in doubts on the matter. Now, what value do you attach to the testimony of so many popes, such as *Leo X (1521), Pius V (1572), Gregory XIII (1585), Sixtus V (1590), Clement VIII (1605), Alexander VII (1667), Bl. Innocent XI (1689), Clement XI (1721), Innocent XIII (1724)* and others who unanimously attribute the institution of the rosary to St. Dominic, the founder of the Dominican Order, an apostolic man who might be compared to the apostles themselves and who, undoubtedly due to the inspiration of the Holy Spirit, became the designer, the author, promoter, and most illustrious preacher of this admirable and truly heavenly instrument, the rosary.[5]

The Bollandists offered no response.

It soon became clear that the Divine Craftsman and the Queen of Heaven were very pleased with Cardinal Lambertini and his defense of the pious tradition. In 1740, he was elected pope and took the name Pope Benedict XIV. An interesting historical side note: It was in the 1750s that the Jesuits began to be banned and kicked out of many countries. For example, Portugal, France, Spain (including Spanish colonies such as the Philippines), Malta, Sicily, and many other countries around the world kicked the Jesuits out of lands under their control. In 1773, the Holy See itself stepped in and suppressed the entire Jesuit community. Although the reasons given for the suppression are unrelated to the Bollandist issue over the pious tradition, one cannot help but be amazed at the timing. The Jesuits would only be fully restored as a religious community in 1814.

After the second reading from the Dominican Breviary was inserted into the Roman Breviary, it was read every year on Rosary Sunday from 1726 to 1913. The Breviary no longer contains these readings because St. Pope Pius X commissioned a revision of the Roman Breviary in the early 20th century. As part of the revisions (undertaken from 1911 to 1913), the pope expressed a desire to eliminate any feast that occurred on a Sunday. Because of this, Rosary Sunday was re-assigned to October 7 instead of the first Sunday of October (Rosary Sunday). Since the feast would no longer be celebrated on a Sunday, it no longer required two readings, so the second reading was dropped. It should be noted that St. Pope Pius X did not do this to disregard the pious tradition. He himself was a firm believer in it and had once even informed the Master General of the Dominicans, Blessed Hyacinth Cormier, that he had thought about joining the Dominicans early in his life. Saint Pope Pius X greatly loved the Dominicans and the pious tradition. Nevertheless, he wanted to emphasize the importance of Sunday in the liturgical life of the Church.

The following excerpts provide a sample of what the Church had her children read every year on Rosary Sunday from 1726 to 1913:

When he [St. Dominic] had been advised by her [the Queen of Heaven], as the tradition says, that he should preach the rosary to the people as a singular protection against heresies and vices, he carried out the task enjoined on him with wonderful fervor and success.[6]

When, after the death of the Blessed Dominic, through the negligence of men and the cunning of the evil spirits, the rosary was nearly forgotten, the Blessed Virgin appeared, surrounded by light, to Brother Alanus of Brittany, a renowned preacher, and exhorted him to revive, in union with his brethren, the forgotten devotion of the holy rosary.[7]

Words fail to express how widely this divine devotion spread amongst Christian people at the preaching of the Friars; and how many societies were formed to the honor of the Mother of God in the name of the rosary, and how kings and emperors, and the princes of the Church, deemed it an honor to join them.[8]

Our Lady of Las Lajas

In 1754, an event took place in Colombia that continues to baffle geologists and other scientists. This event was the miraculous appearance of the image of Our Lady of Las Lajas (Our Lady of the Rocks). As the story goes, one day a woman named María Mueses de Quiñones was walking with her deaf and mute daughter, Rosa, through a very treacherous and rocky area on their way home from a nearby village. When a storm broke out, Maria and her daughter took shelter in the rocky cliffs of a canyon. All of a sudden, little Rosa spoke for the first time, declaring that she saw a beautiful woman who was calling her. Maria did not see or hear the woman, but was amazed that her daughter could now speak. A few days later, Rosa disappeared from the village. Her mother instinctively knew to return to the rocky canyon where she would find her little girl. Incredibly, when Maria went to the rocks, she found Rosa playing with a little child whose mother stood nearby. It was an apparition of the Virgin Mary and the Child Jesus. Maria and her daughter decided to keep this event secret, but would frequently return to the rocks to pray and ask Our Lady for her intercession.

After a few months, little Rosa suddenly fell ill and died. Distraught, Maria took her deceased daughter to the rocks to ask Our Lady to intercede with her Son to bring Rosa back to life. Miraculously, Rosa came back to life. When Maria returned to the village and the people saw that Maria was alive, their interest was piqued about this place where little Rosa had miraculously recovered her speech and even come back from death. The villagers followed Maria and Rosa to the rocks to see the place themselves. While they were there, someone noticed a beautiful image of Our Lady on the rocks. Neither Maria nor Rosa had seen the image there before. No one knew who had painted it or where it had come from. In the beautiful image, Our Lady is holding the Child Jesus and handing St. Dominic a rosary; the Child Jesus is extending a friar's cord to St. Francis of Assisi (see page 376).

After an investigation, the civil authorities and scientists determined that the scene was not a painting at all. The image is miraculously part of the rock itself. Geologists have since bored core samples from several places in the rock and discovered that there is no paint, dye, or pigment on the surface of the rock. The colors of the mysterious image are the colors of the rock itself and extend several feet deep inside the rock! The only man-made aspects of the miraculous image are the crowns above the heads of Jesus and Mary that were later added by local devotees. For more than two centuries, the location has been a place of pilgrimage and devotion. In 1951, the Church authorized devotion to Our Lady under the title of "Our Lady of Las Lajas," and the church built around the image has been declared a minor basilica.

Saints, Martyrs, Musicians

After the insertion of the pious tradition into the Roman Breviary and the miraculous appearance of the image of Our Lady of Las Lajas, a tremendous champion of the rosary came on the scene: St. Alphonsus Liguori (1696–1787). Saint Alphonsus was a bishop, a moral theologian, the founder of the Redemptorists, and a zealous promoter of the rosary. It is remarkable that he had absolutely no knowledge of the manuscripts of St. Louis de Montfort's works *True Devotion* or *The Secret of the Rosary*. Although both manuscripts lay buried in a field in France, the Holy Spirit filled the heart and mind of St. Alphonsus with insights similar to those of St. Louis de Montfort. In 1750, St. Alphonsus put his Marian thoughts in writing, thus creating what has become the most printed book on the Virgin Mary in the history of the Church: *The Glories of Mary*. To date, this book has sold more copies and undergone more printings than any other Marian book. It is truly a Mariological masterpiece. Similar to *The Secret of the Rosary*, it contains many statements and stories that describe the power of the rosary over evil and sin. Although St. Alphonsus did not present a history of the rosary in his book, his intention was to restore the Virgin Mary and her rosary to the hearts and minds of the faithful in an age that thought little of Catholicism and Marian devotion. This great champion of the rosary has been declared a Doctor of the Church.

Blessed William Joseph Chaminade (1761–1850) was another great champion of the rosary during this era. Though he lived well into the 19th century, he also carried out a very fruitful apostolate during the late 18th century and wrote many beautiful things about the rosary. A great promoter of the Marian Sodality, he founded a religious community dedicated to Mary under the title of the Society of Mary (Marianists) and helped restore the Marian sodalities in France after the French Revolution. As a holy priest, he had resisted the Civil Constitution of the Clergy in France, putting himself at risk of possible execution by the anti-Catholic government. There were many heroic men and women championing the rosary in different parts of the world who shed their blood for Christ during this era. One such martyr was Yi Seung-hun (1756–1801), the first convert to Catholicism from among the Korean people. A zealous evangelist, he became a lover of the rosary and smuggled rosaries into Korea from China in order to help share the Catholic faith with his people. He was beheaded for his faith in 1801.

Near the end of the 18th century, Vietnamese Catholics also began to be persecuted for their faith by an anti-Catholic government. It has been estimated that there were as many as 300,000 Vietnamese martyrs during a persecution that lasted almost 100 years. These Vietnamese martyrs suffered some of the worst forms of torture known to man. They often had their faces branded by hot irons with the Vietnamese phrase *ta dao,* which means "false religion." They were then publically humiliated and mutilated, torn limb from limb. Entire villages were brutally tortured and exterminated. Among the large numbers of Vietnamese martyrs were many Dominicans. One such Dominican was St. Vicente Liem de la Paz (1732–1773), an ardent promoter of the rosary and the first native priest to shed his blood for the Catholic faith in Vietnam: He was beheaded.

As part of the ongoing resistance to the persecution in Vietnam, groups of Catholics used to gather secretly every evening to pray the rosary. One of the most well-known gathering places was in the forest of La Vang. In 1798, a group of devout Vietnamese Catholics gathered in the forest to pray the rosary and were privileged to receive an apparition of Our Lady. Shortly after the apparition, the group was apprehended by the authorities and martyred for their faith. After their martyrdom, Our Lady began to appear frequently in La Vang and strengthened the faith of the persecuted. So much blood was being shed in Vietnam that it did not take long for news of the persecution to reach Europe. Horrified by the news, even the cloistered nun St. Thérèse of Lisieux expressed a desire to go to Vietnam, serve as a missionary, and become a martyr. Once the persecution was finally over, the faithful built a basilica dedicated to Our Lady of La Vang. To this day, it remains one of the most popular pilgrimage sites in all of Vietnam.

Famous musicians bore witness to the rosary during this century, too. The many biographies of Wolfgang Amadeus Mozart (1756–1791) note that he prayed the rosary throughout his entire life. When he was a young man, he delighted in playing the organ at the Basilica of St. Dominic in Bologna, Italy, where the remains of St. Dominic are preserved. Franz Joseph Haydn (1732–1809), a close friend of Mozart, once stated that he, Haydn, was inspired to write his greatest musical scores after having prayed the rosary. Haydn's influence on musicians was tremendous. Not only was he a friend of Mozart, but he was also the instructor of Ludwig van Beethoven.

The French Revolution

The 18th century began with the Enlightenment and concluded with the radically anti-Catholic French Revolution. The French Revolution began in 1789 and intensified a few years later into an all-out war against Catholicism. Between May of 1792 and October of 1794, the French government carried out a "de-Christianization" policy in the course of the Reign of Terror. During this time, many Marian shrines were abolished; numerous bishops caved under pressure and submitted to the order that all images, rosaries, and statues of Mary be removed from churches. Even the Confraternity of the Rosary came under attack by both the government and ecclesiastical authorities.

Their ultimate assault on Our Lady occurred in 1793, at the Cathedral of Notre Dame (Our Lady) in Paris when some of the leaders of the Revolution enthroned the "Goddess of Reason" in the sanctuary. In order to publicly manifest their anti-Catholicism, the revolutionaries brought a prostitute into the sanctuary of the cathedral. They made her act out the part of the so-called "Goddess of Reason" and had her desecrate the altar by lying on it in provocative attire. As she lay on the altar half-naked, the people inside the Cathedral made a mockery of the Angelic Salutation by shouting: "Hail Goddess, full of reason!"

The persecution was so intense that in 1794, when a group of courageous Carmelite nuns and lay women known as the Martyrs of Compiègne defied the Civil Constitution and its call for the suppression of their convent, they were taken one by one to the guillotine to be beheaded. The religious community that St. Louis de Montfort had founded, the Company of Mary, was unable to recruit any new members. By royal decree, the Montfort Fathers were prohibited from having more than 12 priests. Nine of these priests and brothers were martyred; only five priests and two brothers remained in the community at the end of the century.

Part of the reason the French authorities hated the Montfort Fathers was that the Company of Mary's fervent preaching on the rosary in France in the 18th century had helped lead to a Catholic counter-revolutionary movement in western France. This resistance movement brought about the Vendée Wars, which lasted from 1793 to 1795. The Vendéens were a Catholic army that prayed the entire rosary every day and wore the rosary around their necks as a sign of their adherence to Catholicism and their disdain for the French Revolution. Many battles were fought between the Vendéens and the French government, but most of the members of the Vendée movement were slain, making many new martyrs. These events reaffirm that if either the members of the Company of Mary or the Vendéens had had *The Secret of the Rosary* in their possession, the document would most likely have been burned and lost forever. It is a fact that many of the documents set on fire during this insane revolution were documents on the rosary. The Civil Constitution of the Clergy was the government's way of seeking to destroy Catholicism and the rosary.

THE 19TH CENTURY:
Lourdes and the Pope of the Rosary

In the wake of the French Revolution, many people in early 19th century Europe had become indifferent to the rosary. Catholic piety and devotion in general waned as the effects of rationalism carried over into the new century. The rosary seemed to have been forgotten again. The fact that Napoleon Bonaparte seized the papal archives in 1810, transferring 3,239 cases of documents to Paris, did not make the situation any better. A few years later, when attempts were made to return the secret archives taken by Napoleon to the Vatican, many documents were lost and/or destroyed because of high transport costs. Without a doubt, many of the documents destroyed and lost contained invaluable information about the rosary and its history.

In 1820, the German mystic Blessed Anne Catherine Emmerich (1774–1824) lamented the fact that the rosary had been abandoned and forgotten. Through one of her mystical visions, heaven blessed her with an understanding of the story of the rosary. Though her vision is rather cryptic, part of it seems to recount the story of the Franciscan novice from 1422 who was given the Franciscan Crown Rosary. She was also given a mystical interpretation of the mysteries of the rosary and its beads based off of the Old and New Testaments. After her vision on the rosary had ended, Bl. Anne Catherine offered the following commentary on what she had seen and experienced:

> This is the rosary that the Mother of God gave to man as the devotion dearest to her; but few have said it in this way! Mary also [in centuries past] showed it to St. Dominic; but, in course of time, it became from neglect and disuse so soiled and sullied with dust that she covered it with her veil as with a cloud, through which, however, it still glimmers. Only by special grace, by great piety and simplicity can it now be understood. It is veiled and far away — only practice and meditation can bring it near![1]

Though the sword was veiled and far away, it did still glimmer. There were a handful of saints at the beginning of the 19th century who still prayed it. It would not be until the great Marian apparitions in Lourdes, France, and the coming of the Pope of the Rosary that the sword would once again be fully unsheathed.

Saints

At the beginning of the 19th century, Catholic books continued to be burned and destroyed by rationalists. Certain political leaders, such as Napoleon Bonaparte, who was a great admirer of Islam, were in constant conflict with the Church. As a result, there was little motivation among Catholic authors to compose books of piety since such books would most likely end up being burned. Yet, to underscore that the rosary was still being prayed during this time, the Servant of God Pope Pius VII attached a plenary indulgence to the rosary in a document titled *Ad Augendam* in 1808 (the same year he excommunicated Napoleon Bonaparte). The indulgence he granted could be obtained once a year by all the faithful.

Some of the more prominent figures during this time who loved the rosary and who occasionally wrote about it were St. Clement Hofbauer (1751–1820), St. John Vianney (1786–1859), Blessed William Joseph Chaminade (1761–1850), and St. Vincent Pallotti (1795–1850). Saint John Vianney, the patron saint of priests, loved the rosary so much that he started the practice at his parish of praying the rosary with his parishioners every evening. He was also very supportive of the Confraternity of the Rosary. One of his close friends was Venerable Pauline Marie Jaricot (1799–1862), who had been greatly edified by his priestly zeal, devotion to St. Philomena, and love for the rosary. She herself would become one of the greatest champions of the rosary of the 19th century. Venerable Pauline had experienced a healing through the intercession of St. Philomena and, shortly before the Industrial Revolution began in 1830, she founded the Association of the Living Rosary of St. Philomena in 1826 in Lyon, France, in thanksgiving for the healing. She desired to help others understand Catholicism better since so many people were ridiculing and mocking it in her day. Her method was to have groups of 15 people join together under the patronage of St. Philomena and pray the rosary. This organization was the only major new rosary movement founded during the early 19th century.

Jaricot was very zealous in spreading the faith and had already founded the Society for the Propagation of the Faith at the age of 20; she founded the Association of the Living Rosary of St. Philomena at age 27. Both of her organizations were missionary in nature and sought to revitalize Catholic life through supporting Catholic missions, giving instruction in Catholic doctrine, and teaching people the rosary. She often stated that the rosary is not *a* devotion to Mary but *the* devotion to Mary. In recognition of her great work, Pope Gregory XVI formally approved the Association of the Living Rosary on January 27, 1832, in the papal document *Benedicentes*. In addition to being influenced by St. John Vianney, she had also been inspired by the life and writings of St. Alphonsus Liguori. She so revered him that she attended his canonization in 1839.

Two other saintly women who championed the rosary during this time were Blessed Anna Maria Taigi (1769–1837) and Blessed Elisabeth Canori Mora (1774–1825). Though neither of these women wrote about the rosary, they are great champions of the rosary because through the rosary, they received grace and strength in order to be holy in the face of a great challenge: They were both married to very difficult husbands. It was through praying the rosary that they became heroic wives and maintained peace in their homes. Blessed Anna Maria gathered her family together every evening to pray the rosary; Bl. Elisabeth prayed the rosary every day and taught her daughters to do the same. A mystic, Bl. Elisabeth foretold that, after her death, her husband would have a profound conversion and become a devout Catholic. Not only did he become a devout Catholic — he also became a Franciscan priest!

Historians have noted that in the Russian Orthodox Church, St. Seraphim of Sarov (1754–1833) prayed something similar to the rosary during the 19ᵗʰ century. Though its roots are hotly debated, some historians believe that the rosary-type prayer he recited, the "Rule of the *Theotokos*," is of ancient origin. It consists of praying 150 Angelic Salutations, divided up into 15 decades. A key difference between this prayer and the Dominican rosary is that the Rule of the *Theotokos* does not have mysteries from the life of Christ attached to it, but rather petitions and reflections on the life of Mary. This is why it is called the Rule of the *Theotokos*. It also has only one Our Father, instead of 15 or 20 as in the Dominican rosary; that one Our Father is prayed at the beginning of the Rule. The person praying the Rule is also free to make up their own reflections to suit their particular needs. Saint Seraphim Zvezdinsky (1883–1937), a bishop, martyr, and saint of the Orthodox Church, was also known to have prayed the Rule of the *Theotokos* during the 19ᵗʰ and 20ᵗʰ centuries. Perhaps someday discoveries will be made that will shed light on the historical origins of this beautiful prayer from the East.

Though not a saint in the official sense, Fr. Henri-Dominique Lacordaire (1802–1861) was one of the best-known Dominicans of his time, renowned for his sanctity. A provincial superior for the Dominicans and an extremely erudite theologian and historian, he is famous for re-introducing the Dominican Order into post-Revolutionary France. Lacordaire often referred to the rosary as the "Gospel on its knees."[2] With the characteristic clarity of the mind of a Dominican, he once offered one of the best explanations of how it came to be that St. Dominic used the antecedents of the rosary as the foundation for the Dominican rosary. He wrote:

> Christians [in the 13ᵗʰ century] were indeed accustomed to turn their hearts to Mary, but the immemorial use of this [Angelic] salutation was without rule or solemnity. The faithful did not unite to address it to their beloved protectress; each one obeyed the impulse of his love. Dominic, who was not ignorant of the power of association in prayer, believed it would be useful to apply it to the angelic salutation, and that this united cry of an assembled people would ascend to heaven with an irresistible power. The very brevity of the angel's words rendered it necessary that they should be repeated a certain

number of times, like those uniform acclamations poured forth by the gratitude of a nation during the progresses of their sovereigns. But repetition would engender distraction of mind. Dominic provided against this by distributing the oral salutations in many series, to each of which he attached the thought of one of the mysteries of our redemption, which was in turn for Blessed Mary a subject of joy, of sorrow, and of triumph. In this way interior meditation was united to public prayer, and the people, while saluting their Mother and their Queen, followed her in their hearts through each of the principal events of her life. Dominic formed a confraternity, the better to assure the duration and solemnity of this mode of supplication.[3]

Lourdes

For centuries, France has often been described as the "Eldest Daughter of the Church." It was one of the first countries to be evangelized by the early Church and has produced some of the greatest saints in Christian history. In the mid-19th century, heaven would give another gift to this land of saints. In 1858, Our Lady blessed a little French girl named St. Bernadette Soubirous with a series of apparitions at the grotto of Massabielle in Lourdes. It had been exactly 650 years since she had appeared in Prouille, France, and given the rosary to St. Dominic. When Mary appeared to little Bernadette, the Blessed Mother held in her hands a golden rosary with white beads. Similar to the era in which St. Dominic lived, the France of the 19th century was facing many difficulties and in need of spiritual renewal.

Devotion to the rosary had been much reduced in most of Europe by the time Our Lady made the first of 18 appearances to St. Bernadette on February 11, 1858. In each apparition, St. Bernadette saw Our Lady with a golden rosary draped over her right arm. In preparation for each apparition, St. Bernadette went to the grotto and prayed the rosary. This practice of St. Bernadette quickly caught on, and many of the people who went to the grotto in preparation for the next apparition also prayed the rosary.

The Lourdes apparitions occurred at one of the rare places in Europe where the rosary was still being prayed by young and old. In fact, it was the custom in Lourdes to add an additional decade of Hail Marys without a mystery attached to it. This decade was prayed for the holy souls in purgatory. There are still vestiges of this practice in Lourdes today. Most pilgrims to Lourdes are unaware of it, but many of the statues of Our Lady of Lourdes at the Shrine show Mary holding a six-decade rosary. For example, the largest statue of Our Lady of Lourdes in Lourdes itself — the one in Rosary Square facing the Basilica of the Rosary — depicts Mary with a six-decade rosary.

As word of the Marian apparitions at Lourdes began to spread around the world, the apparition became known as a rosary apparition. For the first time in any Marian apparition in the history of the Church, Mary prayed parts of the rosary with the visionary. Our Lady did not pray the Hail Mary because she is already in heaven and does not pray to herself. During the Our Fathers and the Hail Marys, Our Lady let her fingers glide over the beads as St. Bernadette prayed them; when it came time to pray the Glory Be, she joined her voice to that of St. Bernadette.

This aspect of the Lourdes apparitions (Our Lady with her rosary) became dear to Catholics around the world. Our Lady of Lourdes with a rosary draped over her right arm became one of the most popular images on prayer cards and in paintings or sculptures. In 1862, when the Lourdes apparitions were approved by the local bishop and affirmed by Bl. Pope Pius IX, a worldwide renewal of rosary devotion was sparked. The Sanctuary of Our Lady of Lourdes itself emphasizes the importance of the rosary. One of the buildings constructed in the vicinity of the apparitions is called the Basilica of Our Lady of the Rosary. This impressive edifice was completed in 1899 and consecrated in 1901. The large area in front of the Basilica became known as Rosary Square. To this day, people from all around the world gather every evening in Rosary Square to conduct a torchlight procession and pray the rosary in various languages. The Feast of Our Lady of the Rosary, held on October 7, is one of the largest celebrations at the Shrine every year.

The "Age of the Rosary"

According to those who specialize in Marian studies, the mid-19th century witnessed the beginning of an "Age of Mary." Mariologists generally agree that it started in 1830 with the visions given to St. Catherine Labouré about the Miraculous Medal and ended with the Marian Year of 1954. Within the span of 125 years, there occurred eight major Marian apparitions and the official declarations of two new Marian dogmas:

1830 – St. Catherine Labouré (Miraculous Medal)
1846 – Our Lady of La Salette
1854 – Dogma of the Immaculate Conception
1858 – Our Lady of Lourdes
1871 – Our Lady of Pontmain
1879 – Our Lady of Knock
1917 – Our Lady of Fatima
1932 – Our Lady of Beauraing
1933 – Our Lady of Banneux
1950 – Dogma of the Assumption of Mary
1954 – Marian Year

Almost all of the Marian apparitions listed above have a rosary dimension, since Mary either came holding a rosary or the respective visionaries prayed the rosary in anticipation of the next apparition. Although the rosary did not factor into the Miraculous Medal apparitions of 1830, St. Catherine Labouré was very devoted to the rosary. The apparitions at La Salette in 1846 have even been considered by many a preparation for the great rosary apparition at Lourdes since at La Salette, Mary instructed the child visionaries Melanie Mathieu and Maximin Giraud to pray the Our Father and the Hail Mary. It was also during the Age of Mary, in 1911, that the first French edition of St. Louis de Montfort's *The Secret of the Rosary* would be published; the first English edition would make its appearance in 1954. From this perspective, it can be stated that, beginning with the apparitions at Lourdes in 1858, an "Age of the Rosary" was initiated that would last until the 1950s.

The "Eldest Daughter of the Church" had suffered much over the centuries and had only recently experienced the end of the French Revolution. Now, the Mother of the Church was going to use her eldest daughter to teach the greatness of the rosary to all her younger siblings around the world. The Holy Trinity had not been pleased with the *Ave* of the rationalists: "Hail Goddess, full of reason." A rosary revolution was about to happen. Champions of the rosary would be raised up who would thunderously proclaim the true *Ave*: "Hail Mary, full of grace!"

Publications and Converts

One of the first features of the rosary revolution was that people once again desired to write about the rosary. Since many books on the rosary had been burned during the French Revolution, there was much that needed to be put on paper once again.

Incredibly, the manuscript for *True Devotion to the Blessed Virgin* was found in 1842 in a chest in a field. It contained many beautiful thoughts on the rosary, but it would take over 20 years for Church authorities to authenticate its authorship. However, once it was proven to have been written by Fr. Louis de Montfort, the manuscript began to go into print everywhere. The first English edition of *True Devotion* made its appearance in 1863, only six years after the Lourdes apparitions.

The Secret of the Rosary had also been rediscovered in the mid-19th century, but since *True Devotion* was authenticated first, it took longer for *The Secret of the Rosary* to be authenticated and put into print. In many ways, the rosary content in *True Devotion* was a preparation for the publication of *The Secret of the Rosary*. After having taught the world what it meant to have true devotion to Mary and live a life of total consecration to her, *The Secret of the Rosary* served as the perfect follow up by arming those consecrated to Mary with the sword of the rosary.

Before the first editions of *The Secret of the Rosary* were printed in the early 20th century, other publications came into existence that greatly promoted the rosary. In 1865, *Ave Maria* magazine was founded at the University of Notre Dame in South Bend, Indiana. It was published under the auspices of the Congregation of the Holy Cross and sought to foster devotion to Mary, as well as to her rosary. *Ave Maria* magazine remained in circulation until 1970. In 1872, the Dominicans in England began *The Monthly Magazine of the Holy Rosary*. Then, in 1891, the Dominicans in the United States began *The Rosary* magazine. *The Rosary* magazine was extremely popular in the United States and had a large readership. The historical studies done on the rosary in this magazine, as well as the stories of the saints and their love for the rosary, are of great value. Unfortunately, like almost all devotional magazines, this inspiring resource ceased publication in the 1960s when a decrease in Marian devotion once again swept the globe.

However, the 19th century also saw famous converts to the Catholic Church who determinedly promoted the rosary. Father Frederick William Faber (1814–1863), a convert from Anglicanism, was scandalized by the lack of knowledge of the faith among Catholics and told cradle Catholics that a truly Catholic mind could hardly be formed without the rosary. He could not perceive how a person could be deeply united to Christ without habitually praying the rosary. His sermons for Rosary Sunday became famous. In his orations and writings, he greatly promoted the pious tradition. He also urged people to pray the rosary for the souls in purgatory. He learned many of these important aspects of the devotion from the newly discovered *True Devotion*. He knew *True Devotion* well because he was the first person to translate it into English. His English translation was published in 1863, the same year that he died.

A more famous convert to Catholicism from this period was Blessed John Henry Newman (1801–1890). He, too, was a fervent devotee of the rosary. In his sermons, he often spoke eloquently and beautifully about the rosary and its power, endorsing the pious tradition.

The effects that Lourdes and the many rosary-themed publications had on people would be evidenced in the other major Marian apparitions that occurred later in the century. In 1871, when Our Lady appeared to several children in Pontmain, France, the apparition lasted for three hours. During the apparition, the adults and others who had gathered all instinctively began to pray the rosary.

Something similar happened in Knock, Ireland, in 1879. When Mary appeared in Knock, the people who saw the vision immediately began to pray the rosary, even though it was raining intensely and they were outside getting soaking wet. At the time of the Knock apparition, the rosary was so popular in Ireland that it was referred to as the "Irish Catechism." Mary did not speak during either the Pontmain or the Knock apparitions. Rather, she let the people gather at her feet and give voice to what was on their hearts. The preferred prayer of the people was the rosary.

Scientists, Politicians, Miracles

During the rosary revolution, a famed scientist and a devout president championed the rosary, and many rosary miracles began to occur. A story is told that one day, a young university student boarded a train in France and sat next to a rather tattered-looking old man. The university student noticed that the old man was silently thumbing his rosary beads, letting the beads slip quietly through his fingers. It greatly disturbed the university student. Considering himself well-educated and scientifically accomplished, the young man asked the old man why he bothered with such outdated and silly things. The university student informed the old man that science had proven things like the rosary useless and a waste of time, and said that Catholic piety was meaningless. The elderly man answered that he was unfamiliar with the kind of "science" the youth was describing and asked the young scholar to explain it to him. Tears welled up in the old man's eyes as he listened to the university student explain his scientific rebuttal of things related to Catholicism. As the train stopped at the station where the old man was to disembark, the student continued to instruct him and even informed the uneducated old man that if he wanted to learn more, he could get in touch with the young scholar. Before exiting the train, the old man fumbled through his coat, found a card, and gave it to the student. After the doors closed and the train continued on, the university student looked at the card. It read: "Louis Pasteur: Director of the Institute of Scientific Research, Paris." The old man was France's leading scientist, Louis Pasteur (1822–1895). Pasteur's scientific genius led to the first vaccines against rabies and anthrax, and he is acclaimed as one of the founders of the scientific discipline of bacteriology. He had also made major advances in vaccination and microbial fermentation, and had invented the process of pasteurization, which is named after him. Pasteur prayed the rosary every day and always carried two rosaries on his person in case he lost one.

There is also the heroic witness of the Catholic president of Ecuador, Gabriel Garcia Moreno (1821–1875). His presidency had been foretold by Our Lady to Venerable Mariana de Jesus Torres (1563–1635) during the approved apparitions in Quito, Ecuador, in the 15th and 16th centuries. During the 19th century, Ecuador was a country in turmoil, suffering greatly from a very anti-clerical and anti-Catholic movement. As a devout Catholic, Gabriel Moreno was not pleased with the direction Ecuador was taking and sought public office to try to turn things around. He ran for the presidency of the country and won! As part of his reform movement, he led the people by both prayer and example. He attended Mass on a daily basis, gave a good example to his people by being very active in a Marian sodality, and prayed the rosary every day. On some days, he would even go out into the streets and pray the rosary with his citizens. He so loved his country that he gave his salary to charity. Moreno led Ecuador to become the leader amongst Latin American countries in science, higher education, and literacy during the 19th century. He also consecrated Ecuador to the Sacred Heart of Jesus. This consecration greatly disturbed the Freemasons in the country, and they sought to kill him. After having been elected president for a third term, a secret society — most likely the Freemasons — murdered him in 1875. He was shot six times and stabbed 14. His last words to his executioners were: "I die, but God does not die!"[4] Shortly after his death, Bl. Pope Pius IX stated that President Moreno had died a victim for the faith. Moreno was one of the greatest Catholic presidents the world has ever known.

Around the same time that President Moreno was praying the rosary with his people in South America, rosary miracles were occurring in North America. In 1859, the Belgian-born laywoman Adele Brise (1831–1896) received a series of apparitions from the Virgin Mary in rural Wisconsin. The apparition, during which Mary appeared under the title "Our Lady of Good Help," was approved in 2010 and is the first approved Marian apparition to have occurred in the United States. Shortly after the Marian apparitions to Adele Brise occurred, a small chapel was built and dedicated to Our Lady of Good Help. In 1871, the area was ravished by a terrible outbreak of fires, including the Great Peshtigo Fire of Wisconsin. The Peshtigo fire occurred on the same day as the Great Chicago Fire, but is not as well-known, due to its rural setting. However, the Peshtigo fire remains the single most deadly fire in United States history to date: An estimated 2,000-plus people burned to death. The Peshtigo fire was so powerful that it was described as a "fire-tornado," and at times even had hurricane-force winds. It traveled at a speed that left everything in its path completely destroyed.

While this fire raged, Sr. Adele Brise, along with many local residents, headed to the chapel dedicated to Our Lady of Good Help and began a rosary procession around the chapel in the hope of protecting it. As they processed around the chapel, they carried a statue of Mary and prayed the rosary nonstop. The raging inferno came extremely close to the chapel, but even facing the threat of suffocation from lack of air and heavy smoke, the people continued the rosary procession. The next morning both the people and the chapel were miraculously left standing, though everything else in the area was completely destroyed. It was as if the chapel had had a protective shield around it. The rosary had saved the chapel!

Another rosary miracle occurred in 1879 at Cap-de-la-Madeleine in Quebec, Canada. This miracle is known as the "miracle of the rosary bridge." During the winter of 1879, a new church was about to be constructed in that area. The Confraternity of the Rosary had been established there in 1694, but due to infrequent visits from priests, the practice of praying the rosary had waned and the local church was in need of spiritual renewal. In 1864, Fr. Luc Desilets, a fervent and pious priest, was sent to the area to help restore the faith and renew piety. He restored the Confraternity of the Rosary, encouraged the family rosary, and began the practice of praying the rosary after every Mass. In his zeal, he decided to erect a new church dedicated to Our Lady in 1879. The problem was that it was winter and he had decided to build the church on a tiny island located in the main river. There was no permanent bridge to the island. Undeterred, the priest held out hope that the river would ice over, allowing all the equipment to be brought over on the ice. However, the winter that year was very mild and the river did not freeze. Since the river had not iced over, the priest asked the people to pray the rosary for a miracle. After many rosaries, a miracle indeed happened. Ice chunks appeared out of nowhere and formed on the river. The ice stayed in position long enough for the heavy stones, timber, and other supplies to cross the river. Everyone in the area attributed this anomaly to the power of the rosary and called the ice a rosary bridge. A few years later, a saintly Franciscan priest named Blessed Frédéric Jansoone (1838–1916) was sent to work in the area. He was a zealous preacher and became a champion of the rosary throughout the region.

More Saints

As the rosary grew in popularity, more and more saints who were very devoted to it began to appear. Saint Don Bosco (1815–1888) promoted the rosary in his apostolic work with young men, teaching them and everyone who would listen to him that all of hell's demons can be conquered through the prayer of the rosary. Saint Anthony Mary Claret (1807–1870), a very zealous bishop and fervent son of Mary, was responsible for founding a religious community known as the Missionary Sons of the Immaculate Heart of Mary (Claretians). Saint Anthony prayed numerous rosaries throughout the day and wrote a book on the devotion that explained its power and worth. The Queen of Heaven was very pleased with his efforts in spreading the rosary. In his autobiography, he humbly revealed one reason why he was so fervent in spreading the rosary. He asserted that on several occasions, Mary had appeared to him and explicitly told him that he was to serve as a "new St. Dominic" in his promotion of the rosary. The fact that Our Lady associated the rosary with St. Dominic gives us an insight into how heaven views the history and origins of the rosary. Saint Claret was obedient to Our Lady and became what she asked him to be. When he became the archbishop of Santiago, Cuba, he mandated that the rosary be recited in all the churches of his archdiocese on Sundays and feast days. To make sure this was being done, he would intentionally and frequently make unscheduled visits to parishes to check up on the priests.

Another man of deep prayer who championed the rosary was the Benedictine monk Blessed Columba Marmion (1858–1923). He promoted devotion to the rosary in both the 19th and 20th centuries, and is considered one of the most influential writers of his time. Blessed Marmion compared the Hail Marys of the rosary to the tiny pebbles David used in his sling to bring down the giant Goliath.

It was also during this century that the Dominican priest Fr. Damien-Marie Saintourens (1835–1920) founded the Dominican Nuns of the Perpetual Rosary in Calais, France, in 1880. Father Saintourens had been a diocesan priest for eight years before joining the Dominicans and becoming a zealous promoter of the rosary. As a champion of the rosary, he erected confraternities all over Europe, as well as in the United States. In 1891, he established a monastery for the Dominican Nuns of the Perpetual Rosary in New Jersey. He had a special devotion to Blessed Alphonsus Navarrette, as well as to the 205 Martyrs of Japan, whom he referred to as martyrs of the rosary since many of them were members of the Confraternity of the Rosary. He was so devoted to them that he made it a point to attend their beatification in Rome in 1867. Father Saintourens died in Camden, New Jersey, in 1920.

In 1882, when Venerable Michael J. McGivney (1852–1890) founded the Knights of Columbus in New Haven, Connecticut, he wanted the Knights to embrace the rosary as a spiritual weapon. In a certain sense, the Knights of Columbus are also Knights of Mary. The spiritual sword is part of their initiation ceremony: Every Knight is given a rosary and makes a promise to pray it as often as he is able. One Knight of Columbus who wielded his spiritual sword against the powers of darkness was St. Miguel de la Mora (1874–1927). During the Mexican Cristero War in the 1920s, many Knights of Columbus became martyrs. Saint Miguel was one of these martyred knights: He was shot while praying his rosary. The Ugandan martyrs in Africa, who were killed in 1886 as martyrs for purity and fidelity to the faith, were also associated with the rosary. These martyrs were champions of the rosary, never letting it fall from their hands even as they were burned alive.

Another champion of the rosary was Blessed Rita Amada de Jesus (1848–1913). Though she was not a martyr, she lived during an era of anti-Catholic persecution in Portugal and suffered much for her faith. Her response to the hatred and anti-Catholic sentiment of the enemies of the faith was to instruct others in the faith by teaching them the rosary.

Saintly Dominicans continued to promote the rosary, as well. One such Dominican was Blessed Hyacinth Cormier (1832–1916). He was the Master General of the Dominican Order from 1904 to 1916 and had a tender love for Our Lady. He composed beautiful prayers in honor of the rosary. The one below was so well received by the Church that St. Pope Pius X granted an indulgence to anyone who recited it:

> O Virgin Mary, grant that the recitation of thy rosary may be for me each day, in the midst of my manifold duties, a bond of unity in my actions, a tribute of filial piety, a sweet refreshment, an encouragement to walk joyfully along the path of duty. Grant, above all, O Virgin Mary, that the study of thy fifteen mysteries may form in my soul, little by little, a luminous atmosphere, pure, strengthening, and fragrant, which may penetrate my understanding, my will, my heart, my memory, my imagination, my whole being. So shall I acquire the habit of praying while I work, without the aid of formal prayers, by interior acts of admiration and of supplication, or by aspirations of love. I ask this of thee, O Queen of the Holy Rosary, through Saint Dominic, thy son of predilection, the renowned preacher of thy mysteries, and the faithful imitator of thy virtues. Amen.[5]

Another Dominican promoting the rosary during the 19th century was St. Francisco Coll y Guitart (1812–1875). He was a close friend of St. Anthony Mary Claret (the new St. Dominic) and also founded a religious community dedicated to Mary. During a civil war in Spain, St. Francisco sought to revitalize Spain and bring peace to his native land by having people join the Confraternity of the Rosary and pray the perpetual rosary. Saint Anthony Mary Claret himself was so inspired by the preaching and missionary activity of St. Francisco that he urged the pope to make St. Francisco an apostolic missionary, which Bl. Pope Pius IX then did. During his missionary activities, St. Francisco published small booklets on the rosary and freely distributed them to the people who attended his missions.

Pope Leo XIII (The Pope of the Rosary)

As all Mariologists know, there has never been a papacy as dedicated to the rosary as that of Pope Leo XIII (1810–1903). The oldest pope in church history — he was 93 years old when he died — Pope Leo XIII held the office of Vicar of Christ for 25 years. During those 25 years, he wrote no fewer than 11 encyclicals on the rosary, as well as countless rosary-themed letters, exhortations, and messages. His 11 rosary encyclicals were written between the years 1883 and 1898. During those years, he wrote a rosary encyclical almost every year. Listed below are his 11 rosary encyclicals in chronological order:

1883 – *Supremi Apostolatus Officio*
1884 – *Superiore Anno*
1887 – *Vi È Ben Noto*
1891 – *Octobri Mense*
1892 – *Magnae Dei Matris*
1893 – *Laetitiae Sanctae*
1894 – *Iucunda Semper Expectatione*
1895 – *Adiutricem Populi*
1896 – *Fidentem Piumque Animum*
1897 – *Augustissimae Virginis Mariae*
1898 – *Diuturni Temporis*

It should be noted that, although Pope Leo XIII did not write a rosary encyclical in 1885, he continued to promote the rosary that year in another encyclical titled *Quod Auctoritate*. In that non-rosary encyclical, which did contain a large section dedicated to the rosary, he proclaimed an extraordinary Jubilee and entrusted it to the patronage of Our Lady of the Rosary. Even when he was not authoring an official document on the rosary, he continued to promote it in almost everything he did. Almost all of his 11 rosary encyclicals were written in preparation for the month of October, and he is largely responsible for turning October into a month dedicated to the rosary. In his youth, he had been very familiar with farm life and knew that October was the month for harvesting. That's why, during his papacy, he chose to promote the rosary in October to signify that the rosary is a way of reaping an abundant harvest of souls.

The Pope of the Rosary affirmed all the rosary indulgences that the Church had offered throughout the centuries, as well as offering his own. He particularly promoted the indulgences offered to the members of the Confraternity of the Rosary and those offered for Rosary Sunday. He was so fond of rosary indulgences that after authoring his last rosary encyclical in 1898, he approved a complete and exhaustive list in 1899 of all the indulgences attached to the rosary. This 1899 document listed indulgences from more than 15 popes and was such a comprehensive list that the Dominicans published it in their January 1900 issue of *The Rosary* magazine. Prior to Pope Leo XIII's list, most people relied on the one published in 1886 by the Dominican priest Fr. Thomas Maria Leikes, from the German province of Dominicans. His extensive list of rosary indulgences was called the "*Rosa Aurea*." Father Leikes' document provided 214 official papal documents on the rosary. It included the names of 39 popes, from Pope Alexander IV all the way to Pope Leo XIII. It remains an invaluable resource for any historian of the rosary.

For Pope Leo XIII, is was clear who had founded the rosary: St. Dominic. Following in the footsteps of his papal predecessors, he repeatedly affirmed the pious tradition. Almost all of his 11 rosary encyclicals refer to St. Dominic as the founder of the rosary. He was such a champion of the rosary that he added the title "Queen of the Most Holy Rosary" to the Litany of Loreto; encouraged the development of the "Living Rosary" founded by Venerable Pauline Jaricot; and beatified Louis de Montfort in 1888. It was a special joy for Leo XIII to beatify Louis de Montfort since it was the writings and witness of this great saint which had instilled in him a great love for Mary and her rosary.

In 1853, when Rome declared that the recently discovered writings of then-Venerable Louis de Montfort were free of theological error, the man who would become Pope Leo XIII familiarized himself with these writings and became a priest on fire with love for the Blessed Virgin Mary. All throughout his priestly ministry, but especially after he was elected pope, Leo XIII wrote prolifically to promote the rosary. Like all the champions of the rosary who came before him, he understood the rosary to be a spiritual weapon, an evangelical tool for expanding the kingdom of Christ, and a most effective instrument for establishing peace in families, society, and the entire world. Reading the newly discovered writings of St. Louis de Montfort proved to be a major influence on both the priestly and papal life of Leo XIII.

The other great influence encouraging Pope Leo XIII's love for the rosary was Lourdes. When the apparitions at Lourdes happened in 1858, he was already 48 years old and had been a priest for more than 20 years. Lourdes became very dear to his heart. He was particularly fond of the fact that Mary prayed parts of the rosary with St. Bernadette. In 1890, as pope, he established the Feast of Our Lady of Lourdes and set February 11 as the annual date for the celebration of the feast.

Blessed Bartolo Longo and Our Lady of the Rosary of Pompeii

One of the most incredible testimonies to the ability of the rosary to bring back a soul from the brink of hell is the life of Blessed Bartolo Longo (1841–1926). Bartolo grew up in southern Italy during a time when Italy was experiencing a very strong nationalist movement. The movement was particularly known for turning people away from Catholicism and her teachings. Bartolo got caught up in this movement during his college years in Naples and fell away from the faith. He became so infatuated with the movement and its ideology that not only did he abandon the Catholicism of his youth, but he also became heavily involved in the practice of spiritualism and the occult. His fascination with mediums and witchcraft led him to participate in many séances, and he was eventually ordained a priest of spiritualism. Later in life, he would state that he had in fact become a servant of the devil and a priest of Satan.

Contrary to what he was promised by the practitioners of the occult, abandoning Catholicism and being ordained a satanic priest did not provide Bartolo with peace and happiness. The opposite actually occurred. After his "ordination," he began to experience deep depression and suffered extreme bouts of anxiety. Eventually these spiritual, psychological, and emotional problems led him to seek out the help of a Catholic priest. He was led to a devout Dominican priest, Fr. Alberto Radente, by the advice of friends. A very learned man, Fr. Radente instructed Bartolo in the faith, helping him turn from the occult and renounce his involvement in spiritualism. Bartolo discovered that, once he did this, he began to experience peace and have a deep desire for a conversion of heart. It did not take long for him to completely reject and renounce the false teachings and practices of spiritualism. In his zeal, he even once barged into a séance, raised a rosary high above the attendees, and rebuked the assembly for what they were doing. He warned them that their practices were false and they needed to turn to Catholicism to find truth.

A lawyer by profession, Bartolo continued his legal practice after his initial conversion. Since he had been brought back to Jesus, Mary, and the Church through the instruction of a Dominican, Bartolo decided to become a Third Order Dominican himself. His initiation ceremony took place on the Feast of Our Lady of the Rosary on October 7, 1871. As part of the ceremony, he was given the name "Br. Rosario." After becoming a Third Order Dominican, he made a trip to Pompeii in order to help a wealthy countess named Marianna de Fusco with her legal matters. Upon his arrival in Pompeii, he was taken aback by the state of the city, and especially the degradation of the people, both spiritual and material. He was shocked to find that very few practiced Catholicism or understood its teachings. Many people had even fallen into the occult and were practicing the same forms of spiritualism that he had once observed. This situation greatly distressed him because he knew that he himself had led many people away from Catholicism during his stint in the occult.

Historically, the city of Pompeii had not experienced any major development since it had been buried in volcanic ash in 79 AD. Now, as a fruit of the anti-Catholic movement in Italy, the people of Pompeii had fallen away from their Catholic heritage and become spiritually dead. Seeing these things all around him caused Bartolo to fall into a terrible depression. He realized that it was people like him who had helped extinguish the light of faith in souls through the anti-Catholic and spiritualist movements. He feared that, because he had been an ordained satanic priest, the devil still had a stranglehold on his soul. Though Bartolo had undergone a conversion, the situation of Pompeii reminded him of his past and haunted him. He was on the verge of total despair and even contemplated suicide.

As his heart sank deeper and deeper into despair, Bartolo forced himself to reflect upon what Fr. Radente had once said about the life and preaching of St. Dominic. He remembered that the rosary had brought erring souls back to the truth and restored hope to lost souls during the life of St. Dominic. He remembered that the Dominican priest had taught him about how Mary had once made the promise to St. Dominic that those who promote the rosary will find salvation. These words kept repeating in Bartolo's mind and heart, and were the answer to his despair. The rosary became his way of beating the bondage of Satan forever. At this point, in 1873, he made a firm decision to stay in the valley of Pompeii and promote the rosary. He started immediately by initiating the restoration of an old dilapidated church.

In addition to fixing up the church, he also sought to establish the Confraternity of the Rosary in Pompeii. By means of the rosary, its mysteries, and its Confraternity, he would seek to re-educate the people in the truths of Catholicism. In those days, however, it was required that confraternities have an image of Our Lady of the Rosary. The image had to depict Our Lady giving the rosary to St. Dominic. Bartolo had no such image, but was able to acquire one through the generosity of Fr. Radente, who had purchased it at a junk sale for practically nothing. Due to his many responsibilities, however, Bartolo was not able to return to Naples to pick it up himself, so it was held by a nun in Naples until it could be delivered to Pompeii. When the image finally arrived in Pompeii in 1875, it arrived on a cart of manure and was in very bad condition. Upon seeing the image, Bartolo was so taken aback by how unattractive it was — this was his first time seeing it — that he thought of sending the image back. He described it as an old, worn, faded painting that had an unattractive depiction of St. Dominic and St. Rose. He thought the depiction of St. Dominic in the image to be so horribly distasteful that he did not even think it was worth the little it had cost.

However, out of respect for the nun and the kindness of Fr. Radente, he humbly accepted the image.

As Bartolo had sought to restore the church building, so now did he also seek to have the image restored. He desired that St. Rose be replaced with an image of St. Catherine of Siena, in keeping with the practice of other confraternities. The restoration resulted in a beautiful depiction of Mary and the Baby Jesus giving the rosary to St. Dominic and St. Catherine. Unbeknownst to Bartolo, the image would become very popular. God would use it to work miracles and build a world-famous basilica around it.

In his newfound zeal for helping others, Bl. Bartolo established religious communities, orphanages, hospitals, schools, and many other institutions and foundations as part of his plan to bring Catholicism back to the area and restore the ancient city of Pompeii. Heaven was very pleased with his efforts, and in 1884, something wonderful happened that caused the entire Catholic world to turn its gaze toward the forgotten city of Pompeii. A little girl named Fortuna Agrelli claimed to have received a vision of the Mother of God and experienced a healing through Bl. Bartolo's rosary image. Fortuna had been suffering from a variety of illnesses for several years. All the physicians her parents had consulted had given up on her. The family, however, did not give up. They began a series of three novenas, praying the rosary for 27 days total, asking for a healing for little Fortuna. At the end of the novena, the Queen of Heaven appeared to Fortuna looking exactly like her depiction in the confraternity image restored by Bl. Bartolo: She appeared holding the Baby Jesus and giving the rosary to St. Dominic and St. Catherine of Siena. During the apparition, the little girl begged Mary for a healing by calling on Mary specifically as "Our Lady of the Rosary." In response, Mary informed the girl that this title was most pleasing to her, and that she would be healed. Mary also informed her that, in the future, anyone who desired to receive graces from God should pray this 27-day rosary novena and add an additional 27 days (three more novenas of rosaries) in thanksgiving. This novena became known as the 54 Day Rosary Novena and is often called the "Irresistible Novena to Our Lady of the Rosary of Pompeii."

News of Fortuna's healing spread quickly. When word of it finally reached Rome, Pope Leo XIII became even more inspired to promote the rosary, and began to write an encyclical on the rosary almost every year. The miracle through the image of Our Lady of the Rosary of Pompeii strongly confirmed the pope's teaching that the pious tradition was worthy of belief. Heaven itself had affirmed the pious tradition through the apparition given to Fortuna, since the miracle was given through an image that depicted the rosary being given to St. Dominic.

In 1885, Bl. Bartolo married Countess Marianna de Fusco, and together they continued to develop the Shrine and its good works. As time went by, Bl. Bartolo and his wife observed how devoted Pope Leo XIII was to the rosary. The couple decided to donate the entire Shrine of Our Lady of the Rosary of Pompeii to the Holy See when Pope Leo XIII died in 1903. It took several years to work out all the details, but the Shrine was finally handed over to the Holy See in 1906.

Blessed Bartolo lived for 20 more years and continued to conduct great works of charity in Pompeii. His apostolate was very fruitful, even helping to form his collaborators into saints. Bartolo instilled in his physician, St. Joseph Moscati (1880–1927), a great love of the rosary. Saint Moscati had become a close friend of Bl. Bartolo over the years, and would make frequent visits from Naples to Pompeii in order to see his friend and visit the Shrine. The saintly physician prayed the rosary every day and never went anywhere without his beads in his pocket.

Today, the church restored by Bl. Bartolo Longo has been declared a basilica and officially designated as the Pontifical Shrine of Our Lady of the Rosary of Pompeii. It receives millions of pilgrims each year. Blessed Bartolo Longo has gained the honor of being one of the greatest champions of the rosary in the history of the Church.

THE 20ᵀᴴ CENTURY:
Marian Apparitions and Apostles of the Rosary

The Queen of Heaven raised up an unprecedented number of champions of the rosary during the 20th century. There were great threats against the Church, and heroic men and women were needed to wield the spiritual sword. At the beginning of the century, Modernism and the abuse of the historical-critical method of scholarship posed serious threats to the Church and her teachings. Modernism desired to do away with the traditions of the past, and the incorrect use of the historical-critical method sought to reinterpret the miraculous events of the past and dismiss them as mundane legends. This caused confusion among the faithful and greatly affected those who prayed the rosary.

When the lengthy papacy of Leo XIII came to an end in 1903, Modernists and critics immediately launched an all-out assault on the history of the origins of the rosary. Pope Leo XIII had been aware of the criticisms leveled against the pious tradition, but paid them no attention. Now, however, the Modernists and critics were everywhere — even within the Dominican Order. In fact, a son of St. Dominic began to lead the charge against the pious tradition. Nevertheless, heaven had anticipated the new critics. In 1911, the first edition of *The Secret of the Rosary* went into print and provided answers to the questions/claims/charges/rumors circulated by Modernists and critics. Unfortunately, however, most of the critics treated *The Secret of the Rosary* as an unreliable source and ignored it. This caused the Divine Craftsman to send the Virgin Mary in apparition after apparition, emphasizing the rosary by holding it in her hand, exhorting others to pray it, and raising up a rosary army. In one of these apparitions, she even provided a heavenly perspective on the validity of the pious tradition.

One of the greatest champions of the rosary in the 20th century would be the Servant of God Joseph Kentenich (1885–1968). He summed up the dangers that Modernism posed to souls and the great triumph that Mary would have over it and all other heresies. He stated:

> The Modernism of our day, that summary of all heresies, may shake the foundations of our holy faith with renewed violence; even Catholic scholars around the world may consciously or unconsciously be striving to lead the Church to death — we need not fear. The Queen of the Apostles will be on guard for her office. As in the past, so now again the Church shall emerge from the battle victorious.[1]

The 20th century would, indeed, be a century of Modernists, skeptics, and critics, but it would also be a century of apparitions, mystics, martyrs, and great heroes of the rosary.

Fr. Thomas Esser, OP

Less than one year after the death of Pope Leo XIII, a German Dominican began to strongly critique the pious tradition. This priest's name was Fr. Thomas Esser (1850–1926). Father Esser was an erudite and well-known Dominican serving as a secretary for the Sacred Congregation of the Index in Rome. At the time, this sacred congregation was in charge of the Index of Prohibited Books. During the papacy of Leo XIII, Fr. Esser had already published several articles that were critical of the pious tradition, but most of the articles went unnoticed by the general public since they were published in scholarly journals.

Father Esser was one of the first Dominicans to question the pious tradition. Other scholars were surprised to observe that a son of St. Dominic was questioning his own order's tradition. To his credit, however, Fr. Esser knew the position of Pope Leo XIII and his predecessors on the matter, and always maintained in his articles that his ideas were only theories. Yet in 1904, after the death of Pope Leo XIII, Fr. Esser began to publish articles for the general public that strongly critiqued the pious tradition. Specifically, from 1904 to 1906, he published a series of eight articles in the German periodical *Der Katholik* in which he made his arguments against the pious tradition.

The theories presented by Fr. Esser were basically re-presentations of the critique of the Bollandists, especially Fr. Cuypers, from the 18th century. His first theory was that the rosary preexisted St. Dominic, since he had found ancient documents attesting that a Psalter of Mary was prayed on a string of beads before St. Dominic's lifetime. Father Esser believed that this proved that St. Dominic was not the founder of the rosary. This argument hinged on Fr. Esser's claim that there were no ancient documents either by St. Dominic or the early Dominicans that mentioned the rosary. The weakness of his argument (one that he himself fully acknowledged) was that the Psalter of Mary that existed before St. Dominic did not have any mysteries associated with it, and therefore was not really the same thing as the Dominican rosary we know today. Realizing the weakness of this argument, he offered a second theory.

In much the same fashion as the Bollandists, Fr. Esser maintained that since no documents existed concerning the rosary by St. Dominic or the early Dominicans, the rosary might have come into existence at a later date. Having found what he thought were the earliest texts on the rosary in the writings of the 15th-century Dominican Bl. Alan de la Roche, he asserted that Bl. Alan was the founder. There was a problem, though. In his writings, Bl. Alan never claimed to be the founder of the rosary. He himself always maintained that St. Dominic was the founder of the devotion. Blessed Alan only claimed to be the one who renewed the rosary. Needing a way around this predicament, Fr. Esser made the strange claim that Bl. Alan de la Roche had confused the 13th-century founder of the Dominicans (St. Dominic) with the 15th-century Carthusian monk Dominic of Prussia. In Fr. Esser's mind, it was Dominic of Prussia who was the author of the rosary and not St. Dominic. He asserted this, not simply because the two

Dominics shared the same first name, but because in the ancient document by Dominic of Prussia, the Carthusian stated that he was the first person to ever write down mysteries of the rosary.

Father Esser's conclusions are fraught with weakness, so much so that even he acknowledged their limitations. In fact, as new discoveries have been made since his death, his theories have fallen apart and the credibility of the pious tradition has been reinforced. For example, when presenting his first theory, Fr. Esser was correct to note that much of the rosary existed before the life of St. Dominic. Today, no one doubts that the Psalter of Mary and prayer beads existed before St. Dominic. What Fr. Esser failed to fully grasp, however, was that he had discovered the antecedents to the rosary and not the rosary itself. There can be no rosary where there are no mysteries.

Regarding his second theory, at the time he was writing, a purely historical-critical approach to the subject would have validated his findings. However, documents have since been discovered that prove that Dominic of Prussia was not the first to write down mysteries of the rosary. Specifically, in 1977, a document dating from 1300 was found that contains the mysteries of the rosary. (See the "New Discoveries" section of this chapter to find out more about this and other recent discoveries.)

The critiques of Fr. Esser against the pious tradition abruptly ended in 1907, and for good reason. In 1907, St. Pope Pius X promulgated his famous encyclical against Modernism, *Pascendi Dominici Gregis*. Four years later, in 1911, *The Secret of the Rosary* went into its first printing. The history of the rosary presented by the recently beatified Third Order Dominican Louis de Montfort went completely against the theories of Fr. Esser. It affirmed that St. Dominic was the founder of the rosary, firmly held to the pious tradition, and (much to the consternation of the critics) even gave honorable mention to Dominic of Prussia and his contemplative version of the rosary, but in no way stated that he was the founder. The book also affirmed that Bl. Alan de la Roche was not the founder of the rosary, but only the Dominican responsible for renewing it in the 15th century. With these emerging pieces of evidence cutting against his theories, Fr. Esser ceased his critique and no longer desired to have any involvement in the arguments against the rosary tradition.

Interestingly, after laying down his pen against the pious tradition, Fr. Esser was consecrated a titular bishop in 1917. To be a titular bishop is to hold an episcopal position in which one is not in charge of a diocese. In his new role, he was to work in Rome for the Holy Office. In 1917, the same year that he became a bishop, the Sacred Congregation of the Index ceased to exist. The responsibilities of the defunct congregation were transferred to the Holy Office, now known as the Sacred Congregation for the Doctrine of the Faith. The year 1917 was also the year that the rosary-themed apparitions at Fatima occurred. Unfortunately, even though Fr. Esser had ceased his critique of the rosary tradition, his previous articles laid the foundation for others to attack the pious tradition. One very

Modernist-leaning Jesuit in particular would pick up where Fr. Esser's criticism had left off and begin to present his theories as if they were facts.

Fr. Herbert Thurston, SJ

For anyone who has studied the history of the rosary, it is very clear that the English Jesuit Fr. Herbert Thurston (1856–1939) is responsible for convincing *almost* the entire Catholic Church that the pious tradition is a myth.

This pseudo-Bollandist wrote incessantly on every topic imaginable during his time. His daily routine consisted of researching and writing articles for publication in journals and periodicals that were read all over the world. It is estimated that he wrote more than 800 articles and authored more than a dozen books during his lifetime. At least 150 of his articles were written for the first edition of the *Catholic Encyclopedia*, launched in 1907. When the encyclopedia was finished in 1914, it was circulated throughout the entire Catholic world. Most readers of the articles in the encyclopedia understood them to represent the official Catholic position on the topic at hand. Father Thurston's most influential article in the *Catholic Encyclopedia* was on the rosary. This article was read around the globe by laity, priests, and bishops, and taken to be the official position of the Church on the rosary and its origins.

In the same year that the *Catholic Encyclopedia* was launched (1907), St. Pope Pius X published his encyclical against Modernism, *Pascendi Dominici Gregis*. In this profound document, the pope railed against those who spread the errors of Modernism, noting that Modernists were able to influence many because they were believers, theologians, historians, critics, apologists, reformers, and oftentimes priests. Saint Pius X emphasized that the greatest danger from the Modernists was their ability to compose both praiseworthy articles on the faith and writings inimical to the Church and her traditions. Regarding the latter, Pope Pius X noted the following:

> If they [Modernists] write history, it is to search out with curiosity and to publish openly, on the pretext of telling the whole truth and with a species of ill-concealed satisfaction, everything that looks to them like a stain in the history of the Church. Under the sway of certain *a priori* rules they destroy as far as they can the pious traditions of the people, and bring ridicule on certain relics highly venerable from antiquity. They are possessed by the empty desire of being talked about, and they know they would never succeed in this were they to say only what has been always said. It may be that they have persuaded themselves that in all this they are really serving God and the Church — in reality they only offend both, less perhaps by their works themselves than by the spirit in which they write and by the encouragement they are giving to the extravagances of the Modernists.[2]

The above statement should be kept in mind as we take a deeper look at the spirit with which Fr. Thurston — a believer, theologian, historian, critic, apologist, reformer, and priest — conducted his historical and theological research on the rosary.

One would have expected Fr. Thurston, a Jesuit priest, to have been a member of a Marian Sodality, a defender of the pious tradition, and a champion of the rosary. Unfortunately, the opposite was the case. Almost all of Fr. Thurston's articles on Catholic topics expressed an extreme skepticism toward miracles, especially miracles associated with the lives of the saints. It was no secret during his lifetime that he had strong Modernist tendencies and was a controversial and captious historical critic, often at odds with the traditions and teachings of the Church. Oddly, however, his critique of the pious tradition was praised by many in the Church and understood to be scientifically irrefutable. As St. Pope Pius X had warned in *Pascendi Dominici Gregis,* Modernism had infiltrated the Church.

What made Fr. Thurston's presentation of the origins of the rosary particularly compelling and authoritative was that he was able to cite a son of St. Dominic (Fr. Esser, discussed in the previous section) who had critiqued the pious tradition and was now a bishop in Rome. Also, Fr. Thurston's zealous use of the very popular historical-critical method almost made him untouchable, since so many other scholars were using the same method in their research and theological inquiries. To question Thurston's methodology would be to question anyone's use of historical criticism. In essence, Fr. Thurston's ideas were no different from those that had been previously put forward by the Bollandists, Fr. Cuypers, and Fr. Esser. In his articles, however, Fr. Thurston did not present his ideas merely as theories. Rather, he "dogmatized" his conclusions and presented them as facts. If anyone dared to question his scholarship or conclusions, Fr. Thurston retaliated by publishing antagonistic and defamatory articles in defense of his positions.

There were many, however, who were willing to engage in theological combat with Fr. Thurston over his attempts to change the Church's position on the pious tradition. Father Joseph Crehan, SJ, the biographer of Fr. Thurston, made the following remark in this regard: "His [Fr. Thurston's] researches [on the rosary] caused a great stir and controversy was thrust upon him, for it seemed to some that his aim was not to promote understanding of the rosary but to discourage the practice of the devotion."[3] Indeed, a battle was raging over the origin of the spiritual sword, and it wasn't a battle being fought merely by flesh and blood combatants. It was a battle that involved spirits — some holy; others, not holy at all.

Quite a few saintly Dominicans came to the defense of the Dominican rosary tradition and took Fr. Thurston to task over his desire to rewrite the history of the rosary through his ubiquitous publications. Dominican scholars such as Fr. John Proctor, Fr. Reginald Walsh, and Fr. Wilfrid Lescher defended the rosary tradition and engaged in literary altercations with Fr. Thurston in various widely-read Catholic publications. One such altercation occurred between Fr. Thurston and Fr. Andrew Skelly, OP, a priest of the western province of the Dominicans in the United States, over the *Catholic Encyclopedia* rosary article. The debate lasted from October of 1912 to February of 1913.

Father Thurston lived for the drama of controversy and loved to engage in debates with Dominicans. This led to the controversy between Fr. Thurston and Fr. Skelly when the latter preached a parish mission in Oregon that included statements describing St. Dominic as the founder of the rosary. An anonymous writer stated in a local paper that Fr. Skelly's claim was contrary to the recent authoritative article by Fr. Thurston on the history of the rosary that had appeared in the *Catholic Encyclopedia*. When Fr. Skelly offered a rebuttal to the claims of the article, Fr. Thurston himself submitted an article to the local paper arguing against Fr. Skelly. In response, Fr. Skelly countered with many articles proving that St. Dominic was the founder of the rosary. The response from Fr. Thurston to the scholarly and well-written articles by Fr. Skelly was complete silence. Father Thurston had met his match.

Aware that the writings of Fr. Thurston had caused major confusion, Fr. Skelly wrote more about the issue and organized his defense of the pious tradition into a pamphlet, *St. Dominic and the Rosary or Was He Its Founder?*, which made its appearance in October of 1913. In the introduction, Fr. Skelly explains why he put the pamphlet together:

> As Father Thurston has not thought good to continue correspondence, and as his ill-informed and misleading article in the 'Catholic Encyclopedia' is a continual challenge to the truth of the tradition, and a source of disturbance to the piety of the faithful in this and other English-speaking countries, I thought it well to issue the correspondence in pamphlet form.[4]

Father Skelly considered Fr. Thurston to be a "notorious iconoclast" and his rosary article in the *Catholic Encyclopedia* an historical and theological travesty. He knew full well that the article in the *Catholic Encyclopedia* would be taken as the official Church position and deeply regretted that it was allowed to be printed. He summed up his concern in these words:

> What does seem to me as unfortunate is that this adverse view [of Fr. Thurston], rashly put forward, as some think, in opposition to the overwhelming tradition of the Church to the contrary, should be transferred from the ephemeral pages of a magazine where it could be met and its worthlessness shown up, to the columns of a permanent work of reference, such as is the "Catholic Encyclopedia."[5]

Father Skelly's concerns were completely justified; unfortunately, over time, what he had feared became reality. Father Thurston's article in the *Catholic*

Encyclopedia was taken to be fact and understood to represent the official position of the Church on the issue. Regardless of the fact that his position contradicted the pious tradition, almost everyone accepted his conclusions. In this regard, Fr. Thurston's biographer was correct in noting: "His [Fr. Thurston's] labours [against the pious tradition] may be said to have changed the trend of Catholic teaching on the subject."[6]

How it came to pass that one man was able to singlehandedly destroy the pious tradition is an enigma. After all, his conclusions were founded on negative arguments and contradicted the teaching of the popes. His arguments were negative in that they relied upon a "lack" of documentary evidence on the rosary from the life of St. Dominic. He was never able to put forth any positive proof that the rosary had not been founded by St. Dominic. The 180-degree shift in Catholic thought on this matter is indeed puzzling, especially since only a few years earlier the great rosary encyclicals of Pope Leo XIII had been published, as well as Louis de Montfort's masterpiece *The Secret of the Rosary*. The only possible way to understand how Fr. Thurston was able to accomplish what he did is to look at the spirit behind his scholarship. The pen and the one who holds it cannot be separated, and it simply cannot be denied that when one looks into the life and influences of Fr. Thurston, there are aspects of his life and intentions that are both devious and disturbing. In particular, there are three areas from his life that may help explain how one man could have had the power to alter a Catholic tradition: 1) his lifelong fascination with the occult and involvement in spiritualism; 2) his Modernist tendencies and association with the excommunicated Jesuit priest Fr. George Tyrrell; and 3) his extreme skepticism toward miracles, especially in the lives of the saints.

From his youth, Herbert Thurston always maintained a scandalous familiarity with spiritualism and its practices. According to his own written testimony, his association with spiritualism began when he was eight years old. His father developed a deep friendship with a man by the name of J. H. Powell, a famous practitioner of spiritualism and the editor of the spiritualist periodical *Spiritual Times*. Throughout Fr. Thurston's youth, J.H. Powell was, Fr. Thurston claims, "a constant visitor at our house."[7] During these visits, Powell engaged in the spiritualist practices of mesmerism, mind-control, and hypnotism.[8] These early experiences left the young boy with a very sympathetic and favorable attitude toward spiritualism before becoming an ordained Jesuit priest. As a Jesuit priest, Fr. Thurston, in imitation of his father, also formed a very close friendship with a famous medium, Bertha Hirst. When they got together, it wasn't to pray the rosary or ask for the intercession of the saints.[9]

Years before establishing his friendship with Bertha Hirst, Fr. Thurston's friend Fr. George Tyrrell, the infamous excommunicated Jesuit priest, had encouraged Thurston to become a member of the Society for Psychical Research (SPR). From the beginning of their friendship, Fr. Tyrrell had encouraged Thurston's interest in spiritualism, and desired to see his Jesuit confrere attain the "courage" to think outside the box of Catholic dogma and papal pronounce-ments. Thus, encouraged and supported by Fr. Tyrrell, Fr. Thurston became an official member of the SPR in 1919. He joined the SPR knowing full well that it was a group devoted to exploring the many practices performed by spiritualists and that his attendance at such events was obligatory. The SPR was also well known to be inimical to the beliefs, teachings, and devotions of the Catholic Church. It was not an organization interested in the saints, mystics, and miracles of Catholicism. The SPR focused its research on mediums, poltergeists, ghosts, vampires, and magicians, as well as those who participated in such things as séances, necromancy, channeling, telepathy, and clairvoyance. The SPR held that a person could only be considered an "expert in spiritualism" by being present at paranormal events and attending séances, all dangerous territory, especially for a Catholic priest. Father Thurston never publicly admitted that he attended séances — he knew this was something absolutely forbidden by the Catholic Church — yet he also never publicly denied it. His friends in the SPR would, however, publicly state that he attended séances as part of the organization.[10] His association with the SPR explains why he adamantly refused to be described as a Catholic teacher or instructor in spiritual or mystical theology. He always insisted that he be referred to as an "expert in spiritualism."

The members of the SPR hardly even considered Fr. Thurston a Catho-lic priest since he was so sympathetic toward their views and practices. In fact, many spiritualists likened him to one of their own. When Fr. Thurston died on November 3, 1939, the November 11 edition of the *Psychic News* praised him as a great friend of spiritualists and affirmed that he had indeed attended many séances. This news caused great confusion among the faithful. Taking their cue from such a famed Jesuit scholar, many Catholics began to attend séances as well. To this day, many of Fr. Thurston's books are widely read and promoted by members of the New Age movement and occult practitioners.

The saying is true: When a man plays with fire, he ends up getting burned. Such a man also leaves the odor of fire upon everything he touches. This proved especially true in the writings of Fr. Thurston. The damaging effects of the flames of spiritualism were manifested in the vast majority of his writings that dealt with Catholic devotions and practices of piety. On occasion, his writings intention-ally went against Catholic teaching. For example, in the English periodical *The Month*, he presented necromancy (communicating with the dead) favorably.[11] These articles had to be examined by four theologians in Rome, due to the ways they conflicted with Church teaching. His Jesuit superiors in England also conducted their own investigation into Fr. Thurston's position on necromancy. In early 1917, after the investigations were concluded, both the Vatican and his Jesuit superiors reprimanded him for having promoted teachings contrary to the faith. In April of 1917, in an attempt to correct the damage Fr. Thurston had done, the Holy Office in Rome issued an official letter informing Catholics that they were absolutely forbidden to practice necromancy.[12] Surprisingly, Fr.

Thurston's unorthodox ideas in other areas continued to appear in his writings and go unquestioned.

Another problematic area in the life and writings of Fr. Thurston was his Modernist approach to historical and theological topics. When St. Pope Pius X wrote the encyclical *Pascendi Dominici Gregis* against Modernism in 1907, one of Fr. Thurston's best friends immediately responded by writing articles against it. This priest was Fr. George Tyrrell. Like Thurston, he was also a Jesuit, a Modernist, and in opposition to many teachings of the Church. Eventually Fr. Tyrrell was suspended from the priesthood, kicked out of the Jesuits, and excommunicated by St. Pope Pius X. Sadly, Fr. Tyrrell died in 1909 without reconciling with the Church.

Before Fr. Tyrrell's death, Fr. Thurston had written a letter to the Vatican in an attempt to defend the Modernist positions of Fr. Tyrrell, even audaciously claiming that because the ecclesial authorities in Rome did not have a thorough enough grasp of the English language, they were incapable of understanding or appreciating the genius of Fr. Tyrrell's thought. Father Thurston even tried to sway the Vatican into allowing the excommunicated Jesuit to continue to celebrate Mass, despite Fr. Tyrrell's lack of belief in the Real Presence of Jesus Christ in the Eucharist.[13]

Father Thurston's negative impact on the Church didn't end with his attack on the rosary or the attempted reversal of Fr. Tyrrell's excommunication. His Modernist agenda continued in his attempts to re-write the history of the Shroud of Turin. He tried to purge from the minds of Catholics the belief that the Shroud of Turin was the burial cloth of Jesus by writing lengthy articles against the tradition of the Shroud and dogmatically declaring it to be a fake. Naturally, the place where his thought on the matter would have the greatest readership and influence was the *Catholic Encyclopedia*, and he readily offered his services to compose the official article on the Shroud. He knew full well that it would be read around the world, and therefore whatever he wrote would have global influence. Initially, his "well-researched" article convinced many members of the Church, including priests and bishops, that the Shroud was a fake. However, due to Fr. Thurston's faulty scholarship and a lack of respect for the papal tradition on the matter, the article was taken out of the second edition of the *Catholic Encyclopedia*.

Unfortunately, Fr. Thurston sought to de-mythologize many such traditions in other "well-researched" articles that were not taken out of the *Catholic Encyclopedia*. For example, in addition to deconstructing the history of the rosary, he is also responsible for re-defining as myth the centuries-old tradition that the Holy House of Loreto — the house of Jesus, Mary, and Joseph in Nazareth — had been mystically transported to Italy by angels. Thanks to his Modernist scholarship, this tradition has been downgraded to a myth. Instead of being recognized as a miracle performed through holy angels, the transportation of the house is now thought to have a purely human explanation.

Father Thurston's revisionist approach to traditional accounts of miracles leads us to the third problematic aspect of his thought; He was an extreme skeptic. In many of his writings he declared himself to not only be a skeptic, but also a "doubting Thomas" and "the devil's advocate." His skepticism is easily discerned in what became one of his most infamous projects. From 1926 to 1938, he took it upon himself to completely revise the classic 17th century work by Fr. Alban Butler known as the *Lives of the Saints*. His revision expunged the vast majority of miracles associated with the saints out of the text. Many who have compared the two versions have noted that he wielded his pen savagely as if it were an axe. He even ridiculed, mocked, and belittled the saints themselves, and referred to many of them as hysterics, neurotics, and masochists. His criticism was so ruthless that one of his Jesuit confreres made one last request as he lay on his deathbed. He begged Fr. Thurston to spare the Blessed Trinity his axe!

Father Thurston spared the Trinity, but continued to have a theological vendetta against saints and miracles. He gave no credence to the belief that Mary had appeared to St. Dominic and given him the rosary. He also considered Bl. Alan de la Roche a fanatic who suffered from delusional visions and hallucinations. Catholics aren't bound to believe in private revelation, but Fr. Thurston stepped beyond disbelief to write disparagingly about holy men and women from the past.

And there were many other holy persons that he criticized and belittled: He wrote disparagingly about Gemma Galgani (now St. Gemma Galgani), Anne Catherine Emmerich (now Blessed Anne Catherine Emmerich), and maintained that the stigmata of Padre Pio (now St. Pio of Pietrelcina) were fake. According to Fr. Thurston's writings, there have been no authentic instances of the stigmata since the time of St. Francis of Assisi.[14] He labeled Venerable Mary of Agreda an hysteric and claimed her bilocations were more accurately described as a "clairvoyant ability." He also ridiculed the visions of St. Simon Stock regarding the origins of the Brown Scapular and wrote that the Sabbatine privilege associated with the scapular tradition was a fraudulent fairytale.

Father Thurston's skepticism and criticism is almost without limit. He believed that the incorrupt bodies of saints could all be explained by natural causes. He was very critical and demeaning toward the relics of saints and offered cold sneers toward the annual miracle associated with the blood of St. Januarius. He believed any person — including canonized saints — who claimed to have lived solely on the Eucharist for long periods of time to be liars and frauds. He rejected any notion that an image, statue, or crucifix could bleed or exude oil. He also held a particular disdain for Marian apparitions, referring to them as various forms of hypnosis or instances of natural telepathy and psychical phenomena. He wrote that the Marian apparitions of La Salette and Beauraing were to be understood as more psychological in nature than spiritual.[15]

All of the things detailed above serve to reveal the many disturbing aspects of the life and thought of the man who intentionally sought to change the accepted history of the rosary. He is the one responsible for teaching the world that the rosary is not of divine origin, but simply a human invention. Yet, three years before Fr. Thurston died, Pope Pius XI made the following statement in his 1936 rosary encyclical *Ingravescentibus Malis:*

> If men in our century, with its derisive pride, refuse the holy rosary, there is an innumerable multitude of holy men of every age and every condition who have always held it dear. They have recited it with great devotion, and in every moment they have used it as a powerful weapon to put the demons to flight, to preserve the integrity of life, to acquire virtue more easily, and in a word to attain real peace among men.[16]

Heaven, too, had something to say regarding the criticism of the rosary tradition. Around this time, the Divine Craftsman brought about an unprecedented number of rosary-themed apparitions.

Marian Apparitions

The 20th century witnessed more reported Marian apparitions than any previous century in Church history. Of more than 500 reported Marian apparitions, an unprecedented number of them have been approved, some have been condemned, and the vast majority remain under investigation by the local bishop or a Vatican commission.

When speaking of apparitions, it is always important to emphasize that no Catholic is bound to believe in a private revelation. What is required for our salvation has been given to us in Public Revelation (that is, Sacred Scripture and Tradition). This does not mean, however, that the private revelations approved by the Church are unimportant. The *Catechism of the Catholic Church* notes the following:

> Throughout the ages, there have been so-called "private" revelations, some of which have been recognized by the authority of the Church. They do not belong, however, to the deposit of faith. It is not their role to improve or complete Christ's definitive Revelation, but to help live more fully by it in a certain period of history. Guided by the magisterium of the Church, the *sensus fidelium* knows how to discern and welcome in these revelations whatever constitutes an authentic call of Christ or his saints to the Church.[17]

Using this definition from the *Catechism*, there can really be no doubt that the emphasis placed on the rosary in all of the approved private revelations of the 20th century constitutes an authentic call of Christ and his saints to the Church. What follows below is a brief presentation of the rosary themes from the more significant approved Marian apparitions of the 20th century.

Fatima, Portugal (1917)

The Marian apparitions that took place in Fatima, Portugal, to Blessed Jacinta Marto, Blessed Francisco Marto, and the Servant of God Lucia Dos Santos are essentially rosary apparitions. In these apparitions, Mary appeared to the little children six times (from May to October). Each time she appeared, she held a rosary. In the previous century, Mary had shown her delight in the rosary by praying parts of it with St. Bernadette during the Lourdes apparitions, but at Fatima, the Blessed Mother's witness to the importance of the rosary took the form of a maternal command. In each of the Fatima apparitions, Mary said that the rosary should be prayed daily for peace in the world and an end to the war (World War I). A person once asked Bl. Jacinta what Our Lady emphasized the most in her apparitions, and she responded that it was the daily rosary. At Fatima, the Queen of Heaven sought to bring the rosary into the daily life of the Christian.

Our Lady also desired a new development in the prayer of the rosary. Her specific request was for the children to recite the following prayer after the Glory Be: "Oh my Jesus, forgive us our sins, save us from the fires of hell, and lead all souls to heaven, especially those in most need of thy mercy." Regarding the addition of this prayer, Venerable Fulton J. Sheen noted that just as the second half of the Hail Mary had developed in the 14ᵗʰ century due to the constant threat of death from the Black Plague, so now the Fatima prayer was given in the context of World War I, which would bring about more than 10 million deaths. Heaven responded to both of these horrors by adding a prayer to the rosary so that the souls who prayed it would have Mary's intercession, the hope of God's mercy, and be more likely to be saved from the fires of hell. The prayer Mary gave the children at Fatima was officially recognized and promoted by the Sacred Apostolic Penitentiary of the Holy See in 1956.

Another significant aspect of the Fatima apparitions came during the last apparition on October 13, when Mary referred to herself as "Our Lady of the Rosary." During this apparition, the children and more than 70,000 other people witnessed the Miracle of the Sun, when the sun changed colors, spun, "danced" across the heavens, and even seemed about to fall toward the gathered crowd. This phenomenon is especially fascinating when one remembers that the earliest accounts of the pious tradition state that St. Dominic witnessed a ball of fire in the sky when he was given the rosary.[18] After the Fatima apparitions ended, Mary appeared to Sr. Lucia again in 1925 at the convent where she lived in Pontevedra, Spain, and spoke to Sr. Lucia about the Five First Saturdays of reparation. An essential dimension of this devotion is praying the rosary and meditating on the mysteries.

Beauraing, Belgium (1932–1933)

In November of 1932, Our Lady began appearing to five little children in Beauraing, Belgium. In total, she appeared 33 times. After the initial apparition, the local parish priest asked the children to pray the rosary in anticipation of the next apparition. When the next apparition occurred on December 6, Mary appeared with a rosary draped over her right arm. In every subsequent apparition until the last one on January 3, 1933, the Queen of Heaven continued to appear with the rosary draped over her right arm.

Banneux, Belgium (1933)

Less than two weeks after the last apparition in Beauraing, Our Lady began appearing to a young girl named Mariette Beco in Banneux, Belgium. In total, Mary appeared to her eight times. Mariette did the exact same thing as the visionaries at Beauraing, where the children began to pray the rosary in anticipation of the next apparition. In the second apparition of Banneux, Mary appeared with a beautiful rosary draped over her arm. For the rest of the apparitions, until they concluded on March 2, Mary appeared with the rosary draped over her arm.

St. Faustina Kowalska (1930s)

Though the private revelations given to St. Faustina in the 1930s are primarily concerned with the Divine Mercy message and devotion, there is also a very strong rosary dimension to these apparitions. Many people are unaware that the Virgin Mary appeared to St. Faustina almost as many times as Jesus did. Saint Faustina was very devoted to Our Lady, and in her *Diary*, there are numerous references to her love for the rosary. One of St. Faustina's most remarkable devotional practices was to pray a novena of 9,000 Hail Marys in preparation for the Solemnity of the Immaculate Conception, which was her favorite Marian feast day.

In his apparitions to St. Faustina, Jesus gave her the Divine Mercy Chaplet. It was revealed to St. Faustina that this new form of devotion to God's mercy was to be prayed on ordinary rosary beads. This important aspect of her revelations can help us to better understand how the rosary was given to St. Dominic in the year 1208. The apparitions given to St. Faustina reveal that the Divine Craftsman can forge a completely new weapon out of antecedent elements. In other words, as the rosary was forged together by using the various antecedents that came before it, so also the Divine Mercy Chaplet was put together using the preexisting rosary beads. However, Our Lord did not ask St. Dominic to keep a diary and record how he received the rosary. In an age when most things were not written down, St. Dominic was told to *preach* the rosary and thus pass it on orally. There was no major incentive to write about the rosary if only a small percentage of the population could read.

There is a further lesson to be learned from the life of St. Faustina and her private revelations. Shortly after St. Faustina began composing her *Diary*, Satan tricked her into burning it. Her *Diary* was to be the written testimony that contained her revelations about the new forms of devotion to God's mercy, which included the Divine Mercy Chaplet. Satan did not want the message to get out. After she burned the first *Diary*, Jesus later appeared to her and informed her that she had been tricked by the enemy. Our Lord then instructed her to begin writing her diary again. This episode teaches us that Satan does in fact seek to destroy and burn the original documents recounting the source of a new devotion, since he knows that devotion will bring about immense good for souls. History also attests that if the devil is unable to destroy the original sources, he will seek to tamper with the evidence, corrupt texts, or cause confusion. This happened with the *Diary* of St. Faustina. Years after her death, a faulty and unauthorized translation of her *Diary* appeared, resulting in the Vatican placing the *Diary* — and all the new forms of devotion inside it — under a ban. This prohibition lasted for nearly 20 years (1959–1978). Are we to think that, after Satan repeatedly tried to destroy the primary source that testified to the origins of the Divine Mercy chaplet, he would not have done something similar centuries ago when the rosary was given to St. Dominic? It is not far-fetched to think that the evil one tried to destroy much of the evidence that witnessed to the Dominican origins of the rosary (and quite possibly succeeded).

Lipa, Philippines (1948)

As we discuss rosary-themed apparitions occurring in the 20th century, the tumultuous history of the alleged Marian apparitions in Lipa, Philippines, needs to be mentioned.

In 1948, Our Lady allegedly appeared to a young girl named Teresita Castillo who had recently entered the Carmelites in Lipa. In this alleged apparition, Teresita claimed Our Lady came dressed in a lovely white dress and held a beautiful golden rosary with her right hand. She described herself to the visionary as the Mediatrix of All Grace. During the alleged apparitions, Teresita and many other people began to experience showers of heavenly rose petals with beautiful images on them. During the alleged apparitions, Our Lady stressed the importance of prayer and penance, and specifically asked the Carmelite nuns to make an act of consecration to her on October 7 (the Feast of Our Lady of the Rosary) according to the consecration method promoted by the recently canonized St. Louis de Montfort. In 1951, it was determined by ecclesiastical authorities in the Philippines and in Rome that there was nothing supernatural about the apparitions in Lipa. In 1991, however, the new archbishop of Lipa decided to reopen the case and appointed a new commission to investigate. This same archbishop would officially grant ecclesiastical approval to the apparitions on September 12, 2015, specifically noting that the apparitions were worthy of belief and supernatural in character. Then, in an unprecedented move, Cardinal Gerhard Müller, prefect of the Congregation for the Doctrine of the Faith, wrote a letter to the archbishop of Lipa on December 11, 2015, informing him that the 1951 decision of the Holy See was to be maintained, thus making the archbishop's September 12, 2015 approval of the Lipa apparitions null and void.

In the alleged apparitions in Lipa, the rosary was at the heart of the message. For example, in the alleged apparition on September 26, 1948, Mary recounted to Teresita how many of the other Marian apparitions had not been heeded; that was why she had come again to ask for the daily recitation of the rosary. In the alleged apparition that occurred on November 12, 1948, Our Lady instructed Teresita that she was to spread the rosary, telling people that they were to pray it every day with devotion. The Mediatrix of All Grace also informed Teresita that the instrument through which peace will come about in the world is the rosary. In 2008, Teresita published a memoir of her apparitions and noted that she had written a diary of the original messages from Our Lady in 1948 — messages that contained words from Our Lady on the rosary — but Church officials required the messages be burned after the apparitions were declared not to be supernatural in nature.[19] Even the writings on the apparitions by the other sisters and the Mother Superior of the convent were burned.[20]

Akita, Japan (1973)

The 1973 Marian apparitions to Sr. Agnes Sasagawa of the Handmaids of the Eucharist in Akita, Japan, are somewhat connected to the Fatima apparitions and the approved apparitions given to Ida Peerdeman in Amsterdam from 1945–1959.[21] The Akita revelations contain very apocalyptic messages, as well as a strong emphasis on praying the rosary.

Sister Agnes was a former Buddhist who had converted to Catholicism at the age of 42. Though completely deaf, Sr. Agnes entered a religious convent in May of 1973. One month after her entrance into the convent, she fell ill and was taken to the hospital. While she was praying her rosary in the hospital, her guardian angel appeared to her and instructed her to begin to pray the following prayer after each decade of the rosary: "Oh my Jesus, forgive us our sins, save us from the fires of hell, and lead all souls to heaven, especially those in most need of thy mercy." It is remarkable that Sr. Agnes was asked to pray this prayer, since the prayer is the exact same one that Mary taught the children at Fatima. Yet Sr. Agnes had never heard the prayer before since Japan has never had a large Catholic population. Also, the prayer had not become known in many parts of the world yet, since it had only been officially recognized by the Vatican in 1956.

In June of 1973, one month after her guardian angel taught her the prayer to be added to the rosary, Mary herself began to appear to Sr. Agnes. The messages given to Sr. Agnes were very apocalyptic. On October 13, 1973, Our Lady informed Sr. Agnes that unless mankind repented and turned from sin, it would experience a terrible punishment. This particular message was so strong and placed such an emphasis on the rosary that the pertinent sections need to be presented here. Mary said:

> If men do not repent and better themselves, the Father will inflict a terrible punishment on all humanity. It will be a punishment greater than the deluge, such as one will never have seen before. Fire will fall from the sky and will wipe out a great part of humanity, the good as well as the bad, sparing neither priests nor faithful. The survivors will find themselves so desolate that they will envy the dead. The only arms which will remain for you will be the rosary and the sign left by my Son. Each day recite the prayers of the rosary. With the rosary, pray for the Pope, the bishops and the priests. The work of the devil will infiltrate even into the Church in such a way that one will see cardinals opposing cardinals, bishops against other bishops. The priests who venerate me will be scorned and opposed by their confreres. Churches and altars will be sacked. The Church will be full of those who accept compromises and the demon will press many priests and consecrated souls to leave the service of the Lord. The demon will be especially implacable against souls consecrated to God.[22]

Due to the gravity of the messages, Sr. Agnes offered herself as a victim soul for the sins of mankind. She performed great penances and was also given the gift of the stigmata. On one occasion, a statue of Our Lady of All Nations based on the Amsterdam apparitions was in the convent chapel and began to weep tears of blood. This miraculous statue continued to weep tears of blood on and off for the next six years. In total, the tears appeared 101 times. This miracle is reminiscent of the miracle of the weeping statue of Our Lady in Syracuse, Italy. It began weeping in 1953, an occurrence approved as authentically supernatural by Venerable Pope Pius XII in 1954. These weeping statues would have made Fr. Thurston cringe, but the miraculous healings associated with them attest to their validity. Sister Agnes herself, the completely deaf victim soul for Jesus, was miraculously healed of her deafness in 1981.

Cuapa, Nicaragua (1980)

Of all the approved Marian apparitions in the 20th century, the ones that occurred in the Central American country of Nicaragua in 1980 provide the clearest insight into how heaven views the origins of the rosary.

In May of 1980, Our Lady began appearing to a 49-year-old sacristan named Bernardo Martinez in rural Nicaragua. Bernardo was a simple man, quite poor and not well-educated. Though Mary would only appear to him several times, the messages she delivered were very powerful. The rosary is considered *the* primary theme of the Cuapa apparitions. She instructed him about the importance of the daily rosary, told him to make sure to pray it with devotion, and also showed him a vision of the origins of the rosary, about which he knew absolutely nothing. She also taught him the Five First Saturdays devotion and told him that she didn't want the people to only pray the rosary during the month of May (a common practice in that region). Rather, she wanted the rosary prayed every month and every day. She particularly stressed the importance of praying the rosary as a family. Bernardo was so transformed by these messages that he discerned a vocation to become a priest. After many years of study, he was ordained in 1995 at the age of 64. He faithfully served as a priest for five years before dying on October 30, 2000, at the age of 69.

During the first apparition of Mary, Bernardo was informed by Mary that she wanted people to pray the rosary every day. She also informed him that she was not pleased when the rosary was prayed mechanically or in a rushed manner, and recommended that Bernardo and others pray the rosary with the aid of biblical excerpts. Not knowing exactly what Mary meant, Bernardo confessed to Our Lady that he was unaware that the rosary was a biblical prayer and asked her to tell him where he could find the relevant biblical passages. In response, Mary directed him to look up certain citations from the Bible. During this first apparition, Mary also instructed Bernardo to renew the practice of the Five First Saturdays devotion. Bernardo admitted that in earlier years, the people in his area had performed this practice faithfully, but, over time, it had fallen into disuse.

During his second vision, on June 8, 1980, Bernardo was shown the history of the rosary. At one point during the vision, Mary instructed Bernardo to look up at the sky. When he looked up, he saw something like a movie being played before him. He witnessed a large procession of saints dressed in white singing joyfully and beautifully. At the head of the procession were the early Christians, catechumens, and martyrs. As he saw this scene, Mary asked Bernardo if he wanted to be a martyr. He was not sure what it meant to be a martyr, and so Mary explained to him that it meant dying for one's faith. After seeing the procession of martyrs, there followed a group of saints dressed in white and carrying luminous rosaries in their hands. The rosaries had extremely white beads and gave off light in a variety of different colors. What Bernardo saw next in the heavenly procession is presented below in a translation of the exact words he wrote down when he was asked to give an account of the apparition to the local bishop:

One of them [the saints dressed in white in the procession] carried a very large open book. He would read, and after listening they silently meditated. They appeared to be as if in prayer.

After this period of prayer and silence, they then prayed the Our Father and ten Hail Marys. I prayed with them. When the rosary was finished, Our Lady said to me: "These are the first ones to whom I gave the rosary. That is the way that I want all of you to pray the rosary." I answered the Lady that yes we would. Some persons have told me that this possibly has to do with the Dominicans. I do not know that religious Order, and to this date have never seen anyone from that Order.

Afterwards, I saw a third group, all of them dressed in brown robes. But these I recognized as being similar to the Franciscans. Always the same, with rosaries and praying.

As they were passing after having prayed, Our Lady again told me: "These received the rosary from the hands of the first ones." After this, a fourth group was arriving. It was a huge procession; now, as we are dressed [in lay clothes]. It was such a big group that it would be impossible to count them. In the earlier ones I saw many men and women; but now, it was like an army in size, and they carried rosaries in their hands. They were dressed normally in all colors.[23]

The above account is extremely important from an historical perspective. Though St. Dominic is not named, it is obvious he is the one at the beginning of the procession carrying the very large open book. It is a very subtle affirmation of the pious tradition. The vision also underscores that it was from the Dominicans that the Franciscans and all others received the rosary. Some might opine that the vision could refer to the Carthusians (in particular, Dominic of Prussia), since the Carthusians also have a white habit. However, at no point in history has it ever been taught that the Carthusians gave the rosary to the Franciscans. As a matter of fact, unbeknownst to Bernardo, St. Louis de Montfort recounted a similar vision in *The Secret of the Rosary* that Mary had given to Dominic the Carthusian.[24] According to St. Louis de Montfort's account, Dominic of Prussia was *already* devoted to the rosary when he had his vision of a heavenly procession of saints praying the rosary. At no time during the vision given to Dominic of Prussia did he receive the rosary as if for the first time. He himself was already praying it before he had his vision. All in all, Mary's vision to Bernardo offers an affirmation of the pious tradition exactly as it has been presented in the oral tradition of the Church and the writings of the popes and saints.

Kibeho, Rwanda (1981–1989)

One of the most heartbreaking Marian apparitions of this century occurred in Africa when Our Lady appeared to several adolescents in Rwanda from 1981 to 1989. During these apparitions, Mary showed the young visionaries that unless people repented, there would be rivers of blood in their land. As a way of preventing the bloodshed, Mary instructed the children to pray the Rosary of the Seven Sorrows. None of the children had ever heard of this prayer and thought it was a brand new type of rosary. Therefore, like any good mother would, Mary began teaching the prayer to the children in 1982 and even commissioned one of the visionaries, Marie Claire Mukangango, to spread knowledge of this rosary to the world.

The children learned from Mary that the Seven Sorrows Rosary was not something new. It had been founded by the Order of Servites in the 13th century (the same century in which St. Dominic founded his rosary). As St. Dominic's rosary had been forgotten and then revived by the apparitions given to Bl. Alan de la Roche in the 15th century, so too had the Seven Sorrows Rosary been forgotten, but now Mary desired it to be revived through the apparitions at Kibeho. Mary also made clear that the Seven Sorrows Rosary was not to replace the Dominican rosary, since she encouraged the children to pray both forms of the rosary. In fact, during many of the apparitions, the children would bring ordinary rosaries that belonged to the people and hold them up so that Our Lady could bless them. Nonetheless, in a country on the verge of bloodshed and genocide, the Sorrowful Mother wanted to emphasize the Seven Sorrows Rosary. Mary even gave the children visions of the forthcoming genocide that would ensue if the people did not repent and pray. She instructed the children to inform the people that if they prayed the Seven Sorrows Rosary, they would find strength to repent and be converted.

Sadly, as history attests, most of the people did not listen to the message of Our Lady. In 1994, the Rwandan genocide occurred. Almost 1 million people were massacred, most by machete. Even Marie Claire, the visionary commissioned to spread the devotion of the Seven Sorrows Rosary, was killed during the genocide. A famous survivor of the Rwandan genocide, Immaculée Ilibagiza, has made it her mission to spread awareness of the apparitions at Kibeho as well as to carry on the mission given to the visionary Marie Clare of spreading the Seven Sorrows Rosary. In one of her books on the Kibeho apparitions, Immaculée noted: "The Rosary of the Seven Sorrows, I discovered, had been used by Christians for hundreds of years, but had somehow become lost in history. Until, that is, after Marie-Claire's apparition — at which point the special rosaries began to appear all over Rwanda."[25]

San Nicolás, Argentina (1983–1990)

In 1983, there began a series of apparitions in Argentina to a simple, uneducated woman named Gladys Quiroga de Motta. As in so many other apparitions in this century, the rosary would be the central theme. From the start of the apparitions, Mary appeared to Gladys holding the Baby Jesus in one arm and displaying a large rosary that stretched across both her hands. In the apparition of November 26, 1983, Mary expressed the desire to be known as "Our Lady of the Rosary of San Nicolás." On the following day, Gladys visited the Cathedral of Our Lady of the Rosary in Rosario (a town near San Nicolás) and saw a statue of Our Lady that she claimed was an exact representation of what Mary looked like during the previous day's apparition. Upon inquiring, Gladys was informed that this particular statue of Our Lady of the Rosary had been given to Argentina in 1884 by Pope Leo XIII for use in the cathedral of Rosario. At some point during construction on the cathedral, it had been placed in the bell tower and forgotten. Below is the account that Gladys gave regarding this episode:

> For the first time, I saw a statue of the Virgin that is the same as what I see. It had been stored away at the Cathedral. This image of Our Lady of the Rosary, that had been brought from Rome to San Nicolás 100 years ago, for the inauguration of the Cathedral, [and was] blessed for that intention by Pope Leo XIII. Our Lady said to me: "They had me in oblivion, but I have reappeared; place me there [where Mary requested a Shrine be constructed] because you see me such as I am."[26]

In 1990, the local bishop gave his approval for the publication and distribution of the messages given to Gladys by Our Lady. There were no less than 1,800 messages! Even after the local bishop gave his approval for the spread of the messages, Gladys continued to have almost daily apparitions. As early as 1984, Our Lady had requested that a medal be cast with the image of Our Lady of the Rosary of San Nicolás on one side and the Holy Trinity with seven stars on the other side. Mary also requested that the rosary be prayed every day, especially among families and in groups, and specifically asked that a perpetual novena of the rosary be undertaken by the local people. The response of the locals was so great that a shrine dedicated to Our Lady of the Rosary of San Nicolás was erected. To this day, the Shrine is a place of pilgrimage and great devotion. These apparitions were officially approved by the diocesan bishop on May 22, 2016.

An entire dissertation could be written on the rich teaching on the rosary presented in the San Nicolás apparitions. For the sake of brevity, it is sufficient to note that Mary described the rosary as a song that God loves to hear and a tie that binds us to our spiritual mother. Our Lady stressed that the rosary is so powerful that it can change the heart of anyone for the better. She also stated that the rosary has the greatest influence in overcoming evil; every danger can be faced with the rosary. As she had done when appearing at Lourdes, during the apparitions the Immaculata prayed the Glory Be at the end of each decade with Gladys. One of the most powerful messages Mary gave about the rosary was from April 10, 1986, when she said: "The holy rosary is the weapon which the enemy fears. It is also the refuge of those who look for relief for their sufferings, and it is the door to enter into my heart."[27]

Saints, Mystics, Martyrs

Along with the many rosary-themed apparitions of this century, there also began to appear on the scene many saints, mystics, and martyrs of the rosary. Many of these champions were very young. For example, the Servant of God

Faustino Perez-Manglano (1946–1963) was a youth on fire with love for the rosary. This young boy was from Spain and, at an early age, made a promise to Our Lady to pray the rosary every day. Whenever he missed a day or two, he would make it up by praying more than one rosary. Faustino was a member of a Marian Sodality and had a strong desire to join the Marianists and become a missionary in South America. Sadly, after a battle with Hodgkin's disease, he died at the age of 17. This young Spaniard has been lauded by the Church as a "hero of the rosary."

Another young champion of the rosary that hailed from Spain was the very beautiful Venerable Teresa Quevedo (1930–1950). As a young girl, Teresa was very devoted to Our Lady, and desired to follow Jesus as a Carmelite nun and serve in the missions in China. From the age of five, she had been a member of a Marian Sodality and prayed the rosary every day. She often noted that it was her devout father who had given her the example of making the rosary a part of her daily spiritual routine. She lived during the era in which *True Devotion to the Blessed Virgin* was becoming more and more known, and used de Montfort's method of consecration to give her life completely to Mary.

A slightly older Italian saint who was also very dedicated to the rosary was St. Richard Pampuri (1897–1930). He obtained a doctorate in medicine at age 25 and was another saint known to pray the rosary throughout his busy day. Across the Atlantic Ocean in the United States, Blessed Miriam Teresa Demjanovic (1901–1927), the first person ever to be beatified on United States soil, also prayed the rosary every day with great fervor and devotion as she carried out her work. She was born in New Jersey in 1901, grew up to be a nun of the Sisters of Charity, and died at the young age of 26. She was beatified on October 4, 2014, in Newark, New Jersey.

Examples of those who lived long lives and were devoted to the rosary abounded as well. One such person was Venerable Práxedes Fernández García (1866–1936). As a Third Order Dominican, she was very devoted to the rosary and prayed it multiple times throughout the day. In her zeal for helping souls, she carried out great works of mercy during a tumultuous time in her native Spain. One of Práxedes' sons even became a Dominican priest. Some of the more prominent champions of the rosary during this century include St. Marie Alphonsine Ghattas (1843–1927), St. Luigi Orione (1872–1940), the Servant of God Joseph Kentenich (1885–1968), the Servant of God Dolindo Ruotolo (1882–1970), Blessed James Alberione (1884–1971), St. Josemaría Escrivá (1902–1975), St. Teresa of Calcutta (1910–1997), and the Servant of God John Hardon (1914–2000).

There were even examples of souls who had lived far from God for much of their lives but, through the rosary, experienced a deep conversion and were given new life in Christ and freedom from their addictions. Venerable Matt Talbot (1856–1925) of Ireland was one such man. He had spent his young adult life (and a good portion of his adult years) as a drunkard and a great sinner.

After many years of hard living, he turned his life over to God, joined a Marian sodality, and became a Third Order Franciscan. Before Alcoholics Anonymous was founded in 1935, Venerable Matt Talbot employed a method of rehabilitation and freedom from addictions that involved relying on Jesus, Mary, and the devotions of the Catholic Church, as opposed to a nebulous and unidentified "higher power." He understood the Catholic Church, with her Sacraments, teachings, and devotions to be God's rehabilitation center for the wounded soul. His method did not involve 12 steps, but the observance of the 10 Commandments and turning from a life of vice to a life of virtue. He spent hours in prayer every day and wore the rosary around his neck as a sign of belonging to Jesus and Mary. His daily rosary served as an antidote to sin. When he died in 1925, numerous chains were found underneath his clothing that he had worn as a form of penance for his former life. The wisdom and example of Venerable Matt Talbot has much insight to offer modern man regarding the power of the rosary to heal addictions.

Incredible mystics who championed the rosary flourished during this time, as well. The most well-known was St. Pio of Pietrelcina (better known as Padre Pio; 1887–1968), who almost never let the rosary leave his hands. People who knew St. Pio have stated that he often prayed as many as 100 rosaries a day!

Another rosary mystic was Blessed Alexandrina Maria da Costa (1904–1955). She was from Portugal, and was widely acclaimed for her incredible sanctity and virtue. A victim for souls, she lay bedridden for more than 30 years and offered all of her suffering for others. In 1949, she received a vision from Mary in which Our Lady came with a rosary and told her that the world was in agony, dying in sin. Our Lady's desire was for prayer and penance. Our Lady also informed Bl. Alexandrina that, as the Mother of God, Mary protects the world and all those who are devoted to her by means of the rosary. Blessed Alexandrina was given to understand that the Eucharist and the rosary are the stairs that lead souls to heaven. On one occasion, Jesus himself commanded her to tell souls about the power of the rosary.

Similarly, Blessed Elena Aiello (1895–1961), an Italian mystic, stigmatist, and founder of a religious community, was told by Our Lady in a vision that many souls are saved through the power of the rosary. Lastly, one of the most overlooked mystics of the 20ᵗʰ century, the convert Adrienne von Speyr (1902–1967), also wrote extensively on the rosary. Adrienne's spiritual director was Fr. Hans Urs von Balthasar, one of the greatest theologians of the 20ᵗʰ century. As her spiritual director, von Balthasar meticulously wrote down the dictations of von Speyr during her mystical experiences and put them in book form. In one particular series of mystical experiences, von Speyr was given special insight into the lives and personalities of many of the great saints. In one of these visions, she saw St. Dominic and dictated to von Balthasar insights into both St. Dominic's personality and virtues. She specifically noted the following regarding her vision of St. Dominic: "There are years in his [St. Dominic's] life in which he prays the rosary very often, as if it were his primary prayer."[28]

Another mystic devoted to the rosary, considered worthy of being declared a martyr by many, is the Servant of God Marcel Nguyen Tân Van (1928–1959). A Redemptorist lay brother, he received frequent visions from Jesus, Mary, and St. Therese of Lisieux. Throughout his youth, he prayed a daily rosary with his mother. When he grew up, he promoted the rosary everywhere he went. In 1954, when northern Vietnam became Communist, he was captured and sent to an internment camp where he was sentenced to 15 years hard labor. After a few years in the camp, he died from sheer exhaustion.

When the same Communist ideology made inroads in Croatia, the martyr Blessed Miroslav Bulešic (1920–1947) championed the rosary by fervently promoting its communal recitation as a means of defeating Communism. He was eventually stabbed in the neck by Communist sympathizers.

Another young martyr from this era was St. Jose Sanchez del Rio (1913–1928). He grew up during the anti-Catholic revolution in Mexico. As a 14-year-old boy and a member of the Cristero movement — devout Catholics who opposed the anti-Catholic government — St. Jose had the courage to stand against the enemies of the Church and lay down his life for Jesus. When he was captured by the anti-Catholic authorities, he was placed in prison, treated like an animal, and constantly urged to renounce his faith. In response, the young Cristero prayed the rosary every day and gave hope to the grown men who were his cellmates. In subsequent attempts to try to get the teenager to renounce his faith, his evil captors sliced his feet with knives and forced him to walk through the town toward the cemetery. Their intention was to frighten the youth and make him renounce Catholicism. They were so wicked that after they had cut off the soles of his feet and made him walk through the streets, they continued to cut and stab him with machetes. Fearlessly, the little Cristero shouted back to the armed men, "Viva Cristo Rey!" Unable to break him, the shameless agents of the government shot him.

Another Mexican hero of the faith and champion of the rosary from this time was the Jesuit priest Blessed Miguel Pro (1891–1927). A year before St. Jose Sanchez del Rio gave his life for Christ, Bl. Miguel was martyred for his faith by being shot by a firing squad. As he stood before the firing squad, Bl. Miguel imitated Jesus by holding his arms outstretched as though on a cross. As he extended his arms, he held a crucifix in one hand and a rosary in the other. Before he was shot, he cried out: "Viva Cristo Rey!"

Blessed Ceferino Giménez Malla (1861–1936), the Spaniard called a "martyr of the rosary" by two popes, was a gypsy who loved the rosary. At one point during the Spanish Civil war (1936–1939), after having been arrested by secular authorities and instructed to surrender his rosary beads or risk being shot, he adamantly refused to hand over his rosary. He preferred to be shot and killed rather than give up his spiritual weapon. As a result, he took a bullet out of love for Jesus and Mary and died with the rosary in his hand. There were many other martyrs for the rosary who gave witness to this great devotion during times of war and persecution. Though she is relatively unknown outside of Eastern Europe, the young and beautiful Polish girl Blessed Karolina Kózka (1898–1914) championed the rosary shortly after the beginning of World War I. As a young girl, she would walk great distances to church every day to spend time with Jesus. During the long walks, she took her rosary with her and prayed it multiple times as she walked to and from church. Her fervor for the rosary inspired many in the local area. Blessed Karolina is often referred to as the Maria Goretti of Poland because a Russian solider tried to rape her, but she heroically resisted his attempts. Unable to overpower her, the Russian soldier killed her by violently stabbing her multiple times with his bayonet.

Two other great Polish martyrs of the rosary were Blessed Władysław Demski (1884–1940) and Blessed Józef Kowalski (1911–1942). Blessed Władysław was a diocesan priest who was taken prisoner by the Nazis in 1939 and eventually sent to the concentration camp in Sachsenhausen. While there, his rosary accidentally fell out of his pocket. A guard nearby saw it and threw it into the mud. The guard then mocked the priest and said that if he cared that much about it, he could find it in the mud and kiss it. Immediately Fr. Władysław knelt down, found the rosary in the mud, and kissed it while making the Sign of the Cross on his lips with it. This action infuriated the guard and prompted the guards to beat the priest to death.

Blessed Józef Kowalski's story is similar. He was a Salesian priest who had been arrested by the Gestapo in 1941 and sent to the Auschwitz concentration camp. One day during roll call, a guard knocked the rosary out of Fr. Józef's hand and commanded him to trample upon it. Father Józef refused and was brutally tortured and drowned in a sewer shortly after. Saint John Paul II, who knew Bl. Józef Kowalski before the war, beatified both him and Fr. Demski in 1999 as two of the 108 Polish Martyrs of World War II.[29]

Another martyr devoted to the rosary was Blessed Oscar Romero (1917–1980). When he was a child, he was very fond of the rosary, and carried his devotion into his priesthood. As a priest, Fr. Romero was known to encourage people to join associations of prayer dedicated to the rosary. He himself prayed the rosary every single day. As the archbishop in El Salvador, Archbishop Romero spoke out against poverty and injustice. For his outspokenness, he was assassinated while celebrating Holy Mass. When Bl. Romero was laid to rest, he was buried with a rosary in his hands.

Publications and Movements

The number of rosary-themed publications and movements that developed during the 20th century is also monumental. On October 7, 1901, two people who were then members of the Anglican Church, the Servant of God Paul Wattson (1863–1940) and Mother Lurana White (1870–1935), formed a movement called The Rosary League of Our Lady of the Atonement. The purpose of the movement was to pray and work for the restoration of Mary's Dowry (England) to the Mother of God. Each member promised to pray at least three decades of the rosary a day for this intention. In 1909, Fr. Paul Wattson, Mother Lurana, and 15 others converted to Catholicism.

When the first French edition of *The Secret of the Rosary* was published in 1911, its message spread like wildfire and helped usher in a plethora of writings on the rosary. Gilbert Keith (G.K.) Chesterton (1874–1936) was one of the most prolific authors of the 20th century and loved the rosary. He prayed the rosary frequently and always kept a rosary hanging from his bedpost. Though he did not write a specific book on the rosary itself, he did pen the epic poem "Lepanto" that recounted the famous rosary victory over the Ottoman Turks. The Catholic historian Hilaire Belloc referred to this poem as the greatest poem of his generation.

Blessed Michael Sopocko (1888–1975) was another influential author writing during this time. The spiritual director of St. Faustina Kowalska and a zealous promoter of the Divine Mercy message and devotion, he was also a fervent devotee of the rosary. He often mentioned the power of the rosary in his many writings on theology.

The martyr of charity, St. Maximilian Kolbe (1894–1941), was another saintly Polish rosary priest. He founded the worldwide Catholic evangelization movement called the Militia Immaculatae and intended the rosary to be part of the daily spiritual practice of its members. Founded in 1917, St. Maximilian's chivalrous movement was formed in response to a Freemason protest against the papacy that he witnessed during his studies in Rome. In his zealous efforts to promote devotion to the Immaculata and her power to crush all opposition to Christ and his Church, St. Maximilian emphasized the importance of the Miraculous Medal and the rosary, and founded a Marian magazine titled *The Knight of the Immaculata*.

Almost all of the Marian magazines that came into existence during this time included frequent articles on the rosary. Magazines such as *Our Lady's Digest* (established in 1925), the *Marian Helpers Bulletin* (1945), and *Soul* (1950) all greatly promoted the rosary. *Soul* magazine was the literary apostolate of the Blue Army, which was founded by Msgr. Harold J. Colgan in New Jersey in 1946. Monsignor Colgan founded the Blue Army in gratitude for a healing he received through the intercession of Our Lady and as a way of helping others to live out the message of Fatima. He deliberately chose the color blue since it is often associated with Our Lady, and it was the "blue" of Our Lady that would overcome the "red" of Communism and Satan. The Blue Army is now known as the World Apostolate of Fatima. Each member of this organization is dedicated to praying the rosary and encouraging others to pray it, as well. The *Marian Helpers Bulletin* (now called *Marian Helper* magazine) was founded by the Marian Fathers of the Immaculate Conception in 1945 and quickly gained an international readership. Shortly after the Marian Fathers founded the *Marian Helpers Bulletin,* they began the Thirteenth of the Month Club in 1948. Members of the Thirteenth of the Month Club commit to praying the rosary each month on the thirteenth for the intentions of the club and its members. To this day, the Thirteenth of the Month Club continues to pray the rosary and spread devotion to Our Lady, and its members receive a monthly newsletter (see page 445).

One of the most lauded Marian movements in the early 20ᵗʰ century was the Legion of Mary, founded by the Servant of God Frank Duff (1889–1980) in 1921. Duff was a devout Irishman, deeply inspired by the Marian spirituality of St. Louis de Montfort. His intention in founding the Legion of Mary was to combine Montfortian Marian devotion with an active apostolate. The movement was to be a spiritual army willing to fight spiritual battles on behalf of Jesus, Mary, and the Church. Part of the Legion of Mary's spirituality was the daily rosary. The rosary was so prominent in the movement that sometimes the Legion of Mary also went by the name the "Army of the Rosary." The members of each respective legion group were encouraged to join the Confraternity of the Rosary in order to reap all the benefits and indulgences offered by the Church to those who pray the rosary. Frank Duff required that the rosary be prayed in common during each weekly meeting of the members. To date, the Legion of Mary remains one of the largest Marian organizations in the world.

As the Irishman Frank Duff was carrying out a very fruitful international Marian apostolate through the Legion of Mary, the Irish-born Servant of God Fr. Patrick Peyton (1909–1992) was carrying out an extremely popular worldwide rosary apostolate known as the Family Rosary Crusade. In the early 1940s, Fr. Peyton began his promotion of the rosary by writing to bishops in the United States and encouraging them to promote the family rosary. In 1947, Fr. Peyton officially launched his rosary crusades on a national and international scale. On fire with a desire to bring the rosary to the entire world, Fr. Peyton traveled to more than 40 countries and was able to gather more than 28 million people to pray the rosary! Remarkably, during the 1950s, he was even able to gather together some of the leading actors in Hollywood to publicly pray the rosary on the radio and national television. When the turbulent era of the 1960s began, Fr. Peyton was one of the few figures who were able draw large groups of people to pray the rosary. In San Francisco in 1961, he was able to bring together more than a half-million people for a rosary gathering for the archdiocese. Unfortunately, this would be the last great rosary event in the United States before the cultural revolution of the 1960s was in full swing and efforts began that would largely push the rosary out of parochial and family life.

The 1960s did not stop Fr. Peyton from promoting the rosary, though. He took his rosary crusade to countries that were more receptive to his message. He gathered millions of people together in rosary rallies in places such as Colombia, Brazil, and the Philippines. His rosary apostolate flourished in those countries, even though the rosary was being forgotten and abandoned in more developed countries. The abandonment of the rosary greatly saddened Fr. Peyton, so he wrote a personal letter to Pope Paul VI asking him to turn back the tide by declaring the rosary a liturgical prayer. Father Peyton so desired the rosary to be prayed by everyone that he even suggested the possibility of adding additional other mysteries from the public life of Jesus. Many of these mysteries are the exact same ones that St. John Paul II would give to the Church in 2002 in the Luminous Mysteries. To this day, Fr. Peyton's rosary efforts remain unparalleled.

Even before Fr. Peyton brought his great rosary crusades to South America, the Schoenstatt movement had already initiated a rosary revival in Brazil in 1950. This movement was known as the Schoenstatt Rosary Campaign. The Schoenstatt movement itself had been founded in Germany in 1914 by the very holy Servant of God Fr. Joseph Kentenich (1885–1968). As a Marian catechetical movement, Schoenstatt's beginnings were closely associated with the ancient Marian sodalities and used their framework as an initial starting point. Father Kentenich himself had a very high regard for the Marian Sodality and was also a great promoter of the rosary. He understood the rosary to be a catechetical tool, a friend in the spiritual life, and a weapon for overcoming the theological and anthropological heresies prevalent in modern times. Initially, from 1950 to the early 1980s, the Schoenstatt Rosary Campaign was only promoted in South American countries, but in 1985, as the Schoenstatt movement celebrated the centennial anniversary of the birth of Fr. Kentenich, the Schoenstatt Rosary Campaign went international and began to spread around the world.

In 1951, a holy bishop from the United States, Venerable Fulton J. Sheen (1895–1979), founded the World Mission Rosary (also called the Missionary Rosary). In 1950, he was appointed the national director for the Society for the Propagation of the Faith, an office he would hold until 1966. As part of his efforts, he came up with a unique color-coded rosary that was to be prayed specifically for the missions. Each decade of the World Mission Rosary would be a different color, signifying a different geographical region of the planet. White represents Europe where the Holy Father resides; yellow represents Asia where the morning sun rises; blue represents the islands of the Pacific, including Australia; green represents Africa because of its forests and grasslands; and red represents the Americas, since the fire of faith had been brought there by missionaries.

Lastly, the first English edition of *The Secret of the Rosary* made its appearance in 1954. This edition would have multiple printings and be spread all over the English-speaking world.

Popes

The rosary was a major theme in the teachings of the popes during the 20th century. Following in the footsteps of Pope Leo XIII, St. Pope Pius X (1835–1914) praised the rosary and frequently mentioned the zeal his papal

predecessor had had for spreading the devotion. Since Pope Leo XIII had writ-
ten 11 rosary encyclicals, St. Pope Pius X did not write a lot about the rosary, but
promoted it in other ways. When he was elected to the papacy in 1903, one of
his first private audiences was held with the Master General of the Dominicans,
Bl. Hyacinth Cormier. During the visit, St. Pope Pius X informed the Master
General that during his early life he himself had thought about becoming a
Dominican. Although it was not God's will that he join the order, St. Pope
Pius X took great delight in telling the Master General that he considered it
a sign from God that he had been elected to the See of Peter on the feast day
of St. Dominic. Saint Pope Pius X was a Dominican at heart, and proved it by
promising the Master General that he would continue the great work of Pope
Leo XIII in promoting the rosary. In fact, in 1907, he issued an indulgence
for those who recited a prayer composed by Bl. Hyacinth. The prayer affirms
the pious tradition (see page 125). In 1908, he wrote a letter to the Perpetual
Rosary Association thanking them for their continued offering of the rosary for
the welfare of the Church. In the *Motu proprio* of October 3, 1913, he revised
the liturgical calendar and the Roman Breviary, and re-assigned the Feast of the
Rosary to October 7 instead of the first Sunday of October. He did this because
he desired the Feast of the Rosary to be an annual commemoration of the Battle
of Lepanto, won on October 7. Unfortunately, this transfer did mean that the
second reading was dropped from the Breviary, and Rosary Sunday was no
longer an official feast day in the Church. However, Rosary Sunday continued
to be celebrated in an "unofficial" way in many churches, especially Dominican
churches, since the indulgences attached to it remained in effect. It would not be
until Blessed Pope Paul VI promulgated a revised manual of indulgences in 1967
that the plenary indulgence attached to Rosary Sunday would be dropped. Even
today, though Rosary Sunday no longer appears in liturgical books and there is
no longer a plenary indulgence attached to it, many Dominicans continue to
have special celebrations, processions, and pilgrimages on the first Sunday of
October in honor of the rosary.

After the incredible papacies of Pope Leo XIII and St. Pope Pius X, popes
continued to affirm the pious tradition. In 1921, in an extremely beautiful encyclical on St. Dominic titled *Fausto Appetente Die,* Pope Benedict XV (1854–1922)
wrote the following:

> How pleased was the Heavenly Queen with her pious servant [St.
> Dominic] may be easily gathered from this, that she used his ministry
> to teach the Most Holy Rosary to the Church, the Spouse of her Son;
> that prayer which, being both vocal and mental, in the contempla-
> tion especially of the mysteries of religion, while the Lord's Prayer is
> fifteen times repeated together with as many decades of the Hail Mary,
> is most adapted to fostering widely piety and every virtue. Rightly,
> then, did Dominic order his followers, in preaching to the people, to

inculcate frequently this manner of prayer, the utility of which he had experienced. He knew, on the one hand, Mary's authority with her Son to be such that whatever graces he confers on men she has their distribution and apportionment. On the other hand, he knew that she is of a nature so kind and merciful that, seeing that it is her custom to succor the miserable of her own accord, it is impossible she should refuse the petitions of those who pray to her. Accordingly the Church, which is wont to salute her "the Mother of Grace and the Mother of Mercy," has so found her always, but especially in answer to the rosary. Wherefore the Roman Pontiffs have let pass no occasion of commending the rosary and have enriched it with Apostolic Indulgences.[30]

One of the strongest affirmations of the pious tradition came during the papacy of Pope Pius XI (1857–1939). Pope Pius XI was very much aware of the scholars who were writing against the pious tradition and the great influence their ideas were having among the hierarchy. During the early 1930s, the critical writings of Fr. Thurston against the pious tradition had been so widely disseminated that even saintly men in the upper reaches of the hierarchy like Blessed Alfredo Schuster (1880–1954), a Benedictine cardinal, began to doubt the pious tradition. Desiring to make his position on the issue heard, Pope Pius XI clearly affirmed the pious tradition in several important documents. The first was a personal letter he wrote in 1934 to Fr. Martin Gillet, the Master General of the Dominicans, titled *Inclytam ac perillustrem*. In this letter, he stated that Prouille was the cradle of the rosary, and addressed the following remarks to all Dominicans: "Among the weapons St. Dominic used to convert the heretics the most efficacious, as the faithful well know, was the Marian rosary, the practice of which, taught by the Blessed Virgin herself, has so widely spread throughout the Catholic world."[31] Then, in 1937, he authored one of the most powerful encyclicals on the rosary ever written, *Ingravescentibus Malis*. In it, Pope Pius XI expressed his gratitude for the rosary teachings of Pope Leo XIII and, among many other gems of Marian teaching, offered a papal affirmation of the pious tradition. He wrote: "This practice of piety [the rosary], Venerable Brethren, admirably diffused by St. Dominic, not without the heavenly suggestion and inspiration of the Virgin Mother of God, is without doubt easy for all, even for the ignorant and the simple."[32] An important aspect of Pope Pius XI's affirmation of the pious tradition is that it was written during the same time that Fr. Thurston's reinterpretation of the origins of the rosary was receiving universal praise. Pope Pius XI could have chosen to leave the origins of the rosary out of his encyclical, but he did not. In fact, he deliberately chose not to use the phrases "as is believed" or "according to the tradition," as many previous popes had done when referring to the pious tradition. He intentionally affirmed the pious tradition without any qualifiers, ambiguity, or possibility of misinterpretation. He didn't need to do this, but intentionally went out of his way to make his point.

Venerable Pope Pius XII wrote a personal letter to the Master General of the Dominicans on July 11, 1957, similar to the personal letter that Pope Pius XI had written to the Master General of the Dominicans in 1934. Pius XII's letter greatly praises the rosary and the Dominicans' zeal in spreading it. Venerable Pope Pius XII concluded the letter with an exhortation to all Dominicans. He said: "Continue, then, as you are doing, zealously, diligently and devoutly promoting the Marian rosary and the various associations that take their name from it; this is a particular mark of your Order, and the pious service of that same Order does not stand in last place in the eyes of the exalted Mother of God, of the Church or of the Catholic religion."[33]

Dominicans

Ironically, the century that witnessed many of the sons of St. Dominic begin to question the pious tradition also saw the rosary finally become an official part of the Dominican habit. The rosary had been an unofficial part of the Dominican habit for centuries — it might even have been incorporated into the original habit — but, as in most ecclesial matters, the time finally arrived when the "normative" practice became the "official" practice and was set down in writing.

Even as some among their number began to criticize the pious tradition, the Dominicans were not lacking defenders of their rosary heritage. The Dominican rosary magazines in England and the United States produced article after article that defended the tradition against the attacks of the critics. These articles were scholarly and edifying. Even the provincial superior of the Dominicans in England, Fr. John Proctor, became involved in the controversy, and wrote an historical and theological defense of the rosary titled *The Rosary Guide for Priests and People*. This masterpiece was written to correct the errors of the historical critics and reassure both priests and people that St. Dominic was the founder of the rosary.

Another defender was the Dominican Fr. Wilfrid Lescher. His articles in defense of the tradition appeared in many popular magazines and eventually became a book titled *St. Dominic and the Rosary*. Father Lescher considered arguments against the pious tradition a form of rebuke against the papacy itself, since the Dominican origin of the rosary is not simply a pious tradition, but also a papal tradition. He noted that the many popes who wrote about the rosary in their encyclicals and letters could have chosen to only mention the prayer of the rosary and leave out mention of its history, but they intentionally chose to include references to St. Dominic as the founder of the rosary. Father Lescher was of the strong opinion that to mention the rosary without St. Dominic was to tear apart the rosary tradition and repudiate its heavenly origins.

In 1934, when Pope Pius XI wrote his personal letter to Fr. Martin Gillet, the Master General of the Dominicans, the Vicar of Christ reminded the Dominicans of their own rosary tradition and offered the following reminder to all the sons of St. Dominic: "The rosary is, as it were, the principle and foundation on which the Order of St. Dominic rests for perfecting the lives of its members, and obtaining the salvation of others."[34] In the same document, the pope went on to note that the town of Prouille, France, was where the rosary was born. He stated:

> Saint Dominic founded the Order of Friars Preachers which Pope Honorius III placed under his own special protection and patronage and whose members he acclaimed, as it were, prophetically, "true lights of the world," and "champions of the faith." The first monastery was founded at Saint Mary of Prouille, which was, indeed, the cradle of the rosary of Mary itself.[35]

A Dominican who took the message of the pope to heart was Blessed Buenaventura Garcia de Paredes (1866–1936). He had served as the Master General of the Dominicans from 1926–1929. After his tenure as Master General, he worked in Spain during the country's anti-Catholic uprising and was martyred for his faith in 1936. When his body was finally found, a Breviary and a rosary were beside his dead body.

Another saintly Dominican living during this period was Fr. Marie Étienne Vayssière (1864–1940). A devout Dominican priest, he was known to "live the rosary" since he prayed it throughout the day. He often mentioned to others that his evening rosary was his "evening Communion." In explaining why he referred to the evening rosary in this way, he said, "It [the rosary] is not merely a series of *Ave Marias* piously recited; it is Jesus living again in the soul through Mary's maternal action."[36]

Blessed Pier Giorgio Frassati (1901–1925) also championed the rosary in the early 20th century. His great love for Dominican spirituality and the rosary led him to become a Third Order Dominican in 1922. This handsome young man was a lover of the rosary and slept with it in his hand every night. He considered his rosary a weapon and always wanted it to be within reach. Once, when asked if he read the Bible, he quickly responded by stating that he carried his New Testament — his rosary — in his pocket! The rosary is, indeed, a portable Bible. An outdoorsman and lover of nature, Bl. Pier Giorgio would often go hiking in the mountains with his friends. During these hikes, he would always invite his friends to pray the rosary with him.

Acclaimed by many as one of the greatest and most erudite Dominican theologians of the 20th century, Fr. Reginald Garrigou-LaGrange was a strong Dominican voice affirming the pious tradition. Garrigou-LaGrange was a teacher of theology at the Angelicum in Rome; one of his pupils, Fr. Karol Wojtyła, ended up becoming St. Pope John Paul II. A learned historian and theologian, Fr. LaGrange was aware of the arguments against the pious tradition. However, he also knew the tradition was not a legend or a myth, and offered the following reflection on the matter:

Our Blessed Lady made known to St. Dominic a kind of preaching till then unknown, which she said would be one of the most powerful weapons against future errors and in future difficulties. Under her inspiration, St Dominic went into the villages of the Albigensians, gathered the people, and preached to them the mysteries of salvation — the Incarnation, the redemption, eternal life. As Mary had taught him to do, he distinguished the different kinds of mysteries, and after each short instruction, he had ten Hail Marys recited — somewhat as might happen even today at a Holy Hour. And what the word of the preacher was unable to do, the sweet prayer of the Hail Mary did for hearts. As Mary promised, it proved to be a most fruitful form of preaching.[37]

The words of Fr. Garrigou-LaGrange are not to be taken lightly. A very learned Dominican theologian, he was well versed in historical matters, especially the Dominican tradition. He was also renowned as an erudite Mariologist. He was so well respected that he was asked by Venerable Pope Pius XII to be a theological consultant as the Holy Father formulated the dogmatic declaration of the Assumption of Mary, promulgated in 1950.

At the International Rosary Congress held in Rome in 1963, Fr. Anicetus Fernandez, a former Master General of the Dominicans, spoke of the pious tradition and impressed upon his confreres the grave obligation imposed upon them to promote it. He stated: "Given that the rosary came to us from the hands of Our Lady herself, a most grave obligation devolves on us. The popes have given us [Dominicans] and no one else the full power and responsibility for bringing it to the people."[38] At the same Rosary Congress, another former Master General of the Dominicans, Cardinal Michael Browne, also made a poignant remark to his Dominican confreres: "The future of the Dominican Order and its apostolate rests on its faithfulness in preaching the rosary."[39] Then in 1976, the acting Master General of the Dominicans, Fr. Vincent de Couesnongle, made a very strong statement on both the pious tradition and the role of all Dominicans in promoting the rosary. He said: "A tradition recognized in the Church makes us heirs of the mission given to our Father Dominic by the Blessed Virgin: 'Go and preach my rosary.' This is a heritage of which we should be proud and from which we should be the first to benefit in our lives and in our prayer."[40]

One of the greatest Dominican promoters of the rosary during this century was the Irishman Fr. Gabriel Harty. His rosary apostolate spanned the second half of the 20ᵗʰ century and extended into the 21ˢᵗ century. Born in 1921, Fr. Harty had been ordained a diocesan priest in his native Ireland. Then, after only four years as a diocesan priest, he joined the Dominicans in 1950. His superiors immediately recognized that he had a particular charism and enthusiasm for promoting the rosary, so they allowed him to focus his talents in this area. As part of his rosary apostolate, he initiated the "Industrial Rosary." By this apostolate, he brought the rosary into the workplace and was able to encourage great numbers

5-9-2019

of people to pray the rosary at work, especially in factories, workshops, and warehouses. He also wrote many books on the rosary and zealously preached on the rosary well into his late nineties. He is often referred to as the "Rosary Priest of Ireland."

Lastly, in 1991, the Third Order Dominican Robert Feeney published a comprehensive and up-to-date book on the rosary titled *The Rosary: The Little Summa*. Feeney's book acknowledges the developments that have taken place throughout the history of the rosary, but also strongly endorses the pious tradition. His book has been through many printings and editions, and bears the endorsement of Vatican officials, nine cardinals, many archbishops, the apostolic nuncio to the United States, the Master General of the Dominicans, and includes a foreword by a cardinal. For those who hold the position that the pious tradition is a legend, Feeney offers the following reflection in this impressive book:

> The popes, in regards to the rosary tradition, are superior to secular historians. They are guided by the Holy Spirit and have the ability to speak with the highest authority. Papal decrees, bulls, and encyclicals have authority in the historical sphere. As heads of the Vatican Library the popes have had learned men assist them in the composition of papal documents. A pope does not accept facts without reasonable proofs. The facts go through tests of research and verification before they are officially approved. The tradition of the rosary is what it is because the popes have made it so.[41]

While not making the claim that the popes are infallible in matters of history, Feeney does make the point, and rightly so, that papal writings in matters of history carry great weight.

The 1960s and 1970s

The turbulent era of the 1960s and 1970s caused a major decrease in Marian devotion throughout the Church. In spite of the dogmatic definition of the Assumption of Mary in 1950 and the Marian year in 1954, interest in Our Lady, and especially interest in the rosary, went into a major tailspin. Contrary to the spirit of the times, however, St. Pope John XXIII (1881–1963) made many beautiful statements about the rosary. He desired it to be prayed by families and even asked people to pray the rosary for the fruitfulness of the Second Vatican Council. Unfortunately, even though the Second Vatican Council never specifically mentioned the rosary, most post-conciliar Catholics were incorrectly informed that the Church no longer desired to promote the rosary. The laity was instructed that the Church was no longer to be described as the Church Militant, at war with the forces of darkness; therefore, the rosary was no longer needed. This widespread misunderstanding resulted in many mistakenly believing the weapon of the rosary had become obsolete and shelving it. The abuse of the historical-critical method, the promotion of radical feminist ideologies, and false methods of conducting ecumenism only added to the decrease in devotion to the rosary. Appropriately, historians and theologians have labeled the decade from 1965 to 1975 as the "decade without Mary" and/or the "decadent decade."

During the first half of the 20ᵗʰ century, it was common practice for Catholic families to gather together every evening and pray the rosary. All of this changed as a result of the cultural and theological shifts in the 1960s. In fact, very few good books were written on Mary in the years immediately after the 1950s. The classic theological works on Mary, including those devoted to the topic of the rosary, began to collect dust on library bookshelves in Catholic institutions of higher learning until the early 1980s. This took place in Catholic seminaries, too. During this time, many men who were studying for the priesthood were even discouraged from praying the rosary. In some seminaries, the rosary was banned from public and common recitation in the seminary chapel! This proved extremely detrimental to the formation of future priests. The Catholic seminary is analogous to boot camp where soldiers are molded. During boot camp, soldiers learn how to fight and use weapons against the enemy. At the end of boot camp, a soldier is commissioned with a weapon to be used on the battlefield. The spiritual weapon for a priest is the sword of the rosary. A priest without a rosary is like a knight without a sword. The lack of devotion to Mary in seminaries during the decadent decade is partly to blame for the production of effeminate men among the ranks of the priesthood. Effeminate men are not known to march into battle and slay dragons. Sadly, many seminarians during this time were even taught that there were no longer any dragons to slay.

Saint Pope John XXIII had anticipated the dangers that lay ahead for priests and wrote a prophetic 1959 encyclical letter on St. John Vianney, the patron saint of priests. In the encyclical, he alerted priests to the danger of losing spiritual power by neglecting their prayer life, an important part of which ought to be the rosary. He wrote:

> This constant union with God [through prayer] is best achieved and preserved through the various practices of priestly piety; many of the more important of them, such as daily meditation, visits to the Blessed Sacrament, recitation of the rosary, careful examination of conscience, the Church, in her wise and provident regulations, has made obligatory for priests. As for the hours of the Office, priests have undertaken a serious obligation to the Church to recite them. The neglect of some of these rules may often be the reason why certain churchmen are caught up in the whirl of external affairs, gradually lose their feeling for sacred things and finally fall into serious difficulties when they are shorn of all spiritual protection and enticed by the attractions of this earthly life.[42]

Unfortunately, his prophetic words were not taken to heart, and many men in the 1960s and 1970s ended up leaving the priesthood in pursuit of the attractions of an earthly life. The Family Rosary Crusades being organized in Central and South America by the Servant of God Patrick Peyton were exceptions to the general decline in the practice of the rosary, however. One of the reasons he took his rosary crusades to other countries was the progressive cultural shift in the United States, which had become so prevalent that his efforts began to fall on deaf ears. It is shocking to think that, only a few years after Fr. Peyton carried out a successful rosary rally of 500,000 people in 1961 in San Francisco, the "Gathering of the Tribes for Human Be-In" was held at the exact same location in Golden State Park in 1967. Historians have described this event as *the* event that ushered in the sexual revolution. Six months later, the infamous "Summer of Love" took place.

Satan was out to get the rosary and anything associated with it. Not only did devotion to the rosary decrease during the decadent decade, but the *Diary* of St. Faustina, containing a new form of devotion to God's mercy prayed on ordinary rosary beads, was banned, as well. As a result of a faulty translation, her *Diary* was placed under a ban by the Holy See from 1959-1978. Father Peyton himself was so alarmed over the rapid decline in devotion to the rosary that he wrote an impassioned letter to the pope in 1971, pleading for the Church to rectify the crisis by declaring the rosary a liturgical prayer. It was a bold proposition, and it was up to Bl. Pope Paul VI (1897–1978) to address it.

Blessed Pope Paul VI had been elected the Vicar of Christ just before the decadent decade had begun. He was very much aware of the decline in Marian devotion and sought to do everything he could to renew interest in Mary and her rosary. In 1964, one year after becoming pope, he gave permission for all priests to bless rosaries in a document titled *Inter Oecumenici*. Up until 1964, the blessing of rosaries was reserved to priests of the Dominican Order. In 1966, one year after the close of the Second Vatican Council, he wrote the encyclical *Christi Matri*. The encyclical was written to promote prayers for peace during the month of October, and the rosary was a prominent theme in the encyclical. Blessed Pope Paul VI strongly encouraged his brother bishops to promote the rosary, even mentioning that the Second Vatican Council itself had encouraged the rosary devotion. He wrote:

> If evils increase, the devotion of the People of God should also increase. And so, venerable brothers, we want you to take the lead in urging and encouraging people to pray ardently to our most merciful mother Mary by saying the rosary … this prayer is well-suited to the devotion of the People of God, most pleasing to the Mother of God and most effective in gaining heaven's blessings. The Second Vatican Council recommended use of the rosary to all the sons of the Church, not in express words but in unmistakable fashion in this phrase: "Let

them value highly the pious practices and exercises directed to the Blessed Virgin and approved over the centuries by the Magisterium."[43]

Unfortunately, by 1966 when *Christi Matri* was released, the decadent decade was well underway, and the efforts of Bl. Pope Paul VI to renew interest in the rosary met with little enthusiasm. Redoubling his efforts, in 1967, he tried to spark a renewed interest in the rosary by revising the indulgences offered by the Church for those who prayed it. This action made the indulgences much easier to understand. Instead of there being a set number of days, quarantines (40 years), or other specified years attached to the indulgences, the revised *Enchiridion of Indulgences* simplified the indulgences attached to the rosary by making them either partial or plenary (see page 350). In 1969, he promulgated the decree that the Optional Memorial of Our Lady of the Rosary celebrated on October 7 was now to be celebrated as an obligatory memorial by the entire Church. He was doing everything he could to bring people back to the rosary.[44]

The bishops in the United States were seeking to do the same thing. In 1970, during a meeting of the United States bishops, John Cardinal Carberry proposed that they write a pastoral letter on Mary and address the decline in Marian devotion after the Second Vatican Council. The letter sought to encourage Catholics to turn back to Mary and especially her rosary. The Mariologist chosen to draft the document was the Carmelite priest Fr. Eamon Carroll. Ironically, during the time that Fr. Carroll was drafting the document, Elvis Presley, a non-Catholic, recorded a hit song in May of 1971 entitled "The Miracle of the Rosary."

Father Carroll finally finished the draft in 1973, and the American bishops published it under their name. It was given the title *Behold Your Mother: Woman of Faith*. In the rosary section of the letter, it poignantly acknowledged the decline in devotion to the rosary in the following statement:

> Only a few years ago, use of the rosary was a common mark of a Catholic, and it was customarily taught to children, both at home and in courses in religious instruction. Adults in every walk of life found strength in this familiar prayer that is biblically based and is filled with the thought of Jesus and his Mother in the mysteries. The praying of the rosary has declined. Some Catholics feel that there has even been a campaign to strip the churches of statues of Our Lady and the saints.[45]

In order to promote the rosary anew, the document both encouraged the traditional rosary and offered the suggestion that new forms of praying it were possible. Specifically, it mentioned that new sets of mysteries could be added to the rosary that emphasized the public life of Jesus. One example they gave was the wedding feast at Cana. The pastoral letter strongly emphasized that, though the rosary had fallen into disuse, it was not to be abandoned.

Less than three months after the American bishops promoted their pastoral letter, Bl. Pope Paul VI gave the Church the apostolic exhortation *Marialis Cultus* (February 2, 1974). During the time that Fr. Carroll had been drafting a document for the American bishops, Bl. Pope Paul VI had appointed a sacred congregation in Rome to draft a Marian document for the entire Church that would address the same issues. Blessed Pope Paul VI sought to have such a document created largely because of the impassioned letter of Fr. Peyton in 1971, requesting that the rosary be declared a liturgical prayer. Father Peyton's request would not be granted, but his letter had addressed a critical issue in the post-Vatican II Church and motivated Bl. Pope Paul VI to address the crisis in Marian devotion. The sacred congregation to which Bl. Pope Paul VI entrusted the writing of this document was the Congregation for Divine Worship.

The theologian, liturgist, and Mariologist assigned to draft the document was the Servite priest Fr. Ignacio Calabuig. The project took three years and underwent four major revisions. Blessed Pope Paul VI was very involved in the project. Each time a draft was completed, he looked it over as soon as it was available. Blessed Pope Paul VI insisted on being directly involved in the project because he was concerned that the pious tradition would be re-interpreted by the theologians drafting the document since many scholars in Rome had fallen into the abuse of the historical-critical method. Sure enough, every time a draft was sent to him, he found fault with it and sent it back because each draft sought to reinterpret the traditional rosary based on modern historical-critical research. Blessed Pope Paul VI was not in favor of changing the tradition, which resulted in a tug of war between him and the historical-critical theologians; the pope kept sending the drafts back to the sacred congregation for further revision until they produced a satisfactory document. Finally, after several years of constant give-and-take, the pope accepted the fourth revision. The document was published in 1974 under the title *Marialis Cultus*.

As part of the exhortation, Bl. Pope Paul VI acknowledged that many of his contemporaries were seeking to rediscover the rosary through historical studies and various other means. He included bishops, priests, laity, and Dominicans among those he credits, the last of whom he specifically described as, "by tradition, the guardians and promoters of this very salutary practice."[46] He also acknowledged the work of historians, but deliberately noted that their work was not to be directed at "defining in a sort of archeological fashion the primitive form of the rosary but at uncovering the original inspiration and driving force behind it."[47] This statement was important because there were indeed theologians who were conducting their research on the rosary as if it were an archeological dig, theologians who desired to deny the pious and papal tradition, repudiating what they could not find in written documents in order to create a revisionist history of the rosary based exclusively on the written records that had survived from the time of St. Dominic. Blessed Pope Paul VI respected the many statements made by his predecessors on the history and origins of the rosary and did not want to go against the papal tradition in *Marialis Cultus*. He only appeased the critics by acknowledging their work.

Interestingly, as the papacy of Bl. Pope Paul VI was coming to an end, one of his last acts was to lift the ban on the *Diary* of St. Faustina on April 15, 1978. By his actions, the Church and the world were now ready to welcome back the rosary and also receive a new form of devotion to God's mercy that involved using traditional rosary beads for a new prayer. The time was ripe for the Church to elect an extremely Marian pope who loved the rosary and was an apostle of mercy.[48]

St. John Paul II

After the death of Bl. Pope Paul VI, the Servant of God Pope John Paul I (1912–1978) was elected to the See of Peter. He was very devoted to the rosary and stated that it helped him become like a little child — but his papacy only lasted for 33 days. He was not the man designated to be the papal champion of the rosary at the close of the century.[49]

As the 20th century had started with the pope of the rosary, Pope Leo XIII, it was to end with a pope considered a papal version of St. Louis de Montfort. This great pope would be St. John Paul II (1920–2005). When Cardinal Karol Józef Wojtyła was elected to the papacy on October 16, 1978, it was a sign that a new springtime of rosary promotion had begun. On October 29, 1978, less than two weeks after his election, he announced to the whole world that the rosary was his favorite prayer. He even noted that the rosary offered a prayer-commentary on the chapter in the Second Vatican Council's dogmatic constitution *Lumen Gentium* that dealt with Our Lady. Saint John Paul II quickly became the most traveled pope in history and preached incessantly about Our Lady and her rosary everywhere he went in a way reminiscent of the apostolic endeavors of St. Louis de Montfort. He even took a phrase from the writings of St. Louis de Montfort as his papal motto: *Totus Tuus*. These words mean "All Yours" and are the shortened version of de Montfort's Marian consecration formula: *Totus Tuus ego sum, et omnia tua sunt. Accipio te in mea omnia. Praebe mihi cor tuum, Maria.* ("I am all yours, and all that I have is yours. I take you for my all. Mary, give me your heart.") With these words as his papal motto, St. John Paul II set out on the highways and byways of the world as an indefatigable spiritual warrior and champion of the rosary.

The roots of St. John Paul II's tremendous love for the rosary can be found in his youth. As a young man, he was greatly influenced by the Marian spirituality of the Servant of God Jan Tyranowski (1900–1947). In 1940, at the age of 20, Karol Wojtyła became a member of a Living Rosary group that had been started in the Krakow area by Jan Tyranowski. This group met every week to share their love for Mary, pray the rosary, and share their insights into the mysteries of the rosary. Each member of the Living Rosary was assigned a particular mystery to meditate on for one month, and promised to say a decade of the rosary a day while meditating on their assigned mystery. It was during these meetings that Jan Tyranowski gave Wojtyła a copy of St. Louis de Montfort's *True Devotion to the Blessed Virgin*. This book had a deep impact on Karol Wojtyła.

Many have stated that, had it not been for Tyranowski, Karol Wojtyła would not have become a priest. In fact, Tyranowski's strong Marian devotion and interest in Carmelite mysticism served as major influences on Wojtyła. After Wojtyła became a priest, the teachings and example of Tyranowski continued to influence his life. When Fr. Wojtyła received his first parish assignment in Niegowic in 1948, he immediately started a Living Rosary group for the youth of the community in memory of his friend Jan Tyranowski, who had died on March 15, 1947. After he became pope, St. John Paul II frequently spoke of how Jan Tyranowski had influenced him, and referred to him as a great man and an apostle of the Living Rosary.

Through the efforts of St. John Paul II, the rosary once again became the most popular Marian devotion among Catholics during the last two decades of the 20th century. In 1987, he declared a Marian Year for the Church, initiating the year with a televised recitation of the rosary that he himself led. A great lover of Marian shrines, he strengthened the bond between the rosary and places of pilgrimage by visiting Marian shrines and praying the rosary at them on almost every trip he made. Saint John Paul II taught the world that to pray the rosary is to make a pilgrimage, since those who pray the rosary mentally and spiritually revisit the holy places associated with the lives of Jesus and Mary.

Saint John Paul II was aided in his efforts to promote the rosary by many other groups in the Church during this time. In 1981, near the very beginning of his papacy, a global Catholic television network (EWTN) was founded by Mother Angelica in Alabama. Part of the network's initial programming was a daily, worldwide broadcast of the rosary. This program inspired many people to take up the rosary again.

In 1984, Cardinal Leo Suenens and the laywoman Veronica O'Brien founded the Fiat Rosary. One day, Veronica O'Brien received a private revelation from Jesus in which he gave her a shorter version of the rosary that was to serve as a simple way of re-introducing the traditional rosary back into the lives of his people. A slightly abbreviated rosary, the Fiat Rosary consists of meditating on selected mysteries from the full-length rosary (Joyful, Sorrowful, Glorious) by covering the key mysteries of the full-length rosary in one prayer session.

Veronica O'Brien was also a zealous promoter of the Legion of Mary, responsible for bringing the Legion of Mary to France, Belgium, Turkey, and Greece. Cardinal Suenens was a well-known advocate for the definition of a new Marian dogma declaring Mary the Mediatrix of All Grace. Jesus would use both of these Marian devotees to correct the severe neglect of the rosary during the 1960s and 1970s.

Heaven offered much assistance to the efforts of St. John Paul II to spread the rosary during this time. During his pontificate, numerous rosary-themed apparitions began to occur around the world. They began with Cuapa, Nicaragua, in 1980, followed by Kibeho, Africa, in 1981, and San Nicolás, Argentina, in 1983. It should also be noted that the alleged Marian apparitions in Medjugorje began in 1981. Although, to date, the Medjugorje apparitions have not been approved, it cannot be denied that these alleged apparitions played a major role in bringing the rosary back into parish and family life around the world. If a Catholic parish during the 1980s or 1990s had a group of people who prayed the rosary before or after Mass, often many members of that group had gone to Medjugorje and participated in the rosary prayed every day at St. James Church. Medjugorje served as a major catalyst for individuals, as well as parish communities, to pray the rosary again.

It was also during the pontificate of St. John Paul II that the rosary was promoted in the most important documents of the Church. When the Church promulgated the new Code of Canon Law in 1983, replacing the 1917 Code, the section that dealt with the formation of priests explicitly sought to counteract the neglect of the rosary experienced in seminaries during the 1960s and 1970s by noting the following: "The veneration of the Blessed Virgin Mary, including the Marian rosary, mental prayer, and other exercises of piety are to be fostered."[50] The new Code of Canon Law even mentioned that members of religious communities were to foster a particular love of the rosary. Shortly after the new Code of Canon Law was released, the bishops of the United States issued the *Program of Priestly Formation*. This important document explicitly noted that opportunities for praying the rosary were to be provided in seminaries. The decadent decade was over; it was time to bring the rosary back to the seminary chapel.

The greatest document published during the pontificate of St. John Paul II was the 1992 *Catechism of the Catholic Church*. This doctrinal tome emphasized the importance of the rosary by having numerous references to the prayer throughout its pages. As a teaching document, the primary focus of the *Catechism* is on the official doctrines and dogmas of the Church. As a doctrinal book, the *Catechism* does not reference any particular private revelation. For this reason, it is not the intention of the *Catechism* to offer a history of the rosary. Therefore, the *Catechism's* silence on the heavenly origins of the rosary should not be taken to imply that the rosary does not have such an origin. The heavenly origins of the rosary are not mentioned because that aspect of the rosary involves private revelation. The *Catechism* deals exclusively with the teachings of the faith according to Public Revelation. Since no private revelation is binding upon the faithful, the *Catechism* does not list any specific private revelation by name, not even Guadalupe, Lourdes, or Fatima (all of which have associated feasts on the Church's liturgical calendar). Papal documents, letters, bulls, exhortations, homilies, and speeches often mention private revelations, but even then, private revelation is not binding upon the faithful. Thus, in its brief mention of the history of the rosary, the *Catechism* simply states the following: "Medieval piety in the West developed the prayer of the rosary as a popular substitute for the

Liturgy of the Hours."[51] Once again, in no way does this statement contradict the pious tradition.

Incredibly, as the second Christian millennium was drawing to a close and people were returning to the rosary with great fervor, a whole new series of alleged Marian apparitions containing strong rosary themes began to take place in such areas as Litmanová, Slovakia (1990), Aokpe, Nigeria (1992), and Itapiranga, Brazil (1994). The end of the second Christian millennium was truly experiencing a rosary revival. Even non-Catholics knew there was something special about the blessed beads. This was evident in 1997, when the whole world watched Princess Diana of Wales, a non-Catholic, be buried with one of her most cherished possessions: the rosary that was given to her by St. Teresa of Calcutta.

Miracles and Victories

Most of the famous miracles and victories associated with the rosary during the 20th century occurred during times of war or oppressive governmental regimes. When the United States dropped atomic bombs on the Japanese cities of Hiroshima and Nagasaki, both bombing sites experienced miracles associated with the rosary. When Hiroshima was bombed on August 6, 1945, an entire house of Jesuits survived, completely unaffected by the bomb. The Jesuit house was located only eight blocks from where the atomic bomb went off and should have been completely annihilated. A church attached to the Jesuit house and everything else around it for miles was obliterated, but the house with the Jesuits in it survived largely intact. Furthermore, none of the Jesuits suffered any ill effects from radiation or loss of hearing whatsoever. In fact, all eight Jesuits lived healthy lives for years after the event. One of the survivors, Fr. Hubert Schiffer, SJ, gave public testimony more than 200 times about what had miraculously happened to him and his confreres. He testified that he firmly believed that they were spared because they prayed the rosary every day in that house in response to the request of Our Lady at Fatima.

Similarly, when the atomic bomb was dropped on Nagasaki on August 9, 1945, it exploded in the Urakami district of the city. That district had been the heart and soul of Catholicism in Japan since the 16th century. It was in this area that St. Maximilian Kolbe founded a Conventual Franciscan mission in the 1930s, calling it the "Garden of the Immaculate." When St. Maximilian settled on that particular property, he was informed that he had made a poor decision. It was in a horrible location, he was told, since the property was facing away from the city, behind a hill, and situated in an area that nobody desired to visit. The saint was unmoved, however, and the house was built on that property. Miraculously, when the atomic bomb was dropped, the Franciscans' house was left standing and all the friars inside were unharmed. Just as the Jesuits had done at their house in Hiroshima, the Franciscans prayed the rosary every day in their house. Our Lady had guided St. Maximilian to obtain a piece of property that would be protected from the bomb blast.

Another rosary miracle occurred after World War II in the country of Austria. After World War II, various parts of Austria were divided up and parceled out to other countries. The most Catholic section of Austria, which included Vienna, was given to Russia. Russia was still Communist at that time, and was very happy to have been given the richest section of Austria. The Viennese were not happy about the divisions, since many of them were now under Russian governance. The Austrian people desperately desired to find a way to escape their oppressive political situation. The answer came through the rosary. In 1946, a devout priest named Fr. Petrus Pavlicek made a pilgrimage to the principal Marian shrine in Austria, the Marian Basilica in Mariazell. During his pilgrimage, he was reminded of what the rosary had done for the Christian world during the Battle of Lepanto and heard an interior voice instructing him to do something similar. The voice said to him, "Do as I say and there will be peace." Desiring to obey this heavenly instruction, Fr. Pevlicek organized a Holy Rosary Crusade of Reparation in 1947, consisting of the Viennese people conducting a public rosary procession in the streets of their city. The explicit intention for the rosary crusade was to bring about an end to Communism in their country and the entire world. Initially, the processions were not that well attended, but over time, the number of participants grew to enormous proportions. By 1955, after eight years of rallying support from among the Austrian people, the public recitation of the rosary drew more than a half million people, equaling one-tenth of the entire population of Austria. Then, to everyone's surprise, on May 13, 1955, the Soviets announced that they were leaving Austria of their own accord, with the last forces leaving in October of the same year. Everyone attributed this miraculous turn of events to the rosary. In fact, a few months before she died in 1962, the German mystic and Servant of God Theresa Neumann (1898–1962) was asked why Russia had left Austria. She said it had taken place because of the rosaries prayed by the Austrian people.

One of the most inspiring rosary victories during this century took place in Brazil in 1964. When the country was being governed by the Communist-leaning president João Goulart, large groups of people turned to the rosary and rose up in rebellion against their oppressive leaders. Rosary groups were formed and were able to break up Communist rallies by marching in the streets and praying the rosary loudly. One famous event occurred in the city of Belo Horizonte, where a Communist rally was taking place under the direction of President Goulart. The president had already appointed many Communists to high positions in the government and was now rallying support in Belo Horizonte for a Communist revolution in Brazil. The archbishop of Rio de Janeiro, Cardinal de Barros Camara, spoke against the President by going on national radio to ask the people of Brazil to live the message of Fatima as a means of overcoming the Communist threat. President Goulart was so enraged by the archbishop's messages that he insulted the people of Brazil in a public speech and ridiculed the rosary, saying that it was his Communist ideas that would reform and save Brazil, not the rosaries of simple women. These words greatly upset the Brazilian people, and they decided to confront the Communists during the rally in Belo Horizonte.

The rally in Belo Horizonte was led by Goulart's brother-in-law, Leone Brizola, and it was to be one of the largest Communist rallies in the country. As it was taking place, more than 20,000 women marched into the streets with rosaries in their hands to engage in spiritual battle! They marched right into the midst of the Communist rally and prayed the rosary so loudly that it shut the rally down. On March 19, only six days after the women broke up the Communist rally, more than 600,000 people marched through the streets of São Paolo praying the rosary in the famous "March of the Family with God toward Freedom." Initially this march was called the "March to Make Amends to the Rosary" since President Goulart had insulted the rosary in his public speech. However, the name was changed so that non-Catholics would be encouraged to participate as well. Many non-Catholics did attend the march and prayed the rosary with the Catholics as they marched in defiance against the Communist vision of the president. Goulart was so intimidated by the rosary army that within two weeks he had fled the country! In thanksgiving for the rosary victory, the people of Brazil organized another march in gratitude to Our Lady and her rosary. It was held on April 2, 1964, one day after President Goulart fled the country. This march was called the "March of Thanksgiving to God." More than a million people marched through the streets of Rio de Janeiro celebrating their freedom from the threat of Communism.

In the Philippines in 1986, the People Power Revolution used the rosary to overcome the oppressive dictatorship of President Ferdinand Marcos. On the Sunday before the collapse of the Marcos regime, tens of thousands of Filipinos rose up in protest against the dictator by lining up and kneeling in front of armed tanks to pray the rosary. At the front of the lines were devout nuns who ceaselessly led the people in the recitation of the sacred mysteries. Risking their lives, thousands and thousands of people joined in with the sisters and prayed the rosary on their knees before the tanks. When they were ordered to move or be run over, the large group prayed the rosary even louder. Dominican priests arrived with a replica of the statue of Our Lady, La Naval de Manila, and carried it in procession in front of the tanks. On one side of the famous EDSA road where the people had gathered in front of the tanks, a large billboard with an image of Fr. Patrick Peyton could be seen bearing the inscription, "The family that prays together, stays together." Miraculously, there was never a shot fired, the tanks never touched the people, and President Ferdinand Marcos and his wife, Imelda, fled the country. Cardinal Jaime Sin, the archbishop of Manila, later recounted to the media what he had been told by many of the soldiers who were there that day. They said that they were about to run over the people with the tanks when they saw an extremely beautiful lady who instructed them that they were to stop their tanks and do no harm to the people because she was the queen of the island.

Not every rosary miracle in the 20ᵗʰ century involved wars and revolutions, though. In 1978, the rosary saved a young woman from being raped and killed by the infamous serial killer Ted Bundy. Responsible for at least 30 brutal and sadistic murders, Ted Bundy was eventually caught and executed by electric chair in 1989. Before his death, he testified to an aspect of one of his killing sprees in Florida that not even he understood. On the evening of January 15, 1978, Bundy broke into a sorority house at Florida State University in Tallahassee and brutally assaulted and killed several young women. However, one of the women in the house remained completely untouched, even though she had come face-to-face with the killer. When police arrived at the scene of the brutal murders, they found the young woman in a near catatonic state, unwilling to speak to anyone but a priest. A local priest, Monsignor William Kerr, was called to the scene to speak to the woman. She told him that after Ted Bundy had killed two of her sorority sisters and severely harmed two others, he opened the door to her room, ready to kill her. Oddly, when Bundy opened the door and saw her lying in bed, he dropped his weapon and ran away. The young woman told Msgr. Kerr that before she had gone off to college, she had promised her mother that every night before going to bed, she would pray a rosary for protection. That particular night, she had fallen asleep while praying the rosary. The rosary was in her hand when Bundy opened the door and looked at her. Incredibly, when Ted Bundy was on death row, he asked for spiritual guidance from Msgr. William Kerr, the same priest that had talked to the young woman on the night of the murders. In the course of their conversation, Bundy informed Msgr. Kerr that he had no idea why he had not killed the young woman. He said that when he had gotten to her room, he had had every intention of killing her, but a mysterious force prevented him from entering the room, and he dropped his weapon and fled. He didn't know it, but that mysterious force was the rosary!

New Discoveries

There were many new discoveries made connected to the rosary during the 20ᵗʰ century. The greatest was the re-discovery of the lost masterpiece *The Secret of the Rosary* by St. Louis de Montfort. After many other documents on the history of the rosary had been destroyed by plagues, wars, the Protestant rebellion, and the French Revolution, the Divine Craftsman allowed the greatest history of the rosary to remain hidden until it was needed the most. After the manuscript was re-discovered, it was printed for the first time in French in 1911, followed by a German edition in 1920 and an English edition in 1954. Incredibly, all the 20ᵗʰ century critics of the rosary tradition intentionally chose to ignore it, despite the fact that St. Louis de Montfort used ancient historical sources, was a Third Order Dominican, and was very knowledgeable about the Dominican Order's oral tradition. They chose to ignore *The Secret of the Rosary* because its contents repudiated all their re-interpretations of history.

Despite the critics' refusal to acknowledge *The Secret of the Rosary*, there were other discoveries made during the second half of the 20th century that challenged their conclusions. In 1945, the famous author Masie Ward made the following observation regarding the new discoveries:

> On the negative side [of the history of the rosary] discussions of what happened in the Middle Ages are apt to be obscured by the fact that so many documents have been lost, especially during the ravages of the Black Death. On the positive side, however, more and more discoveries are constantly made, so that if we cannot say with certainty that a particular thing was *not* done by our ancestors, we can often say with certainty that a particular thing was done.[52]

Masie Ward would not be alone in her critique of the negative arguments of the critics.

In 1954, the noted author and historian John S. Johnson took the critics of the rosary tradition to task and highlighted how one new discovery in particular completely undermined their conclusions:

> The critics relied mainly on the argument of silence to question the ancient tradition that the Blessed Virgin gave the rosary to St. Dominic. They should have known that many documents referred to by Blessed Alan may have existed, but did not survive the burning scourge of the Huguenots, who destroyed convents, monasteries, libraries, among the countless institutions they committed to the flames. The critics went so far as to say that Blessed Alan had invented the rosary devotion ... and had attributed it to St. Dominic to tie it in with a famous name. But the two persons Alan relies on for his story of the origin of the rosary had their "Mariales" [Marian books] preserved at the Convent of Gand [Belgium]: which library was burnt during the wars on religion. There are other rosary documents which have been discovered in later years which were from before Blessed Alan's time. The long poem, Rosarius, antedates him by a hundred years or so and clearly refers the rosary to St. Dominic and the battle of Muret. This removes Blessed Alan from all suspicion of inventing his sources.[53]

The "*Rosarius*" poem mentioned by Johnson is in itself proof that the rosary was not "invented" by Bl. Alan but already existed in the 13th century. Writing in 1963, the very learned priest Fr. William Most had this to say regarding the content of the "*Rosarius*" poem and its implications for affirming the pious tradition:

> The most impressive evidence prior to the time of Alan has appeared since [Fr.] Thurston wrote. In his work *The Rosary and its Historical Antecedents*, Mathieu Gorce, a French Dominican, has made a careful

analysis of a set of verses by a French Dominican which seem to be from the early fourteenth century — that is, about a century after the time of St. Dominic. These verses (to sum up the conclusions of Gorce) seem to represent St. Dominic as having a mission from heaven to save the world in preaching a devotion to the *Ave Maria,* which is associated with meditation on some mysteries of our faith. The document is entitled *Rosarius.* The analysis of Gorce shows that the document *Rosarius* probably reflects the view that the preaching-praying method is due to St. Dominic, with divine support. As to the name of this document we must note that the term at the age (early 14th century) was not restricted to meaning a set of prayers and meditations, such as our rosary, but could also refer to a set of sermons. This would fit admirably well with the view that St. Dominic employed a preaching-praying method [of praying the rosary].[54]

As more discoveries were made, the conclusions of the critics continued to fall to pieces. For example, one of the arguments put forth by the advocates of the historical-critical revision against the pious tradition was that, since Dominic of Prussia claimed to be the first to attach meditations to the rosary, he should be called the real founder of the rosary. Nevertheless, recent discoveries have proven that Dominic of Prussia was not the first to attach mysteries to the Dominican rosary. In 1977, Dr. Andreas Heinz, a well-respected historian and member of the theological faculty at the University of Trier, discovered a manuscript describing a rosary containing meditations on the life of Christ that is much older than the one of Dominic of Prussia. It is dated around 1300, and may even have been used in the late 13th century. He discovered this manuscript in a collection of prayers from the Cistercian convent of St. Thomas near Trier.[55] Since the critics claimed that meditations on the rosary only came into existence in the 15th century, this discovery proves that the critics were wrong.

Further affirmation that the rosary was preached by St. Dominic in the 13th century can be seen in the studies done by Fr. André Duval, OP. He conducted extensive studies on the subject and published his findings in 1988. He discovered that the first *written* account about St. Dominic preaching on the Marian Psalter (the rosary) is not in the writings of Bl. Alan de la Roche but rather in the homilies of the Dominican bishop Jean de Monte in the early 15th century.[56] In addition, thanks to the historical research on the rosary conducted in libraries across Europe by Fr. Gabriel Harty, OP, copies of the original Confraternity Book of the Dominican priest Fr. Michael Insulis, dating from 1486, were found in the National Library of Paris. Father Insulis was a priest who had helped Bl. Alan de la Roche in his revival of the rosary and the rosary Confraternity. As part of this discovery, Fr. Harty learned that the lost copies of the Confraternity book had ended up in the National Library of Paris, due to the ransacking of the Vatican archives in 1810 by Napoleon Bonaparte. Napoleon, for all his many faults, considered these books to have been so beautifully produced and so priceless that he had them brought to Paris as "war booty" during his ravaging of parts of Italy. These books are significant because they defend the pious tradition by stating that the rosary and the Confraternity were founded by St. Dominic. Father Insulis insists that neither Bl. Alan de la Roche nor Fr. Jacob Sprenger were the originators of the rosary, but only the revivers of it. This discovery is historically invaluable. These treasures still sit on shelves in the National Library of Paris. In his autobiography, Fr. Harty makes a fraternal plea to his Dominican confreres, especially the Dominican Generalate in Rome, to earnestly seek to acquire at least one copy from the National Library in Paris so that the Dominicans themselves can "rediscover the lost treasure that is the Rosary Confraternity."[57]

Recent artistic discoveries have also shed light on the history of the rosary. In the National Gallery of Art in London, a painting known as "The Arnolfini Marriage" by Jan van Eyck offers tremendous insights into the history of the rosary. Painted in 1434, the painting features two figures about to be married. At first glance, it seems like a simple painting, yet when the image is magnified so that more detail can be seen, something remarkable appears on the wall behind the two figures: a rosary! The rosary is hanging on a wall next to a large mirror framed by a wooden picture rosary featuring 10 mysteries. This painting gives witness that the rosary was already popular enough in the early 15th century to be displayed in people's homes. Interestingly, Jan van Eyck painted in Bruges, a location not that far from Ghent, where the Beguines had the tradition of praying the rosary. "The Arnolfini Marriage" proves that the rosary already existed before the contemplative version promoted by Dominic of Prussia emerged or the renewal led by Bl. Alan de la Roche took place. In fact, during his lifetime, Van Eyck painted other works of art that also featured the rosary. All of these works of art prove that the Ulm picture rosary of 1483 was not the first of its kind.

It is almost certain that future discoveries will be made regarding the history of the rosary, as well. When they occur, the pious tradition as taught by popes and saints will receive further affirmation.

THE 21ST CENTURY:
Luminous Mysteries in Dark Days

There are many forces opposing Christianity in the third Christian millennium. Some of these threats are old, but many of them are new. To face these attacks, the Divine Craftsman has re-sharpened the sword of the rosary and given it a whole new set of mysteries. With the establishment of Divine Mercy Sunday and the universal promotion of the Chaplet of Divine Mercy, the rosary is clearly not only a weapon of truth, but also an instrument of mercy. The Secretary of Divine Mercy, St. Faustina, once wrote in her *Diary*: "I shall fight all evil with the weapon of mercy."[1] In the third Christian millennium, the rosary will be used by men, women, and children to combat the enemies of the Cross and also to bring souls to the mercy of Christ. Popes will be relentless in promoting it, bishops will have visions about it, and new heroes and champions will emerge who will instruct others to wield it in the darkness of a world that has abandoned both reason and Divine Revelation.

Weapon of Truth and Instrument of Mercy

The first canonized saint of the third Christian millennium was St. Faustina Kowalska. She was canonized on Divine Mercy Sunday, April 30, 2000. It was on that same day that St. John Paul II declared that the second Sunday of Easter would be officially known and celebrated throughout the entire Church as Divine Mercy Sunday. The Divine Mercy message and devotion was already the fastest growing grassroots movement in the history of the Church, but Faustina's canonization would help further popularize one of the most important aspects of her visions, namely, the Divine Mercy Chaplet. As a result of St. Faustina's canonization, the rosary became even more commonly used since the Divine Mercy Chaplet is prayed on ordinary Dominican rosary beads. The rosary is now officially understood as both a weapon of truth and an instrument of mercy. The importance of this two-fold dimension to the rosary would be made even more plain one year later when Muslim terrorists attacked the World Trade Center in New York City and the Pentagon in Washington, D.C., on September 11, 2001, killing almost 3,000 people. The response of St. John Paul II was to ask the world to pray the rosary during the month of October for protection against future attacks and as a way of obtaining peace.

After the terrorist attacks on 9/11, St. John Paul II began to emphasize the rosary even more than he had before. He foresaw terrible things on the horizon for humanity and was greatly worried. During the same month that he requested the rosary be prayed for protection against terrorism (October 2001), he beatified Blesseds Luigi and Maria Beltrame Quattrocchi, the first married couple in the history of the Church to be beatified together. During the beatification homily, he intentionally emphasized the important role that the daily rosary played in their marriage. He stated: "At the center of their life was the daily Eucharist as well as devotion to the Virgin Mary, to whom they prayed every evening with the rosary."[2] The beatified couple had been married for 45 years, making for a lot of rosaries prayed together as a couple, to which St. John Paul II sought to draw people's attention. Then, in December of 2001, he approved and confirmed the publication of the Vatican's new *Directory on Popular Piety and the Liturgy*. This important document greatly emphasized the rosary and the Divine Mercy devotion, further promoting both of these important devotions throughout the entire Church. All of this prepared the world for what he would do in 2002 when he sharpened the blade of the rosary by giving it a whole "new" set of mysteries and granting a plenary indulgence to all who celebrate Divine Mercy Sunday. The Divine Craftsman and the Queen of Heaven had been preparing the world for these things.

Luminous Mysteries in the Third Christian Millennium

Before 9/11 took place and St. John Paul II stepped up his efforts to promote the rosary, an almost unnoticed beatification occurred on May 9, 2001. Divine Providence had intentionally planned for a holy man to be beatified and canonized during this time because of the insights he offered on the rosary in the mid-20th century. The name of the man being beatified was Blessed George Preca (1880–1962) (now St. George Preca; he was canonized in 2007). Saint Preca was the founder of the Society of Christian Doctrine in Malta and was popularly known as the "Second Apostle of Malta" (the first being St. Paul.) The timing of his beatification was providential: It took place one year before St. John Paul II added an additional set of mysteries to the rosary. Unbeknownst to most people, it was St. George Preca who had proposed a new set of mysteries, called the "mysteries of light," in 1957. The mysteries he desired to see promoted were the same five mysteries that St. John Paul II used to sharpen the blade of the rosary in his 2002 apostolic letter *Rosarium Virginis Mariae*. As we have already noted, there were others throughout history who sought to promote new mysteries for the rosary (for example, St. Louis de Montfort and the Servant of God Patrick Peyton, among others). However, it was specifically the Luminous Mysteries of Fr. George Preca that St. John Paul II embraced and promoted.

In 2002, when St. John Paul II promulgated *Rosarium Virginis Mariae*, he not only added a new set of mysteries, but also acknowledged the development of the rosary and offered a subtle affirmation of the pious tradition. In the first paragraph of the letter, he noted that the rosary "gradually took form in the second millennium under the guidance of the Spirit of God."[3] This statement underscores that the rosary is not to be understood as a static devotion, but rather as one that continues to be shaped over time. Then, in the second paragraph, he intentionally singled out a previous papal document that had strongly emphasized the pious tradition. He wrote: "Numerous predecessors of mine attributed great importance to this prayer [the rosary]. Worthy of special note in this regard is Pope Leo XIII who on September 1, 1883, promulgated the encyclical *Supremi Apostolatus Officio*, a document of great worth."[4] His choice to refer to this particular encyclical of Pope Leo XIII is interesting because it explicitly stated that St. Dominic "composed" the mysteries of the rosary and was the "first to institute" it. Of all the documents St. John Paul could have referenced, he intentionally chose to reference one that affirmed the pious tradition. By doing this, he offered a subtle affirmation of the pious tradition himself. He did not rely entirely on the words of Pope Leo XIII, however, since he himself alluded to the pious tradition when he wrote the following:

> The history of the rosary shows how this prayer was used in particular by the Dominicans at a difficult time for the Church due to the spread of heresy. Today we are facing new challenges. Why should we not once more have recourse to the rosary, with the same faith as those who have gone before us?[5]

It is obvious that the "difficult time for the Church due to the spread of heresy" to which St. John Paul II was referring was the Albigensian heresy that St. Dominic overcame through the rosary. In his letter on the rosary, St. John Paul II depicted the rosary as a living sacramental of the Church that has its origins in both time and eternity. The development of the rosary over time is not in contradiction to the pious tradition since the rosary has the ability to adapt to particular needs, eras, and epochs of history.

In response to St. John Paul II's letter on the rosary, the Master General of the Dominicans, Fr. Carlos Alfonso Azpiroz Costa, wrote a letter to the pope thanking him for his insights on the rosary. In the Master General's letter, he, too, acknowledged both the pious tradition and the developments that have taken place in the history of the rosary. He wrote:

> The Order of Preachers, throughout the centuries, wanted especially to spread the rosary. Popular devotion, in fact, recognizes St. Dominic as the "founder" of the rosary, and Christian art, for many centuries, represents him thus receiving the rosary from the hands of the Blessed Virgin Mary. The Constitutions of the Friars affirms that the practice and the preaching of the rosary are to be held "*ut nota Ordinis peculiaris*" (as a characteristic peculiar to the Order). I also thank you for inviting us to meditate on the "Mysteries of Light!"[6]

Unfortunately, not everyone welcomed the Luminous Mysteries of St. John Paul II. Many ultra-traditionalists rejected the Luminous Mysteries on the grounds that they were an invention of a post-Vatican II pope. Yet as we have seen, the Luminous Mysteries pre-date the Second Vatican Council. Furthermore, any Christian who sincerely believes that Jesus and Mary are displeased when people meditate on such mysteries as the proclamation of the kingdom of God and the institution of the Eucharist need to seriously examine their hearts and intentions. All St. John Paul II did was to sharpen the blade of the ancient rosary and equip the Church with the needed weapons for the issues of our times, especially meditation on the importance of Baptism, the sanctity of marriage, the necessity of conversion, the divinity of Christ, and the Real Presence of Jesus in the Eucharist. As a prophet for the third Christian millennium, St. John Paul II brought the rosary into modern times and transformed the spiritual sword into a lightsaber capable of conquering the forces of darkness.

The Need for Champions Continues

After the publication of *Rosarium Virginis Mariae*, St. John Paul II proclaimed a Year of the Rosary, to be held from October 2002 to October 2003. During this special year, parishes and dioceses were to place particular emphasis on the rosary by offering celebrations in its honor. At the beginning of the Year of the Rosary, St. John Paul II led by example when he wrote a personal letter to the Servant of God Chiara Lubich (1920–2008) and asked her to promote the rosary in a particular way during this year by organizing a major event. Chiara was the founder of the international Focolare movement, a very popular figure in the Church, and a great lover of the rosary. In response to the request of the Pope, she organized a Marian Congress in Rome in April of 2003. The theme of the Congress was the rosary.

After the Year of the Rosary, St. John Paul II continued to promote the rosary ardently. He visited the Basilica of the Rosary in Lourdes in 2004, and requested that the Luminous Mysteries be incorporated in a visual way into the Basilica. This resulted in beautiful images depicting the Luminous Mysteries being placed on the outside façade of the Basilica.

After the death of St. John Paul II in 2005, Pope Benedict XVI continued to fervently promote the rosary. Like his predecessor, he not only promoted the rosary and referred to it as a spiritual weapon, but also the Divine Mercy message and devotion, especially by establishing the World Apostolic Congress on Mercy. On many occasions during his pontificate, especially in the cool of the evening, he was observed walking through the Vatican gardens praying his rosary. He, too, made a pilgrimage to the Shrine of Our Lady of the Rosary of Pompeii. In his *Angelus* message on Tuesday, October 7, 2008, the Memorial of Our Lady of the Rosary, he acknowledged the ancient practice of Rosary Sunday and offered a subtle affirmation of the pious tradition:

> This first Sunday of October [October 5, 2008] offers us two reasons for prayer and reflection: the *Memorial of Our Lady of the Rosary*, which is celebrated precisely today [October 7, 2008], and *missionary commitment*, to which this month is especially dedicated. The traditional image of Our Lady of the Rosary portrays Mary who with one arm supports the Child Jesus and with the other is offering the

rosary beads to St. Dominic. This important iconography shows that the rosary is a means given by the Virgin to contemplate Jesus and, in meditating on his life, to love him and follow him ever more faithfully. It is this message that Our Lady has also bequeathed to us in her various apparitions. I am thinking in particular of the apparition in Fatima that occurred 90 years ago. Presenting herself as "Our Lady of the Rosary," she insistently recommended the daily recitation of the rosary to the three little shepherd children, Lucia, Jacinta and Francisco, in order to obtain the end of the war. Let us also accept the Virgin's motherly request, pledging to recite the rosary with faith for peace in families, nations and throughout the world.[7]

It was during the papacy of Benedict XVI that the rosary brought about several well-known miracles in South America. In 2008, Colombia was on the verge of going to war with its neighbors Ecuador and Venezuela. The reason for the conflict was a raid conducted within Ecuador's borders by Colombia in an attempt to extinguish a group of Marxist terrorists. This action was authorized by Columbia's president Alvaro Uribe, and caused Ecuador and its ally Venezuela to stand ready to go to war with Colombia. As tensions increased and war was about to break out, the Colombian president called upon his staff to pray the rosary as a means of ending the tensions and bringing about peace. The rosary was prayed in the chapel in the presidential palace and dedicated to Our Lady of the Rosary of Chiquinquirá, the patroness of Colombia, Ecuador, and Venezuela. Miraculously, two days after the rosary was prayed, all three presidents shook hands during the Group of Rio summit. The threat of war was ended by means of the rosary.

The other rosary miracle occurred in 2010 in Chile, when 33 miners were trapped in an underground mine for 69 days. Pope Benedict XVI personally blessed 33 rosaries and sent them to the miners so that they could pray the rosary and know that Mary was with them. The blessed rosaries were sent down the small shaft to the men, and they began to pray them and wear them around their necks. Miraculously, all 33 men survived and were rescued from the mine on October 13, the anniversary of the Miracle of the Sun at Fatima!

After the papacy of Benedict XVI, the first ever Jesuit pope was elected to the See of Peter — Pope Francis, who had been known as Jorge Mario Bergoglio.

Pope Francis has a great love for the rosary, inspired by St. John Paul II in 1985. During an apostolic visit, the future Jesuit pope attended a papal event and witnessed St. John Paul II devoutly praying the rosary on his knees. The limitless confidence that he saw in St. John Paul II as he prayed the rosary greatly moved him to emulate the saintly pope. Bergoglio realized that he needed to increase his own devotion to Mary, especially by means of the rosary. As he has proclaimed to the world, from that day forward he has prayed 15 mysteries of the rosary every day. (His practice started before the Luminous Mysteries were given to the Church by St. John Paul II in 2002.)

At the papal conclave in 2013, as he began to receive many votes to become the next pope, other cardinals noticed that he was devoutly praying the rosary. After his election, he informed the world that praying the rosary during the vote gave him a tremendous sense of peace, since he knew Our Lady was with him. Then, the day after he was elected to the papacy, he made a visit to the Basilica of Santa Maria Maggiore in Rome to entrust his pontificate to Mary. It was during that visit that he surprised everyone when he walked over to the tomb of St. Pope Pius V, knelt down, and prayed for an extended time. Saint Pope Pius V was the 16th century Dominican pontiff who formed the Holy League and brought about the rosary victory over the Ottoman Turks at the Battle of Lepanto.

On November 17, 2013, Pope Francis recommended to pilgrims visiting Rome something called "*Misericordina,*" a medicine box that contained a rosary, an image of the Divine Mercy, and a prescription for prayer. He had volunteers hand them out to the people present and underscored that *Misericordina* is spiritual medicine for the soul. He specifically noted the following: "This is a rosary, with which you can pray the Chaplet of Divine Mercy."

On April 3, 2014, in an address to the bishops of Rwanda in Africa, Pope Francis reminded the bishops of the importance of living the message of Our Lady of Kibeho, especially of prayer, fasting, and the rosary. According to Msgr. Alfred Xuereb, one of Pope Francis's secretaries, the only time the pope stops working is to pray the rosary. Pope Francis encourages priests, families, and children to pray the rosary every day, too. In imitation of the two previous pontiffs, he, too, made a pilgrimage to the Shrine of Our Lady of the Rosary of Pompeii in March of 2015. He has stated that the rosary sustains us in our battles against the evil one. Pope Francis' papal witness as an apostle of Divine Mercy, praying the daily rosary, and encouraging others to do the same is extremely important for the Church in the 21st century.

The Church and her faithful are under attack by a world hostile to Jesus Christ and his sacred mysteries. The times are so serious that the spiritual sword of the rosary must find itself in the hands of new champions. It needs to be taken to the front lines of the battle in order to combat the following threats and conquer them with truth and mercy:

Abortion

Abortion is the silent and invisible holocaust of our times. Since the legalization of abortion in the United States in 1973, it is estimated that more than 1.5 billion abortions have occurred worldwide. In the United States alone, more than 60 million abortions have taken place since 1973. This amounts to an average of 1.2 million abortions occurring annually in the United States. Globally, more than 125,000 abortions are committed every day. Such groups as the World Health Organization and Planned Parenthood are being used by Satan to destroy the human race.

Homosexual "Marriage"

Many countries throughout the world have now legalized so-called homosexual "marriage." Renegade courts and the votes of misguided citizens have made homosexual "marriage" a constitutionally guaranteed right and the law of the land in many countries. Regardless of the fact that only 4 percent of the population claims to be homosexual, the majority of people in the world today are in favor of homosexual "marriage" and all the disorders that flow from it, namely, sodomy, the adoption and raising of children by homosexual couples, and the teaching of all forms of sexual deviancy and disorder in public education.

Contraception

The objectification of the human person and the pursuit of hedonism and pleasure without responsibility have seen the destruction of the family. Contraception is at the root of this moral pandemic. It is estimated that as many as 90 percent of married Catholics use some form of artificial birth control, a moral travesty that lies at the root of many of the moral crises in the world.

Divorce

Divorce rates are at an all-time high. It is estimated that one-third of all marriages today end in divorce. Divorce results in many children being raised in broken homes. The breakdown of the family causes men, women, and children to suffer emotional, psychological, and spiritual wounds that are difficult to heal. Many children today grow up without a father. Annulment rates in the Catholic Church are also at an all-time high. Though the Church allows for valid separation through the annulment process, it is still a sad fact that the annulments in the United States account for 60 percent of the Catholic Church's annulments worldwide.

Pornography

Pornography is a lustful plague unleashed on the earth by the demons of hell. It is estimated that the majority of males today are first exposed to pornography around the age of 13. Many of these young men will become addicted to pornography and seek to act out their lustful fantasies in both sinful and criminal ways. Shockingly, even many women today find themselves addicted to pornography. Many psychological and healthcare professionals have emphasized that addiction to pornography is oftentimes directly linked to pedophilia, homosexuality, and other sexual disorders.

Euthanasia

A lack of respect for the dignity of the human person has caused many people to desire to terminate the life of another. This is known as euthanasia. Etymologically, the word "euthanasia" means "happy death." Yet, at its core, euthanasia is nothing more than the "legal" killing of another person. In a number of states and countries today, if a person is viewed as a financial and/or societal burden, they are liable to be put to death.

Suicide

Suicide rates worldwide are at an all-time high. The word "suicide" means "to kill oneself." Worldwide, a suicide occurs every 30 seconds. In total, there are more than 1 million suicides every year on this planet. Many are due to the extremely high rates of depression, divorce, and hopelessness experienced by a godless global society. Many so-called "right-to-die" movements have arisen worldwide that seek to put into law the "right" of a person to end their own life.

The Occult

When people turn away from belief in God, they often turn to the occult and/or self-deification. Preferring to be "spiritual" rather than religious, people who are involved in occult practices desire to have power and control over others. Evidence of the rise of the occult today is seen in the worldwide fascination with witches, spells, zombies, yoga, Reiki, Santeria, Santa Muerte, aliens, astrology, black magic, covens, Tarot cards, fortune telling, mediums, Ouija boards, psychics, Satanism, etc. It is no wonder that an increase in demonic possession has occurred globally.

Lukewarm Catholics

The majority of Catholics today do not know the Ten Commandments, how many Sacraments there are, what sin is, or that Jesus is present, Body, Blood, Soul, and Divinity, in the Eucharist. Generations experiencing poor catechesis and a lack of heroic Christian witnesses have led to ignorance and confusion in the Church. Lukewarm Catholics are largely responsible for electing deeply problematic politicians and presidents. The majority of Catholics are suffering from a deep theological crisis. Many have chosen to leave Catholicism and join Protestant sects or abandon religion altogether.

Radical Islam

Masquerading as a religion of peace, radical Islam has a two-fold goal: the universal practice of Sharia Law and the elimination of all non-Muslims. Using terrorism as their method, many followers of the false prophet Mohammed have, from the beginning of Islam's existence, openly expressed a desire to conquer Rome and destroy Christianity. Sadly, the rate of contraception being practiced in many formerly Christian countries, especially in Western Europe, will soon lead to the majority of persons in these countries being Muslim. Radical Islam poses a real threat to the foundations of civilization throughout the world. In our day, the Church must continue to promote the rosary and initiate a new crusade and Holy League against radical Islam. The weapon of this crusade must be the spiritual sword of the rosary. In recent times, Jesus himself has informed us of this important truth.

In late 2014, Jesus appeared to a Catholic bishop in Nigeria and instructed him that the rosary was the weapon to be used to overcome radical Islam. Bishop Oliver Dashe Doeme of the diocese of Maiduguri, Nigeria, claims that one evening, while he was praying his rosary, Jesus appeared to him holding a sword. During the vision, Jesus extended the sword toward the bishop. When the bishop went to take the sword from Jesus, it was miraculously transformed into a rosary! Once the bishop had the rosary-sword in his hands, Jesus looked at him and said three times, "Boko Haram is gone! Boko Haram is gone! Boko Haram is gone!" Boko Haram is the notorious radical Muslim group that violently slaughters non-Muslims by such means as decapitation or burning alive. This group also kidnaps young girls, rapes them, and then sells them as sex slaves. After the bishop of Maiduguri had his vision, he began to promote the rosary in Nigeria and around the world. In many of his interviews, he repeats his vision and informs his listeners of his interpretation of the vision in the following words: "As soon as I received the sword, it turned into a rosary. I didn't need any prophet to give me the explanation. It was clear that with the rosary we would be able to expel Boko Haram."[8]

Indeed, it is the sacred mysteries of Jesus Christ that have the power to overcome abortion, homosexual "marriage," contraception, divorce, pornography, euthanasia, suicide, the occult, lukewarm Christianity, and Islam. Do you not see the need, dear reader, for praying the rosary? Are you not alarmed by the situation?

In 2008, the 800ᵗʰ anniversary of the birth of the rosary (1208–2008), God himself inspired the Master General of the Dominicans, Fr. Carlos Azpiroz Costa, to write a letter to all the sons of St. Dominic in preparation for the 800ᵗʰ anniversary of the founding of the Order of Preachers (1216–2016). In that letter, he declared a Dominican Year of the Rosary (2008–2009) and noted the following:

> In order to provide a focus for this next year, I am proposing that we begin to renew our preaching way of life through re-discovering the rosary as a means of contemplation and an instrument of prophetic preaching. In many ways the rosary, as a uniquely Dominican contribution to the life of the Church, has slipped from our [Dominican] grasp.[9]

Father Azpiroz Costa went on to emphasize how important the rosary has been in world affairs and how it needs to be used in the world today as a means of bringing about peace:

> Our world is one that seems to be constantly torn apart by war. Uppermost in my mind is war-torn Iraq, and of course not far behind is the continual bloodshed between Israelis and Palestinians.

The 20th century was a century of wars and devastation across the planet. In the worst of these moments, people turned to the rosary praying for peace. Indeed, was that not the focus of the Fatima devotions for the conversion of Russia and was not Mary invoked as the Queen of Peace? At the same time, let us not minimize those cold wars that can go on within families, communities, and within our own hearts and souls. Cannot the rosary bring us to peace?

I have come to see the rosary as indeed a beloved universal prayer. Whether in Italy or the Ukraine, Mexico or the United States, the Philippines or Vietnam, Kenya or Nigeria, the rosary is found, prayed and loved. I believe one reason for this is because it is a tangible reality as well as a prayer. It is something almost every Catholic owns. It is given as a gift. It is a ritual whether said alone or together. It is something we can touch, hold, and even grasp at difficult moments of our life; it is like grasping the hand of Mary herself. The rosary is placed in our hands both at the "hour of our death" and afterwards when we are buried. The prayers of the rosary are summaries of our faith. Learning these prayers is like learning to talk; it is the beginning of our prayer life; and yes, it is also the end of our life of prayer "your will be done" "now and at the hour of our death." We are given a rosary in our youth, we receive a rosary when we take the habit, and a rosary is at our side when we are buried.

Brothers and Sisters, let us walk this road of renewal together. Let us set out having the confidence that Dominic had in Mary, the Mother of God.[10]

Saint Paul once instructed the Ephesians: "Take up the helmet of salvation and the sword of the Spirit, which is the word of God" (Eph 6.17). The rosary is the sword of the Spirit, forged in the New Testament, and waiting to be used by the soldier of Christ today. Father Gabriel Harty, the great Irish Dominican promoter of the rosary, wielded the sword of the rosary well into his nineties and once made the following poignant statement:

When a Dominican is clothed with the habit, he is invested with large rosary beads to hang from his belt. He is like an army officer commissioned with a sword of office, as was David when given the very sword with which he had slain Goliath: "There is no other sword like it; give it to me" (1 Sam 21:9). Any good preacher of the rosary is meant to use it not only for his own private prayer, but as an instrument of his missionary work and as a weapon of salvation. There is none like it.[11]

Who, dear reader, will wield the spiritual sword of the rosary for the Queen of Heaven today and become a champion against the darkness of our present times? Is it you?

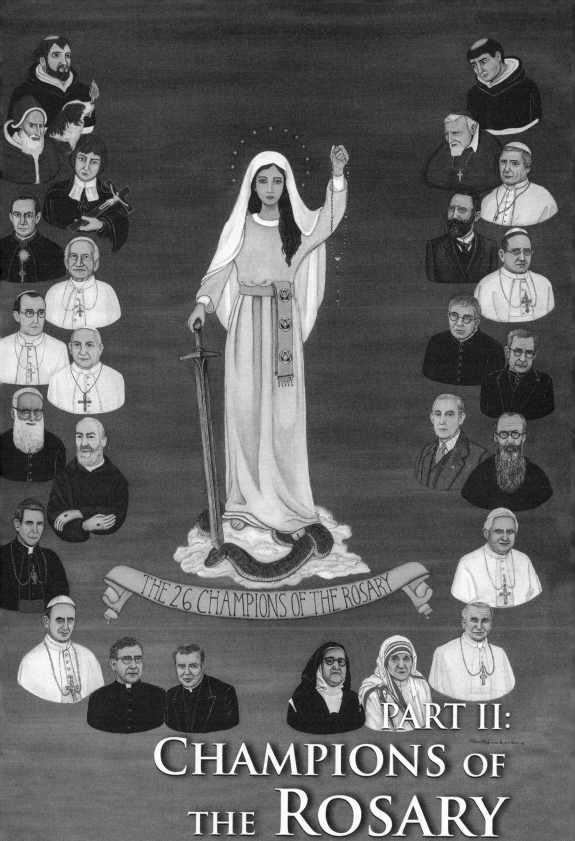

THE 26 CHAMPIONS OF THE ROSARY

PART II:
CHAMPIONS OF
THE ROSARY

I want no respite in this battle, but I shall fight to the last breath for the glory of my King and Lord. I shall not lay the sword aside until he calls me before his throne; I fear no blows, because God is my shield.

~ St. Faustina Kowalska

Put on the whole armor of God, that you may be able to stand against the wiles of the devil. For we are not contending against flesh and blood, but against the principalities, against the powers, against the world rulers of this present darkness, against the spiritual hosts of wickedness in the heavenly places. Therefore take up the whole armor of God, so that you may be able to withstand on the evil day, and having done everything, to stand firm. Stand therefore, and fasten the belt of truth around your waist, and put on the breastplate of righteousness. As shoes for your feet put on whatever will make you ready to proclaim the gospel of peace. With all of these, take the shield of faith, with which you will be able to quench all the flaming arrows of the evil one. And take the helmet of salvation, and the sword of the Spirit, which is the word of God.

~ Ephesians 6:11-17

ST. DOMINIC

The Founder of the Rosary
1170–1221

CANONIZED: July 3, 1234 by Pope Gregory IX
FEAST DAY: August 8

SAINT DOMINIC, born in Caleruega, Spain, was the founder of the Order of Preachers. His mother, Blessed Juana of Aza, while still carrying him in her womb, had a vision of a dog setting the world on fire with a torch that it carried in its mouth. The vision proved to be prophetic. In 1216, St. Dominic founded the Dominicans, who quickly became known as the *Domini canes* (the dogs of God). A renowned preacher of Christian truths, St. Dominic founded the "dogs of God" to be a band of well-formed itinerant preachers, sniffing out heresy and bringing the lost sheep of God's flock back to pasture. Through his preaching, St. Dominic was able to bring back many souls from the errors of the Albigensian heresy. He died at age 51 in Bologna, Italy.

Marian Devotion

Saint Dominic was a Marian saint who, as he walked from town to town preaching the Gospel, raised his voice in song to Our Lady by preaching her Psalter and singing the *Ave Maris Stella* (Hail, Star of the Sea). His early biographers mention that he frequently received visions of the Virgin Mary and preached about her with great fervor. In one particular vision, Jesus himself informed St. Dominic that the Dominicans were entrusted to the protection of Mary. According to Dominican tradition, part of the Dominican habit itself is said to have been given to the order by Our Lady. Saint Dominic's tender devotion to the Virgin Mary is considered to be the very foundation upon which the Order of Preachers rests. His love for Mary is further evidenced by the fact that the primitive Constitutions of the Order required all the members to profess obedience to both God *and* the Virgin Mary.

Pope Benedict XVI, in a general audience on February 3, 2010, summarized the primary elements that went into making the life and apostolic action of St. Dominic fruitful and made clear that St. Dominic's devotion to Mary took pride of place. The pope said: "In the very first place is Marian devotion which he [St. Dominic] fostered tenderly and left as a precious legacy to his spiritual sons who, in the history of the Church, have had the great merit of disseminating the prayer of the holy rosary, so dear to the Christian people and so rich in Gospel values: a true school of faith and piety."

Champion of the Rosary

According to the Dominican tradition, St. Dominic founded the rosary in the year 1208. After having devoted all his efforts to trying to win back the hearts and minds of those who had been swept away by the Albigensian heresy, St. Dominic retreated to a forest near Prouille, France, to seek guidance from heaven. It was there that the Virgin Mary entrusted the rosary to St. Dominic, instructing him in its use and implementation, and effectively making him the father of a new form of preaching and praying. With the spiritual sword of the rosary in his hand, St. Dominic's new style of preaching became effective against the Albigensians and won many back to the fullness of Christian teaching in the Catholic Church.

As part of her instructions to St. Dominic about the rosary, the Queen of Heaven informed him that the rosary was to be understood as a weapon of war and a battering ram against heresy. With this in mind, St. Dominic founded the Order of Preachers, a band of brothers known as the "dogs of God" and the Order of the Rosary. In time, the rosary would be officially recognized as part of the Dominican habit and worn on the left side in order to symbolize a sword ready to be unsheathed and taken into spiritual combat. The greatest stories of the power and effectiveness of the rosary in the life of St. Dominic are recorded in *The Secret of the Rosary* by the Third Order Dominican St. Louis de Montfort.

Saint Dominic is also credited with founding the Confraternity of the Rosary. In his zeal for promoting truth and saving souls, St. Dominic founded this association of prayer to accompany the rosary and assure its spread throughout the world. Much like the rosary itself, this movement was initially known by various other names and titles. Yet it has been affirmed by many popes that this confraternity of prayer was originally founded by St. Dominic. In all likelihood, the Confraternity of the Rosary began in the Church of St. Sixtus in Rome in 1216 and was brought to other countries such as Spain and France by St. Dominic himself.

Rosary Gems

Wonder not that until now you [St. Dominic] have obtained so little fruit by your labors; you have spent them on a barren soil, not yet watered with the dew of divine grace. When God willed to renew the face of the earth, he began by sending down on it the fertilizing rain of the Angelic Salutation. Therefore, preach my Psalter.

~ Our Lady's words to St. Dominic

Through the merits of the Virgin Mary herself and the intercession of Saint Dominic, [who was] once the excellent preacher of this Confraternity of the Rosary, this entire world was preserved.

~ Pope Alexander VI

The Albigensian heresy, then raging in a part of France, had blinded so many of the laity that they were cruelly attacking priests and clerics. Blessed Dominic lifted his eyes to heaven and turned them toward the Virgin Mary, the Mother of God. Dominic invented this method of prayer, which is easy and suitable to everyone and which is called the Rosary or the Psalter of the Blessed Virgin Mary. It consists of venerating the Blessed Virgin by reciting 150 Angelic Salutations, the same number as the Psalms of David, interrupting them at each decade by the Lord's Prayer, meanwhile meditating on the mysteries which recall the entire life of our Lord Jesus Christ. After having devised it, Dominic and his sons spread this form of prayer throughout the Church.

~ St. Pope Pius V

When he [St. Dominic] had been advised by her [Our Lady], as the tradition says, that he should preach the rosary to the people as a singular protection against heresies and vices, he carried out the task enjoined on him with wonderful fervor and success.

~ Servant of God Pope Benedict XIII

Saint Dominic, seeing that the gravity of people's sins was hindering the conversion of the Albigensians, withdrew into a forest near Toulouse where he prayed unceasingly for three days and three nights. During this time he did nothing but weep and do harsh penances in order to appease the anger of Almighty God. He used his discipline so much that his body was lacerated, and finally he fell into a coma. At this point Our Lady appeared to him, accompanied by three angels, and she said: "Dear Dominic, do you know which weapon the Blessed Trinity wants to use to reform the world?" "Oh, my Lady," answered Saint Dominic, "you know far better than I do because next to your Son Jesus Christ you have always been the chief instrument of our salvation." Then Our Lady replied: "I want you to know that, in this kind of warfare, the battering ram has always been the Angelic Psalter [the Hail Mary] which is the foundation stone of the New Testament. Therefore if you want to reach these hardened souls and win them over to God, preach my Psalter."

~ St. Louis de Montfort

As long as priests followed Saint Dominic's example and preached devotion to the holy rosary, piety and fervor thrived throughout the Christian world and in those religious orders which were devoted to the rosary. But since people have neglected this gift from heaven, all kinds of sin and disorder have spread far and wide.

~ St. Louis de Montfort

All during life, Saint Dominic had nothing more at heart than to praise Our Lady, to preach her greatness and to inspire everybody to honor her by saying the rosary.

~ St. Louis de Montfort

Saint Dominic was so convinced of the efficacy of the holy rosary and of its great value that, when he heard confessions, he hardly ever gave any other penance.

~ St. Louis de Montfort

Blanche of Castille, Queen of France, was deeply grieved because twelve years after her marriage she was still childless. When Saint Dominic went to see her he advised her to say her rosary every day to ask God for the grace of motherhood, and she faithfully carried out his advice. In 1213 she gave birth to her eldest child, Philip, but the child died in infancy. The Queen's fervor was nowise dulled by this disappointment; on the contrary, she sought Our Lady's help more than ever before. She had a large number of rosaries given out to all members of the court and also to people in several cities of the kingdom, asking them to join her in entreating God for a blessing that this time would be complete. Thus, in 1215, Saint Louis was born — the prince who was to become the glory of France and the model of all Christian kings.

~ St. Louis de Montfort

When our Blessed Lady gave the holy rosary to Saint Dominic she ordered him to say it every day and to get others to say it daily. Saint Dominic never let anyone join the Confraternity unless he were fully determined to say it every day.

~ St. Louis de Montfort

After St. Dominic had founded the Order of Preachers, it was his desire to put an end to the errors of the Albigensians. Moved by divine inspiration, he began to implore the help of the Immaculate Mother of God, to whom alone it has been given to wipe out all the heresies in the universe, and he preached the rosary as an infallible protection against heresies and vices.

~ Blessed Pope Pius IX

You know how the [rosary] devotion came about; how, at a time when heresy was very widespread, and had called in the aid of sophistry, that can so powerfully aid infidelity against religion, God inspired St. Dominic to institute and spread this devotion. It seems so simple and easy, but you know God chooses the small things of the world to humble the great. Of course, it was first of all for the poor and simple, but not for them only, for everyone who has practiced the devotion knows that there is in it a soothing sweetness that there is in nothing else.

~ Blessed John Henry Newman

Under her [Mary's] inspiration, strong with her might, great men were raised up — illustrious for their sanctity no less than for their apostolic spirit — to beat off the attacks of wicked adversaries and to lead souls back into the virtuous ways of Christian life, firing them with a consuming love of the things of God. One such man, an army in himself, was Dominic Guzman [St. Dominic]. Putting all his trust in Our Lady's rosary, he set himself fearlessly to the accomplishment of both these tasks with happy results.

~ Pope Leo XIII

Great in the integrity of his doctrine, in his example of virtue, and by his apostolic labors, he [St. Dominic] proceeded undauntedly to attack the enemies of the Catholic Church, not by force of arms; but trusting wholly to that devotion which he was the first to institute under the name of the holy rosary, which was disseminated through the length and breadth of the earth by him and his pupils. Guided, in fact, by divine inspiration and grace, he foresaw that this devotion, like a most powerful warlike weapon, would be the means of putting the enemy to flight, and of confounding their audacity and mad impiety. Such was indeed its result. Thanks to this new method of prayer — when adopted and properly carried out as instituted by the Holy Father St. Dominic — piety, faith, and union began to return, and the projects and devices of the heretics to fall to pieces. Many wanderers also returned to the way of salvation, and the wrath of the impious was restrained by the arms of those Catholics who had determined to repel their violence.

~ Pope Leo XIII

That great saint [St. Dominic], divinely enlightened, perceived that no remedy would be more adapted to the evils of his time than that men should return to Christ, who "is the way, the truth, and the life," by frequent meditation on the salvation obtained for us by him, and should seek the intercession with God of that Virgin, to whom it is given to destroy all heresies. He therefore so composed the rosary as to recall the mysteries of our salvation in succession, and the subject of meditation is mingled and, as it were, interlaced with the Angelic Salutation and with the prayer addressed to God, the Father of Our Lord Jesus Christ.

~ Pope Leo XIII

The Mother of God taught the rosary to the patriarch [St.] Dominic in order that he might propagate it.

~ Pope Leo XIII

Loving the Blessed Virgin as a Mother, confiding chiefly in her patronage, Dominic started his battle for the Faith. The Albigenses, among other dogmas, attacked both the Divine maternity and the virginity of Mary. He, attacked by them with every insult, defending to the utmost of his strength the sanctity of these dogmas, invoked the help of the Virgin Mother herself, frequently using these words: "Make me worthy to praise thee, Sacred Virgin; give me strength against thine enemies." How pleased was the Heavenly Queen with her pious servant may be easily gathered from this, that she used his ministry to teach the most holy rosary to the Church, the Spouse of her Son; that prayer which, being both vocal and mental, in the contemplation especially of the mysteries of religion. Rightly, then, did Dominic order his followers, in preaching to the people, to inculcate frequently this manner of prayer, the utility of which he had experienced.

~ Pope Benedict XV

The battle around the humanity of Christ begins anew with the Albigensians in the Middle Ages. St. Dominic steps forth and selects as foundation for his effectiveness the proclamation of the faith in the illustrious motherhood of Mary, the frequent repetition of the Hail Mary. The rosary becomes a Summa Theologica, *a catechism for the people which has the double character of being both a prayer and teacher. From it, the Dominican preachers drew both the contents and armor for their sermons.*

~ Servant of God Joseph Kentenich

To her [Mary] is given the office of destroying heresies throughout the world. Dominic received from her, according to tradition, the admonition to preach the rosary as a singularly effective weapon against heresy and vice, and the fervor and success with which he carried out the task entrusted to him are truly amazing.

~ Blessed James Alberione

In his spirituality, St. Dominic used to have recourse also to material means in prayer; and among other endeavors he made use of the beads to count the "Hail Marys." Then, noting the people's ignorance concerning religion, and having to combat the Albigensians who denied the fundamental truths of Christianity, Dominic, inspired by God, thought it well to have the people meditate a truth or mystery every ten "Hail Marys." Thus, while giving to the people an easy manner of praying, he also gave a simple means of instruction.

~ Blessed James Alberione

St. Dominic wanted these mysteries [of the rosary] recalled every day, that they might be well impressed on the mind and never be forgotten.

~ Blessed James Alberione

St. Dominic, who died in 1221, received from the Blessed Mother the command to preach and to popularize this devotion [the rosary] for the good of souls, for conquest over evil, and for the prosperity of Holy Mother Church and thus gave us the rosary in its present classical form.

~ Venerable Fulton J. Sheen

The tradition given great weight by many popes has it that early in the thirteenth century the Blessed Mother told St. Dominic to preach the rosary. By means of this formidable weapon he was able to roll back another great tide of heresy threatening the Church, and with St. Francis of Assisi, to leave a revitalized faith to the Middle Ages.

~ Servant of God Patrick J. Peyton

The traditional image of Our Lady of the Rosary portrays Mary with one arm supporting the Child Jesus and with the other offering the rosary beads to Saint Dominic. This important iconography shows that the rosary is a means given by the Virgin to contemplate Jesus and, in meditating on his life, to love him and follow him ever more faithfully.

~ Pope Benedict XVI

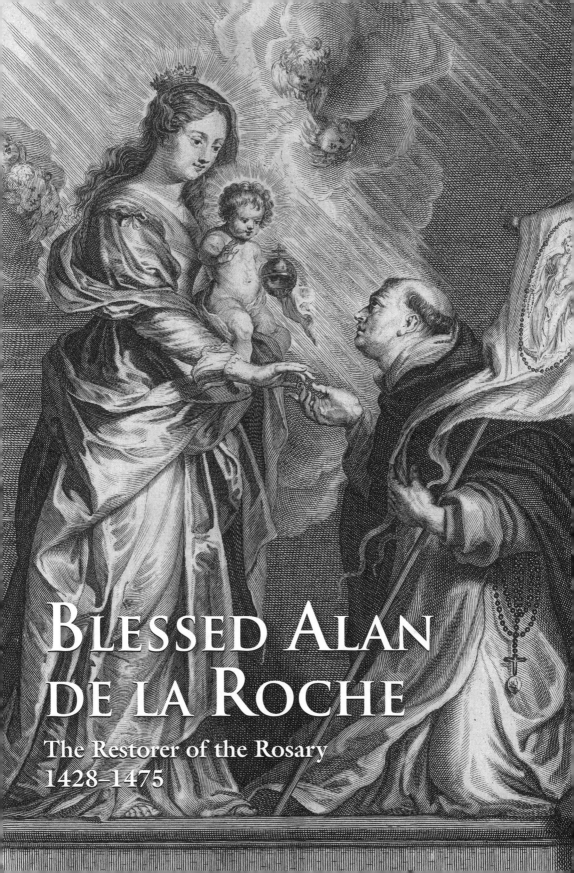

Blessed Alan de la Roche

The Restorer of the Rosary
1428–1475

BLESSED ALAN DE LA ROCHE was born in Brittany and entered the Dominicans at an early age. He was a faithful spiritual son of St. Dominic. After making his profession of vows, he studied in Paris, where he became a distinguished lecturer of sacred theology. As a priest, he taught theology in Lille, Douai, and Ghent, and at one point was also designated by his superiors to serve as the official visitator for Dominican houses in central Europe. He was a renowned preacher and got involved in the Observant Reform Movement within the Dominicans that sought to return their order to the faithful observance of the ideals of their founder. Blessed Alan died on September 8, 1475, the Feast of Our Lady's Birth, in Zwolle, Holland.

The Dominicans have traditionally accorded Alan the title of "Blessed," and he is universally acclaimed by the Church as such, though he has never been formally beatified. In certain countries, Catholic parishes have been named after him and have even bestowed on him the title "St. Alan." There are many devotional statues depicting Bl. Alan in churches around the world, and many Dominican priests and brothers continue to take "Alan" as part of their religious name. In the old Dominican Breviary, Bl. Alan was celebrated with a special feast day. Today, though he has no official feast, he is unofficially honored on the date of his death, September 8.

Marian Devotion

According to Dominican tradition, Bl. Alan experienced a deeper conversion of life through the intercession of the Blessed Virgin Mary. In *The Secret of the Rosary,* the Third Order Dominican St. Louis de Montfort noted that, in his youth, Bl. Alan was horribly tempted by devils and fell into many sins, but, through Mary's intercession, was given the ability to overcome Satan and his devices. The English translation of Bl. Alan's name is "Alan of the Rock." After his conversion, he adhered firmly to the teachings of the Church, joined the Dominicans, and became a devout friar and zealous preacher in the service of the Queen of Heaven. It is said that during his priestly life, he never began any endeavor, whether mundane or sacred, without first saying a Hail Mary.

Blessed Alan's love for Mary was so intense that, like many other chivalric saints, he was given the title "new spouse of Mary." His love for the Virgin of virgins was so pure and virtuous that he was considered another St. Joseph. Other Marian saints who were privileged to bear this same title include St. Edmund Rich, St. Hermann Joseph, and St. John Eudes. For his part, in his visions, Bl. Alan was even given a necklace made of Mary's hair and presented with a ring that symbolized the spiritual marriage existing between himself and the Virgin. In one of his visions, Mary appeared to him and placed the ring on his finger herself. (See the image on the previous page for an artistic depiction of this event).

Champion of the Rosary

During his life, Bl. Alan received many visions from Jesus, Mary, and St. Dominic. Almost all of these visions centered on the rosary and heaven's desire for him to renew it. Commanded and commissioned to be the one to restore the rosary devotion, Bl. Alan was at first reluctant to follow heaven's directions. It was only after being rebuked by Jesus for having the knowledge and influence as a son of St. Dominic to bring about a renewal in the rosary and failing to do so that Bl. Alan put all his fears behind him and became the great restorer of the rosary devotion and the Confraternity of the Rosary.

In order to restore the rosary and its Confraternity, Bl. Alan wrote several historical books and manuals that taught others how to pray the rosary. His manuals helped to bring about the restoration of the Confraternity of the Rosary in Douai, France, in 1470. Five years after his successful renewal of the rosary and its Confraternity, his Dominican confrere Fr. Jacob Sprenger established a confraternity in Cologne, Germany, on September 8, 1475, the very day that Bl. Alan died. The confraternity in Cologne would be the first officially recognized confraternity to be renewed because the Holy Roman Emperor Frederick III was a member and petitioned the pope for approval. Unfortunately, due to wars, persecutions, and the burning of many Catholic libraries, especially those of the Dominicans, none of Bl. Alan's original manuscripts exist today.

Rosary Gems

The rosary in particular is a sign of predestination. Our fidelity in reciting it is a sure sign of salvation.

~ Blessed Alan de la Roche

All priests say a Hail Mary with the faithful before preaching, to ask for God's grace. They do this because of a revelation that Saint Dominic had from Our Lady. "My son," she said one day, "do not be surprised that your sermons fail to bear the results you had hoped for. You are trying to cultivate a piece of ground which has not had any rain. Now when Almighty God planned to renew the face of the earth, he started by sending down rain from heaven — and this was the Angelic Salutation. In this way God made over the world.

~ Blessed Alan de La Roche

One day when he [Blessed Alan] was saying Mass, Our Lord, who wished to spur him on to preach the holy rosary, spoke to him in the Sacred Host: "How can you crucify me again so soon?" Jesus said. "What did you say, Lord?" asked Blessed Alan, horrified. "You crucified me once before by your sins," answered Jesus, "and I would willingly be crucified again rather than have my Father offended by the sins you used to commit. You are crucifying me again now because you have all the learning and understanding that you need to preach my mother's rosary, and you are not doing so. If you only did this you could teach many souls the right path and lead them away from sin — but you are not doing it."

~ St. Louis de Montfort

Our Lady, too, spoke to him [Blessed Alan] one day to inspire him to preach the holy rosary more and more: "You were a great sinner in your youth," she said, "but I obtained the grace of your conversion from my Son. Had such a thing been possible I would have liked to have gone through all kinds of suffering to save you because converted sinners are a glory to me. And I would have done this also to make you worthy of preaching my rosary far and wide."

~ St. Louis de Montfort

Saint Dominic appeared to Blessed Alan as well and told him of the great results of his ministry: he [St. Dominic] had preached the holy rosary unceasingly, his sermons had borne great fruit and many people had been converted during his missions. He said to Blessed Alan: "See the wonderful results I have had through preaching the holy rosary! You and all those who love Our Lady ought to do the same so that, by means of this holy practice of the rosary, you may draw all people to the real science of the virtues."

~ St. Louis de Montfort

One day Our Lady said to Blessed Alan: "Just as Almighty God chose the Angelic Salutation to bring about the Incarnation of his Word and the redemption of mankind, in the same way those who want to bring about moral reforms and who want people reborn in Jesus Christ must honor me and greet me with the same salutation. I am the channel by which God came to men, and so, next to my son Jesus Christ, it is through me that men must obtain grace and virtue."

~ St. Louis de Montfort

One day Our Lady said to Blessed Alan: "I want people who have a devotion to my rosary to have my Son's grace and blessing during their lifetime and at their death, and after their death I want them to be freed from all slavery so that they will be like kings wearing crowns and with scepters in their hands and enjoying eternal glory."

~ St. Louis de Montfort

Our Lady also said to Blessed Alan: "I want you to know that, although there are numerous indulgences already attached to the recitation of my rosary, I shall add many more to every fifty Hail Marys (each group of five decades) for those who say them devoutly, on their knees — being, of course, free from mortal sin. And whosoever shall persevere in the devotion of the holy rosary, saying these prayers and meditations, shall be rewarded for it; I shall obtain for him full remission of the penalty and of the guilt of all his sins at the end of this life."

~ St. Louis de Montfort

One day Our Lord said to Blessed Alan: "If only these poor wretched sinners would say my rosary, they would share in the merits of my passion and I would be their Advocate and would appease my Father's justice."

~ St. Louis de Montfort

Blessed Alan said that a man he knew of had desperately tried all kinds of devotions to rid himself of the evil spirit who possessed him, but without success. Finally he thought of wearing the rosary around his neck, which eased him considerably. He discovered that whenever he took it off the devil tormented him cruelly, so he resolved to wear it night and day. This drove the evil spirit away forever, because he could not bear such a terrible chain. Blessed Alan also testified that he had delivered a large number of people who were possessed by putting the rosary around their necks.

~ St. Louis de Montfort

Blessed Alan says that he has seen several people delivered from Satan's bondage after taking up the holy rosary, even though they had previously sold themselves to him in body and soul by renouncing their baptismal vows and their allegiance to Our Lord Jesus Christ.

~ St. Louis de Montfort

Blessed Alan writes that many of the [Dominican] brethren had appeared to them while reciting the rosary, and had declared that next to the Holy Sacrifice of the Mass there was no more powerful means than the rosary to help the suffering souls [in purgatory]. Numerous souls were released daily who otherwise would have been obliged to remain in purgatory for years.

~ St. Alphonsus Liguori

Blessed Alan relates the story of a noble lady of Aragon named Alexandra, who had been the cause of jealousy and hatred among several young men of her city. As a result of this rivalry, she was killed, and her body cast into a well. St. Dominic, who had converted her, recommended her to the Confraternity of the Holy Rosary, and himself said many prayers to Mary for the repose of the lady Alexandra's soul. The latter appeared to thank him in the name of the souls who were suffering in purgatory with her, and to beg him to preach everywhere the practice of the rosary in suffrage, because they enjoyed the greatest relief through it.

~ Blessed James Alberione

May he [St. Joseph] obtain for us the ability of Father St. Dominic, St. Vincent Ferrer, and Blessed Alan de la Roche to promote the rosary.

~ Blessed Gabriele Allegra

St. Pope Pius V

The Dominican Pope of the Rosary
1504–1572

PAPACY: 1556–1572
BEATIFIED: May 1, 1672 by Pope Clement X
CANONIZED: May 22, 1712 by Pope Clement XI
FEAST DAY: April 30

SAINT POPE PIUS V was 14 years old when he entered the Dominicans. A disciplined and learned man, Divine Providence elevated him to the papacy to be the "dog of God" who would bark against the Protestant rebellion and attack the Islamic Turks who desired to conquer Christianity and Western Civilization. As a reforming pontiff, he was very zealous in reforming the laxity of the clergy as well as the moral corruption of many in the hierarchy. He is responsible for the successful implementation of the decrees of the Council of Trent and the standardization of the liturgy. Though extremely busy as the Vicar of Christ, he remained very devoted to his religious order and wore his white Dominican habit under his papal attire. According to most historians, he set the precedent for all subsequent popes to wear a white cassock as part of their papal attire.

Marian Devotion

In his zeal for standardizing the liturgy, St. Pope Pius V revised the Divine Office (Liturgy of the Hours) in 1568. As part of the revision, he inserted the complete version of the Hail Mary prayer (already in use in other breviaries) into the universal Roman Breviary. This action officially established the complete Hail Mary prayer — the exact version we pray today — as the universally approved formula. The complete version of the Hail Mary did not originate with the pontificate of St. Pope Pius V, since it had been in use since the 14th century, but to his perpetual honor and credit, he established it as the universal norm.

In response to the Protestant rebellion, St. Pope Pius V issued the *Catechism of the Council of Trent*. This catechism included the official Church teachings on the Virgin Mary. As a friend of St. Charles Borromeo, the reforming cardinal and bishop of Milan, St. Pope Pius V was very supportive of Borromeo's efforts to champion the rosary against the Protestants. He especially supported Borromeo's defense of Catholicism by emphasizing the necessary role of the Virgin Mary in the life of Christ and the Church. Saint Pope Pius V is buried in the greatest Marian church of the Catholic world, the Basilica of Santa Maria Maggiore in Rome.

Champion of the Rosary

Saint Pope Pius V was one of the greatest papal champions of the rosary. He authored two extraordinary documents on the rosary, promoted the rosary as *the* means of conquering Islam, and established a liturgical feast in honor of the rosary. His first document on the rosary, titled *Consueverunt Romani Pontifices,* was promulgated on September 17, 1569. Along with praising the rosary, this apostolic letter contains many statements affirming the pious tradition and encourages the frequent recitation of the rosary, especially in response to ongoing threats from the Muslims.

In response to the threat of invasion from the Ottoman Turks (Muslims), St. Pope Pius V formed a Holy League, an army to beat back the forces of Islam. Knowing the power of the rosary, he intentionally established the Holy League on the Feast of St. Dominic. As part of his efforts to defeat the Muslims, he asked Christians throughout the world, especially in Italy, to pray for victory over the Muslims by gathering together and praying the rosary. He himself gathered people together in Rome at the Dominican church of Santa Maria Sopra Minerva and prayed the rosary for this intention. His prayers and the prayers of all the faithful were heard. As historical records attest, before news had reached Rome that the Muslims had been defeated at the Battle of Lepanto, St. Pius V had already received a vision in which he saw Our Lady and knew with certainty that the battle had been won by the Holy League.

In gratitude for the victory at Lepanto, and convinced that the victory had come through the rosary campaign he initiated, he promulgated his second rosary document, *Salvatoris Domini,* on March 15, 1572. In this document, he directed that a feast be celebrated every year on October 7 as a commemoration of the victory over the Muslims. The feast was appropriately titled Our Lady of Victory. In the same document, in order to give special recognition to the role the rosary played in the Battle of Lepanto, he also established Rosary Sunday. This annual liturgical celebration was to be held on the first Sunday of October, and those who participated in the celebrations were granted a plenary indulgence. He also granted a plenary indulgence to anyone who joined the Confraternity of the Rosary.

Rosary Gems

[Saint] Dominic invented this method of prayer, which is easy and suitable to everyone and which is called the Rosary or the Psalter of the Blessed Virgin Mary. It consists of venerating this Blessed Virgin by reciting 150 Angelic Salutations, the same number as the Psalms of David, interrupting them at each decade by the Lord's Prayer, meanwhile meditating on the mysteries which recall the entire life of our Lord Jesus Christ.

~ St. Pope Pius V

After having devised it [the rosary], Dominic and his sons [the Dominicans] spread this form of prayer throughout the Church. The faithful welcomed it with fervor, were soon set on fire by this meditation and were transformed into other men; the darkness of heresy receded; the light of the faith reappeared, and the Friars of the same Order, legitimately commissioned by their Superiors, founded associations of the rosary everywhere, in which the faithful had themselves enrolled.

~ St. Pope Pius V

This devotion [the rosary], which reverently honors both the principal mysteries of Christ and her who alone has crushed every heresy of the 13th century and later on, often defeated the enemies of the Church. Rightly, therefore, we must hope that the same power [of the rosary] will repulse the errors of hell, will annihilate the machinations of godlessness, will remove from the people the errors that have been propagated and, with it, the great upheaval that convulses all mankind.

~ St. Pope Pius V

By the rosary the darkness of heresy has been dispelled, and the light of the Catholic Faith shines out in all its brilliancy.

~ St. Pope Pius V

Inspired by the Holy Ghost, as is piously believed, Blessed Dominic, Founder of the Order of Friar-Preachers, in a time like the present, when France was infested by the Albigensian heresy, which had blinded so many followers of this world that they raved against the priests of the Lord, raising his eyes to heaven, and seeking some easy and good method of prayer to God, which should be within the reach of all, devised the Rosary or Psalter of the Blessed Virgin.

~ St. Pope Pius V

Saint Pius V, one of the greatest Popes who ever ruled the Church, said the rosary every day.

~ St. Louis de Montfort

It is said that the Pontiff [St. Pius V] knew by Divine Revelation of the victory of Lepanto achieved at that very moment when through the Catholic world the pious sodalities of the holy rosary implored the aid of Mary in that formula initiated by the Founder of the Friar Preachers and diffused far and wide by his followers.

~ Pope Benedict XV

In the 16th century, the archenemy [the Turks] threatened all the port cities of the Mediterranean with its terrible fleet. Pius V brought together an armada in union with Spain, Venice, and the Knights of Malta, with Don Juan as admiral. Pius himself, a second Moses, set himself at the head of a storm of prayer. At his word, the rosary was prayed by all Christianity in order to secure Mary's favor in the decisive battle upon which the fate of Italy and all Europe depended.

~ Servant of God Joseph Kentenich

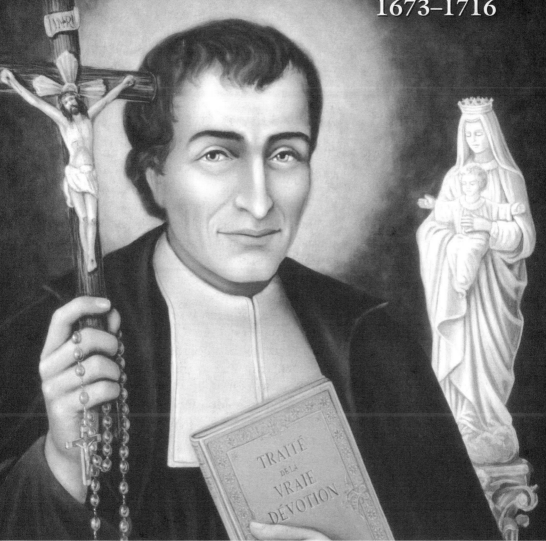

St. Louis de Montfort

The Preacher of the Rosary
1673–1716

BEATIFIED: January 22, 1888 by Pope Leo XIII
CANONIZED: July 20, 1947 by Venerable Pope Pius XII
FEAST DAY: April 28

SAINT LOUIS DE MONTFORT was born in Brittany in 1673. As a zealous preacher of the eternal wisdom of Jesus Christ, the Cross, and the Virgin Mary, he walked over 18,000 miles on foot all throughout Europe in the course of his evangelization efforts. In 1706, Pope Clement XI confirmed the fruitfulness of his preaching ministry and commissioned him to be an apostolic missionary. He founded two religious communities: the Missionaries of the Company of Mary (Montfort Fathers) and the Daughters of Wisdom. He conducted missions at over 200 parishes and authored many books that are acclaimed as classics of Catholic theology and spirituality. On one occasion while preaching, he punched and knocked out several intoxicated hecklers because they were mocking the subject of his message, namely, Jesus and Mary. Saint Louis de Montfort was a force to be reckoned with! He died at age 43 and was buried in Saint-Laurent-sur-Sèvre, France, in the basilica named after him. He was canonized in 1947.

Marian Devotion

Saint Louis de Montfort is one of the greatest Marian saints of all time, if not *the* greatest. His most famous work on Our Lady is the Marian masterpiece *True Devotion to the Blessed Virgin*. For 126 years, it lay hidden in a chest buried in a field until it was re-discovered in 1842. After it was found and published, it quickly became *the* primary Mariological work referenced by all subsequent Marian saints, scholars, and popes. *True Devotion to the Blessed Virgin* has been published in over 300 editions and translated into more than 20 languages. Saint Louis de Montfort is known as *the* saint of Marian consecration. He also authored the very popular book *The Secret of Mary*.

The Marian devotion of St. Louis de Montfort is superlative. Synthesizing the Marian teachings of the first 17 centuries of the Church, he preached and wrote about Mary as the "Lady of breathless beauty," the masterpiece of God's creation, and the surest and most effective way to truly follow Jesus Christ. There have been few saints who have so beautifully and succinctly expressed the essence of Marian devotion as St. Louis de Montfort. He taught that as the Mother of God and the spiritual mother of God's children, Mary is the aqueduct and Mediatrix of All Grace, the heart of the Mystical Body of Christ, the air we breathe, the quickest and easiest way to Jesus, and the mold of saints. As the mold for creaturely holiness, Mary is understood by St. Louis to be the ultimate saint-maker and thus a necessary mediatrix in our sanctification. For anyone who desires to go deeper into Marian devotion and piety, there is no substitute for reading the original works of St. Louis de Montfort. In God's time, St. Louis de Montfort's Marian genius may well be cause for the Church to declare him a Doctor of the Church.

Champion of the Rosary

Saint Louis de Montfort is the author of the greatest book ever written on the rosary, *The Secret of the Rosary*. Similar to *True Devotion,* it was unknown during his lifetime and only re-discovered in the mid-19th century. Since it was first published in 1911, millions and millions of copies have been made and countless translations undertaken. Through *The Secret of the Rosary,* the Church and the world were once again made aware of the importance of the rosary in the lives of St. Dominic and Bl. Alan de la Roche. Saint Louis de Montfort titled his book *The Secret of the Rosary* because so few souls truly know the secret of sanctity that is contained and hidden in the blessed beads of Our Lady. There is no other book that gives so much honor to the rosary. Its author can truly be said to be an apostle, a champion, and the greatest writer on the rosary in the history of the Church.

Saint Louis de Montfort loved the rosary so much that he became a Third Order Dominican on November 10, 1710. He obtained permission from the Master General of the Order of Preachers to preach the rosary everywhere he went and established confraternities of the rosary during his missions. It is estimated that he enrolled over 100,000 people in the Confraternity of the Rosary during his lifetime. He especially recommended the rosary to priests as a means of converting as many souls as possible and taught that the rosary offers grace in this life and glory in the next. Just as St. Dominic used the rosary to overcome the Albigensians in the 13th century, so did St. Louis use the rosary to preach against the Jansenists in the 18th century. As an apostolic missionary and a Third Order Dominican, he wore a 15-decade rosary from his belt as a spiritual sword. The practice of including the Apostles' Creed, the initial Our Father, and three Hail Marys at the beginning of the rosary, as well as assigning a fruit to each mystery, is attributed to his preaching.

Rosary Gems

This [the rosary] is one of the greatest secrets to have come down from heaven.

~ St. Louis de Montfort

It would hardly be possible for me to put into words how much Our Lady thinks of the holy rosary and of how she vastly prefers it to all other devotions.

~ St. Louis de Montfort

Almighty God has given it [the rosary] to you because he wants you to use it as a means to convert the most hardened sinners and the most obstinate heretics. He has attached to it grace in this life and glory in the next.

~ St. Louis de Montfort

When the Holy Spirit has revealed this secret [of the rosary] to a priest and director of souls, how blessed is that priest! If a priest really understands this secret he will say the rosary every day and will encourage others to say it.

~ St. Louis de Montfort

Let all men, the learned and the ignorant, the just and the sinners, the great and the small praise and honor Jesus and Mary, night and day, by saying the most holy rosary.

~ St. Louis de Montfort

I beg of you to beware of thinking of the rosary as something of little importance — as do ignorant people and even several great but proud scholars. Far from being insignificant, the rosary is a priceless treasure which is inspired by God.

~ St. Louis de Montfort

Since the holy rosary is composed, principally and in substance, of the prayer of Christ and the Angelic Salutation, that is, the Our Father and the Hail Mary, it was without doubt the first prayer and the first devotion of the faithful and has been in use all through the centuries, from the time of the apostles and disciples down to the present.

~ St. Louis de Montfort

When people say the rosary together it is far more formidable to the devil than one said privately, because in this public prayer it is an army that is attacking him. He can often overcome the prayer of an individual, but if this prayer is joined to that of other Christians, the devil has much more trouble in getting the best of it. It is very easy to break a single stick, but if you join it to others to make a bundle it cannot be broken.

~ St. Louis de Montfort

Our Lady has shown her thorough approval of the name Rosary; she has revealed to several people that each time they say a Hail Mary they are giving her a beautiful rose and that each complete rosary makes her a crown of roses.

~ St. Louis de Montfort

The rose is the queen of flowers, and so the rosary is the rose of all devotions and it is therefore the most important one.

~ St. Louis de Montfort

Nobody can condemn devotion to the holy rosary without condemning all that is most holy in the Catholic Faith, such as the Lord's Prayer, the Angelic Salutation and the mysteries of the life, death and glory of Jesus Christ and of his holy Mother.

~ St. Louis de Montfort

I promise you that if you practice this devotion and help to spread it you will learn more from the rosary than from any spiritual book.

~ St. Louis de Montfort

Never will anyone who says his rosary every day become a formal heretic or be led astray by the devil. This is a statement that I would gladly sign with my blood.

~ St. Louis de Montfort

Arm yourselves with the arms of God — with the holy rosary — and you will crush the devil's head and you will stand firm in the face of all his temptations. This is why even the material rosary itself is such a terrible thing for the devil, and why the saints have used it to enchain devils and to chase them out of the bodies of people who were possessed.

~ St. Louis de Montfort

It must not be thought that the rosary is only for women and for simple and ignorant people; it is also for men and for the greatest of men.

~ St. Louis de Montfort

Please do not scorn this beautiful and heavenly tree, but plant it with your hands in the garden of your soul, making the resolution to say your rosary every day.

~ St. Louis de Montfort

Somebody who says his rosary alone only gains the merit of one rosary, but if he says it together with thirty other people he gains the merit of thirty rosaries. This is the law of public prayer. How profitable, how advantageous this is!

~ St. Louis de Montfort

If a Church or a chapel is not available, say the rosary together in your own or a neighbor's house.

~ St. Louis de Montfort

If you say the rosary faithfully until death, I do assure you that, in spite of the gravity of your sins you shall receive a never fading crown of glory. Even if you are on the brink of damnation, even if you have one foot in hell, even if you have sold your soul to the devil as sorcerers do who practice black magic, and even if you are a heretic as obstinate as a devil, sooner or later you will be converted and will amend your life and save your soul, if — and mark well what I say — if you say the holy rosary devoutly every day until death for the purpose of knowing the truth and obtaining contrition and pardon for your sins.

~ St. Louis de Montfort

To become perfect, say a rosary a day.

~ St. Louis de Montfort

True servants of the Blessed Virgin, like Dominic of old, will range far and wide, with the holy Gospel issuing from their mouths like a bright and burning flame, and the rosary in their hands, and being like your watchdogs, burn like fire and dispel the darkness of the world like a sun.

~ St. Louis de Montfort

ST. ALPHONSUS LIGUORI

The Doctor of the Rosary
1696–1787

BEATIFIED: September 15, 1816 by Pope Pius VII
CANONIZED: May 26, 1839 by Pope Gregory XVI
DOCTOR OF THE CHURCH: March 23, 1871 by Bl. Pope Pius IX
FEAST DAY: August 1

SAINT ALPHONSUS LIGUORI was born near Naples and lived to be 90 years old. Gifted with an incredible intellect, he obtained a doctorate in law from the University of Naples at the age of 16. After many years practicing law, he abandoned his law practice, studied to become a priest, and quickly became one of the greatest moral theologians in the history of the Church. He authored a mammoth collection of theological and devotional writings, penning more than 100 publications. During his lifetime, he was consecrated a bishop, founded the Congregation of the Most Holy Redeemer (Redemptorists), and was a major promoter of frequent visits to the Blessed Sacrament.

Marian Devotion

From his youth, St. Alphonsus had a pious and filial love toward the Virgin Mary. He learned much of his Marian devotion from his devout and saintly mother. On the day of the conferral of his doctorate degree — at the age of 16 — he knelt down before the entire faculty of the University of Naples and professed a solemn oath to defend the truth of Mary's Immaculate Conception. In his day, this truth was not defended by all Catholics because the dogma of the Immaculate Conception would not be defined until 1854. Throughout his life and priestly ministry, he always promoted and defended the Immaculate Conception of Mary in all of his Marian writings. After his death, heaven rewarded his efforts to promote the Immaculate Conception. In 1871, he was declared a Doctor of the Church by the same pope, Bl. Pope Pius IX, who proclaimed the Dogma of the Immaculate Conception in 1854.

The story of how St. Alphonsus responded to the call from God to become a priest manifests his unmistakable Marian character. When he gave up his legal practice and decided to become a priest, he went to the statue of Our Lady of Mercy in the Church of Our Lady of Ransom in Naples, knelt down, took off his cavalier's sword and placed it at the feet of the statue of Mary. This action symbolized that he no longer desired to be a servant of the mundane, but a servant and knight of the Queen of Heaven. He fasted every Saturday in honor of Our Lady. As a priest and theologian, he became one of the most important Marian authors of the 18th century. His Marian influence on clergy and laity alike was tremendous. He often preached on the notion that Mary was a new Noah's ark in which sinners could find refuge from the storms of life.

In 1750, he published his Marian masterpiece, *The Glories of Mary*. This book took him 16 years to write. Because St. Louis de Montfort's books were not discovered until 1842, *The Glories of Mary* had a head start, and so has the privilege of being the most widely distributed Marian book of all time. It has gone through over 800 editions and been translated into dozens of languages. Though he had no knowledge of the Marian works of St. Louis de Montfort, *The Glories of Mary* has many similarities to the works of St. Louis de Montfort and was likewise meant to counter the Jansenism of his day. Like St. Alphonsus had done with all of his books, it was written in front of an image of Our Lady of Good Counsel that the saint kept on his desk. In the opening paragraphs of *The Glories of Mary*, he states that he owes everything to Mary and notes that it is his great desire to spread devotion to her. He taught that Mary's mantle serves as a protective cloak for sinners and, after the honor we owe Jesus Christ, we are to give chief place in our hearts to the love of Mary, our spiritual mother. He composed hymns to Mary, painted images of her, and wrote a commentary on the *Salve Regina*. He was so well loved by the pope that he was consecrated a bishop at the Dominican Church of Santa Maria Sopra Minerva in Rome in 1762. He died as the *Angelus* was being prayed, holding an image of Mary in his hands.

Champion of the Rosary

As a Doctor of the Church, St. Alphonsus is sometimes also referred to as the "Doctor of Prayer." One of the prayers he prayed every day was the rosary. He was so devoted to the rosary that, toward the end of his life when his memory was slowly fading, he often expressed concern to those around him if he was uncertain that he had prayed his rosary on that particular day. The rosary was his daily companion till the end.

It is truly amazing to think that St. Alphonsus lived in the same century as St. Louis de Montfort, but did not know of the existence of *The Secret of the Rosary*. Yet St. Alphonsus proved himself to be a true champion of the rosary by both his life and *The Glories of Mary*. In his book, he gave many examples of the power of the rosary in the lives of those who prayed it, even providing stories of people who were miraculously saved through the power of the rosary. He himself encouraged people to join the Confraternity of the Rosary and emphasized that people should pray the rosary to help the souls in purgatory. To this day, a 15-decade rosary is part of the religious habit of the Redemptorists.

Rosary Gems

There is no devotion so generally practiced by the faithful of all classes as that of the rosary.

~ St. Alphonsus Liguori

The rosary should be said with devotion.

~ St. Alphonsus Liguori

It is well to say the rosary kneeling, before an image of Mary, and, before each decade, to make an act of love to Jesus and Mary, and ask them for some particular grace.

~ St. Alphonsus Liguori

The immense good that this noble devotion [the rosary] has done to the world is well known. How many, by its means, have been delivered from sin! How many led to a holy life! How many to a good death, and are now saved!

~ St. Alphonsus Liguori

In an earthquake a poor woman was buried under the ruins of a house which was overthrown. A priest had the stones and rubbish cleared away, and under them found the mother with her children in her arms, alive and uninjured. On being asked what devotion she had practiced, she replied, that she never omitted saying the rosary, and visiting the altar of our Blessed Lady.

~ St. Alphonsus Liguori

A person who was leading an immoral life had not the courage to give it up; he began to say the rosary and was converted.

~ St. Alphonsus Liguori

A person who maintained a sinful friendship, by saying the rosary felt a horror of sin; she fell a few more times into sin, but by means of the rosary was soon quite converted.

~ St. Alphonsus Liguori

Saint Vincent Ferrer said to a man who was dying in despair, 'Why are you determined to lose your soul, when Jesus Christ wishes to save you?' The man answered that, in spite of Christ, he was determined to go to hell. The Saint replied, 'And you, in spite of yourself, shall be saved.' He [St. Vincent] began with the persons in the house to recite the rosary; when, behold, the sick man asked to make his confession; and having done so with many tears, expired.

~ St. Alphonsus Liguori

He [St. Stanislaus Kostka] never did anything without first turning to her [Mary's] image to ask her blessing. When he said her office, the rosary, or other prayers, he did so with the same external marks of affection as he would have done had he been speaking face to face with Mary.

~ St. Alphonsus Liguori

If we want to help the souls in purgatory then we should say the rosary for them because the rosary gives them great relief.

~ St. Alphonsus Liguori

Suffice it to know that this devotion [the rosary] has been approved by the Church, and that the Sovereign Pontiffs have enriched it with indulgences.

~ St. Alphonsus Liguori

BLESSED POPE
PIUS IX

The Servant of
the Rosary
1792–1878

PAPACY: 1846–1878
BEATIFIED: September 3, 2000 by St. John Paul II
FEAST DAY: February 7

BLESSED POPE PIUS IX was pope for 31 years and had the privilege of being the longest reigning pope in the post-apostolic era of the Church. He suffered from epilepsy all throughout his life. When he was a seminarian, he suffered such an intense epileptic seizure that he was dismissed from both the seminary and the Papal Noble Guard. It was only after he threw himself at the feet of the Servant of God Pope Pius VII and begged to be reinstated that the pope allowed him back into the seminary and the Papal Noble Guard. During the first few years of his priesthood, his health required that another priest assist him during Mass due to his unpredictable seizures. Despite his epilepsy, he was made a bishop at the age of 35 and sent by the Pope to Chile and Peru to assist the apostolic nuncio. Because of his service in South America, he was the first man to hold the office of the Vicar of Christ to have set foot in the Americas. When he was elected to the papacy in 1846, he chose the name "Pius" in honor of the Servant of God Pope Pius VII, since it was Pius VII who had encouraged his vocation despite his epilepsy. He wrote 38 encyclicals, was the first pope to be photographed, and, at the First Vatican Council, helped formulate the dogmatic definition of papal infallibility.

Marian Devotion

Blessed Pope Pius IX is known as the "Pope of the Immaculate Conception." On December 8, 1854, it was his privilege to dogmatically define Mary's Immaculate Conception. During the official announcement of the new dogma, as he began to pronounce the authoritative papal formula *declaramus* ("we declare"), a beam of light descended into St. Peter's and shone directly on him. Aware of the honor that was his in declaring this dogma, he immediately began to cry and was so moved that he had to cease reading the declaration until his tears subsided. He truly loved the Immaculate Conception, and even before he declared the dogma in 1854, had already given permission to the bishops of the United States in 1847 to declare the Immaculate Conception the patroness of the country.

In the writings of Bl. Pope Pius IX, Mary is described as more holy than the cherubim and seraphim; all the tongues of heaven and earth do not suffice to praise her as she truly deserves. As the mother of Jesus and our spiritual mother, her prayers have extraordinary power. God delights in answering her prayers since she serves as the Mediatrix of All Grace. To give the faithful a greater awareness of the importance of Mary's intercession, he instituted the Feast of Our Lady of Perpetual Help in 1876.

Champion of the Rosary

In 1858, during the pontificate of Bl. Pope Pius IX, heaven gave the Church a great gift when the Lourdes apparitions took place. Occurring only four years after the declaration of the dogma of the Immaculate Conception, the

Lourdes apparitions brought about a renewed interest in the rosary. Throughout his pontificate, Bl. Pope Pius IX championed the rosary as a protection against vice and heresy, even stating that if he but had an army to pray the rosary, he could conquer the world! On May 7, 1867, he beatified the 205 martyrs of Japan, many of whom were Dominicans and members of the Confraternity of the Rosary.

As a result of the renewed interest in the rosary that emerged after the Lourdes apparitions, Bl. Pope Pius IX frequently preached on the rosary, wrote about it, and affirmed the plenary indulgence available to the faithful on Rosary Sunday. In 1868, at the request of Fr. Joseph Moran, a Spanish Dominican, Bl. Pope Pius IX granted an indulgence to all who attended October observances in honor of the rosary. The rosary was in the hands of this saintly pope to the very end of his life. At the age of 85, while he was praying the rosary with his staff, he died of a heart attack as the result of an epileptic seizure.

Rosary Gems

I could conquer the world if I had an army to say the rosary.

~ Blessed Pope Pius IX

Among all the devotions approved by the Church, none has been so favored by so many miracles as the rosary devotion.

~ Blessed Pope Pius IX

If you desire peace in your hearts, in your homes, in your country, assemble every evening to recite the rosary.

~ Blessed Pope Pius IX

The single richest treasure in the Vatican is the rosary.

~ Blessed Pope Pius IX

When St. Dominic, acting by the inspiration of God, had implored the help of the Immaculate Mother of our Lord to uproot the heresy of the Albigenses, and when he went forth to preach the rosary as a marvelous succor against heresy and sin, this devotion spread itself among the faithful in an admirable manner.

~ Blessed Pope Pius IX

As St. Dominic employed this prayer [the rosary] as a sword to destroy the monstrous heresy of the Albigenses, so likewise in our time the faithful, in using the same weapon — that is to say, the daily recitation of the rosary — will obtain that, by the all-powerful protection of the Mother of God, the many errors infecting the world will be uprooted and destroyed.

~ Blessed Pope Pius IX

Have courage, my dear children! I exhort you to fight against the persecution of the Church and against anarchy, not with the sword, but with the rosary.

~ Blessed Pope Pius IX

As you know, dear sons, it is a celebrated fact that the rosary was entrusted by the Holy Mother of God to St. Dominic as a singular help when he battled against monstrous errors.

~ Blessed Pope Pius IX

At the call and summons of God, St. Dominic, the founder of the Order of Friars Preachers, implored the help of the Immaculate Mother of God, to whom alone it appertains to destroy all heresies in the world, in order to overcome the errors of the Albigenses, and had begun to preach the rosary as a defense of marvelous power against heresies and vices.

~ Blessed Pope Pius IX

Let the rosary, this simple, beautiful method of prayer, enriched with many indulgences, be habitually recited in the evening in every household. These are my last words to you: the memorial I leave behind me.

~ Blessed Pope Pius IX

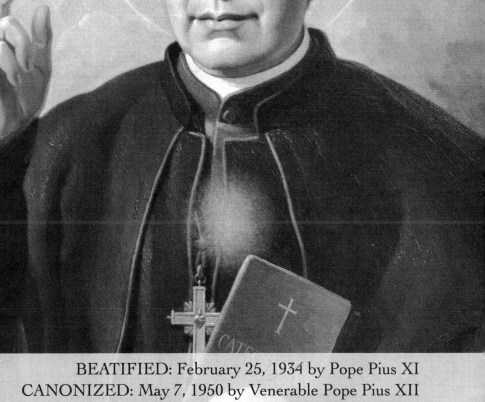

ST. ANTHONY MARY CLARET

The 'St. Dominic' of the Rosary
1807–1870

BEATIFIED: February 25, 1934 by Pope Pius XI
CANONIZED: May 7, 1950 by Venerable Pope Pius XII
FEAST DAY: October 24

S AINT ANTHONY MARY CLARET was born in Sallent, Spain, and although he was only 5-foot-1 in height, he was a giant of the faith. As a young man, he desired to become a Carthusian monk, but due to poor health and the necessary rigors of eremitical life, he was turned away. He then thought of becoming a Jesuit and entered their novitiate, but after further discernment he left the Jesuits and ended up becoming a diocesan priest. He was very zealous in his priestly ministry, and even spent a year and a half preaching an extensive series of retreats in the Canary Islands. In his zeal for spreading the Gospel, he founded the Missionary Sons of the Immaculate Heart of Mary (Claretians) before being made the archbishop of Santiago, Cuba.

Saint Anthony helped bring about a great reform in the clergy and the Catholic Church in Cuba. He confirmed over 300,000 people, validated over 9,000 marriages, and sometimes preached as many as 12 sermons a day. It has been estimated that during his many years as a priest, he preached over 25,000 sermons! He also authored over 100 theological works. His efforts to bring about reform were not welcomed by everyone, however. The Freemasons in Cuba were particularly disturbed by his efforts, and several attempts were made on his life. During one assassination attempt, he was stabbed in the face. After his time in Cuba, he served as the confessor to the queen of Spain and helped with preparations for the First Vatican Council. He was a staunch defender of papal infallibility and helped formulate its definition at the Council. Due to failing health, he spent the last days of his life at a Cistercian monastery in France.

Marian Devotion

From his youth, St. Anthony had a tender devotion to the Blessed Virgin and frequently made visits to the Shrine of Our Lady of Fusimanya to pray the rosary with his sister Rosa. In his inspiring autobiography, he credits Our Lady with saving him on one occasion from drowning in treacherous waves, as well as helping him overcome a great temptation against purity. During a trip to Italy in 1839, for the first time he witnessed people exhibiting a great devotion to the Immaculate Heart of Mary. This helped him to develop a Marian devotion that would become known as the *cordimariana* ("Marian heart") spirituality. He was extremely devoted to the Immaculate Heart of Mary and, in 1847, founded the Archconfraternity of the Heart of Mary in Vic, Spain. Two years later, in 1849, he founded a religious community dedicated to the Immaculate Heart known as the Missionary Sons of the Immaculate Heart of Mary. When members of the community professed their religious vows, they were also required to make a solemn promise to propagate devotion to the Immaculate Heart of Mary.

Similar to St. Alphonsus Ligouri, St. Anthony understood Mary's Immaculate Heart to be a new Noah's ark. By entering her heart, mankind would be able to find a place of safety against the spiritual deluge overtaking the world. He also understood Mary's heart as the "mercy seat" from which all graces of the Holy Trinity are distributed. Saint Anthony's Marian theology was greatly influenced by the writings of St. Alphonsus Liguori. He often instructed people to read *The Glories of Mary*. Saint Anthony also loved the presentation of Mary in *The Mystical City of God* by Venerable Mary of Agreda. He himself wrote at least 10 works on the Virgin Mary. When he became a bishop, he inserted the name "Mary" into his own name. Before leaving for his diocese in Cuba, he made pilgrimages to three of his favorite Marian Shrines: the ones dedicated to Our Lady of Pilar, Our Lady of Montserrat, and Our Lady of Fusimanya. He lived during the era in which Bl. Pope Pius IX declared the dogma of the Immaculate Conception and Mary appeared to St. Bernadette at Lourdes.

Champion of the Rosary

When St. Anthony was very young, his parents gave him a rosary, enrolled him in the Confraternity of the Rosary, and offered him a great parental example by praying a daily rosary in the home. During his youth, he found a book on the rosary owned by his parents. After reading it, he became an ardent champion of the rosary all throughout his adolescence. Saint Anthony was so devoted to the rosary that he would frequently lead both children and adults in its recitation at the local parish. Immediately after becoming a seminarian, he joined the Perpetual Rosary Society and enrolled himself in the local Confraternity of the Rosary. From the beginning of his seminary studies, he took up the practice of praying three rosaries a day, continuing this pious practice for the rest of his life. Once he became a priest, he rarely gave any sermon without having first instructed the people in how to pray the rosary. On many occasions, he would even pray a set of mysteries with everyone present before delivering his sermon.

Saint Anthony was consecrated a bishop on the Feast of Our Lady of the Rosary in 1850. There is sworn testimony from a man who was present at one of St. Anthony's Masses just a few days before his episcopal ordination that there were heavenly lights surrounding him as he offered Mass at a rosary altar. The young man who witnessed this event eventually became a priest and continued to tell others what he had seen during that Mass. As the archbishop of Santiago, Cuba, St. Anthony gave away over 20,000 rosaries and mandated that the rosary be prayed in all the churches in his diocese on Sundays and feast days. To make sure this practice was carried out, he often made surprise visits to parishes. He also authored several works on the rosary, translated a book on the rosary that had been written by another priest, and, in a book he wrote specifically for seminarians, insisted that every seminarian pray the rosary every day. Though he was completely unaware of St. Louis de Montfort's writings on the rosary and died seven years before Pope Leo XIII began writing rosary encyclicals, St. Anthony's explanation of the origins of the rosary are in perfect accord with *The Secret of the Rosary* and the 11 rosary encyclicals of Pope Leo XIII. Providentially, in 1899, one year after Pope Leo XIII wrote his last rosary encyclical, he declared Anthony Mary Claret a Venerable.

With such zeal for promoting the rosary, there is good reason why St. Anthony is acclaimed as the "St. Dominic" of the 19th century. A fellow Spaniard, he greatly loved St. Dominic, imitated him in his preaching-praying style, and always carried a rosary on his person. Of greater significance, however, is the fact that on several occasions, the Virgin Mary appeared to St. Anthony and informed him that he was to serve as the "St. Dominic" for the people of his time by zealously promoting the rosary.

Rosary Gems

When I was a little boy I was given a pair of rosary beads, and I was more pleased with them than with the greatest treasure.

~ St. Anthony Mary Claret

My parents, who are now in heaven, inspired in me a devotion to the holy rosary when I was still very young. They bought me a pair of beads and had me enrolled in the Confraternity of the Rosary in our parish.

~ St. Anthony Mary Claret

Before I had reached the age of reason I knelt daily to say a part of the rosary.

~ St. Anthony Mary Claret

Mother Mary, how good you have been to me and how ungrateful I have been to you! My mother, I wish to love you from now on with all my heart, and not only to love you myself, but to bring everyone else to know, love, serve, and praise you and to pray the holy rosary, a devotion that is so pleasing to you.

~ St. Anthony Mary Claret

On the ninth of the same month [October 9, 1857], at 4:00 in the morning, the Blessed Virgin Mary repeated several times what she had told me on other occasions — that I was to be the "Dominic of these times in spreading devotion to the rosary."

St. Anthony Mary Claret

Let victory be thine, O Mother. Thou wilt conquer. Yes, thou hast the power to overcome all heresies, errors, and vice. And I, confident in your powerful protection, will engage in the battle, not only against flesh and blood, but against the prince of darkness, as the Apostle [Paul] says, grasping the shield of the holy rosary and armed with the double-edged sword of the divine word.

~ St. Anthony Mary Claret

The good priest is not content with being a devotee of Mary, but rather he strives to promote every style of devotion to Mary; for example, teaching others to pray the rosary well.

~ St. Anthony Mary Claret

Have you said the rosary every day with devotion?

~ St. Anthony Mary Claret

Pray the rosary every day.

~ St. Anthony Mary Claret

We should meditate on the mysteries [of the rosary], applying them to the circumstances of our own lives.

~ St. Anthony Mary Claret

I found that another powerful means for doing good was giving away rosaries and teaching people how to use them.

~ St. Anthony Mary Claret

Mary Most Holy will be our Mistress, Directress, and Captainess, and we will be Brothers in the Brotherhood of Mary, Queen of the Rosary.

~ St. Anthony Mary Claret

The ancient peoples of the East had a practice of offering rose-wreaths to be worn as crowns to distinguished persons; and true Christians have the praiseworthy practice of offering each day with great devotion the crown of Marian roses to their beloved Mother, the Blessed Virgin. Such was the practice of St. Louis King of France, the great Bossuet, Fenelon, St. Vincent de Paul, St. Charles Borromeo, St. Francis de Sales, St. Francis Xavier, and others. Ever since the year 1208, during which the glorious St. Dominic taught people to pray it daily, there has not been a saint nor any person distinguished for learning and virtue, nor an observant religious community, nor a well-ordered seminary, which has not had the devotion to the rosary.

~ St. Anthony Mary Claret

It can be said that the rosary is a compendium of our holy religion.

~ St. Anthony Mary Claret

The holy rosary is comprised of many holy elements; no one doubts that this devotion is very pleasing to God and the holy Virgin. The devotion of the most holy rosary is powerful enough to transmit all graces and, as we are aware from experience, it has proven to be a remedy during times of war, plagues, hunger and other calamities;

in addition, those who have been troubled in body or soul, if they had recourse to the rosary, always received consolation.

~ St. Anthony Mary Claret

The most holy rosary is an abundant mine through which Christians, praying and meditating with attention and devotion, become enriched with great merits.

~ St. Anthony Mary Claret

The rosary is a flower garden that contains all kinds of beautiful and aromatic virtues.

~ St. Anthony Mary Claret

The most holy rosary is the most powerful, easy, and gentle means for dispelling ignorance and for removing errors and heresies.

~ St. Anthony Mary Claret

The rosary is the strongest impulse of the human heart, and those who get hooked on it will improve their habits.

~ St. Anthony Mary Claret

Secular people who are well off and lacking in nothing often pray the holy rosary in the morning and the evening when traveling; how much more should seminarians and priests do likewise!

~ St. Anthony Mary Claret

Most Holy Virgin, obtain for us the grace to devoutly pray your most holy rosary.

~ St. Anthony Mary Claret

Long live the holy rosary of Mary!

~ St. Anthony Mary Claret

POPE LEO XIII

The Pope of the Rosary
1810–1903

PAPACY: 1878–1903

P OPE LEO XIII is the longest lived pope in Church history, dying at 93. A brilliant writer, poet, and theologian, he established the Pontifical Academy of St. Thomas Aquinas in Rome in 1879 (now known as the Pontifical University of St. Thomas Aquinas, or the Angelicum). He was passionate about hunting and viniculture, and was known to trap birds and tend a small vineyard within the confines of the Vatican Gardens.

As a pastor of souls and a mystic, Pope Leo XIII was deeply concerned about the social and moral issues of his time, and gave the Church many spiritual weapons to combat these issues. While saying Mass one day, he had a vision of a fierce spiritual battle taking place and was inspired to write the famous Prayer to St. Michael the Archangel. He greatly promoted devotion to St. Joseph, consecrated the entire world to the Sacred Heart of Jesus, promoted the First Friday devotions, and established June as the month dedicated to the Sacred Heart. He is also the pope before whom a young Thérèse of Lisieux knelt, begging to be allowed to enter Carmel at the age of 15. He was the first pope to appear on film and beatified St. Louis de Montfort in 1888.

Marian Devotion

From his youth, Pope Leo XIII had a strong devotion to Mary. Through the discovery of the Marian writings of St. Louis de Montfort in 1846, and the subsequent investigations into these writings as part of de Montfort's beatification cause, Pope Leo XIII was deeply influenced by de Montfort's Marian thought. He was so enamored with *True Devotion to the Blessed Virgin* that he granted an indulgence to anyone who consecrated themselves to Mary using St. Louis de Montfort's method. Another source of Marian inspiration for Pope Leo XIII was the work of Blessed Bartolo Longo in Pompeii.

Pope Leo XIII was very open to private revelation. He promoted the Brown Scapular, instituted the Feast of Our Lady of the Miraculous Medal, wrote an apostolic letter promoting pilgrimages to Marian shrines, especially Lourdes, and received the visionary of La Salette, Mélanie Calvat, in two separate private audiences. He so loved Lourdes that he commissioned the construction of a Lourdes Grotto in the Vatican Gardens. Following the thought of St. Bernard of Clairvaux, he taught that a Christian trying to live their faith without Mary is comparable to a bird trying to fly without wings. In his many Marian writings, he emphasized that it is Our Lady who is capable of bringing about obedience to the Vicar of Christ among all Christians. He was the first pope to have his voice recorded; on the recording, he's singing the Hail Mary.

Champion of the Rosary

Pope Leo XIII is the greatest champion of the rosary to ever hold the office of the Vicar of Christ. During his pontificate, he wrote 11 encyclicals on the rosary, promulgated numerous apostolic letters on the rosary, and gave countless messages on the rosary to various dioceses and religious institutes. His rosary encyclicals contain a summary of all the statements previous popes had made about St. Dominic's role as the father of the rosary and the founder of the Confraternity of the Rosary. In almost every rosary encyclical that he wrote, he affirmed that St. Dominic was the founder of the rosary. He expressly taught that Our Lady herself entrusted the rosary to St. Dominic, and compared St. Dominic's Confraternity to an army of prayer and a spiritual battalion capable of winning souls for Christ.

A pontiff who sought to emphasize the importance of Catholic social teaching, he wrote the encyclical *Rerum Novarum* and also taught that the rosary was part of the solution to the social problems of his day. He tirelessly taught that the rosary was the most effective means of expanding the kingdom of Jesus Christ in the world and was of benefit to both individuals and society at large. He encouraged everyone to pray the rosary every day, and especially encouraged priests and missionaries to preach the rosary, since it has the power to expel evil and heal the sores of the human heart.

Pope Leo XIII dedicated the month of October to the rosary, granted many indulgences to the rosary, approved a comprehensive list of the indulgences attached to the rosary, affirmed Rosary Sunday, supported the construction of the Basilica of the Rosary in Lourdes, inserted the title "Queen of the Most Holy Rosary" into the Litany of Loreto, wrote a charter for the Confraternity of the Rosary, encouraged the Dominicans to promote the rosary, and supported the rosary apostolate of Bl. Bartolo Longo at the Basilica of the Rosary in Pompeii. Even a shortened version of his famous Prayer to St. Michael the Archangel is now commonly prayed at the end of the rosary. The writings of Pope Leo XIII highlighted a special blessing: To pray the rosary is to pray with the holy angels, since it was the Archangel Gabriel who uttered the first *Ave*. Pope Leo XIII will forever be *the* pope of the rosary.

Rosary Gems

It is mainly to expand the kingdom of Christ that we look to the rosary for the most effective help.

~ Pope Leo XIII

It is well known that there have been many persons occupied in most weighty functions or absorbed in laborious cares who have never omitted for a single day this pious practice. Combined with this advantage is that inward sentiment of devotion which attracts minds to the rosary, so that they love it as the intimate companion and faithful protector of life.

~ Pope Leo XIII

Experience has shown that to inculcate love for the Mother of God deeply in souls there is nothing more efficacious than the practice of the rosary.

~ Pope Leo XIII

In Mary, God has given us the most zealous guardian of Christian unity. There are, of course, more ways than one to win her protection by prayer, but as for us, we think that the best and most effective way to her favor lies in the rosary.

~ Pope Leo XIII

The rosary is the most excellent form of prayer and the most efficacious means of attaining eternal life. It is the remedy for all our evils, the root of all our blessings. There is no more excellent way of praying.

~ Pope Leo XIII

For every time we devoutly say the rosary in supplication before her, we are once more brought face to face with the marvel of our salvation; we watch the mysteries of our Redemption as though they were unfolding before our eyes; and as one follows another, Mary stands revealed at once as God's Mother and our Mother.

~ Pope Leo XIII

Meditation on the mysteries of the rosary, often repeated in the spirit of faith, cannot help but please her [Mary] and move her, the fondest of mothers, to show mercy to her children.

~ Pope Leo XIII

The rosary is by far the best prayer by which to plead before her [Mary] the cause of our separated brethren.

~ Pope Leo XIII

The formula of the rosary ... is excellently adapted to prayer in common, so that it has been styled, not without reason, "The Psalter of Mary." And that old custom of our forefathers ought to be preserved or else restored, according to which Christian families, whether in town or country, were religiously wont at close of day, when their labors were at an end, to assemble before a figure of Our Lady and alternately recite the rosary. She, delighted at this faithful and unanimous homage, was ever near them like a loving mother surrounded by her children, distributing to them the blessings of domestic peace, the foretaste of the peace of heaven.

~ Pope Leo XIII

For in the rosary all the part that Mary took as our co-Redemptress comes to us.

~ Pope Leo XIII

The rosary, if rightly considered, will be found to have in itself special virtues, whether for producing and continuing a state of recollection, or for touching the conscience for its healing, or for lifting up the soul.

~ Pope Leo XIII

May Mary, the Mother of God and of men, herself the authoress and teacher of the rosary, procure for us its happy fulfillment.

~ Pope Leo XIII

The spirit of prayer and the practice of Christian life are best attained through the devotion of the rosary of Mary.

~ Pope Leo XIII

In places, families, and nations in which the rosary of Mary retains its ancient honor, the loss of faith through ignorance and vicious error need not be feared.

~ Pope Leo XIII

The rosary of the Blessed Virgin Mary, combining in a convenient and practical form an unexcelled form of prayer, an instrument well adapted to preserve the faith and an illustrious example of perfect virtue, should be often in the hands of the true Christian and be devoutly recited and meditated upon.

~ Pope Leo XIII

The Blessed Virgin alone can save us, and she will renew the wonders of Lepanto.

~ Pope Leo XIII

The origin of this form of prayer [the rosary] is divine rather than human.

~ Pope Leo XIII

They [Confraternities of the Rosary] are, so to speak, the battalions who fight the battle of Christ, armed with his sacred mysteries, and under the banner and guidance of the heavenly Queen.

~ Pope Leo XIII

We may well believe that the Queen of Heaven herself has granted an especial efficacy to this mode of supplication [the rosary], for it was by her command and counsel that the devotion was begun and spread abroad by the holy Patriarch Dominic as a most potent weapon against the enemies of the faith at an epoch not, indeed, unlike our own, of great danger to our holy religion.

~ Pope Leo XIII

Pope Sixtus V, of happy memory, approved the ancient custom of reciting the rosary; Gregory XIII dedicated a day under this title, which Clement VIII afterward inscribed in the Martyrology, and Clement XI extended to the Universal Church. Benedict XIII inserted the feast in the Roman Breviary, and we ourselves, in perpetual testimony of our affection for this devotion, commanded that the solemnity with its office should be celebrated in the Universal Church.

~ Pope Leo XIII

Let all the children of Saint Dominic rise up for the fight and let them, like mighty warriors, be prepared to use in the battle the weapons with which their blessed Father, with so much foresight, armed them. This is what they have to do: Let them plant everywhere the rosary of the Blessed Virgin Mary; let them propagate and cultivate it with fervor; through their assiduous care may the nations be enrolled in these holy militias where the ensigns of the rosary shine; may the faithful learn to avail themselves of this weapon, to use it frequently; may they be instructed in the benefits, graces, and privileges of this devotion.

~ Pope Leo XIII

In the darkness of the times, Leo XIII appeared like a new dawn, and if he diffused much light in the universe through his great genius and indefatigable work, it cannot be denied that everything in him was the fruit of his devotion and love for the Blessed Virgin. He wrote eleven encyclicals on the rosary and enriched this prayer with indulgences.

~ Blessed James Alberione

During a most trying time for the Church, when for a long time a dreadful tempest of evils had been oppressing us, Leo XIII, in a series of encyclical letters, strongly urged the faithful all over the world to recite the holy rosary frequently.

~ Blessed James Alberione

The [rosary] encyclicals [of Pope Leo XIII] had varied contents, but they were all very wise, vibrant with fresh inspiration, and directly relevant to the practice of the Christian life. In strong and persuasive terms they exhorted Catholics to pray to God in a spirit of faith through the intercession of Mary, his Virgin Mother, by reciting the holy rosary.

~ St. Pope John XXIII

BLESSED BARTOLO LONGO

The Apostle of the Rosary
1841–1926

BEATIFIED: October 26, 1980 by St. John Paul II
FEAST DAY: October 5

BLESSED BARTOLO LONGO was born near Naples, Italy, to a devout Catholic family that prayed the rosary. As a young man, he studied law at the University of Naples. After being swept away by various political ideologies, he became anti-Catholic, radically opposed to what he believed were the "old wives' tales" of Catholicism. He particularly disdained the papacy, the priesthood, and the Dominicans. His hatred for the Dominicans was, in part, due to his disdain for their intellectual and academic efforts to defend Catholicism against the secular philosophies Bartolo had embraced. Within a short period of time, he went from adhering to nationalistic ideologies to becoming involved in spiritualism. This led him to attend séances and become an ordained priest of Satan.

Bartolo's involvement with the occult and spiritualism left him empty and unhappy. He suffered from hallucinations, torturous nightmares, frazzled nerves, bodily ailments, and severe depression. Seeking guidance, he turned to a friend and a Dominican priest, and began to experience a radical conversion. Fearing for his soul, he renounced spiritualism and its practices, and turned back to the Catholicism of his youth. In gratitude for having been delivered from the occult, he became a Third Order Dominican and dedicated his life to the spread of the rosary, especially by renewing the Catholic faith in the ancient city of Pompeii and building there the Basilica of Our Lady of the Rosary. He initiated many charitable works as part of his apostolate and was made a knight of the Order of the Holy Sepulchre.

Marian Devotion

Though he turned away from Catholicism during his legal studies in Naples, Bartolo always maintained a reverence for the feminine mystery and treated all women with respect and dignity. His respect for women stemmed from his love for his earthly mother. It was this mother-son bond that God used to bring about his radical conversion through Mary, his spiritual mother. In fact, when he abandoned spiritualism, he set out to make unparalleled efforts to cause Mary to be better known and loved. Our Lady became the Queen of his heart and his great hope of finding salvation in Christ. He relied completely upon her in all his works and efforts to help souls.

When St. John Paul II beatified Bl. Bartolo in 1980, he offered the following thoughts in his homily on Bl. Bartolo's great Marian devotion: "Bartolo Longo, a Third Order Dominican, and founder of the religious institution 'The Daughters of the Most Holy Rosary of Pompeii,' can truly be defined as 'the man of the Virgin': for love of Mary he became a writer, apostle of the Gospel, propagator of the rosary, founder of the famous sanctuary [of the rosary] in the midst of enormous difficulties and adversities; for love of Mary he created charitable institutions, became a beggar for the children of the poor, transformed the city of Pompeii into a citadel of human and Christian goodness; for love of Mary he silently endured calumny and tribulations, passing through a long Gethsemane, always trusting in Providence, always obedient to the Pope and the Church."

Champion of the Rosary

After his reversion back to Catholicism, Bl. Bartolo became a Third Order Dominican on October 7, 1871, and took the name "Br. Rosario," a name whose importance may not have been completely clear to him at that time. The rosary would come to be his anchor and hope of salvation when, during a work-related visit to Pompeii in 1872, he underwent a great challenge to his faith.

During the trip, he discovered that the people living near the ancient city of Pompeii were suffering from a severe lack of catechesis and had succumbed to the errors of spiritualism. Seeing the failing state of Pompeii caused him to go into a severe depression, since he knew that he had once been a priest of Satan, leading many people away from the faith and into the falsehoods of spiritualism. He felt as if he was still under the bondage of the devil, and a deep sense of hopelessness came over him so strongly that he contemplated suicide. There was only one thing that drew him out of his depression: calling to mind Mary's promise to St. Dominic that whoever promotes the rosary will be saved. Relying on this promise, he put away his suicidal intentions and gave his life entirely over to the promotion of the rosary. He began to incorporate the rosary into everything he did. Every evening, he would gather with others to pray the rosary in common in church. The rosary became the sweet chain that bound him to Jesus and Mary, and broke the bondage of Satan.

The promotion of the rosary and the restoration of the Catholic faith in Pompeii became Bartolo's mission in life. In 1873, he began a confraternity in Pompeii, and, inspired by his friend St. Caterina Volpicielli and her work of spreading devotion to the Sacred Heart of Jesus in Naples, he began the construction of a Shrine dedicated to Our Lady of the Rosary in Pompeii. As he was furnishing his rosary shrine, he obtained an image of Our Lady of the Rosary and had it restored. Through this image, God worked miracles so that the whole world would come to believe in the power of the rosary.

In 1877, he published *The Fifteen Saturdays*, a book about miracles associated with the rosary. In 1884, he launched a magazine dedicated to the rosary (still in circulation today) called *Il Rosario e la Nuova Pompeii* (*The Rosary and the New Pompeii*). He became a friend of St. Joseph Moscati, a saintly physician from Naples who prayed the rosary every day. Saint Moscati came to know Bl. Bartolo through serving as his personal physician and grew to love the Shrine of Our Lady of the Rosary of Pompeii. On average, 4 million people visit the Shrine of Our Lady of the Rosary of Pompeii every year. Saint John Paul II, Pope Benedict XVI, and Pope Francis have all made personal pilgrimages to the Basilica of the Rosary in Pompeii to pray and encourage others to pray the rosary. Blessed Bartolo Longo was buried on the Feast of Our Lady of the Rosary (October 7,

1926). In *Rosarium Virginis Mariae*, St. John Paul II's letter on the rosary, he gave Bl. Bartolo the title "the apostle of the rosary."

Rosary Gems

My only purpose in thirty-three years of service has been that of saving my soul and that of my brother by spreading the most holy rosary.

~ Blessed Bartolo Longo

The rosary is a teacher of life, a teacher full of gentleness and love, where people beneath the gaze of Mary, almost without noticing, discover they are being slowly educated in preparation for the second life, that which is authentic life, for it is not destined to end in a very few years, but to go unto eternity.

~ Blessed Bartolo Longo

Just as two friends, frequently in each other's company, tend to develop similar habits, so too, by holding familiar converse with Jesus and the Blessed Virgin, by meditating on the mysteries of the rosary and by living the same life in Holy Communion, we can become, to the extent of our lowliness, similar to them and can learn from these supreme models a life of humility, poverty, hiddenness, patience and perfection.

~ Blessed Bartolo Longo

The rosary, in a gentle, subtle way leads one to the Eucharist, to the Most Blessed Sacrament: those who approach Jesus in thought, yearn to approach him in reality; those who know Jesus cannot but love him; indeed, those who truly love Jesus cannot forego possessing him.

~ Blessed Bartolo Longo

The rosary could very well be called the poem of human redemption. The rosary is a poem that takes its lively but simplistic hues from the pure palette of the Gospel; while at the same time it draws its logical ties, its harmonious responses, its entire intimate dialectic from the highest theology.

~ Blessed Bartolo Longo

If it be true that you [Mary] promised St. Dominic that whoever spreads the rosary will be saved, I will be saved, because I shall not depart from this land of Pompeii without having spread your rosary.

~ Blessed Bartolo Longo

Sweet Queen of my heart, kindly accept the prayer I address to you, that your love may spread in my heart and in the hearts of all those who honor you by reciting the rosary.

~ Blessed Bartolo Longo

Awaken your confidence in the Most Holy Virgin of the Rosary!

~ Blessed Bartolo Longo

O Blessed Rosary of Mary, sweet chain which binds us to God, bond of love which unites us to the angels, tower of salvation against the assaults of hell, safe port in our universal shipwreck, we shall never abandon you.

~ Blessed Bartolo Longo

I thought that perhaps as the priesthood of Christ is for eternity, so also the priesthood of Satan is for eternity. So, despite my repentance, I thought that I was still consecrated to Satan, and that I am still his slave and property as he awaits me in Hell. As I pondered over my condition, I experienced a deep sense of despair and almost committed suicide. Then I heard an echo in my ear of the voice of Friar Alberto repeating the words of the Blessed Virgin Mary: "One who propagates my rosary shall be saved."

~ Blessed Bartolo Longo

My God, you did not look at my past, you did not stop before my weakness; in one hand you placed the rosary, in the other a pen, and you said to me: "Write, they will listen to you, for it is I who will place in your heart the word of life."

~ Blessed Bartolo Longo

You [Mary] are omnipotent by grace and therefore you can help us. Were you not willing to help us, since we are ungrateful children and undeserving of your protection, we would not know to whom to turn. Your motherly heart would not permit you to see us, your children, lost. The Infant whom we see on your knees and the blessed rosary which we see in your hand inspire confidence in us that we shall be heard.

~ Blessed Bartolo Longo

The rosary is a seat, upon which Mary sits as teacher, to teach us the way by which we can attain life.

~ Blessed Bartolo Longo

Bartolo Longo, a Third Order Dominican, and founder of the religious institution "The Daughters of the Most Holy Rosary of Pompeii," can truly be defined as "the man of the Virgin": for love of Mary he became a writer, apostle of the Gospel, propagator of the rosary, founder of the famous sanctuary in the midst of enormous difficulties and adversities; for love of Mary he created charitable institutions, became a beggar for the children of the poor, transformed the city of Pompeii into a citadel of human and Christian goodness; for love of Mary he silently endured calumny and tribulations, passing through a long Gethsemane, always trusting in Providence, always obedient to the Pope and the Church.

~ St. John Paul II

Bartolo Longo is the apostle of the rosary, the layman who fully lived his Christian commitment.

~ St. John Paul II

When we see, in the famous painting of Our Lady of Pompeii, the Virgin Mother and the Child Jesus giving the rosary beads to St. Catherine of Siena and St. Dominic, we immediately understand that this prayer leads us through Mary to Jesus, as Pope John Paul II taught us in his letter Rosarium Virginis Mariae, in which he explicitly mentions Bl. Bartolo Longo and the charism of Pompeii.

~ Pope Benedict XVI

I am pleased to emphasize that like St. Paul, Bartolo Longo was transformed from persecutor to apostle: an apostle of Christian faith, of Marian devotion and, in particular, of the rosary, in which he found a synthesis of the whole Gospel.

~ Pope Benedict XVI

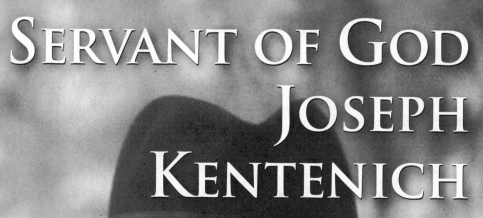

SERVANT OF GOD
JOSEPH
KENTENICH

The Friend of the Rosary
1885–1968

THE SERVANT OF GOD JOSEPH KENTENICH

was born near Cologne, Germany, in 1885, and joined the Pallotines in 1904. As a spiritual director and teacher at the Pallottine seminary in Schoenstatt, Germany, he was inspired to found the Schoenstatt movement in 1914. The Schoenstatt movement is essentially an education movement with a very strong Marian dimension. As an educator of youth and a zealous promoter of the Catholic apostolate, Fr. Kentenich sought to bring about a spiritual, moral, and anthropological renewal in the world through Mary.

In 1941, during World War II, Fr. Kentenich was arrested by the Gestapo and put into prison. In 1942, due to medical reasons, he was given the opportunity to avoid time in a concentration camp, but he made a resolution to offer up his suffering for the Schoenstatt movement. He spent three years in Dachau. His suffering for the movement proved very fruitful, and continued even after he was freed.

Father Kentenich's apostolic work was ahead of his time and would only be fully appreciated after the Second Vatican Council. During his lifetime, his intentions were often misunderstood. At one point, he was forced to surrender control of the Schoenstatt movement to others and was transferred to a Pallottine house in Milwaukee, Wisconsin. Before he left for the United States, he made a pilgrimage to the shrine of Our Lady of the Rosary of Pompeii to entrust everything to Mary. During his time on administrative leave in Wisconsin, he had nothing to do with Schoenstatt for 14 years (1951-1965). Unfortunately, during his exile in Wisconsin, he was the subject of unfounded suspicions and was stripped of his faculties to offer Mass publically for one week. Blessed Pope Paul VI ended Kentenich's exile in 1965, and he was able to return to Germany. Once he returned to Europe, he left the Pallotines and became a diocesan priest. He died on September 15, 1968 (the Feast of Our Lady of Sorrows). On his tomb are the words *Dilexit Ecclesiam* ("He loved the Church"). That is all he wanted written on his grave.

Marian Devotion

When he was nine, Kentenich's mother had to make the difficult decision to leave her son at the orphanage of St. Vincent in Oberhausen, Germany, because she was unable to care for him. Before a statue in the orphanage that depicted Our Lady giving the rosary to St. Dominic and St. Catherine of Siena, his mother consecrated him to Mary and begged the Blessed Virgin to educate her son and be his mother. This event made a lasting impression on the young boy. Throughout his life, he uttered the famous Pallottine phrase *Mater habebit curam* ("Mother takes care") in reference to the maternal assistance of the Blessed Virgin.

Through learning and living the Marian spirituality of the Pallottine community, Kentenich came to understand Our Lady as the great missionary, educator, and teacher. As a novice, he read *True Devotion to the Blessed Virgin* by St. Louis de Montfort and was greatly influenced by it. As a seminarian, he thoroughly studied de Montfort's works and, once ordained, he preached many conferences on the Montfortian method of Marian consecration. He was a zealous promoter of the Marian Sodality. On October 18, 1914, during his talk to the Marian sodality at the minor seminary in Schoenstatt, he asked Our Lady to erect her throne in that place in a special way. This event marked the beginning of the Schoenstatt movement. In the same year, 1914, he also read an article about the zealous apostolic work of Bl. Bartolo Longo in Pompeii and was strongly inspired to turn Schoenstatt into an international movement.

The special characteristic of the Schoenstatt Marian movement is the covenant of love the members make with the Mother Thrice Admirable, giving her a blank check, which means that Mary can do with them whatever she desires. The Schoenstatt form of Marian consecration is lived out by the members loving, imitating, and invoking Mary, as well as by the various apostolic works that they undertake. All members of the movement are called to be apparitions of Mary in the world and lead people closer to Jesus by being an *altera Maria* ("another Mary"). Father Kentenich compared the members of Schoenstatt to the star of the Magi, leading people to Jesus and Mary. In the brilliant mind of Fr. Kentenich, the Marian dogmas of the Church were understood to be a compendium of all the great truths of Catholicism. His anthropological Mariology was a precursor to St. John Paul II's theology of the body. Father Kentenich perceived Mary to be the most beautiful bait that God uses to catch human hearts and bring them back to Christ. Mary, in essence, is a magnet for souls, and God desires to draw her triumphal chariot onto the battlefield of today's crisis-filled era in order to obtain peace and the restoration of all things in Christ.

Champion of the Rosary

Spending three years in the concentration camp of Dachau gave Fr. Kentenich a keen sense of the very real and ongoing spiritual battle between good and evil. He understood Mary to be the great Victress in this battle over all demons and heresies, and always insisted that the rosary is our friend in this battle. The rosary is the choice weapon that Mary gives to her soldiers and knights on the battlefield. A man of his times, Fr. Kentenich compared the rosary to an atomic bomb, noting that the rosary is much more powerful than even the greatest of man-made bombs. He taught that a child of Mary has nothing to fear on the battlefield since she is the victorious Queen and triumphant Mother of God. He would often boldly proclaim: *Servus Mariae Nunquam Peribit!* ("A Servant of Mary will never perish!").

Father Kentenich taught that Mary is our great educator and her classroom is the rosary. By means of the rosary, she teaches her children to avoid anything and everything that brings sadness to our heavenly Father. The rosary is not only our friend in times of battle, but also in times of joy, since it helps us avoid sin. In

1950, in order to advance a new effort of evangelization through the rosary, an apostolate known as the Schoenstatt Rosary Campaign began in Brazil. It spread quickly and, by 1976, extended to other countries in South America. In 1985, for the celebrations taking place to mark the centennial of Fr. Kentenich's birth, the Schoenstatt Rosary Campaign was launched on a global scale and began to spread all throughout the world.

Rosary Gems

The great remedy of modern times which will influence the events of the world more than all diplomatic endeavors and which has a greater effect on public life than all organizational ones, is the rosary.

~ Servant of God Joseph Kentenich

In the Middle Ages the Cathar sect [adherents to the Albigensian heresy] spread like wildfire. Kings fought to destroy it. It was overcome by the rosary.

~ Servant of God Joseph Kentenich

The Hail Marys [of the rosary] transport us into the sacred space of Mary's heart.

~ Servant of God Joseph Kentenich

The rosary is a sort of machine gun and atomic bomb, namely a weapon that is far superior to all the weapons of modern warfare in overcoming the enemy of God.

~ Servant of God Joseph Kentenich

The rosary has proven itself as a friend in the life and work of great men.

~ Servant of God Joseph Kentenich

The rosary is a good friend in joy, but an even better friend in battle. Today the drums continuously beat for battle. Our lives are one big battle. We are dependent on loyal, good friends. The rosary is such a good friend in the big battle of our time.

~ Servant of God Joseph Kentenich

The rosary is our good friend. Being familiar with it configures us to Christ. Through the rosary we become apparitions of Christ and encounters of Christ. How important a good friend is! A friend gives a child a sense of being sheltered even in a strange place. A good friend is a great treasure and a great rarity. Oh, the beautiful things that have been said and sung about friendship! And we may say and sing all this of the rosary, our good friend!

~ Servant of God Joseph Kentenich

What fruits the world and the Church owe to the rosary!

~ Servant of God Joseph Kentenich

Those who pray the rosary do more for the benefit of the whole human race than all the orators and deputies, more than all the organizers, secretaries and writers, more than all the capitalists even if they would make their entire wealth available to the Church.

~ Servant of God Joseph Kentenich

Let us immerse ourselves into the ocean of love which the rosary allows us to drink in richly, and let the glowing love of Christ and his Mother inflame our weak sacrificial spirit.

~ Servant of God Joseph Kentenich

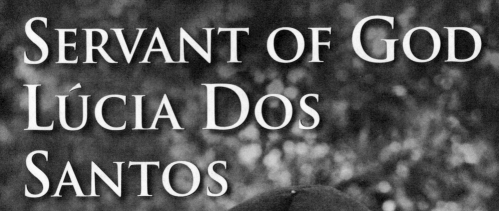

SERVANT OF GOD LÚCIA DOS SANTOS

The Visionary
of the Rosary
1907–2005

THE SERVANT OF GOD LÚCIA DOS SANTOS

was born in Aljustrel, Portugal, in 1907, and lived to be 97 years old. On May 13, 1917, the Blessed Virgin Mary began appearing to little Lúcia and two of her cousins, Jacinta and Francisco Marto, in the nearby village of Fatima. With one exception, Mary appeared to the three little children on the thirteenth of the month from May to October. (In August, Mary appeared a few days later, since the children had been put in jail.) During the last apparition on October 13, 1917, the famous Miracle of the Sun occurred. During that apparition, the Sun gyrated and danced across the sky; more than 70,000 people witnessed it. The messages of Fatima contain many themes, most of which are centered on making reparation to the Immaculate Heart of Mary, doing penance, praying for peace, Marian consecration, and the rosary.

Shortly after the apparitions, Lúcia's two cousins, Jacinta and Francisco, died. Lúcia herself went on to become a Sister of St. Dorothy and then a Discalced Carmelite nun. Jacinta and Francisco were beatified on April 9, 2000, by St. John Paul II. Sister Lúcia was a friend of St. John Paul II and met with him on several occasions. She wrote six memoirs of her life, recounting her experiences of Our Lady and the Fatima messages. When she died on February 13, 2005, Portugal declared a national day of mourning two days later.

Marian Devotion

After the Marian apparitions occurred in Fatima, Sr. Lúcia received several other visitations from Mary during her years in the Dorothean convent in Pontevedra, Spain. During the apparition of December 10, 1925, Our Lady revealed to Sr. Lúcia her desire for the Five First Saturdays devotion in reparation to her Immaculate Heart. With a special mission and vocation to make reparation to the Sacred Heart of Jesus and the Immaculate Heart of Mary, Sr. Lúcia sought to spread devotion to Mary's Immaculate Heart through her memoirs.

When Sr. Lúcia became a cloistered Carmelite nun, she was able to enter into a more prayerful and intense Eucharistic life. Sister Lúcia viewed Mary as the first monstrance that revealed Jesus to the nations. (The word "monstrance" stems from the Latin word *monstrare*, which means "to show.") In her writings, Sr. Lúcia emphasized that Mary is also the living tabernacle of the presence of Jesus Christ. The entire work of our redemption started in Mary's Immaculate Heart.

Champion of the Rosary

When Sr. Lúcia was a young girl, her family prayed a daily rosary together during the month of May every year. Lúcia was considered to be mature and pious for her age and so was allowed to receive her First Holy Communion at the age of six, even though the normal age for that special occasion was 10. After receiving the Eucharist for the first time, she knelt down and prayed before a statue of Our Lady of the Rosary, and later testified that the statue smiled at her.

During the Fatima apparitions, Mary stressed the importance of the recitation of the rosary. All three children became champions of the rosary and encouraged others to pray it with them before each apparition. Little Francisco became so zealous in praying the rosary that, during one of the apparitions, he told Our Lady that he would pray as many rosaries as she wanted. Later in life, when Sr. Lúcia recorded her memories, she frequently mentioned the great fervor that Blesseds Jacinta and Francisco had for the rosary.

Mary also specifically asked Sr. Lúcia to learn how to read and write so that she could communicate to the world the importance of the rosary and the messages Mary was giving her. Our Lady particularly emphasized the daily rosary as a means of bringing about an end to World War I. Mary also revealed to the children a new prayer that she wanted to be added at the end of each decade of the rosary. The prayer was, "Oh my Jesus, forgive us our sins, save us from the fires of hell, and lead all souls to heaven, especially those most in need of thy mercy." Since Blesseds Jacinta and Francisco died shortly after the apparitions, it was Sr. Lúcia who made this prayer more widely known. In essence, the Fatima apparitions were rosary apparitions; Mary confirmed this when, on October 13, the day of the last apparition and the day the Sun danced, Mary revealed to the children that she was Our Lady of the Rosary.

After the Fatima apparitions, Our Lady continued to instruct Sr. Lúcia on the importance of the rosary. During the apparition on December 10, 1925, in Pontevedra, Spain, Mary taught Sr. Lúcia the Five First Saturdays Devotion. An essential aspect of this devotion is that souls are to pray the rosary and spend at least 15 minutes meditating on the mysteries. Sister Lúcia understood the rosary and various forms of devotion associated with it to be concrete ways that all people could co-operate with Jesus, our Redeemer, and Mary, our Co-Redemptrix. She showed this specifically when, during Lent, she would pray the Chaplet of the Five Wounds with her arms outstretched! (The Chaplet of the Five Wounds originated with the Passionists in the early 19th century.) She considered the rosary to be a type of spiritual nourishment and made rosaries to give away to little children. In one of her memoirs, she also wrote beautiful meditations for the mysteries of the rosary.

Rosary Gems

My daughter [Sr. Lúcia], look at my heart surrounded with the thorns with which ungrateful men pierce it at every moment by their blasphemies and ingratitude. You, at least, try to console me, and say that I promise to assist at the hour of death with all the graces necessary for salvation all those who, on the first Saturday of five consecutive months, go to Confession and receive Holy Communion, recite five decades of the rosary and keep me company for a quarter of an hour while meditating on the mysteries of the rosary, with the intention of making reparation to me.

~ Our Lady to the Servant of God Lúcia Dos Santos

At the end of the rosary, she [Bl. Jacinta Marto] always said three Hail Marys for the Holy Father.

~ Servant of God Lúcia Dos Santos

The rosary is the prayer which God, through his Church and Our Lady, has recommended most insistently to us all, as a road to and gateway of salvation.

~ Servant of God Lúcia Dos Santos

During the month of May, we used to recite the rosary as a family every day.

~ Servant of God Lúcia Dos Santos

When lovers are together, they spend hours and hours repeating the same thing: "I love you!" What is missing in the people who think the rosary monotonous is Love; and everything that is not done for love is worthless.

~ Servant of God Lúcia Dos Santos

The prayer of the rosary, after the Holy Liturgy of the Eucharist, is what most unites us with God by the richness of [the] prayers that compose it. All of them [the prayers of the rosary] came from heaven, dictated by the Father, by the Son, and by the Holy Spirit. The "Glory" we pray between the decades was dictated by the Father to the angels when he sent them to sing it close to his Word, the newborn child. It is also a hymn to the Trinity. The "Our Father" was dictated by the Son and it is a prayer to the Father. The "Hail Mary" is all impregnated with Trinitarian and Eucharistic sense. The first words were dictated by the Father to the angel when he sent him to announce the mystery of the incarnation of the Word. Moved by the Holy Spirit, Saint Elizabeth said: "Blessed are thou amongst women, and blessed is the fruit of thy womb." The Church also moved by the Holy Spirit, added, "Holy Mary, Mother of God, pray for us sinners now and at the hour of our death."

~ Servant of God Lúcia Dos Santos

The Most Holy Virgin, in these last times in which we live, has given a new efficacy to the recitation of the rosary to such an extent that there is no problem, no matter how difficult it is, whether temporal or above all spiritual, in the personal life of each one of us, of our families … that cannot be solved by the rosary. There is no problem, I tell you, no matter how difficult it is, that we cannot resolve by the prayer of the holy rosary.

~ Servant of God Lúcia Dos Santos

All well-intentioned people can, and should, recite the five decades of the rosary every day. The rosary should constitute each person's spiritual food.

~ Servant of God Lúcia Dos Santos

Our Lady insists that we pray the rosary every day because she knows our inconstancy, our weakness and our need.

~ Servant of God Lúcia Dos Santos

God, who is our Father and understands better than we do the needs of his children, chose to stoop to the simple ordinary level of all of us in asking for the daily recitation of the rosary, in order to smooth for us the way to him.

~ Servant of God Lúcia Dos Santos

Those who say the rosary daily are like children who, every day, manage to find a few moments just to be with their father, to keep him company, to show him their gratitude, to do some service for him, to receive his advice and blessing. It is an exchange of love, the love of the father for the child and the child for the father; it is a mutual giving.

~ Servant of God Lúcia Dos Santos

After the Holy Liturgy of the Eucharist, the prayer of the rosary is what better draws to our spirit the mysteries of Faith, Hope and Charity. She [the rosary] is the spiritual bread of souls.

~ Servant of God Lúcia Dos Santos

The rosary is the prayer of the poor and the rich, of the wise and the ignorant. To uproot this devotion from souls, is like depriving them of their daily spiritual bread. She [the rosary] is what supports that little flame of faith that has not yet been completely extinguished from many consciences. Even for those souls who pray without meditating, the simple act of taking the beads to pray is already a remembrance of God, of the supernatural.

~ Servant of God Lúcia Dos Santos

The simple remembrance of the mysteries in each decade is another radiance of light supporting the smoking torch of souls. This is why the devil has moved against it such a great war. And the worst part is that he has deluded and deceived souls of great responsibility by their position [on the rosary]. They are blind men leading blind men. They pretend to base their saying [on the rosary] in the [Second Vatican] Council and do not realize that the Holy Council ordered them to preserve all the practices that in course of years had been fostered in honor of the Immaculate Virgin Mother of God. The prayer of the rosary is one of the most important and, according to the decrees of the Holy Council and the orders of the Holy Father, it must be maintained.

~ Servant of God Lúcia Dos Santos

I will pray the rosary every day. For this I must go to the chapel a quarter of an hour before the ringing [of the bell] for Mass and pray the first rosary, meditating on the joyful mysteries. At four o'clock in the afternoon when I am usually alone, I will make a visit to Jesus present in the Blessed Sacrament and pray the second rosary, meditating on the sorrowful mysteries. Then if I have time, I will do the Stations of the Cross. If at this time I cannot, I will do it after the examination of the night. The third rosary I recite with the community at 6:30 pm, and I will meditate on the glorious mysteries.

~ Servant of God Lúcia Dos Santos

There are those who say that the rosary is an antiquated and monotonous prayer because of the constant repetition of the prayers which compose it. But I put the question: Is there anything kept alive without the perseverance in the continual repetition of some actions?

~ Servant of God Lúcia Dos Santos

The holy rosary, according to Lúcia of Fatima, is so powerful that it can solve any problem, material or spiritual, national or international.

~ Blessed Gabriele Allegra

ST. MAXIMILIAN KOLBE

The Knight of the Rosary
1894–1941

BEATIFIED: October 17, 1971 by Bl. Pope Paul VI
CANONIZED: October 10, 1982 by St. John Paul II
FEAST DAY: August 14

SAINT MAXIMILIAN KOLBE was born in Zdunska Wola, Poland, and became a Conventual Franciscan. At a very young age he earned doctorates in both philosophy and theology from pontifical universities in Rome. During his studies in Rome, he was greatly disturbed when he witnessed protests against the Church and the papacy by Freemasons. His response to these protests was to establish the Militia Immaculatae (MI) in 1917, the same year that the Fatima apparitions occurred. The MI was founded to be a Marian movement to counter the Freemasons and the Modernists infiltrating the Church.

Saint Maximilian was on fire with zeal for serving Christ and his Church through apostolic works and even conducted missionary work in the Far East, especially in Japan. In Nagasaki, he established a religious house that would later experience miraculous protection during the atomic bombing of Nagasaki on August 9, 1945 (see page 172). Back in Europe, during World War II, St. Maximilian was arrested by the Gestapo and sent to the Nazi concentration camp of Auschwitz. In a heroic act of selfless Christian charity, he volunteered to die in the place of a total stranger, Franciszek Gajowniczek, since this man had a family. The intention of the Nazis was to kill St. Maximilian and everyone in his cell through starvation. However, after two weeks, St. Maximilian had outlived all the other prisoners, and the Nazis killed him by means of an injection of carbolic acid. His body was cremated at the concentration camp on August 15, 1941, the Assumption of Mary into heaven. For his heroic love, the Church has declared him a martyr of charity. When Maximilian was beatified in 1971 and canonized in 1982, Franciszek Gajowniczek, the man whose life he had saved, was in attendance during the ceremonies.

Marian Devotion

As a young boy, St. Maximilian often expressed a desire to be a soldier. In 1906, after an episode in which his mother asked him what would become of him, he had a vision of Mary in which she offered him two crowns: one crown was white and represented purity; the other crown was red and represented martyrdom. Our Lady asked him which he desired, and, in his soldier-like zeal, he exclaimed that he wanted both! From that moment, his devotion to Mary was like that of a medieval knight for his fair lady. Saint Maximilian helped to re-introduce Marian chivalry into the hearts of many Catholics. In the Kolbe home, the family had an altar dedicated to Our Lady of Czestochowa, the Queen of Poland, where he would spend long hours in prayer before the image of his queen.

Shortly after he joined the Conventual Franciscans, he was sent to Rome to study. It was in Rome that he first heard about the miraculous conversion of Alphonse Ratisbonne. Ratisbonne was a Jewish man who received a vision of Mary in 1842 that ultimately lead to his conversion to Catholicism, becoming a great promoter of the Miraculous Medal, and ordination as a Jesuit priest.

This story inspired in St. Maximilian a desire to use the Miraculous Medal as a means of praying for the conversion of the enemies of the Church, especially the Freemasons and the Modernists. In preparation for founding the MI, he studied the Miraculous Medal apparitions given to St. Catherine Labouré, focusing especially on the promises that Mary made to St. Catherine regarding the medal. He so believed in the power of the Miraculous Medal that, when he founded the MI, he required each member to wear one. Then, once he was ordained a priest, he celebrated his first Mass at the altar of Our Lady in the Church of Sant'Andrea della Fratte in Rome, at the exact spot where Alphonse Ratisbonne had received his vision of Mary. Throughout St. Maximilian's whole life as a priest, he used the Miraculous Medal as a spiritual weapon, referring to it as a spiritual bullet against the enemies of Christ.

In 1927, he founded a monastery in Poland known as the City of the Immaculate (Niepokalanów), sometimes also called Marytown. It quickly became the center of an intense Marian apostolate, including a radio station and publication house that produced literature on Our Lady. At one point, the monastery housed almost 900 friars! Saint John Paul II visited Niepokalanów in 1983.

Saint Maximilian also founded a very popular magazine titled the *Knight of the Immaculate*. In 1930, as a missionary in Japan, he established a mission house in Nagasaki called the Garden of the Immaculate. As a Franciscan, he had a tremendous love for the Immaculate Conception and personalized the title by referring to Our Lady as the "Immaculata." Because of his zeal for the Immaculata, he had a special love for Lourdes since Mary had revealed herself to St. Bernadette as the Immaculate Conception.

Synthesizing the Catholic tradition on Marian consecration and, like nearly every other promoter of consecration to Jesus through Mary, heavily influenced by St. Louis de Montfort, St. Maximilian developed his own formula for Marian consecration. He believed that those who give their lives completely to Mary are to be her docile instruments in bringing about the "marianization" of all things in Christ. Drawing from the Franciscan tradition of Marian thought, he also emphasized Our Lady's role as the Spouse of the Holy Spirit, even stating that she is the quasi-incarnation of the Holy Spirit. He went so far as to say that the true purpose of a follower of Christ is to be "transubstantiated" into the Immaculate. This "transubstantiation" means that all followers of Christ are to become another Mary in their essence, that is, sinless, pure, holy, and immaculate. Saint Maximilian truly desired to win all souls for Christ through the Immaculate Co-Redemptrix and Mediatrix of All Grace.

Champion of the Rosary

Saint Maximilian was a true knight of the rosary and prayed it every day of his priestly life. Though he intended the Miraculous Medal to be the primary weapon of the Militia Immaculatae, he also required that all members pray the rosary every day. He preached and spoke frequently of the power of the rosary, taught his friars about the history of the rosary, and offered a kind of catechesis on the mysteries associated with the rosary. As a knight of the Immaculata, he understood the rosary to be a spiritual sword, and explicitly noted that each Knight and Lady of the Immaculate (members of the Militia Immaculatae) were to wield it with devotion and fervor.

In 1941, when he was captured by the Nazis and sent off to the concentration camp, one of the Nazi officers noticed the rosary hanging from his habit and used it as a means to abuse him. The Nazi officer violently grabbed the rosary, held up the crucifix to the saint's face, and asked him if he truly believed in Jesus Christ and the rosary. Saint Maximilian's response was "yes," for which he was brutally beaten several times in front of all the other prisoners. As a prisoner in Auschwitz, St. Maximilian frequently led the other prisoners in praying the rosary, especially those who shared his cell. Saint Maximilian is both a martyr of charity and a knight of the rosary.

Rosary Gems

The origin of the rosary is well known. A contemporary witness [of St. Dominic], Fr. Tiery of Alpola [Fr. Theodoric of Apolda lived from 1228–1297], a Dominican, recounts it. He says that St. Dominic could not in a particular locality convert the heretics; he turned to the Blessed Virgin Mary, whom he had highly revered since his childhood, and asked for assistance. The Queen of Heaven then appeared to him, showed him the rosary, and instructed him to propagate it. He fervently set to work, and from that time he recovered with ease a great many souls who had strayed, so that soon their number exceeded one hundred thousand. The whole Catholic world eagerly received the holy rosary, and innumerable graces and miracles of conversion testified to its supernatural origin.

~ St. Maximilian Kolbe

The popes have highly recommended it [the rosary], and as [Pope] Hadrian VI asserts: "the rosary defeats Satan." [Pope] Paul III said, "Through the rosary of St. Dominic, God's wrath toward France and Italy was restrained," and [Pope] Julius III proclaims, "The rosary is the ornament of the Roman Church." [Pope] Gregory XIV: "The rosary is the eradication of sin, the recovery of grace, the increase of God's glory." [Pope] Paul V: "The rosary is a treasure of graces." [Pope] Urban VIII: "Through the rosary, the number of most fervent Christians increases." [Blessed Pope] Pius IX: "If you desire peace to reign in your hearts and families, gather together each evening to recite the rosary." Pope Leo XIII in his encyclical on the rosary says, "We strongly urge all the faithful, whether it be publicly in the churches or in private homes and within the family, to pray the rosary and, as far as possible, not to relent in this holy exercise."

~ St. Maximilian Kolbe

In addition to the Lord's Prayer and the Angelic Salutation the essence of the rosary is contemplating the mysteries of the life of Christ the Lord and the most holy Mother of God.

~ St. Maximilian Kolbe

The scapular, the rosary, and the Miraculous Medal: here are three things that the Immaculata herself deigned to offer for the salvation of mankind.

~ St. Maximilian Kolbe

Knights and Ladies of the Immaculata, and all of you who read these words ... recite a third part [five decades] of the rosary daily.

~ St. Maximilian Kolbe

It is true that one is not under pain of sin in regard to praying the rosary — but what kind of love would ours be if it were limited to our strict obligations, neglect of which would be a serious transgression? Such conduct would appear more as the service of a slave than the love of a child towards his best Father in heaven, and most affectionate Mother. No! This is unworthy of a lover of Mary. Such a person seeks rather the opportunity to go to her as often as possible, to remain at her feet as long as possible.

~ St. Maximilian Kolbe

Can a pagan recite the rosary? And why not? Indeed, in that case, he may delve more easily into the truth of our faith. By praying, he may obtain the grace to know the truth in religious matters and the strength to accept such religion much more easily. He will acknowledge it as true, regardless of setbacks or judgments from others who are still unfamiliar with matters of faith.

~ St. Maximilian Kolbe

It [the rosary] is so easy to understand that children, and also simple persons who do not know how to read, can use the rosary as a means to prayer.

~ St. Maximilian Kolbe

One has to have great patience and trust in her. Moreover, one must pray much in times of trouble and suffering. One needs to invoke her most sweet name, "Mary," or say a "Hail Mary," and in the most difficult and most crucial times it will not hurt to even recite a whole section of the rosary.

~ St. Maximilian Kolbe

A prayer both simple and sublime that the Immaculata herself indicated when she appeared in Lourdes is the holy rosary. May it become the sword of each knight of the Immaculata, just as the Miraculous Medal is the bullet that strikes down evil!

~ St. Maximilian Kolbe

May the Miraculous Medal be the bullet in the hand of the Knights of the Immaculata and the holy rosary the sword.

~ St. Maximilian Kolbe

Prayer, therefore, and especially the rosary and penance — here are the Immaculata's orders for us all.

~ St. Maximilian Kolbe

The head of all the varied members of the infernal dragon is undoubtedly in our times — Freemasonry. And she shall crush his head. Further, history teaches us that there was hardly a conversion in which Mary's hand was not particularly seen. All the saints fostered a special devotion to her, and the Holy Father, Leo XIII says in an encyclical on the rosary (September 22, 1891), "It can be affirmed that from the immense treasure of all grace ... nothing is given to us by the will of God, except through Mary, and as no one can approach the Most High Father but by the Son, so ordinarily no one can approach Christ but by his mother."

~ St. Maximilian Kolbe

In October, Catholics have the custom of venerating the Most Holy Mother by reciting the rosary in churches or in private homes, and even the Immaculata, manifesting herself at Lourdes in 1858, appeared with rosary in hand, thus encouraging us by her own example to recite it. We therefore surely give great pleasure to the Mother of God and draw down upon ourselves and our families many blessings from God when we recite the rosary.

~ St. Maximilian Kolbe

In her apparition at Lourdes, in 1858, the Mother of God held in her arms the rosary, and through [St.] Bernadette, recommended to us the recital of the rosary. We can conclude, therefore, that the prayer of the rosary makes the Immaculata happy. Moreover, with this prayer we can easily obtain great graces and divine blessing.

~ St. Maximilian Kolbe

Behold, if we desire to rise even to her [Mary's] knowledge and loving of Jesus, we must whisper "Hail Mary," and repeating it, meditate upon these mysteries [of the rosary] in union with her.

~ St. Maximilian Kolbe

In every Catholic home, even the poorest, it is possible to find a rosary. Above all, in the hour of prayer, in church, or during a funeral, one notices that the faithful keep in their hands a rosary. In moments of joy or sadness, whenever the faithful turn to God in prayer, they recite the rosary and are deeply bonded with it.

~ St. Maximilian Kolbe

The humble prayer to the Immaculata, the holy rosary, together with heartfelt prayers, will indicate when and how to act, because in those moments it is she who directs, in those moments it is she who erases any difficulty.

~ St. Maximilian Kolbe

There is often mention of fifteen promises, by means of which the Most Blessed Virgin exhorts the faithful to recite the rosary. Those who received these promises were St. Dominic and Bl. Alan de la Roche.

~ St. Maximilian Kolbe

SERVANT OF GOD
FRANK DUFF

The Man of the Rosary
1889–1980

The Servant of God Frank Duff was born into a wealthy family in Dublin, Ireland, in 1889. During his youth, he was hit in the ear by a cricket ball; consequently, his hearing was impaired in that ear for the rest of his life. At the age of 24, he became aware of the extreme poverty of many people in the cities of Ireland and tried to make a difference by serving the poor in Dublin through the Society of St. Vincent de Paul. This charitable work gave him a desire to lead a more devout Christian life. As a result, he started to attend two Masses a day beginning in 1914, and continued this practice for the rest of his life.

With his dear friend Venerable Edel Quinn, Duff became a pioneer of lay involvement in apostolic works. He greatly encouraged the Catholic laity to strive for sanctity and engage in charitable works. He was so well respected for his contributions to the apostolate of the laity that Bl. Pope Paul VI invited him to attend the Second Vatican Council as a lay observer. During the final session of the Council, the entire assembly of bishops from around the world stood and gave Frank Duff a standing ovation in recognition of his tremendous work. In his zeal to help souls experience the freedom that the truths of Catholicism bring, he was miraculously able to help bring about the conversion of almost the entire red-light district in Dublin, especially the area associated with prostitution. He was very devoted to the Sacred Heart of Jesus. Frank Duff lived to be 91 years old, dying on a First Friday.

Marian Devotion

In 1917, the same year that Our Lady appeared in Fatima and St. Maximilian founded the Militia Immaculatae, Frank Duff read St. Louis de Montfort's *True Devotion to the Blessed Virgin*. He had overheard a few men discussing the book and became interested in acquiring a copy himself. When he found a first edition of the English translation in a bookstore, he purchased it. At first, he did not understand the book due to its depth and lofty Marian expressions, but, after reading it half a dozen times, he finally got it. This devotion set his soul aflame. He understood that Mary was not just another saint and member of the Church, but the greatest of all saints and the very heart of the mystery of Christianity. From this point on, he began to teach everyone that if they did not understand Mary, they were incapable of understanding Christianity.

As a result of his fervent devotion to Our Lady, he founded the Legion of Mary on September 7, 1921. Having been greatly influenced himself by the writings of St. Louis de Montfort, Duff established that the Legion was to be very Montfortian in its Marian devotion and piety. The purpose and goal of the Legion was to assist Mary, the Mediatrix of All Grace, in the spiritual combat perpetually waged between the Church and the powers of darkness. He named his organization the Legion of Mary because he viewed it as an army of the Mother of God, championing the cause of her divine Son. Through this army's use of prayer and apostolic works, he wanted the Legion to help the Church bring all souls to Jesus through Mary. It would prove to be an extremely fruitful Marian apostolate during the 20th century, with members in almost every diocese in the world. Blessed Pope Paul VI described the Legion of Mary as the greatest movement to help souls since the establishment of the great mendicant religious orders in the 16th century! It was so effective at bringing about conversions to Christ and spread so quickly to every part of the globe that Mao Tse-tung, the Communist leader and father of the People's Republic of China, referred to the Legion of Mary as "Public Enemy Number One."

Champion of the Rosary

A devoted son of the Church, Frank Duff spent at least four hours a day in prayer. On most days, he would even sacrifice his lunch break to spend an hour in prayer. The rosary was always part of his daily prayer routine. He was very fond of recommending the daily rosary to everyone he met. He had a unique understanding of the rosary, saying it is the "prime devotion to the Holy Spirit." What he meant was that when a person prays the rosary, they are immediately overshadowed by the Holy Spirit, since Mary is the Spouse of the Holy Spirit and can never be separated from her spouse. This dimension of his thought is quite fascinating, since people rarely associate devotion to the Holy Spirit with the recitation of the rosary. In the mind of Frank Duff, the rosary opens up hearts to the workings of the Holy Spirit because in the rosary we celebrate and remember the principal interventions of the Holy Spirit in the drama and mysteries of salvation.

The largest Marian association in the world, the Legion of Mary is made up of small local groups called "Praesidiums." This terminology comes from the Roman technique of protecting a particular area by maintaining a fortified garrison or military line. A Legion of Mary Praesidium conducts apostolic works and meets weekly to pray. Frank Duff mandated that each Praesidium pray the rosary as part of their weekly prayer meeting. He also encouraged each member to join the Confraternity of the Rosary.

Frank Duff always stressed that the rosary is the core of the Legion of Mary's spirituality. As such, he desired that the rosary be prayed with dignity and respect. He did not want it prayed too quickly or in a chaotic fashion, but rather, with a meditative rhythm. He particularly emphasized that those praying the second half of the Hail Mary were not to start before the person praying the first half of the Hail Mary had said the Holy Name of Jesus. Duff considered the rosary to be so essential to the Legion of Mary that, when he wrote the Legion of Mary handbook, he said that what breathing is to the human body, the rosary is to the Legion of Mary.

Rosary Gems

The rosary was established about the year 1200 and it took from the first minute. It was proposed to people and they were encouraged to use it. It proved itself to have an affinity for the people. Ever since, it has been intertwined with Catholic life. It has been prominent in devotional literature; an element in the lives of the holy ones of the Church; the subject of the teachings of the Popes and the Doctors. The rosary has been carried by Our Lady in many of the accepted apparitions. It has entered into many of the recorded miraculous events, some of which have saved the world. It is believed to have been responsible for innumerable favors. I wonder has there been any saint since the 13th century who did not use it?

~ Servant of God Frank Duff

Anyone who says the rosary will have a reasonably complete and vivid idea of the Christian narrative.

~ Servant of God Frank Duff

If the rosary be hurt [neglected], Mary's place will be diminished and so will the quantity of prayer in our lives.

~ Servant of God Frank Duff

The rosary is a prayer which fits itself to changing circumstances. At times of sickness or of exhaustion, there is no other so useful.

~ Servant of God Frank Duff

As we say the rosary, we try to stage the mysteries before our minds. However meager our powers to meditate, we cannot help learning all those mysteries. They expand into so many "photographic" situations, linking themselves up with the various pictures we have seen or the accounts which we have heard or read of those events. We may be sure too that grace takes hold of that "picturisation," intensifies it and renders it fruitful.

~ Servant of God Frank Duff

Every word of the rosary is a prayer to God.

~ Servant of God Frank Duff

The rosary counteracts any tendency to relegate her [Mary] to a sub-compartment in the Christian life.

~ Servant of God Frank Duff

The rosary should be recited reverently.

~ Servant of God Frank Duff

The rosary is irreplaceable.

~ Servant of God Frank Duff

POPE PIUS XI

The Watchman of the Rosary
1857–1939

PAPACY: 1922–1939

Pope Pius XI held the chair of St. Peter during the period between World War I and World War II. A man of blunt speech and a no-nonsense style of leadership, he took the name "Pius" because of the great admiration he had for the pope of his youth, Bl. Pope Pius IX. Pius XI was a very accomplished scholar and, before becoming pope, had served as the chief librarian for the Ambrosian Library in Milan; the Archbishop of Milan; and the prefect of the Vatican Library in Rome. He earned three doctorate degrees (in philosophy, theology, and canon law) from the Gregorian University in Rome and specialized in paleography (or the study of ancient handwriting), focusing on medieval manuscripts and documents. At one point, he also served as the apostolic nuncio to Poland and had such a tremendous zeal for Christian unity that he desired to be a martyr in Russia.

During his papacy, he canonized St. Bernadette Soubirous, St. John Vianney, St. Don Bosco, and St. Thérèse of Lisieux. He also established the Feast of Christ the King as a means of trying to ease tensions between various nations. He established Vatican Radio in 1931 and was the first pope to broadcast on radio. Like his predecessors, he strongly condemned Modernism and promoted unity and peace. An avid mountain climber, he reached the summit of many famous peaks, including the Matterhorn. There is even a glacier named after him in Chile.

Marian Devotion

Before he became pope, Pius XI was a member of a Jesuit sodality of Our Lady and was known to be a very Marian priest. When he became the archbishop of Milan, he started a Marian sodality in his archdiocese. He so loved the Sodality of Our Lady that he compared it to the Milky Way, stretching from horizon to horizon and encompassing countless souls. It was during his pontificate and with his knowledge and consent that the Fatima apparitions received approval by the Church. He called Lithuania the "*Terra Mariana*" ("the land of Mary") and, in 1930, declared the Immaculate Conception (under the title of "Our Lady of Aparecida") the Patroness of Brazil. He also greatly loved Lourdes and, one year before he was elected pope, made an official pilgrimage to Lourdes. Once pope, he canonized St. Bernadette Soubirous on December 8, 1933.

Providentially, it was one year before Pius XI was elected to the papacy that the Servant of God Frank Duff founded the Legion of Mary. During Pius XI's papacy, the Legion of Mary spread throughout the world, and on September 16, 1933, Pope Pius XI imparted a special blessing to all the members of the Legion of Mary. As part of this blessing, he noted that, just as Mary had cooperated in redemption, the members of the Legion of Mary were to be cooperators with Christ in his salvific mission. Pope Pius XI clearly taught that Mary rightly deserves the titles Mediatrix of All Grace and Co-Redemptrix.

Champion of the Rosary

During his pontificate, Pius XI dealt with the aftermath of World War I, the possibility of another world war, and the anti-Catholic persecutions in Mexico, Spain, and the Soviet Union. He warned the world of the errors of Fascism, Communism, and Nazism, and urged the recitation of the most holy rosary. To this purpose, in 1937, he wrote the rosary encyclical *Ingravescentibus Malis* (*The Ever-Worsening Evils*). In this powerful encyclical, he affirmed that St. Dominic was the founder of the rosary, underscored that the rosary is a weapon to be used against all heresies, ideologies, and threats against truth, and made an appeal to all people to pray it. He taught that the rosary is a weapon for combating the evil spirits at work in the world and bringing about peace in the hearts of men. During his pontificate, many of the faithful who became martyrs gave witness to the rosary: Blessed Miroslav Bulešic, Blessed Ceferino Giménez Malla, Blessed Miguel Pro, and many others. Pius XI knew that the rosary had the power to conquer all ideologies, especially that of Communism.

A champion of the rosary, Pope Pius XI issued a decree ordering that the Basilica of Our Lady of the Rosary of Pompeii be expanded and enlarged so that more people could go there on pilgrimage. He emphasized that the rosary was not a vainly repetitious prayer, but rather could be compared to a person saying to their beloved "I love you" over and over again. He wrote a personal letter to the Master General of the Dominicans affirming the pious tradition, explicitly stating that Prouille was the cradle of the rosary, and told the Dominicans that the rosary is at the center of their charism and should be zealously promoted by the friars. He saw the rosary as a teacher of the moral and theological virtues, capable of cultivating in souls a desire for holiness and a greater love for Christ and the Church.

Rosary Gems

Among the weapons St. Dominic used to convert the heretics the most efficacious, as the faithful well know, was the Marian rosary, the practice of which, taught by the Blessed Virgin herself, has so widely spread throughout the Catholic world. Now where does the efficacy and power of this manner of praying come from? Certainly from the very mysteries of the Divine Redeemer which we contemplate and piously meditate so that we may rightly say that the Marian rosary contains the root and foundation on which the Order of St. Dominic depends, in order to procure the perfection of life of its own members and the salvation of other men.

~ Pope Pius XI

Saint Dominic founded the Order of Friars Preachers which Pope Honorius III placed under his own special protection and patronage and whose members he acclaimed, as it were, prophetically, "true lights of the world," and "champions of the faith." The first monastery was founded at Saint Mary of Prouille, which was, indeed, the cradle of the rosary of Mary itself.

~ Pope Pius XI

When very frequently we receive newly married couples in audience and address paternal words to them, we give them rosaries, we recommend these to them earnestly, and we exhort them, citing our own example, not to let even one day pass without saying the rosary, no matter how burdened they may be with many cares and labors.

~ Pope Pius XI

How could love not be made more fervent by the rosary? We meditate on the suffering and death of our Redeemer and the sorrows of his afflicted Mother.

~ Pope Pius XI

Kings and princes, burdened with most urgent occupations and affairs, made it their duty to recite the rosary.

~ Pope Pius XI

Among the various supplications with which we successfully appeal to the Virgin Mother of God, the holy rosary without doubt occupies a special and distinct place.

~ Pope Pius XI

The rosary enlivens the hope for things above that endure forever. As we meditate on the glory of Jesus and his Mother, we see heaven opened and are heartened in our striving to gain the eternal home.

~ Pope Pius XI

The fathers and mothers of families particularly must give an example to their children, especially when, at sunset, they gather together after the day's work, within the domestic walls, and recite the holy rosary on bended knees before the image of the Virgin, together fusing voice, faith and sentiment. This is a beautiful and salutary custom, from which certainly there cannot but be derived tranquility and abundance of heavenly gifts for the household.

~ Pope Pius XI

Those wander from the path of truth who consider this devotion [the rosary] merely an annoying formula repeated with monotonous singsong intonation, and refuse it as good only for children and silly women!

~ Pope Pius XI

This mystic crown [the rosary], not only is found in and glides through the hands of the poor, but it also is honored by citizens of every social rank.

~ Pope Pius XI

Everyone can understand how salutary it [the rosary] is, especially in our times wherein sometimes a certain annoyance of the things of the spirit is felt even among the Faithful, and a dislike, as it were, for the Christian doctrine.

~ Pope Pius XI

The holy rosary not only serves admirably to overcome the enemies of God and Religion, but is also a stimulus and spur to the practice of evangelic virtues which it injects and cultivates in our souls. Above all, it nourishes the Catholic Faith, which flourishes again by due meditation on the sacred mysteries, and raises minds to the truth revealed to us by God.

~ Pope Pius XI

The rosary elevates minds to the truths revealed by God and shows us Heaven opened. The Virgin Mary herself has insistently recommended this manner of praying. All graces are conceded to us by God through the hands of Mary.

~ Pope Pius XI

BLESSED JAMES ALBERIONE

The Evangelist of the Rosary
1884–1971

BEATIFIED: April 27, 2003 by St. John Paul II
FEAST DAY: November 26

BLESSED JAMES ALBERIONE was born in northern Italy and was one of the greatest pioneers in the field of Catholic media. When asked by his first grade teacher what he wanted to be when he grew up, he said that he wanted to be a priest. An erudite theologian, he earned a doctorate in theology and served for a time as a seminary professor and spiritual director. In his zeal to use modern means of social communication to spread the Gospel, he founded the Pauline family, consisting of 10 religious institutes for priests, religious, and laity.

He was ahead of his time in his ardor for using social communication as a means of spreading the Gospel. His work was so well respected that he was invited to attend every session of the Second Vatican Council as a theological consultant. Blessed Pope Paul VI greatly admired and supported his work, and took the time to visit Bl. James on his deathbed; an hour after the papal visit, Bl. James died. He was buried in the basilica he had had constructed in Rome, the Basilica of Mary, Queen of Apostles. Saint John Paul II referred to him as the first apostle of the New Evangelization and beatified him on Divine Mercy Sunday in 2003.

Marian Devotion

From his earliest days, Bl. James manifested a profound devotion to Mary. Shortly after his birth, his mother consecrated him to Our Lady at the Shrine of Our Lady of the Flowers in northern Italy. All throughout his youth, he frequented this Marian shrine and spent countless hours in prayer to Mary. As a priest, he desired that everything be done under the watchful and maternal gaze of Mary. Some of his greatest Marian influences were Blessed William Joseph Chaminade, St. Vincent Pallotti, and Pope Leo XIII. Blessed Alberione's Marian devotion led to personal sanctification and zealous apostolic activity. For this reason, in addition to stressing the importance of Mary's motherhood for each Christian, he also emphasized Mary's important apostolic work as our teacher and Co-Redemptrix. One of his favorite titles for Our Lady was "Queen of the Apostles."

Blessed Alberione wrote many prayers to Our Lady and also composed a chaplet to Mary, Queen of Apostles. He so loved Mary's title "Queen of the Apostles" that he saw to the construction of a new basilica in Rome to honor her under that same title. Mary was his favorite and most frequent topic when he preached. His writings on Our Lady total over 1,700 pages! He never missed an opportunity to introduce Mary into his many activities and apostolic works.

Champion of the Rosary

Blessed James Alberione often remarked that if Our Lady were to become more known, imitated, invoked, and loved, the world would be completely "Christianized." He particularly stressed that the Christianization of the world would come about through the weapon of the rosary. Like so many before him, he believed in the pious tradition about the rosary's origins and frequently referenced the many battles that had been won for Christ and the Church through the power of the rosary. Whether he was teaching, preaching, or authoring books, he always provided numerous examples of the power of the rosary in the lives of the saints. He loved to refer to the heroic example of the saints who found in the rosary a great source of sanctity, strength, protection, and zeal in their apostolic actions.

Whenever Bl. Alberione was about to give a talk, it was his practice to pray a rosary before delivering the talk. When traveling by car, he would pray non-stop rosaries until he reached his destination. He held that the rosary is an easy and efficacious prayer, especially helpful for growing in virtue and overcoming the enemies of the spiritual life. Knowing the rosary to be a prayer most pleasing to Our Lady, he emphasized praying the rosary with faith, devotion, and a firm purpose of reforming one's life. For this reason, he strongly encouraged people to pray the rosary on their knees when possible. He himself gave this pious example.

Rosary Gems

What is the rosary? It is the object of our hope. Afflicted sons and daughters, as soon as they hold the rosary in their hands, feel a new hope arising again in them, a hope which is strong and serene. After the cross I do not know of anything which can give comfort to a soul more than the rosary. The Church recommends the rosary to everyone, and desires that religious have it always with them so that they may live under the continual protection of Mary.

~ Blessed James Alberione

In the early times of the Church, the faithful made use of a kind of rosary consisting of a thin cord with many knots to count the prayers which they repeated. St. Dominic, inspired by God, gave a definite form to the rosary beads. This is a common belief and is also confirmed by many pontifical documents.

~ Blessed James Alberione

The Albigensians, a revolutionary and sacrilegious group, were denying truths of the Faith and devastating beautiful regions in France, Spain and Italy. At first St. Dominic tried to oppose them with his apostolic words, but to no avail. He then had recourse to Mary. He recited the holy rosary and had all the people recite it, too, while meditating on the mysteries. Mary won, and peace returned.

~ Blessed James Alberione

St. Dominic is the apostle of truth, but he is also the devout apostle of devotion to the rosary.

~ Blessed James Alberione

The Albigensians were conquered and converted in large numbers by St. Dominic with the holy rosary.

~ Blessed James Alberione

From her [Mary], St. Thomas Aquinas sought celestial wisdom daily with the holy rosary.

~ Blessed James Alberione

The rosary has obtained great conversions such as those of Ratisbonne and Hermann Cohen; it has given strength in battles against violent temptations, as experienced by St. Alphonsus and St. Francis de Sales; it has preserved baptismal innocence, as in St. Louis Gonzaga and in St. Rose of Lima.

~ Blessed James Alberione

St. Philip Neri walked the streets of Rome with the rosary in his hand; he sought out wayward souls and by means of the rosary inspired them to repent.

~ Blessed James Alberione

Whenever St. Vincent Pallotti, apostle of Rome, went to visit the dying, he would recite the rosary on the way.

~ Blessed James Alberione

St. Clement Hofbauer, apostle of Vienna, attributed to Mary the great conversions he obtained among sinners and the dying. Before dealing with them, he would recite and have others recite a part of the rosary.

~ Blessed James Alberione

St. Francis de Sales was a most meek and most strong priest; a bishop of inexhaustible zeal, a writer and preacher of true devotion; a marvel because of his prodigies. Why? He overcame the hardest trials by making a vow to recite the entire rosary daily, and he kept his vow faithfully.

~ Blessed James Alberione

St. John Berchmans died clutching the crucifix, the rosary, and the rules of his order. "These were the three things dearest to me during my life," he kept saying, "with these I die happily."

~ Blessed James Alberione

St. Louis IX, King of France, recited the rosary even while leading his army in time of war.

~ Blessed James Alberione

He [St. Charles Borromeo] instituted the Confraternity of the Rosary [in his diocese] and ordained that a solemn procession in honor of Mary, during which the Litany of the Blessed Virgin Mary was sung, be held in every parish on the first Saturday of every month. One night he was saying his evening prayers and the holy rosary, when a scoundrel broke into his quarters and fired a shot at him from close range. At the sound of the shot, the prayer ceased. Astonishment and terror seized those present, and although apparently mortally wounded, the saint smiled and calmly indicated to proceed with the prayers. At their conclusion, St. Charles Borromeo rose, and to his great surprise saw the bullet, which had barely ripped his outer garment, fall at his feet.

~ Blessed James Alberione

The rosary is an easy, powerful, and common devotion.

~ Blessed James Alberione

How often a rosary, a medal of the Blessed Mother, devout novenas, penances for the salvation of obstinate sinners who are ill, have obtained real prodigies from this Mother!

~ Blessed James Alberione

Let us recite the holy rosary often and well.

~ Blessed James Alberione

Toward Mary we must have an enlightened and limitless confidence and love; the most heartfelt, expansive, and tender devotion; the most common and constant practices of the rosary, the Angelus, the three Hail Marys, the chaplet, Saturday, etc.

~ Blessed James Alberione

The rosary is a compendium of the Holy Gospel; it is a summary of the lives of Our Lord and the Virgin Mary; it is a summary of the entirety of Christian doctrine. Therefore, it has justly been called the Christian's Breviary.

~ Blessed James Alberione

The rosary is an easy devotion. It is composed of prayers which everyone learns as a child — prayers which can be said without any effort or difficulty. The rosary can be recited at any time, in any place and in any circumstance. The rosary is pleasing to the Blessed Virgin, because of its origin and its excellence. In fact, the rosary is not the product of human fancy; it was suggested to men by the Blessed Virgin herself, and she had the most sublime purpose for doing so. Mary personally gave us this precious token of salvation, and she also taught us the manner of using it. Is there any devotion [to Mary] more excellent than this?

~ Blessed James Alberione

More than once, through the rosary, those who were disseminating grave errors have been defeated. Through it many sinners have been converted to God; through it love of God and of his mother has bloomed anew. The Church herself has found in the rosary her shield of defense. With this mighty weapon she has defeated Satan, just as with a sling David defeated the giant Goliath. It is not without reason that the Supreme Pontiffs have strongly recommended this practice, enriching it with indulgences.

~ Blessed James Alberione

As long as the rosary remains in a family, Jesus, [the] Way and Truth and Life, remains.

~ Blessed James Alberione

Mary's merits for our redemption shine forth in the mysteries of the rosary.

~ Blessed James Alberione

Without the rosary, I felt I was incapable of even giving an exhortation.

~ Blessed James Alberione

Let us resolve to pray to the Blessed Virgin especially with the recitation of the rosary.

~ Blessed James Alberione

Always, everything was built more with the rosary than with other means.

~ Blessed James Alberione

Queen of the Most Holy Rosary, in these times of such brazen impiety, manifest thy power with the signs of thine ancient victories.

~ Blessed James Alberione

Jesus cried over Jerusalem, which did not want to listen to him. He cried seeing the punishment that would touch this city. And when you are not received, feel sad, not for yourselves, but for them, and recite the rosary for them.

~ Blessed James Alberione

Say many and beautiful rosaries. We show our devotion to Mary, Queen of Apostles, especially through the simple form of the rosary.

~ Blessed James Alberione

The rosary, which the Church so highly recommends, is not only the font of many graces for the living, but also a most powerful means of aiding the dead.

~ Blessed James Alberione

The rosary is a prayer for the evangelization of the pagans, for the conversion of heretics, for the return of schismatics, for making lukewarm and superficial Christians fervent; for leading good Christians to sanctity.

~ Blessed James Alberione

The rosary of Mary is the great lever, it is the anchor of salvation for society and for individuals. Lepanto and Vienna are names associated with the rosary. The victories over the Albigensians, over French philosophism, over liberalism and modernism find their explanation in the rosary.

~ Blessed James Alberione

Following one's vocation means waging a continuous battle because the devil will make every effort to ruin vocations. Thus, the rosary is the great means of victory.

~ Blessed James Alberione

The rosary can be recited everywhere: on the street, in the train, in the bus, in church, in waiting rooms — all places can be considered suitable for reciting the rosary.

~ Blessed James Alberione

Recite the rosary with the humility of [St.] Bernadette or of the three little shepherds of Fatima.

~ Blessed James Alberione

VENERABLE POPE PIUS XII

The Pastor of the Rosary
1876–1958

PAPACY: 1939–1958
VENERABLE: December 19, 2009 by Pope Benedict XVI

Venerable Pope Pius XII was born in Rome in 1876 to a devout family who instilled in his heart a deep desire for prayer. His father was a particularly pious Third Order Franciscan and helped his young son discern a call to the priesthood. Ordained on Easter Sunday, he served in a variety of capacities as a priest. Pope Benedict XV consecrated him a bishop in the Sistine Chapel on the same day that Mary was making her first appearance in Fatima (May 13, 1917). Years later, after having served the Church as the papal nuncio to Germany, he was elected to the chair of St. Peter and took the name "Pius" because of his great respect for Pope Pius XI.

Always a critic of Nazism, Pius XII helped many Jewish people escape from Poland during WWII, and even hid many Jews in the Vatican. These actions so impressed the chief rabbi of Rome, Rabbi Israel Zolli, that in 1945, after the war, he converted to Catholicism. Pius XII is responsible for making Karol Wojtyła (the future St. John Paul II) a bishop at the young age of 38. Pius XII wrote 41 encyclicals and canonized a number of great Marian saints, including St. Louis de Montfort, St. Catherine Labouré, and St. Anthony Mary Claret. After the Sacred Scriptures, he is the most frequently cited authoritative source in the documents from the Second Vatican Council. Venerable Pope Pius XII died on October 9, 1958, and was buried at St. Peter's on October 13, the anniversary of the Miracle of the Sun at Fatima.

Marian Devotion

Venerable Pope Pius XII is often called the "Pope of Mary" because of his tender love for the Virgin. When he was a young boy, he would spend hours in prayer before an image of Mary at the Gesu, the Jesuit church and general headquarters in Rome. This pious practice often made him late for dinner. When he was ordained a priest, he requested that his first Mass be celebrated before the altar of the *Salus Populi Romani* image of Mary in the Basilica of Santa Maria Maggiore. Upon becoming pope, he explicitly placed his pontificate under the care of Our Lady of Good Counsel and encouraged all priests to have a tender devotion toward her.

He is also known as the "Pope of the Assumption" because, in 1950, he officially declared the dogma that Mary was assumed, body and soul, into heaven. According to Sr. M. Pascalina Lehnert, his housekeeper for 40 years, Pius XII saw the "miracle of the sun" — similar to that which occurred at Fatima — on four separate occasions. Three of these occurrences were within days of the proclamation of the dogma of the Assumption, and one of them occurred on November 1, 1950, the actual day of the definition.

Pius XII's writings are rich in Marian theology and devotion. In 1947, addressing the Marian Congress in Ottawa, Canada, he noted that because Mary is the mother of the Vine (Jesus), she is also the mother of the branches (us). During the Marian Year 1953–1954, which he himself declared, he personally crowned the image of the *Salus Populi Romani* and wrote a beautiful prayer, calling her the "Conqueress of evil and death." In *Mystici Corporis*, his theologically profound encyclical on the Church, he described Mary as the neck and heart of the mystical body through which all graces flow. He celebrated the centenary of the proclamation of the dogma of the Immaculate Conception in his letter *Fulgens Corona*, and in *Mediator Dei*, his encyclical on the liturgy, he emphasized that the month of May was to be particularly dedicated to Mary. Additionally, he wrote an encyclical commemorating the centenary of Lourdes, established the Feast of the Queenship of Mary, and wrote the document considered the "magna carta" for the Sodality of Mary, titled *Bis Saeculari*. He so greatly loved the Marian Sodality that he is also known as the "Pope of the Sodalities." He personally erected the World Federation of Sodalities and spoke at the First International Sodality World Congress on September 8, 1954.

Champion of the Rosary

As a devoted son of Mary, it was only natural for Pius XII to also have a deep love for the rosary. In 1942, on the 25th anniversary of the apparitions at Fatima, with World War II raging, he explicitly invoked the intercession of the Queen of the Most Holy Rosary, asking her to bring about peace in the world. Like so many others before him, he understood the rosary to be weapon and, in particular, stressed that the rosary is similar to David's sling: small, but able to bring down the mighty Goliath. He emphasized that the rosary has pride of place among all the devotions to Mary. When he consecrated the world to the Immaculate Heart of Mary in 1942, he explicitly mentioned the Marian title "Queen of the Rosary." In 1946, he wrote a letter to the archbishop of Manila called *Philippinas Insulas*, and referred to the rosary as the "*totius Evangelii breviarum*" ("a summary of the entire Gospel"). During the Marian Congress in the Philippines in 1954, Pius XII delivered a message to it by radio, stating that the rosary is the national devotion of the country and calling the Philippines the "Kingdom of the Holy Rosary." In his audiences with newlyweds, he always exhorted them to pray the rosary throughout their marriage and encouraged parents to teach their children to lay the spiritual flowers of the rosary at the feet of Mary's images.

In 1952, he published the profound rosary encyclical *Ingruentium Malorum (The Approaching Evils)*, stressing that the origins of the rosary are heavenly rather than human. In this deeply beautiful encyclical, he also attaches particular importance to the promotion of the family rosary as a means of preserving the faith in children and helping adults acquire virtue and perseverance in their Christian journey. During his papacy, he prayed the rosary at various times throughout his busy day, and constantly encouraged priests to pray the daily rosary as a means of growing in holiness. In 1957, he wrote a personal letter to the Master General of the Dominicans to remind the sons of St. Dominic that the promotion of the rosary is a particular mark of the Dominican order, and that they were to continue to zealously, diligently, and devoutly promote it.

Rosary Gems

There is no surer means of calling down God's blessings upon the family and espe-cially of preserving peace and happiness in the home than the daily recitation of the rosary. And apart from its supplicatory power, the family rosary can have very far-reaching effects, for if the habit of this pious practice is inculcated into children at a young and impressionable age, they too will be faithful to the rosary in later years, and their faith will thereby be nourished and strengthened.

~ Venerable Pope Pius XII

The Marian rosary is a marvelous garland woven from the angelic annunciation interspersed with the Lord's Prayer and joined together with a course of meditation, a most efficacious kind of entreaty, and most especially fruitful for the attainment of everlasting life. For this reason, in addition to the most excellent prayers of which it is comprised and which are, as it were, plaited into a crown of heavenly roses, it also offers an invitation to stir up one's faith, a help to devotion and outstanding models of virtue through the mysteries presented for contemplation. It therefore cannot fail to be most pleasing to the Virgin Mother of God and to her only Son, who undoubtedly considers any praise, honor and glory rendered to his mother as likewise rendered to himself.

~ Venerable Pope Pius XII

If you recite the family rosary, all united, you shall taste peace; you shall have in your homes concord of souls.

~ Venerable Pope Pius XII

The flowers of the rosary never perish.

~ Venerable Pope Pius XII

We put great confidence in the holy rosary for the healing of evils which afflict our times. Not with force, not with arms, not with human power, but with Divine help obtained through the means of this prayer, strong like David with his sling, the Church undaunted shall be able to confront the infernal enemy.

~ Venerable Pope Pius XII

O sorrowful and Immaculate Heart of Mary, Queen of the Most Holy Rosary, and Queen of the World, rule over us, together with the Sacred Heart of Jesus Christ, our King. Save us from the spreading flood of modern paganism; kindle in our hearts and homes the love of purity, the practice of a virtuous life, an ardent zeal for souls, and a desire to pray the rosary more faithfully.

~ Venerable Pope Pius XII

There are certain exercises of piety which the Church recommends very much to clergy and religious. It is our wish also that the faithful, as well, should take part in these practices. The chief of these are: meditation on spiritual things, diligent examination of conscience, enclosed retreats, visits to the Blessed Sacrament, and those special prayers in honor of the Blessed Virgin Mary, among which the rosary, as all know, has pride of place.

~ Venerable Pope Pius XII

What a sweet sight — most pleasing to God — when, at eventide, the Christian home resounds with the frequent repetition of praises in honor of the august Queen of Heaven! Then the rosary, recited in common, assembles before the image of the Virgin, in an admirable union of hearts, the parents and their children, who come back from their daily work. It unites them piously with those absent and those dead. It links all more tightly in a sweet bond of love, with the most Holy Virgin, who, like a loving mother, in the circle of her children, will be there bestowing upon them an abundance of the gifts of concord and family peace.

~ Venerable Pope Pius XII

The home of the Christian family, like that of Nazareth, will become an earthly abode of sanctity, and, so to speak, a sacred temple, where the holy rosary will not only be the particular prayer which every day rises to heaven in an odor of sweetness, but will also form the most efficacious school of Christian discipline and Christian virtue. This meditation on the Divine Mysteries of the Redemption will teach the adults to live, admiring daily the shining examples of Jesus and Mary, and to draw from these examples comfort in adversity, striving towards those heavenly treasures "where neither thief draws near, nor moth destroys" (Luke 12:33). This meditation will bring to the knowledge of the little ones the main truths of the Christian Faith, making love for the Redeemer blossom almost spontaneously in their innocent hearts, while, seeing their parents kneeling before the majesty of God, they will learn from their very early years how great before the throne of God is the value of prayers said in common.

~ Venerable Pope Pius XII

We consider the holy rosary the most convenient and most fruitful means [to obtain the aid of Mary], as is clearly suggested by the very origin of this practice, heavenly rather than human, and by its nature. What prayers are better adapted and more beautiful than the Lord's prayer and the angelic salutation, which are the flowers with which this mystical crown is formed? With meditation on the Sacred Mysteries added to the vocal prayers, there emerges another very great advantage, so that all, even the most simple and least educated, have in this a prompt and easy way to nourish and preserve their own faith.

~ Venerable Pope Pius XII

Queen of the Most Holy Rosary, Help of Christians, Refuge of Mankind, trium-
phant in all battles for God! We, your suppliants, prostrate ourselves at your throne,
confident that we shall obtain mercy and receive grace, the needed assistance and
protection, during the calamities of these days, not indeed by our own merits, of which
we presume nothing, but solely through the immense goodness of your maternal heart.

~ Venerable Pope Pius XII

Let all try to approach with greater trust the throne of grace and mercy of our Queen
and Mother, and beg for strength in adversity, light in darkness, consolation in
sorrow; above all let them strive to free themselves from the slavery of sin and offer an
unceasing homage, filled with filial loyalty, to their Queenly Mother. Let her churches
be thronged by the faithful, her feast-days honored; may the beads of the rosary be
in the hands of all; may Christians gather, in small numbers and large, to sing her
praises in churches, in homes, in hospitals, in prisons. May Mary's name be held in
highest reverence, a name sweeter than honey and more precious than jewels; may
none utter blasphemous words, the sign of a defiled soul, against that name graced
with such dignity and revered for its motherly goodness; let no one be so bold as to
speak a syllable which lacks the respect due to her name.

~ Venerable Pope Pius XII

This [the rosary] is truly the national devotion of the Philippines, which remains
sometimes the last link with the faith and the union of Christians in certain small
islands of the North, so far that they seem lost in the fog, so remote, that they haven't
seen missionaries for years and years. Philippines! Kingdom of Mary! Philippines!
Kingdom of the Holy Rosary! Run to this throne of grace, to this saving devotion,
because the storm is raging not far away from you. Remain firm in the Holy Faith
of your fathers that you have received at the cradle, just as your islands remain
firm, although shaken by earthquakes and violently besieged by irritated waves. And
never let the sacred fire of your love for your heavenly Mother die in your souls, this
sacred fire represented by these volcanoes erupting from time to time revealing the
furnace hidden in your land.

~ Venerable Pope Pius XII

SERVANT OF GOD DOLINDO RUOTOLO

The White Martyr of the Rosary
1882–1970

THE SERVANT OF GOD DOLINDO RUOTOLO

T HE SERVANT OF GOD DOLINDO RUOTOLO was born in Naples and is almost unknown outside of Italy. His unique name, "Dolindo," means "pain," and indeed, he was a white-martyr throughout his life. Saint Pio of Pietrelcina considered him a saint. Frequently, when people went to San Giovanni Rotondo to visit Padre Pio, he would ask why they were visiting him when there was a saint in Naples! Like St. Pio, Dolindo Ruotolo was zealous for the faith and frequently misunderstood by both the hierarchy and contemporary theologians.

Ruotolo was a priest with a Neapolitan temperament, not known to mince words when it came to opposing the historical-critical method of scripture scholarship. He zealously wrote against its abuse and warned people of its dangers. As a result, he had his priestly faculties to publicly celebrate the Sacraments removed on several occasions. To this day, there is a story circulating in Naples that Our Lady appeared to Venerable Pope Pius XII and exhorted him to give priestly faculties back to Dolindo immediately. Providentially, Pius XII intervened so that Dolindo could once again publicly celebrate the Sacraments. A devout priest and avid scholar, Dolindo has been called the "Scribe of the Holy Spirit." He penned a 33-volume commentary on Holy Scripture, as well as many other theological works. He wanted people to read good books on theology and devotion, and so he founded the Apostolato Stampa press in order to publish orthodox theological works. He was an extraordinary musician, a Third Order Franciscan, and slept less than three hours a night due to his intense prayer life.

Marian Devotion

An erudite theologian and author, Dolindo wrote many works on Our Lady and various commentaries on the Magnificat and the Visitation of Mary to her relative Elizabeth. He understood Our Lady to be at the very heart of Christianity and theology, and included her in almost all of his theological writings. During the last 10 years of his life, he referred to himself as "the Madonna's little old man." In his old age, he suffered from extreme arthritis and paralysis, yet persevered through the pain to write a trilogy of books on Our Lady. His Marian trilogy was written to defend the Marian teachings of the Church.

Dolindo was very devoted to both Our Lady of Lourdes and the message of Fatima. He zealously promoted devotion to the Immaculate Heart of Mary and emphasized that May was Mary's month. The month of May was particularly prominent in his devotion to Mary because he understood the human heart to be like a flower that needs to be cultivated by Mary. He also had a special love for the souls in purgatory. In the course of his various devotions to Mary, he offered up all his actions to Mary in order to help the poor souls in purgatory.

Champion of the Rosary

Throughout his priesthood, it was rare for anyone to see the Servant of God Dolindo Ruotolo without a rosary in his hand. The rosary was his constant companion. An accomplished musician, he was very fond of referring to the rosary in musical terms and considered the rosary to be his "spiritual" instrument. He deeply regretted that Modernism had reduced the prominence of the rosary in the lives of many Catholics, and emphatically preached that the rosary was not a tedious prayer of repetition, but a method for contemplating the saving mysteries of the life of Christ. He always encouraged people to pray the rosary devoutly and stressed that a rosary well prayed is analogous to laying roses at Mary's feet. On the other hand, he was quick to note that a rosary poorly prayed is comparable to laying dead leaves at the feet of the Queen of Heaven.

Dolindo lived through both World War I and World War II. He saw the rosary as a weapon in the spiritual life, referring to the rosary as a sword and a machine gun in our spiritual arsenal. In his homilies, he often informed his listeners that every Hail Mary was a shot fired at Satan and the forces of darkness. He had a profound understanding of Our Lady's necessary role in bringing us closer to Christ, and believed Our Lady to be the Mediatrix of All Grace and the spiritual "power grid" that distributes all the graces of Christ to the members of the Church. Extending the metaphor, he emphasized that the rosary was a major means of tapping into the power grid.

Rosary Gems

In climbing toward God for its salvation, the soul possesses the Key of Heaven in the rosary.

~ Servant of God Dolindo Ruotolo

Amid the disharmony of our chaotic lives, the rosary is the instrument, the harp or the psaltery with its ten chords, for each group of harmonies. With the rosary we continually raise a song of love from earth.

~ Servant of God Dolindo Ruotolo

The rosary has very great riches, both in the Hail Mary and in the mysteries contemplated. It is not a monotonous mumbling. It is a marvelous harmony, just as a musical instrument does not play a dull repetition of a note, but a melodic and harmonious variation, which raises the soul and arouses in it much affection and sweet and pure thoughts. It is almost a vibration of waves and the delicacy of musical chords.

~ Servant of God Dolindo Ruotolo

As an army has its marching music, marking the time for the soldiers, so does the rosary lovingly mark time for the Church militant.

~ Servant of God Dolindo Ruotolo

The rosary is a powerful prayer against Satan and against the assaults of evil. Our Church brought, and continues to bring, great triumphs because of this prayer. The decades of the rosary, from this point of view, are like the belt of a machine gun: every bead is a shot, every affection of the soul is as an explosion of faith that frightens off Satan, and Mary once more crushes his head.

~ Servant of God Dolindo Ruotolo

O Most Holy Rosary, may your flowers bloom on the desolate flowerbeds of unbelievers and let simple and lively faith come to bloom again.

~ Servant of God Dolindo Ruotolo

The holy rosary was always, and still is the most acceptable devotion to the Heart of Mother Mary.

~ Servant of God Dolindo Ruotolo

The rosary is not a tedious prayer just because the person is always repeating the Hail Mary. Each Hail Mary recited, with the contemplation of the mysteries, is always said with a different feeling and the intensity of the prayer is not monotonous. It is an intensity of love. Does not a child call his mother all the time? His cry: "Mom!" is different according to the need that inspires and animates it. Therefore, recite the rosary like a child, invoking our Heavenly Mother and imploring her help.

~ Servant of God Dolindo Ruotolo

If you want to live a holy life, cultivate devotion to Mary in your family. Gather your children in prayer and in the recitation of the holy rosary.

~ Servant of God Dolindo Ruotolo

Praying the rosary is like the rolling of the pictures of a movie, a reminder of the great mysteries of our Redemption, showing them over and over again.

~ Servant of God Dolindo Ruotolo

The rosary saves you from despair and opens to you the luminous ways of charity and holiness. The rosary is your comfort in your life and the sweet chain that unites you to God.

~ Servant of God Dolindo Ruotolo

The rosary is not a tedious prayer in which we repeat always the same thing. This is the belief of those who look for an excuse not to say it.

~ Servant of God Dolindo Ruotolo

A careless rosary is a rosary with torn dead leaves.

~ Servant of God Dolindo Ruotolo

ST. PIO OF PIETRELCINA

The Mystic
of the Rosary
1887–1968

BEATIFIED: May 2, 1999 by St. John Paul II
CANONIZED: June 16, 2002 by St. John Paul II
FEAST DAY: September 23

SAINT PIO OF PIETRELCINA, affectionately known as Padre Pio, was a Capuchin Franciscan and one of the greatest mystics of the 20th century. For more than 50 years, he bore the stigmata (bleeding wound marks) of Christ. He was a man of suffering and frequently misunderstood by his brother priests and religious confreres. Due to these misunderstandings, he was not allowed to hear confessions or celebrate Mass publicly for two years. Pope Pius XI, however, personally ordered the Holy Office to reverse the decisions made against Padre Pio.

Even while Padre Pio was alive, Venerable Pope Pius XII considered him a saint and encouraged people to visit the holy Franciscan mystic in San Giovanni Rotondo, the place where St. Pio lived and eventually opened a hospital. In 1947, Karol Józef Wojtyła, a young Polish priest studying in Rome, visited Padre Pio in San Giovanni Rotondo. Many people believe that during this encounter between the two future saints, the Franciscan mystic informed his Polish visitor of his future election to the papacy. Whether this is true or not, it was providentially planned that Wojtyła would be elected to the papacy, take the name John Paul II, and beatify and canonize St. Pio of Pietrelcina.

Marian Devotion

In line with the great Franciscan tradition of Marian spirituality, St. Pio understood Our Lady to be the tabernacle of the Most High, perpetually surrounded by angels. He was always aware that Mary was standing by his side as his mother and protector. A mystic who experienced frequent visions of Jesus, Mary, the saints, and the angels throughout his life, St. Pio was surprised when he learned that everyone else did not have similar visions. He would often ask his guardian angel to help him love Mary more, and frequently said that during the Mass, he felt the presence of Our Lady and the holy angels at his side.

A devoutly Marian priest, St. Pio offered fraternal guidance to his brother priests regarding Mary. He would inform them that they would only become holy and their ministries fruitful if they welcomed Mary into their hearts and maintained a deep relationship with her. His priestly heart was on fire with love for Mary; he knew that there is no other path leading to life except the one trod by our spiritual mother.

Mary obtained a healing for him on at least one occasion in 1959, when the Fatima Pilgrim Statue was touring through cities in Italy. When the statue came to San Giovanni Rotondo, he desperately wanted to see her, but was so ill that, after making three attempts to view the pilgrim statue, he was not able to lift himself out of bed. As the helicopter carrying the pilgrim statue took off, he poured out his sorrow to Mary, expressing his disappointment at not being able to see her miraculous statue. Then, all of a sudden, the pilot inexplicably turned the helicopter around and headed back toward the monastery where Padre Pio was in bed! The pilot later attested that he had no explanation for why he veered off course and returned to circle several times above the monastery.

Padre Pio and heaven knew the reason. Mary desired to grant her son's wish, and as an additional blessing, at the moment that the helicopter was circling over his monastery, Padre Pio felt his body tremble. He experienced a complete healing. In thanksgiving for the healing, Padre Pio sent a crucifix to Fatima. Then, a few months later, a delegation from the Blue Army presented him with a hand-carved statue of Our Lady of Fatima. He placed it in the sacristy where he prepared for Mass each day. In 1968, he died whispering the name he honored a thousand times a day: "Maria."

Champion of the Rosary

Saint Pio, who clearly lived the life of a victim-soul (one who has been called by God to share in a special way in the sufferings of Jesus and make reparation for the sins of the world), has been referred to as the "Living Rosary" since, as a mystic who bore the wounds of Christ, he lived the mysteries of the rosary more directly than most and always had a rosary in his hand. As a youth, he learned his tremendous love for the rosary from the example provided by his family. Every evening, his family would gather together to pray it. A devout Catholic family, they would even fast in honor of Our Lady of Mt. Carmel. During his youth, as well as during his time as a soldier stationed in Naples, he made frequent visits to the Shrine of Our Lady of the Rosary of Pompeii.

One of the many sufferings imposed on St. Pio by the Church was that he was forbidden to write about his mystical experiences. That is why there exist very few writings by him on the rosary and the other great loves of his holy life. Nevertheless, he bore constant witness to the rosary in his many conversations with people. When priests came to see him, he always recommended the rosary to them. It has been said that his silent sermon was always the rosary. He prayed it constantly throughout the day. Once, when asked by his religious superior how many rosaries he had prayed that day, St. Pio responded, "Thirty-four!" On another occasion, when asked by a Franciscan confrere what prayer was most pleasing to Mary, he quickly responded that it was the rosary because she herself had taught it to us and continued to stress its importance in her various apparitions.

Saint Pio understood the rosary to be a powerful spiritual weapon, able to overcome theological errors and false political regimes. On several occasions, he bilocated to the prison cell of another great champion of the rosary, József Cardinal Mindszenty. Imprisoned for his radical opposition to Communism, Mindszenty was a Hungarian prelate who frequently preached that the rosary was the secret weapon of the Catholic Church against Communism. Padre Pio knew this, too, and greatly desired to hand on the spiritual weapon of the rosary to his spiritual children. The day before he died, when asked to offer a final exhortation to those around him, his advice was to love Mary, make her known, and always pray the rosary. When he died, not only did he have the name of Mary on his lips, but he also had the rosary in his hand.

Rosary Gems

Love the Blessed Mother and make her loved. Always say the rosary.

~ St. Pio of Pietrelcina

The rosary is a weapon in our hands with which we can overcome the devil's attacks.

~ St. Pio of Pietrelcina

Our Lady has never refused me a grace through the recitation of the rosary.

~ St. Pio of Pietrelcina

Go get my weapon [the rosary].

~ St. Pio of Pietrelcina

Love the Madonna and pray the rosary, for her rosary is the weapon against the evils of the world today.

~ St. Pio of Pietrelcina

The rosary, that is my weapon.

~ St. Pio of Pietrelcina

Satan always tries to destroy this prayer [the rosary], but he will never succeed. It is the prayer of her who triumphs over everything and everyone.

~ St. Pio of Pietrelcina

The rosary is the weapon that wins all battles.

~ St. Pio of Pietrelcina

It would be impossible to name all the many saints who discovered in the rosary a genuine path to growth in holiness. We need but mention Saint Louis Marie Grignion de Montfort, the author of an excellent work on the rosary, and, closer to ourselves, Padre Pio of Pietrelcina, whom I recently had the joy of canonizing.

~ St. John Paul II

St. Josemaría Escrivá

The Pilgrim of the Rosary
1902–1975

BEATIFIED: May 17, 1992 by St. John Paul II
CANONIZED: October 6, 2002 by St. John Paul II
FEAST DAY: June 26

SAINT JOSEMARÍA ESCRIVÁ was born in Barbastro, Spain, earned a doctorate in theology from the Lateran University in Rome, and lived his entire life in the 20th century. A very prayerful priest with a deep devotion to the Holy Eucharist, he worked with the poor and sick in the slums of Madrid for many years. In 1928, he founded Opus Dei, an organization of laypeople and priests dedicated to announcing God's universal call to holiness for all people. An extremely fruitful apostolate, Opus Dei received official approval from the Church in 1950 from Venerable Pope Pius XII.

Saint Josemaría Escrivá authored numerous books, many of which have been translated into multiple languages, selling millions of copies worldwide. Viktor Frankl, the famous psychiatrist, neurologist, and survivor of the Holocaust, once met St. Josemaría, and was so impressed and inspired by him that Frankl described him as a "spiritual atomic bomb."

Marian Devotion

At the age of two, St. Josemaría suffered from an unknown illness (most likely epilepsy) and was expected to die. His devout mother took him to the Marian shrine of Torreciudad in Aragon, Spain, and earnestly prayed for him before a statue of Our Lady of the Angels that dates from the 11th century. Miraculously, he recovered. His mother attributed his healing to Our Lady. This event helped to form in him a strong, life-long Marian devotion. As a seminarian, he made frequent visits to the nearby city of Saragossa to the Shrine of Our Lady of Pilar. Upon being ordained a priest, he celebrated his first Mass in that shrine. Later in life, always grateful for his healing as a child, he oversaw the construction of a major shrine to Our Lady in Torreciudad. This shrine continues to be operated by the members of Opus Dei and is a popular pilgrimage destination for people from all over Europe.

Throughout his life, St. Josemaría was known to have a particular love for Marian shrines and places where Mary had appeared in apparitions. He visited Fatima no less than nine times! On several of his trips to Fatima, he made personal visits to speak with the surviving visionary of Fatima, the Servant of God Sr. Lúcia Dos Santos. He loved to wander through the streets of Rome in search of little images of Mary to honor and venerate, visited Lourdes several times, went on a pilgrimage to the shrine of Our Lady of the Rosary of Pompeii, and, in 1951, one year after Opus Dei received official approval, made a pilgrimage to the Holy House of Loreto to entrust Opus Dei completely to Our Lady. One of his favorite shrines was the one dedicated to Our Lady of Sonsoles in Spain. In Spanish, *sonsoles* means "those suns" and refers to the beautiful eyes of the Marian statue there. He made countless pilgrimages to lesser-known Marian shrines in Europe, as well, and in 1970, he traveled to Mexico City to make a novena at the Basilica of Our Lady of Guadalupe. Part of the heritage he left to the members of Opus Dei was his encouragement for the members to make frequent Marian pilgrimages.

Saint Josemaría never trusted any undertaking that didn't somehow manifest a love for Our Lady. He understood clearly that Jesus can only be truly found when we seek Mary, because it is God's will that we receive and return to Jesus through Mary. One of his greatest aspirations that he repeated constantly was the phrase, *"Omnes cum Petro ad Iesum per Mariam!"* (*"All with Peter to Jesus through Mary!"*). He ended almost all of his homilies by mentioning Mary, promoted devotion to the Brown Scapular, and taught that the month of May is a special time for Marian devotions. Every time he went into his room, he would kiss a particular statue of Our Lady; this statue became affectionately known as "The Lady of the Kisses." Once, after St. Josemaría venerated an image of St. Juan Diego giving a rose to Our Lady of Guadalupe, he expressed to those around him a desire to die in such fashion. Providentially, when he died in 1975, he was near a picture of Our Lady of Guadalupe that hung in his room.

Champion of the Rosary

Saint Josemaría's parents were devout Catholics. In his youth, they gave him the edifying example of praying the rosary in the home. At the age of 10, he began to carry the rosary in his pocket everywhere he went. He considered the rosary his weapon, his instructor in the virtues of Jesus and Mary, and a method for telling Mary that he loved her. A constant pilgrim, St. Josemaría always made the rosary a part of his Marian pilgrimages. He would pray the rosary during his journeys to shrines, as well as on the journeys back home. Even while at a shrine, he would make a point of walking around the grounds to pray a rosary.

Throughout his priestly life, he prayed the rosary every day and wrote a beautiful book on the rosary in just one day. In that book, he emphasized that the rosary should be prayed well, with a meditative spirit, and not in a hurried or rushed manner. He also emphasized that the rosary was not only for "little old women," but also for grown men and everyone else. Referencing the exhortation of Christ that only the childlike will enter the kingdom of heaven (see Mt 18:3), he instructed everyone that it is the rosary that most helps us to become childlike and express a daily love for the Blessed Virgin. To this day, the rosary remains a daily devotion at the shrine he founded in honor of Our Lady in Torreciudad, Spain. Part of his legacy to the members of Opus Dei was his example of praying the daily rosary, which he desired they imitate.

Rosary Gems

If you say the holy rosary every day, with a spirit of faith and love, Our Lady will make sure she leads you very far along her Son's path.

~ St. Josemaría Escrivá

Today, as in other times, the rosary must be a powerful weapon to enable us to win in our interior struggle, and to help all souls.

~ St. Josemaría Escrivá

The holy rosary is a powerful weapon. Use it with confidence and you'll be amazed at the results.

~ St. Josemaría Escrivá

To say the holy rosary, considering the mysteries, repeating the Our Father and Hail Mary, with the praises to the Blessed Trinity, and the constant invocation of the Mother of God, is a continuous act of faith, hope and love, of adoration and reparation.

~ St. Josemaría Escrivá

For a Christian, vocal prayer must spring from the heart, so that while the rosary is said, the mind can enter into contemplation of each one of the mysteries.

~ St. Josemaría Escrivá

You always leave the rosary for later, and you end up not saying it at all because you are sleepy. If there is no other time, say it in the street without letting anybody notice it. It will, moreover, help you to have presence of God.

~ St. Josemaría Escrivá

Many Christians have the custom of wearing the scapular; or they recall the central events in Christ's life by saying the rosary, never getting tired of repeating its words, just like people in love.

~ St. Josemaría Escrivá

When we say the rosary, which is a wonderful devotion which I will never tire of recommending to Christians everywhere, our minds and hearts go over the mysteries of Mary's admirable life which are, at the same time, the fundamental mysteries of our faith.

~ St. Josemaría Escrivá

Do you want to love Our Lady? Well, then, get to know her. How? By praying her rosary.

~ St. Josemaría Escrivá

Pray the holy rosary. Blessed be that monotony of Hail Marys which purifies the monotony of your sins!

~ St. Josemaría Escrivá

Pronounce the Our Father and the Hail Marys of each decade [of the rosary] clearly and without rushing: this will help you always to get more and more out of this way of loving Mary.

~ St. Josemaría Escrivá

Take [up] the rosary, one of the most deeply rooted of Christian devotions. The Church encourages us to contemplate its mysteries.

~ St. Josemaría Escrivá

Pause for a few seconds — three or four — in silent meditation to consider each mystery of the rosary before you recite the Our Father and the Hail Marys of that decade. I am sure this practice will increase your recollection and the fruits of your prayer.

~ St. Josemaría Escrivá

St. Pope
John XXIII

The Shepherd of the Rosary
1881–1963

PAPACY: 1958–1963
BEATIFICATION: September 3, 2000 by St. John Paul II
CANONIZATION: April 27, 2014 by Pope Francis with
Pope Emeritus Benedict XVI in attendance
FEAST DAY: October 11

SAINT POPE JOHN XXIII was born in the Lombardy region of Italy and had 13 brothers and sisters. While in the seminary, he became a Third Order Franciscan. Over the course of his priestly life, he served the Holy See in several diplomatic assignments, including an appointment as the papal nuncio to France. During World War II, while nuncio, he helped save many Jewish people from the horrors of the Holocaust. Elected to the papacy in 1958, he was chosen to lead the Church during the initial years of the turbulent 1960s. Aware that there was a cultural shift occurring in society, he opened the historic Second Vatican Council in October of 1962. His frequent habit of sneaking out of the Vatican at night to walk the streets of Rome earned him the nickname "Johnny Walker." He is often referred to as the "Pope of St. Joseph" because he did much to promote devotion to St. Joseph.

He had a great sense of humor. Once, when asked how many people worked at the Vatican, he responded, "About half!" Good Pope John XXIII died of stomach cancer in 1963.

Marian Devotion

From his youth, John XXIII had a great love for Our Lady, especially Our Lady of Perpetual Help. As a priest, he showed a particular love for Marian shrines and visited them frequently. He visited Fatima in Portugal, Czestochowa in Poland, and Lourdes (his favorite Marian shrine) in France. He first went to Lourdes in 1905, and afterwards made numerous pilgrimages there as nuncio. During his time as archbishop of Venice, he consecrated the new Basilica of Lourdes on behalf of the pope.

He believed that piety towards the most holy Virgin was the mark of a truly Catholic heart. He did much to promote devotion to Mary during his pontificate. Prior to the opening of the Second Vatican Council, he journeyed to the Holy House of Loreto to ask for Mary's intercession for the Council. He is responsible for the canonization of many Marian saints, especially St. Vincent Pallotti and St. Peter Julian Eymard.

Champion of the Rosary

As a young child, St. Pope John XXIII loved the rosary and prayed it every evening with his family. He carried this love of the rosary into his priesthood; when he served as archbishop of Venice, he prayed 15 decades of the rosary every day. After he was elected to the papacy, the first encyclical of his pontificate was an encyclical on the rosary titled *Grata Recordatio* (*Grateful memory*). In it, he explicitly referred to and praised the rosary encyclicals of Pope Leo XIII, affirming that the rosary is a social remedy for the troubled times in which he was chosen to lead the Church.

His love of the rosary was so great that he established a daily schedule during his papacy that allowed him to pray the entire rosary every day. He would pray the Joyful Mysteries in the morning, the Sorrowful Mysteries in the afternoon, and, at 7:30 p.m. every evening, he would pray the Glorious Mysteries with the members of the papal household (his secretary, the religious sisters, and the housekeepers). He published a series of meditations on the various mysteries of the rosary, and noted that, after Holy Mass and the Liturgy of the Hours, the rosary has pride of place among all Christian devotions. He greatly supported the Servant of God Patrick Peyton in his efforts to promote rosary crusades and the family rosary, and encouraged everyone to pray the rosary. He considered the rosary to be the simplest and easiest form of prayer.

Rosary Gems

This prayer — the holy rosary — is the simplest and easiest one of all for the Christian people.

~ St. Pope John XXIII

When parents and children gather together at the end of the day in the recitation of the rosary, together they meditate on the example of work, obedience, and charity which shone in the house of Nazareth; together they learn from the Mother of God to suffer serenely; to accept with dignity and courage the difficulties of life and to acquire the proper attitude to the daily events of life. It is certain that they will meet with greater facility the problems of family life. Homes will thereby be converted into sanctuaries of peace. Torrents of divine favors will come to them, even the inestimable favor of a priestly or religious vocation.

~ St. Pope John XXIII

Individuals, whatever their spiritual status may be, will undoubtedly find in the fervent recitation of the holy rosary, an invitation to regulate their lives in conformity with Christian principles. They will, in truth, find in the rosary a spring of most abundant graces to help them in fulfilling faithfully their duties in life.

~ St. Pope John XXIII

The well-meditated rosary consists in a threefold element. For each decade there is a picture, and for each picture a threefold emphasis, which is simultaneously: mystical contemplation, intimate reflection, and pious intention.

~ St. Pope John XXIII

The rosary is a very commendable form of prayer and meditation. In saying it we weave a mystic garland of Ave Marias, Pater Nosters, *and* Gloria Patris.

~ St. Pope John XXIII

As an exercise of Christian devotion among the faithful of the Latin Rite who constitute a notable portion of the Catholic family, the rosary ranks after Holy Mass and the Breviary for ecclesiastics [priests], and for the laity after participation in the sacraments. It is a devout form of union with God and lifts souls to a high supernatural plane.

~ St. Pope John XXIII

May the rosary never fall from your hands.

~ St. Pope John XXIII

The rosary is the glory of the Roman Church.

~ St. Pope John XXIII

Oh, what a delight this blessed rosary is! Oh, what assurance it brings of being heard here on earth and in the eternal heavens!

~ St. Pope John XXIII

I knew Pope John. His love for Our Lady and his devotion to her rosary contributed an essential element to his spiritual growth and stature.

~ Servant of God Patrick Peyton

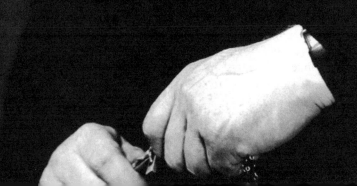

SERVANT OF GOD PATRICK PEYTON

The Rosary Priest
1909–1992

THE SERVANT OF GOD PATRICK PEYTON was born into a poor family in Ireland. At the age of 19, he immigrated to the United States to find employment. He found work as a janitor at the Catholic cathedral in Scranton, Pennsylvania. On one occasion, he was so inspired by a mission preached by the Holy Cross Fathers that he joined their religious community and became a seminarian. While a seminarian, he was healed from tuberculosis as a result of praying a novena to Our Lady. In thanksgiving, he made a promise to Our Lady that he would spend the rest of his life telling families throughout the world how Mary desires to help them and bringing the daily rosary into their homes. In his zeal for spreading the rosary, he became one of the greatest promoters of the rosary in the history of the Church.

After initiating a radio program in Albany, New York, that sought to spread the family rosary, he officially launched the Family Rosary apostolate in 1942. As part of his efforts to spread the family rosary across America, he wrote to every bishop in the United States and asked them to promote the family rosary in their respective dioceses. He coined the catchy slogan, "The family that prays together stays together," and was able to mobilize some of the most famous Hollywood actors and celebrities of his time to support his rosary efforts. He even got many of these celebrities to appear on television programs and radio broadcasts to promote the family rosary. In 1947, he launched Family Theater Productions as a further method for promoting the family rosary through the media, and, in 1948, he began the Family Rosary Crusades apostolate. During his lifetime, he organized rosary events in more than 40 countries, gathering over 28 million people to pray the rosary! He was greatly loved by many popes and was a personal friend of St. Teresa of Calcutta. He is buried in Holy Cross Cemetery, located on the grounds of Stonehill College in Easton, Massachusetts.

Marian Devotion

The fervent Marian devotion of Fr. Patrick Peyton can be traced back to his formative years in Ireland. He was greatly influenced by his devout Catholic parents and the Marian devotion of the Irish people. Every evening, his mother would call the family to prayer, and his father would lead the family rosary in the home.

During his time as a seminarian in the United States, after his healing from tuberculosis took place, his love for Mary turned into an apostolate. He understood his mission in life to be spreading devotion to Mary and her rosary, writing several books and addressing crowds across the world. Mary was his princess. He was honored to bring solid teaching about his princess to every nation, and often referred to himself as "Mary's donkey." The famous actress Loretta Young once made the remark that she had never met a man so in love with a woman as Fr. Peyton was in love with the Blessed Virgin Mary.

His Marian devotion inspired many people all over the world to pray the rosary as a means of peaceful resistance to dictatorial regimes. For example, in

1986, during the People Power Revolution that overthrew the oppressive dictatorship of President Ferdinand Marcos in the Philippines, it was the message of Fr. Patrick Peyton that gave the Filipino people tremendous strength and heroic courage sufficient to enable them to stand in front of armed tanks and pray the rosary. On the famous EDSA freeway, the people were encouraged to stand their ground and pray the rosary when they saw the huge billboards for Fr. Patrick Peyton's Rosary Crusades that lined the street. The billboards read: "The family that prays together stays together" and "A world at prayer is a world at peace." The rosary brought about a peaceful revolution; not a single shot was fired.

Champion of the Rosary

Without exaggeration, the efforts of Fr. Patrick Peyton to spread the family rosary are unparalleled. Truly deserving to be called the rosary priest, he not only founded major movements to promote the family rosary, but also produced 15 short films that used the mysteries of the rosary as their central themes. He was so bold in service to his mission that, in 1971, he wrote a letter to Pope Paul VI requesting the rosary's elevation to the status of a liturgical prayer! He made such a request because he was watching entire nations turn away from the rosary during the 1960s and early 1970s. The rejection of the rosary greatly disturbed him, and he begged the Vicar of Christ to do something about it. The response from Rome came in the form of Bl. Pope Paul VI's famous 1974 apostolic letter *Marialis Cultus*. Though the letter did not elevate the rosary to the status of a liturgical prayer, Bl. Pope Paul VI greatly defended the rosary, encouraged the faithful to pray it, and placed a particular emphasis on the family rosary.

In the mind of Fr. Peyton, the rosary is the Psalter of Redemption because it lovingly intertwines two most beautiful prayers: the Our Father and the Hail Mary. He considered the rosary a method of evangelization and a catechetical tool; for this reason, he always emphasized the importance of reciting the Creed at the beginning of the rosary. Like many others, he expressed a desire for additional mysteries to be associated with the rosary so that people could learn to meditate more frequently on the public life of Jesus. Several of the mysteries he proposed would later be incorporated into the rosary by St. John Paul II. Echoing the words of Bl. Pope Pius IX, Fr. Peyton informed everyone in attendance at his events that when they held the rosary in their hands, they were holding the "single richest treasure in the Vatican." He was convinced that praying the rosary as a family would make virtue and good works flourish in both the home and in society. To further encourage people to pray the rosary, he promoted the 15 promises of Our Lady to those who pray the rosary (see page 349).

Due to the effectiveness and popularity of his Family Rosary Crusades, Fr. Peyton received personal invitations from bishops all around the world to visit their countries and spread the family rosary. In 1961, more than 550,000 people attended his rosary rally in San Francisco. This event was proclaimed by the archdiocesan archivist the most important event in the history of the archdiocese of

San Francisco. In 1962, he gathered more than one million people in Colombia to pray the rosary, and in the same year in Rio de Janeiro, Brazil, he gathered over 1.5 million. In 1964, he gathered 2 million people in Sao Paulo, Brazil, and in 1985, he gathered well over 2 million people in the Philippines to pray the rosary.

Rosary Gems

From my earliest memories, I saw my father with the rosary beads in his hands and my mother holding hers.

~ Servant of God Patrick Peyton

The rosary can bring families through all dangers and evils.

~ Servant of God Patrick Peyton

I want to get ten million families to pray the rosary every day.

~ Servant of God Patrick Peyton

Because of the daily family rosary, my home was for me a cradle, a school, a university, a library, and most of all, a little church.

~ Servant of God Patrick Peyton

It is the rosary prayed by families that will keep the lights of faith glowing in the days of darkness of faith, as it has done in the past.

~ Servant of God Patrick Peyton

Countless families the world over invite Mary to their homes through the family rosary. She comes. They sense her presence. They solve their problems because where Mary is present there is Christ, her Divine Son.

~ Servant of God Patrick Peyton

What a blessed thing it would be if we could pray the rosary over nationwide radio and bring Our Blessed Mother into every home in America.

~ Servant of God Patrick Peyton

We must hold fast to the treasure of the rosary, the gift of Our Blessed Mother.

~ Servant of God Patrick Peyton

We must never forget the rosary and its meaning, the very embodiment of our Christianity.

~ Servant of God Patrick Peyton

Like all the works and events in the Church, the rosary has the power and touch of the Holy Spirit upon it.

~ Servant of God Patrick Peyton

Starting on their wedding day my parents knelt each evening before the hearth to say together the family rosary, that God and Mary might protect and bless their home and fill it with the laughter of children.

~ Servant of God Patrick Peyton

Throughout history the friends of Our Blessed Lady have devised ways and means of asking for her power and intercession, and the most outstanding means is the rosary.

~ Servant of God Patrick Peyton

The one thing I want to do with my life is to devote every minute of it to restoring the family rosary.

~ Servant of God Patrick Peyton

What is so good about the rosary is that it goes all the way in telling the whole story of Jesus and Mary and ourselves.

~ Servant of God Patrick Peyton

It's in that school, in that sanctuary, in that holy home of the rosary, that I discovered Mary! And in discovering Mary, I discovered a protector. I found a friend. I found a mother that would never die. I found a mother filled with affection for me, filled with concern for my welfare, lavishing upon me her strength, her prayers, her guidance, her protection. I'm speaking to you of Mary, the Mother of Jesus Christ. And thanks to the family rosary, this is the greatest fruit that it gave me.

~ Servant of God Patrick Peyton

When combined with the pure contemplative prayer of the rosary meditations, the Hail Mary becomes the most powerful weapon ever placed in the hands of man — a weapon which, through God and his most blessed Mother, will someday change the face of the earth.

~ Servant of God Patrick Peyton

When you look at the rosary in your hand it appears very simple, that little string of beads, yet how far that short chain reaches, what a cosmos it encircles, how closely it binds us to God and to Mary. You hold the power to change your lives.

~ Servant of God Patrick Peyton

BLESSED POPE PAUL VI

The Defender of the Rosary 1897–1978

PAPACY: 1963–1978
BEATIFIED: October 19, 2014 by Pope Francis with
Pope Emeritus Benedict XVI in attendance
FEAST DAY: September 26

B LESSED POPE PAUL VI was born in northern Italy and elected the Vicar of Christ during the turbulent 1960s and 1970s. Before being elected to the papacy, he had earned a doctorate in canon law and served as the Vatican Secretary of State, as well as the archbishop of Milan. Upon the death of St. Pope John XXIII, the Second Vatican Council was halted, but Bl. Pope Paul VI re-opened it and brought about its conclusion in 1965.

Blessed Pope Paul VI was an extremely humble man. After his death, it became known that, during his papal visit to the Philippines in 1970, he had been stabbed in the chest in the Manila airport by a Bolivian poet and artist who had disguised himself as a priest. The man who stabbed him, Benjamin Mendoza, had purchased a dagger in a Muslim thrift shop. Interestingly, the miracle that was approved for Bl. Pope Paul VI's beatification was worked through the relic of the blood left on his vestment from the stabbing. The case involved an unborn child in his mother's womb that had suffered brain defects during pregnancy. The mother's physician advised her to abort the child, but the mother refused. Instead, she asked for the intercession of Pope Paul VI at the urging of a nun who gave her a holy card with a piece of the pope's cassock from the attack in Manila. When the child was born, to the surprise of everyone, there were no brain defects. Interestingly, it had been Bl. Pope Paul VI who wrote the landmark encyclical *Humanae Vitae* that defended all human life and condemned all forms of artificial birth control. Blessed Pope Paul VI was known as the "pope of firsts" because he was the first pope to ever fly on a plane, the first pope to visit Fatima, and the first pope to visit the Holy Land since St. Peter.

Marian Devotion

Blessed Pope Paul VI's tender devotion to Mary is evident in his request that his first Mass as a priest be celebrated in the Basilica of Santa Maria delle Grazie in Brescia. As a bishop and then later as pope, he frequently spoke at Marian congresses and events in order to encourage devotion to Mary. He considered the Sacrament of Baptism a prolongation of the virginal maternity of Mary and boldly taught that for a person to be a true Christian, they needed to be Marian. In all of his teachings on Mary, he always emphasized that Our Lady is the model of Christian perfection.

Like many of his predecessors, he fervently promoted the month of May as a special time for honoring Mary. He even released an apostolic exhortation titled *Mense Maio* (*The Month of May*) on this subject in 1965. The year 1965 was also the concluding year of the Second Vatican Council. At the end of the Council, Paul VI declared Mary the Mother of the Church. On the 50th anniversary of the apparitions at Fatima (May 13, 1967), he became the first pope to visit Fatima. He visited many Marian shrines during his papacy and wrote the apostolic exhortation *Marialis Cultus* in 1974. This landmark document sought to correct the neglect in Marian devotion that had occurred after the

Second Vatican Council. He also beatified the great Franciscan priest and martyr of charity, St. Maximilian Kolbe.

Champion of the Rosary

During the first general audience of his pontificate, Bl. Pope Paul VI extolled praying the rosary as an especially beneficial pious practice for all the faithful. He was very much in favor of the family rosary and spoke about it frequently throughout his papacy. He made frequent reference to the importance of meditation during the rosary, stating that the rosary without contemplation is like a body without a soul. While the Second Vatican Council was taking place, he wrote a letter to the papal legate for the Mariological Congress being held in the Dominican Republic and specifically noted that one of the exercises of Marian piety that the Fathers of the Council were recommending was the rosary. Then, in 1966, one year after the Council, he wrote *Christi Matri*, emphasizing again that the Second Vatican Council had intended to promote the rosary.

In 1967, when he revised the list of indulgences offered by the Church, he simplified the indulgences and limited them to two categories: partial or plenary. The new list contained a section on the rosary and made the indulgences attached to the rosary much easier to understand. In 1969, in honor of the fourth centenary of the document of St. Pope Pius V codifying the form of the rosary, he published the apostolic letter *Recurrens Mensis October* to promote praying the rosary in October and offering the rosary as a means of bringing about peace in the world.

During his pontificate, many theologians wanted him to revise the prayer of the rosary and break from his predecessor's acceptance of the pious tradition of the rosary's origins through St. Dominic. To his perpetual credit, Bl. Pope Paul VI remained staunchly opposed to such ideas. While he understood there had been legitimate adaptations and developments of the rosary over the centuries, he had no intention of changing the rosary or, as many theologians were suggesting he do, rejecting the consensus of his predecessors about the rosary's history. In fact, in the course of preparations for *Marialis Cultus*, his most well-known Marian document, he regularly sent the drafts back to the theological ghostwriters because he did not agree with their attempts to change the rosary or rewrite its history. He did this four times! It was for this reason that *Marialis Cultus* took three years to compose. *Marialis Cultus* was not promulgated until Bl. Pope Paul VI was satisfied with it. He was a staunch defender of the rosary.

Rosary Gems

The rosary is a Gospel prayer.

~ Blessed Pope Paul VI

By its nature the recitation of the rosary calls for a quiet rhythm and a lingering pace, helping the individual to meditate on the mysteries of the Lord's life as seen through the eyes of her who was closest to the Lord.

~ Blessed Pope Paul VI

The succession of Hail Marys [of the rosary] constitutes the warp on which is woven the contemplation of the mysteries.

~ Blessed Pope Paul VI

Meditating on the mysteries of the holy rosary, we learn, after the example of Mary, to have peace in our souls, through the unceasing and loving contact with Jesus and the mysteries of his redemptive life.

~ Blessed Pope Paul VI

The rosary is an exercise of piety that draws its motivating force from the liturgy and leads naturally back to it.

~ Blessed Pope Paul VI

Do not fail to put repeated emphasis on the recitation of the rosary, the prayer so pleasing to Our Lady and so often recommended by the Roman Pontiffs.

~ Blessed Pope Paul VI

We like to think, and sincerely hope, that when the family gathering becomes a time of prayer, the rosary is a frequent and favored manner of praying.

~ Blessed Pope Paul VI

If evils increase, the devotion of the People of God should also increase. And so, venerable brothers [bishops], we want you to take the lead in urging and encouraging people to pray ardently to our most merciful mother Mary by saying the rosary ... this prayer is well-suited to the devotion of the People of God, most pleasing to the Mother of God and most effective in gaining heaven's blessings. The Second Vatican Council recommended use of the rosary to all the sons of the Church, not in express words but in unmistakable fashion in this phrase: "Let them value highly the pious practices and exercises directed to the Blessed Virgin and approved over the centuries by the Magisterium."

~ Blessed Pope Paul VI

The rosary is a devotion that, through the Blessed Mother, leads us to Jesus.

~ Blessed Pope Paul VI

Without contemplation, the rosary is a body without a soul.

~ Blessed Pope Paul VI

As the history of the Church makes clear, this very fruitful way of praying [the rosary] is not only efficacious in warding off evils and preventing calamities, but is also of great help in fostering Christian life.

~ Blessed Pope Paul VI

We now desire, as a continuation of the thought of our predecessors, to recommend strongly the recitation of the family rosary.

~ Blessed Pope Paul VI

We exhort all Catholic families to introduce this devotion [the rosary] into their lives, and to encourage its propagation.

~ Blessed Pope Paul VI

Blessed are we if we are faithful in reciting that very popular and splendid prayer — the rosary — which is a kind of measured spelling out of our feelings of affection in the invocation: Hail Mary, Hail Mary, Hail Mary. Our life will be a fortunate one if it is interwoven with this garland of roses, with this circlet of praise to Mary, to the mysteries of her Divine Son.

~ Blessed Pope Paul VI

VENERABLE FULTON J. SHEEN

The Bishop of the Rosary
1895–1979

VENERABLE: June 28, 2012 by Pope Benedict XVI

VENERABLE FULTON J. SHEEN was born in El Paso, Illinois, and is considered one of the first Catholic televangelists. Archbishop Fulton Sheen was a master orator with a quick wit and an uncanny ability to present deep theological topics in a simple and understandable way. The famed G.K. Chesterton greatly admired him and wrote the introduction to Sheen's first book, published in 1925. As a priest, he reached over 4 million people every Sunday from 1930 to 1952 with his nationally broadcast radio program "The Catholic Hour." In 1952, he was made an auxiliary bishop of the Archdiocese of New York and began a television program called "Life is Worth Living." This program lasted for five years and, on average, reached over 30 million people every week. The program was so popular that he won two Emmy awards. Though he held a doctorate in philosophy, his message was understandable by the vast majority of people and appealed to everyone, including non-Catholics.

Sheen was later made the bishop of Rochester, New York, and eventually an archbishop. In spite of his busy schedule, he still found time to write more than 73 books. Deeply devoted to the Eucharist, he was dedicated to spending a Holy Hour before the Blessed Sacrament every day, and often remarked that all his ability to preach and teach came from that daily devotion. He converted many famous people to Catholicism and served as the National Director of the Society for the Propagation of the Faith. Two months before he died, he met St. John Paul II during a papal visit to St. Patrick's Cathedral in New York City. During that encounter, St. John Paul II embraced him, praised his work, and told him that he was a "loyal son of the Church."

Marian Devotion

When Fulton Sheen was born, his mother consecrated him to the Blessed Virgin Mary. Then, when he received his First Holy Communion, his mother renewed this consecration. All throughout his youth, Sheen had an intense love for the Blessed Mother. During his priestly ministry, Mary was a frequent theme of his sermons, and he often gave inspiring conferences regarding the role of Mary in the spiritual life. When Sheen became a bishop, he chose the phrase *Da per matrem me venire* ("That I may come to you through the Mother") as his episcopal motto. His favorite Marian shrine was Our Lady of Lourdes, which he visited over 30 times throughout his life.

Sheen's eloquence in writing about Our Lady is evidenced in his Marian masterpiece, *The World's First Love: Mary, Mother of God*. In this book, and in many of his other writings, he stressed the central importance of the person of Mary in Christianity, noting that God created his own mother and loved her so much that he gave her 10 times as much of his life as he did his apostles. In other words, Our Blessed Lord gave three years of his life to his disciples, but he gave 30 years to his dear mother. In eloquent prose, Sheen speaks of Mary as the ciborium of the Real Presence, the key to the treasure box that is Jesus, the heart of Christianity, and the one through whom the Muslims will come to Christ. He always emphasized that Jesus and Mary were inseparable, saying that if a person loses the mother, they will eventually also lose the Son.

Champion of the Rosary

As a priest, a bishop, and an archbishop, Fulton Sheen always promoted the rosary. In his numerous philosophical and theological books, he always found a way to fit in a thought or two on the rosary. He firmly believed that the rosary had the power to transform both individuals and society at large. He encouraged people to pray it while walking, working, and driving. In his day, he even noted that the knobs on most steering wheels could be used as counters for the Hail Marys. He considered the rosary to be therapeutic, especially since it is a form of meditative prayer that involves touching the beads of the rosary, caressing the crucifix, and kissing it tenderly.

Sheen taught that the rosary is a prayer for everyone, from the simplest person to the greatest theologian. He often reminded those who considered themselves intellectually elite that they were depriving themselves of great graces if they failed to humble themselves and pray the rosary. From 1950 to 1966, he served as the National Director for the Society for the Propagation of the Faith. In that position, he greatly promoted the rosary in a number of ways, including his creation of the World Mission Rosary. His desire was for everyone to make a prayerful missionary tour of the world by praying a rosary made up of different colors signifying the different geographical regions of the world: Green stands for Africa; blue for the vast Pacific region of Oceania; white for Europe; red for the Americas; and yellow for Asia, since it is the land of the rising sun. His World Mission Rosary became very popular and is still in use today.

Rosary Gems

It is objected that there is much repetition in the rosary inasmuch as the Lord's Prayer and the Hail Mary are said so often; therefore it is monotonous. That reminds me of a woman who came to see me one evening after instructions. She said, "I would never become a Catholic. You say the same words in the rosary over and over again, and anyone who repeats the same words is never sincere. I would never believe anyone who repeated his words, and neither would God." I asked her who the man was with her. She said he was her fiancé. I asked: "Does he love you?" "Certainly, he does." "But how do you know?" "He told me." "What did he say?" "He said: 'I love you.'" "When did he tell you last?" "About an hour ago." "Did he tell you before?" "Yes, last night. He tells me every night." I said: "Don't believe him. He is repeating; he is not sincere."

~ Venerable Fulton J. Sheen

In the rosary, we not only say prayers, we think them.

~ Venerable Fulton J. Sheen

Airplanes must have runways before they can fly. What the runway is to the airplane, that the rosary beads are to prayer — the physical start to gain spiritual altitude.

~ Venerable Fulton J. Sheen

No normal mind yet has been overcome by worries or fears who was faithful to the rosary. You will be surprised how you can climb out of your worries, bead by bead, up to the very throne of the Heart of Love itself.

~ Venerable Fulton J. Sheen

Because the rosary is both a mental and a vocal prayer, it is one where intellectual elephants may bathe, and the simple birds may also sip.

~ Venerable Fulton J. Sheen

If you wish to convert anyone to the fullness of the knowledge of Our Lord and of his Mystical Body, then teach him the rosary. One of two things will happen. Either he will stop saying the rosary — or he will get the gift of faith.

~ Venerable Fulton J. Sheen

The beauty of the rosary is that it is not merely a vocal prayer. It is also a mental prayer. One sometimes hears a dramatic presentation in which, while the human voice is speaking, there is a background of beautiful music, giving force and dignity to the words. The rosary is like that.

~ Venerable Fulton J. Sheen

The rosary is the book of the blind, where souls see and there enact the greatest drama of love the world has ever known; it is the book of the simple, which initiates them into mysteries and knowledge more satisfying than the education of other men; it is the book of the aged, whose eyes close upon the shadow of this world and open on the substance of the next.

~ Venerable Fulton J. Sheen

Concentration is impossible when the mind is troubled; thoughts run helter-skelter; a thousand and one images flood across the mind; distracted and wayward, the spiritual seems a long way off. The rosary is the best therapy for these distraught, unhappy, fearful, and frustrated souls, precisely because it involves the simultaneous use of three powers: the physical, the vocal, and the spiritual, and in that order.

~ Venerable Fulton J. Sheen

All the idle moments of one's life can be sanctified, thanks to the rosary. As we walk the streets, we pray with the rosary hidden in our hand or in our pocket; as we are driving an automobile, the little knobs under most steering wheels can serve as counters for the decades. While waiting to be served at a lunchroom, or waiting for a train, or in a store, or while playing dummy at bridge, or when conversation or a lecture lags — all these moments can be sanctified and made to serve inner peace, thanks to a prayer that enables one to pray at all times and under all circumstances.

~ Venerable Fulton J. Sheen

As the magnifying glass catches and unites the scattered rays of the sun, so the rosary brings together the otherwise dissipated thoughts of life in the sickroom into the white and burning heat of Divine Love.

~ Venerable Fulton J. Sheen

In moments when fever, agony, and pain make it hard to pray, the suggestion of prayer that comes from merely holding the rosary — or better still, from caressing the Crucifix at the end of it — is tremendous.

~ Venerable Fulton J. Sheen

The power of the rosary is beyond description.

~ Venerable Fulton J. Sheen

The mind is infinitely variable in its language, but the heart is not. The heart of a man, in the face of the woman he loves, is too poor to translate the infinity of his affection into a different word. So the heart takes one expression, "I love you," and in saying it over and over again, it never repeats. That is what we do when we say the rosary — we are saying to God, the Trinity, to the Incarnate Savior, to the Blessed Mother: "I love you, I love you, I love you."

~ Venerable Fulton J. Sheen

The rosary is a great test of faith. What the Eucharist is in the order of sacraments, that the rosary is in order of sacramental — the mystery and the test of faith, the touchstone by which the soul is judged in its humility. The mark of the Christian is the willingness to look for the Divine in the flesh of a babe in a crib, the continuing Christ under the appearance of bread on an altar, and a meditation and a prayer on a string of beads.

~ Venerable Fulton J. Sheen

ST. TERESA OF CALCUTTA

The Missionary
of the Rosary
1910–1997

BEATIFIED: October 19, 2003 by St. John Paul II
CANONIZED: September 4, 2016 by Pope Francis
FEAST DAY: September 5

SAINT TERESA OF CALCUTTA was born in Albania and entered the Sisters of Loreto at the age of 18. While living in India, she witnessed the extreme poverty of many people and was inspired to found a new religious community, the Missionaries of Charity. Her greatest desire was to quench the thirst of Jesus in the destitute, abandoned, and the poorest of the poor around the world. Affectionately known as Mother Teresa, she founded orphanages and homes all around the world that are run by her Missionaries of Charity. In 1979, she was honored with the Nobel Peace Prize.

A woman of deep prayer, St. Teresa lived an intensely Eucharistic spirituality. Incredibly, it was revealed after her death that for most of her life she had experienced long periods of dryness in the spiritual life, lengthy absences of any spiritual consolation, and the dark night of the soul. Nevertheless, all throughout her torturous spiritual dryness, she remained joyful and steadfast in her service to Jesus in the poor. Her witness of trust and selfless service to God and neighbor were extremely inspiring. She was greatly loved by many popes, especially St. John Paul II.

Marian Devotion

As a young girl, St. Teresa made an annual pilgrimage with her mother to the mountain Shrine of Our Lady of Cernagore. The annual pilgrimage made a deep impression on her young heart; she later attested that the annual visits to the shrine of Our Lady helped her respond to her religious vocation. Saint Teresa delighted in visiting Marian shrines throughout her life. She had a particular love for Guadalupe and Our Lady of Fatima, and fervently prayed for the conversion of Russia, as Our Lady requested at Fatima.

Saint Teresa had a tremendous devotion to the Immaculate Heart of Mary, as well as the Miraculous Medal. Everywhere she went, she handed out Miraculous Medals to those who were in attendance at her events. In order to carry out this practice, she asked people to obtain large quantities of Miraculous Medals and give them to her in bags so that she could hand them out during her missionary travels. One of her favorite prayers to Our Lady was the *Memorare;* she was known to stop everything in difficult situations and ask others to pray it with her. Her habit of praying nine *Memorares* in a row for immediate assistance from heaven in a difficult situation became known as the "express novena." She had a boundless trust in Our Lady and sought to imitate Mary's virtues, especially her silent and selfless co-redemptive suffering.

Champion of the Rosary

As a young girl, in addition to making the annual Marian pilgrimage, Teresa also belonged to a Marian sodality at her local parish. This sodality instilled in her a life-long love for the rosary. The rosary became her favorite Marian devotion. Before she founded the Missionaries of Charity, the Blessed Virgin spoke to her and instructed her to teach the rosary to little children and the poor. As was her practice with the Miraculous Medal, she almost always had the rosary in her hand and would pray it at various times throughout the day. She considered holding the rosary to be like holding Mary's hand. The rosary was her constant companion and gave her strength during her years of spiritual dryness and interior suffering.

A true champion of the rosary, St. Teresa required the sisters in all the houses of the Missionaries of Charity around the world to pray the rosary in common every day. Observing the Missionaries of Charity praying the rosary in their chapels is an extremely edifying experience, especially since they pray it with great devotion and without the assistance of kneelers. Saint Teresa's own feet were very worn down and her toes twisted from years of kneeling to pray the rosary on hard floors with no kneelers. In her zeal for the rosary, she declared that she wanted to open 15 convents in Russia in honor of the 15 mysteries of the rosary. (This was before St. John Paul II established the Luminous Mysteries.) Providentially, she ended up opening 20 convents in Russia, even though she had no idea that St. John Paul II would add five more mysteries to the rosary five years after her death!

Once, while she was traveling through an airport in a country plagued with war, everyone in line was asked if they had any weapons on their person. To everyone's surprise, Mother Teresa declared that she had a weapon! She gently opened her wrinkled hand and revealed her weapon to everyone: her rosary.

She was a great admirer of the efforts of Fr. Patrick Peyton to spread the family rosary and attended his events on several occasions to show her support. When she died in 1997, her body was placed in a casket with a rosary and a large Miraculous Medal in her hands.

Rosary Gems

Take care of them — they are mine. Bring them to Jesus — carry Jesus to them. Fear not. Teach them to say the rosary — the family rosary, and all will be well.

~ Our Lady's words to St. Teresa of Calcutta

When we walk the streets, in whatever part of the world, the sisters [Missionaries of Charity] carry in their hands the crown of the rosary. The Virgin is our strength and our protection.

~ St. Teresa of Calcutta

Our [Missionaries of Charity's] holy hour is our daily family prayer where we get together and pray the rosary before the exposed Blessed Sacrament the first half hour, and the second half hour we pray in silence.

~ St. Teresa of Calcutta

We are taught to love and say the rosary with great devotion; let us be very faithful to this our first love — for it will bring us closer to our Heavenly Mother. Our [Missionaries of Charity's] rule asks of us never to go to the slums without first having recited the Mother's praises; that is why we have to say the rosary in the streets and dark holes of the slums. Cling to the rosary as the creeper clings to the tree — for without Our Lady we cannot stand.

~ St. Teresa of Calcutta

The other day I can't tell you how bad I felt — there was a moment when I nearly refused to accept — deliberately I took the rosary and very slowly without even meditating or thinking — I said it slowly and calmly — the moment passed — but the darkness is so dark, and the pain is so painful — but I accept whatever he [Jesus] gives and I give whatever he takes.

~ St. Teresa of Calcutta

We honor her [Mary] by praying the rosary with love and devotion and by radiating her humility, kindness, and thoughtfulness towards others.

~ St. Teresa of Calcutta

Do you pray the rosary often?

~ St. Teresa of Calcutta

Pray the rosary every day.

~ St. Teresa of Calcutta

St. John Paul II

The Promoter
of the Rosary
1920–2005

PAPACY: 1978–2005
BEATIFIED: May 1, 2011 by Pope Benedict XVI
CANONIZED: April 27, 2014 by Pope Francis with
Pope Emeritus Benedict XVI in attendance
FEAST DAY: October 22

SAINT JOHN PAUL II was born in Wadowice, Poland, and became the first non-Italian pope since the 16th century. As a young man, he was an actor and an avid skier, kayaker, and outdoorsman. He grew up in a very difficult time under the Nazi and Communist occupations of Poland, which forced him to study to become a priest in secret. An extremely intelligent and erudite man, he was sent to Rome after his ordination and studied under some of the greatest theologians of his time. He never lost his love for the outdoors and was out kayaking on the day the news arrived that Venerable Pope Pius XII had selected him to be an auxiliary bishop. He knew at least 12 languages, was eventually made the archbishop of Krakow, and was a participant at the Second Vatican Council.

He was elected to be the Vicar of Christ in 1978, and quickly became one of the most influential popes in the history of the Church. He brought the Church out of the turbulent 1960s and 1970s, helped end Communism in Europe, visited 129 countries, beatified 1,338 people, and canonized 482 saints. He wrote 14 encyclicals, 15 apostolic exhortations, and 45 apostolic letters. He was also an apostle of the Divine Mercy message and devotion as given to St. Faustina Kowalska, established Divine Mercy Sunday, and offered groundbreaking teaching on topics such as the theology of the body.

On May 13, 1981, the anniversary of the first apparition of Our Lady at Fatima, John Paul II was shot in St. Peter's Square by the radical Turkish Muslim Mehmet Ali Agca. It was later reported that just before St. John Paul II was shot, he had made a slight movement toward a little girl who was holding a holy card of Our Lady of Fatima. Our Lady of Fatima saved him on that day, and he knew it. On October 7 of that same year, the Feast of Our Lady of the Rosary and his first general public audience after his recovery, he made reference to the connection between being shot on May 13 and the Fatima apparitions. Incredibly, a second assassination attempt was made one year later on May 12, 1982, in Fatima itself. During his pilgrimage to Fatima in thanksgiving to Our Lady for having saved his life from the previous year's assassination attempt, a Catholic priest from the Society of St. Pius X, Fr. Juan María Fernández Krohn, attempted to kill St. John Paul II. This mentally disturbed clergyman tried to stab St. John Paul II with a bayonet, but failed. Our Lady of Fatima had saved him again. Then, in 1995, an Al-Qaeda-funded attempt to kill the pope by means of a suicide bomber was foiled one week before its execution while Pope John Paul II was on a trip to the Philippines for World Youth Day. Mary's mantle was over St. John Paul II.

He would live for 10 more years before dying on the vigil of Divine Mercy Sunday in 2005. For his holiness and monumental apostolic activity, St. John Paul II rightly deserves to be known as St. John Paul the Great.

Marian Devotion

Karol Wojtyła had a filial love for Mary. After losing his earthly mother at a very early age, he entrusted himself to Our Lady's care and had complete confidence in her. He was greatly influenced by the Marian writings of St. Louis de Montfort and said that reading *True Devotion to the Blessed Virgin* was a turning point in his life. In fact, when he was elected the Vicar of Christ, he chose as his pontifical motto a Marian phrase from the writings of St. Louis de Montfort: "*Totus Tuus*," that is, "All Yours [Mary]." In his frequent catechetical talks on Mary and her maternal role in Christianity, he emphasized that it is impossible for people to understand the Church unless they look to Mary, since there is no other person who can better introduce us to the knowledge of Christ than his mother.

Saint John Paul II promoted the Marian Sodality and the Legion of Mary everywhere he went. In his many world travels as pope, he greatly delighted in visiting Marian shrines. During many of these visits, St. John Paul II took the opportunity to speak of Our Lady as our maternal Mediatrix, the masterpiece of God's mercy, the pattern of Christian holiness, and the woman of the Eucharist who leads her spiritual children to the Real Presence of Christ. He encouraged all the members of the Church, especially youth, to foster a filial devotion to Mary, and led by example by bringing Our Lady into everything he said and did.

When he was shot in 1981, during the surgery to remove the bullet, he requested that the doctors not remove his Brown Scapular. During his convalescence in the Gemelli Clinic in Rome, he asked for two things: the secrets that Mary had given to the children of Fatima and the *Diary* of St. Faustina Kowalska. In 1984, a few years after his full recovery, he consecrated the world to the Immaculate Heart. According to the Servant of God Lúcia Dos Santos, St. John Paul II's consecration fulfilled Mary's request at Fatima that the world, including Russia, be consecrated to her Immaculate Heart. A few years after the consecration, he declared a Marian Year that was observed from 1987 to 1988 and published the Marian encyclical *Redemptoris Mater*. It was shortly after these events that the USSR fell apart and Communism ended in Russia.

Champion of the Rosary

Saint John Paul II's tremendous love of the rosary can be traced to his young adult years in Poland. Beginning in 1940, Karol Wojtyła attended a weekly Living Rosary group started by the Servant of God Jan Tyranowski. In this group, each member was given a particular mystery to meditate on for one month, saying a decade a day while contemplating that particular mystery. It was during this time in Wojtyła's life that Jan Tyranowski suggested he read St. Louis de Montfort's *True Devotion to the Blessed Virgin*. Tyranowski's example of Marian devotion was a major influence on Wojtyła; quite a few historians have noted that had it not been for Tyranowski, Wojtyła might not have become a priest. As a newly ordained priest, Fr. Wojtyła started a Living Rosary group for the youth at his first parish in 1948. In 1996, Pope John Paul II recalled the memory of his friend and Marian mentor Jan Tyranowski, calling him a "great apostle of the Living Rosary." As a priest, bishop, cardinal, and pope, St. John Paul II was also a great apostle of the rosary.

As a bishop in Krakow, he was known to pay regular visits to Kalvaria Zebrzydowska, the principal Marian shrine of the Archdiocese of Krakow. During these visits, he would walk along the paths praying his rosary. During the winter, when there was snow or ice on the ground, he would clasp a ski pole in one hand and a rosary in the other as he walked the grounds of the shrine. Today, there is a statue of St. John Paul II holding a rosary in his hand in front of this Marian shrine. As a cardinal, he was invited to the Vatican by Bl. Pope Paul VI in 1976 to give a Lenten retreat and affirmed his devotion to the rosary by choosing the rosary and its mysteries as his main theme.

After his election to the papacy on October 16, 1978, it only took him two weeks to announce to the world that the rosary was his favorite prayer (October 29, 1978). He even stated on that same day that the rosary was a prayer-commentary on *Lumen Gentium*, the document from the Second Vatican Council that included a chapter on Mary. For the duration of his pontificate, rarely a year went by in which he did not do something monumental to promote the rosary. On March 3, 1979, he began the practice of praying the rosary over Vatican Radio on the First Saturday of each month. On October 21, 1979, he visited the Shrine of Our Lady of Pompeii, and in 1980, he beatified the great apostle of the rosary Bartolo Longo. In 1981, he promoted the family rosary in the apostolic exhortation *Familiaris Consortio*, and in 1982, he visited the resting place of St. Dominic in Bologna.

Among the many other significant rosary events of his papacy, two in particular stand out. First, on September 19, 1996, he went to Saint-Laurent-sur-Sèvre, France, and prayed at the tomb of St. Louis de Montfort. Second, in 2002, he wrote the apostolic letter *Rosarium Virginis Mariae*, in which he gave the Church the Luminous Mysteries and declared that, from October 7, 2002, to October 7, 2003, the Church would celebrate a Year of the Rosary. He himself closed out the Year of the Rosary by making another visit to the Shrine of Our Lady of the Rosary in Pompeii.

Saint John Paul II was the most traveled pope in history and brought the rosary with him everywhere he went. He gave out rosaries at all of his papal audiences, encouraged young people at World Youth Days to pray it, and gave the edifying example of praying the entire rosary every day. He asked all people to promote the rosary with fervor and conviction, and taught that the rosary is among the finest and most praiseworthy methods of Christian contemplation. His gift to the Church of the Luminous Mysteries of the rosary was a means of "re-sharpening" or "re-loading" the spiritual weapon of the rosary.

Rosary Gems

The rosary is my favorite prayer.

~ St. John Paul II

The holy rosary introduces us into the very heart of faith. With our thoughts fixed on it, we greet repeatedly, joyfully, the holy Mother of God; declare blessed the Son, the sweet fruit of her womb; and invoke her motherly protection in life and in death.

~ St. John Paul II

The rosary, though clearly Marian in character, is at heart a Christocentric prayer.

~ St. John Paul II

How could one possibly contemplate the mystery of the Child in Bethlehem, in the joyful mysteries [of the rosary], without experiencing the desire to welcome, defend and promote life, and to shoulder the burdens of suffering children all over the world?

~ St. John Paul II

With the rosary, the Christian people sit at the school of Mary.

~ St. John Paul II

She [Mary] prays with us. The rosary prayer embraces the problems of the Church, of the See of St. Peter, and the problems of the whole world.

~ St. John Paul II

To recite the rosary is nothing other than to contemplate with Mary the face of Christ.

~ St. John Paul II

It [the rosary] shows, through the vicissitudes of the Son of God and of the Virgin, how constant in human life is the alteration of good and evil, calm and storms, joyful days and sad ones.

~ St. John Paul II

The rosary, reclaimed in its full meaning, goes to the heart of Christian life.

~ St. John Paul II

If properly revitalized, the rosary is an aid and certainly not a hindrance to ecumenism!

~ St. John Paul II

The repetition of the Hail Mary in the rosary gives us a share in God's own wonder and pleasure: in jubilant amazement we acknowledge the greatest miracle in history.

~ St. John Paul II

The rosary belongs among the finest and most praiseworthy traditions of Christian contemplation.

~ St. John Paul II

Daily recitation of the rosary in the family was once widespread. How worthwhile would such a practice be today! Mary's rosary removes the seeds of family breakup; it is the sure bond of communion and peace.

~ St. John Paul II

The family that prays together stays together. The holy rosary, by age-old tradition, has shown itself particularly effective as a prayer which brings the family together. Individual family members, in turning their eyes toward Jesus, also regain the ability to look one another in the eye, to communicate, to show solidarity, to forgive one another and to see their covenant of love renewed in the Spirit of God.

~ St. John Paul II

To return to the recitation of the family rosary means filling daily life with very different images, images of the mystery of salvation: the image of the Redeemer, the image of his most Blessed Mother. The family that recites the rosary together reproduces something of the atmosphere of the household of Nazareth: its members place Jesus at the center.

~ St. John Paul II

To pray the rosary is to hand over our burdens to the merciful hearts of Christ and his Mother.

~ St. John Paul II

To understand the rosary, one has to enter into the psychological dynamic proper to love.

~ St. John Paul II

The rosary can be recited in full every day, and there are those who most laudably do so.

~ St. John Paul II

At times when Christianity itself seemed under threat, its deliverance was attributed to the power of this prayer [the rosary], and Our Lady of the Rosary was acclaimed as the one whose intercession brought salvation.

~ St. John Paul II

In the present international situation, I appeal to all — individuals, families and communities — to pray the rosary for peace, even daily, so that the world will be preserved from the dreadful scourge of terrorism.

~ St. John Paul II

We must be strong and prepared and trust in Christ and in his Holy Mother and be very, very assiduous in praying the holy rosary.

~ St. John Paul II

Dear brothers and sisters, recite the rosary every day. I earnestly urge Pastors to pray the rosary and to teach people in the Christian communities how to pray it. For the faithful and courageous fulfillment of the human and Christian duties proper to each one's state, help the people of God to return to the daily recitation of the rosary.

~ St. John Paul II

The rosary mystically transports us to Mary's side as she is busy watching over the human growth of Christ in the home of Nazareth.

~ St. John Paul II

The history of the rosary shows how this prayer was used in particular by the Dominicans at a difficult time for the Church due to the spread of heresy. Today we are facing new challenges. Why should we not once more have recourse to the rosary, with the same faith as those who have gone before us?

~ St. John Paul II

[Saint] Joseph Vaz was on fire with faith. Guided by the example of his Divine Master, he travelled the whole island [of Sri Lanka], going everywhere, often barefoot, with a rosary round his neck as a sign of his Catholic faith.

~ St. John Paul II

To recite the rosary means to learn to gaze on Jesus with his Mother's eyes, and to love Jesus with his Mother's heart. Today, my dear young people, I am also, in spirit, handing you the rosary beads. Through prayer and meditation on the mysteries, Mary leads you safely towards her Son! Do not be ashamed to recite the rosary alone, while you walk along the streets to school, to the university or to work, or as you commute by public transport. Adopt the habit of reciting it among yourselves, in your groups, movements and associations. Do not hesitate to suggest that it be recited at home by your parents and brothers and sisters, because it rekindles and strengthens the bonds between family members. This prayer will help you to be strong in your faith, constant in charity, joyful and persevering in hope.

~ St. John Paul II

Confidently take up the rosary once again. Rediscover the rosary in light of Scripture, in harmony with the liturgy, and in the context of your daily lives. May this appeal of mine not go unheard!

~ St. John Paul II

Our beloved John Paul II was a great Apostle of the Rosary: we remember him on his knees, his rosary beads in his hands, immersed in the contemplation of Christ.

~ Pope Benedict XVI

POPE BENEDICT XVI

The Theologian
of the Rosary
1927–present

POPE BENEDICT XVI was born in Bavaria, Germany, and is one of the most brilliant men to ever hold the office of pope. Before being elected to the papacy, he was an accomplished pianist, an academic theologian who served as a theological consultant at the Second Vatican Council, and the archbishop of Munich and Freising. During his many years of living in Rome, he held the offices of prefect for the Congregation of the Doctrine of the Faith, dean of the College of Cardinals, president of the International Theological Commission, and president of the Pontifical Biblical Commission. He was elected to the papacy in 2005.

In 2013, due to poor health and old age, Pope Benedict XVI resigned from the papacy, making way for a younger and healthier pontiff to hold the office of the Vicar of Christ. After his resignation, he continued to live in the Vatican and serve the Church through a life of prayer under the title "Pope Emeritus Benedict XVI." He is the first pope to relinquish the office of the papacy since Pope Gregory XII in 1415. Many of his theological works are recognized as spiritual classics.

Marian Devotion

The Marian devotion of Pope Benedict XVI is deeply rooted in a biblical, liturgical, and ecclesial approach to Our Lady. He emphasized in both his Marian devotion and his theological writings on Mary that, from a biblical perspective, she is best understood as the Daughter of Zion, the mother of the Messiah, and our spiritual mother. He also emphasized her relationship to God as the Spouse of the Holy Spirit, which allows her to more deeply fulfill her role as our spiritual mother by bringing the Holy Spirit with her wherever she is present.

Pope Benedict XVI also has a rich liturgical Marian devotion. He delighted in emphasizing that the month of May was to be a time particularly devoted to Mary, and he always stressed that the liturgical season of Advent should be understood as a Marian season because it is in Advent that we await the coming of Jesus through Mary. Like previous popes, he, too, loved to visit Marian shrines. In 2008, he made a special pilgrimage to Lourdes to celebrate the 150th anniversary of the Lourdes apparitions.

The Marian dimension of the Church is where Pope Benedict XVI's devotion to Mary has shone most plainly. He depicts the Church as a Marian mystery and shows that Our Lady has an absolutely necessary role in carrying out the providential plan of God in Christ. Mary serves as the archetype, mirror, and truest image of the Church and the Christian. She is the driving force of catholicity and the person the members of the Church must look to in order to truly understand the truth about Jesus Christ, the Church, and ourselves. He taught that if the Church were to fall silent in her praise and devotion to Mary, the Church itself would no longer be capable of glorifying God as she ought, since the Bible itself teaches the praises of Mary. In the person of Mary, the Church has a maternal protector and intercessor before the throne of the Almighty.

Champion of the Rosary

As a young boy, Pope Benedict XVI witnessed the tender love his parents had for Our Lady and her rosary. His parents would often gather the entire family together to pray the rosary. Every year during the month of May, the entire family went to Church every day to pray the rosary. This youthful love of the rosary carried into his priestly and academic endeavors. As a cardinal, even though he was entrusted with many responsibilities, he would always find time to pray at least a few decades a day. At times, he would even divide up a specific set of mysteries and intersperse the various mysteries throughout his day. When he became pope, he began to pray the rosary every day, sometimes praying it in the morning or in the evening while walking through the Vatican gardens.

To Pope Benedict, praying the rosary is a pilgrimage since the meditations require a person to make mental visits to the holy places associated with the lives of Jesus and Mary. For this reason, whenever he beatified or canonized a person, he delighted in making reference to their devotion to the rosary and how it helped them to become holy as they made their pilgrimage of faith. He was a very humble pope who rarely talked about himself or his personal Marian devotion; rather, he highlighted the Marian devotion of the saints, especially their love for the rosary. He is responsible for canonizing the 14th century rosary promoter St. Nuno Álvares Pereira. Like St. Nuno, he knew that the rosary is a weapon and encouraged everyone, especially the youth, to pray it daily.

Throughout his pontificate, and even after his resignation, Pope Benedict XVI has promoted the rosary. In May of 2008, he led the rosary on the First Saturday of the month in the Basilica of Santa Maria Maggiore in Rome. In October of the same year, he visited the Shrine of Our Lady of the Rosary in Pompeii and spoke very highly of Bl. Bartolo Longo and all that he did to promote the rosary. In May of 2010, he visited Fatima and prayed the rosary publicly with those present. Also, in 2010, when 33 Chilean miners were trapped deep in an underground mine for 69 days, he blessed 33 rosaries in Rome and sent them to the trapped miners. The rosaries were sent down the narrow shaft to the miners, who began to pray the rosary every day and wore the blessed rosaries around their necks. Miraculously, all 33 men survived and were rescued on October 13, the anniversary of the Miracle of the Sun at Fatima, where Our Lady appeared under the title "Our Lady of the Rosary!" During the Year of Faith (2012-2013) he asked all Catholics, especially families, to rediscover the prayer of the rosary and to pray it. On August 28, 2014, one year after he resigned from the papacy, a group of Cuban bishops were visiting the Vatican for the installation of an image of Our Lady of Cobre in the Vatican gardens, and were personally invited by Pope Emeritus Benedict XVI to join him later that evening in the Vatican gardens to pray the rosary.

Rosary Gems

The traditional image of Our Lady of the Rosary portrays Mary who with one arm supports the Child Jesus and with the other is offering the rosary beads to St. Dominic. This important iconography shows that the rosary is a means given by the Virgin to contemplate Jesus and, in meditating on his life, to love him and follow him ever more faithfully.

~ Pope Benedict XVI

The recitation of the rosary allows us to fix our gaze and our hearts upon Jesus, just like his Mother, the supreme model of contemplation of the Son.

~ Pope Benedict XVI

I urge you all to recite the rosary every day, abandoning yourselves with trust in Mary's hands.

~ Pope Benedict XVI

The rosary is the prayer of the Christian who advances in the pilgrimage of faith, in the following of Jesus, preceded by Mary.

~ Pope Benedict XVI

Today, together we confirm that the holy rosary is not a pious practice banished to the past, like prayers of other times thought of with nostalgia. Instead, the rosary is experiencing a new springtime. Without a doubt, this is one of the most eloquent signs of love that the young generation nourishes for Jesus and his Mother, Mary.

~ Pope Benedict XVI

Our Lady invites us every year to rediscover the beauty of this prayer [the rosary], so simple and so profound.

~ Pope Benedict XVI

Through the rosary we allow ourselves to be guided by Mary, the model of faith, in meditating on the mysteries of Christ. Day after day she helps us to assimilate the Gospel, so that it gives a form to our life as a whole.

~ Pope Benedict XVI

The prayer of the rosary, so dear to [St.] Bernadette and to Lourdes pilgrims, concentrates within itself the depths of the Gospel message. It introduces us to con-templation of the face of Christ. From this prayer of the humble, we can draw an abundance of graces.

~ Pope Benedict XVI

St. Józef Bilczewski was a man of prayer. The Holy Mass, the Liturgy of the Hours, meditation, the rosary and other pious practices formed part of his daily life.

~ Pope Benedict XVI

His [Bl. Ceferino Giménez Malla's] deep religious sense was expressed in his daily participation in Holy Mass and in the recitation of the rosary. The rosary beads themselves, which he always kept in his pocket became the cause of his arrest and made Bl. Ceferino an authentic "martyr of the rosary," because he did not let anyone take the rosary from him, not even when he was at the point of death.

~ Pope Benedict XVI

In the 19th century she [Bl. Anna Maria Adorni] was an exemplary wife and mother and then, widowed, she devoted herself to charity to women in prison and in difficulty, for whose service she founded two religious Institutes. Because of her ceaseless prayer, Mother Adorni was known as the "Living Rosary."

~ Pope Benedict XVI

The rosary is a spiritual weapon in the battle against evil, against all violence, for peace in hearts, in families, in society and in the world.

~ Pope Benedict XVI

Spiritually unite yourselves to Jesus Crucified and trustfully abandon yourselves into the hands of Mary, calling upon her unceasingly with the rosary.

~ Pope Benedict XVI

The historical origin of the rosary lies in the Middle Ages. This was a time when the Psalms were the normal form of prayer. But the great number of unlettered persons of that period could not take part in the biblical Psalms. Therefore people looked for some kind of Psalter for them and found the prayers to Mary with the mysteries of the life of Jesus Christ, strung out like beads on a necklace.

~ Pope Benedict XVI

[Saint] Dominic was canonized in 1234 and it is he himself who, with his holiness, points out to us two indispensable means for making apostolic action effective. In the very first place is Marian devotion which he fostered tenderly and left as a precious legacy to his spiritual sons who, in the history of the Church, have had the great merit of disseminating the prayer of the holy rosary, so dear to the Christian people and so rich in Gospel values: a true school of faith and piety. In the second place, Dominic, who cared for several women's monasteries in France and in Rome, believed unquestioningly in the value of prayers of intercession for the success of the apostolic work.

~ Pope Benedict XVI

PART III:
PRAYING
THE
ROSARY

Blessed be the Lord my rock, who trains my
hands for war, and my fingers for battle.

~ Psalm 144:1

Though we live in the world we are not carrying
on a worldly war, for the weapons of our warfare are not worldly but have
divine power to destroy strongholds.

~ 2 Corinthians 10:3-4

For the word of God is living and active,
sharper than any two-edged sword, piercing to the division of soul and spirit,
of joints and marrow, and discerning the thoughts and intentions of the heart.

~ Hebrews 4:12

WHY PRAY THE ROSARY?

Why pray the rosary? The short answer: *It takes a sword to slay a dragon.* Dear reader, there is a serpent dragon with seven vicious heads who seeks to destroy you (see Rev 12:3). A dragon with one head is threatening enough, but a dragon with seven heads requires a heavenly weapon — the heavenly Queen's weapon. Mary will give you this weapon if you ask for it. Remember the words of Pope Leo XIII: "The Mother of God, the Virgin most powerful, who in times past co-operated in charity that the faithful might be born in the Church, is now the intermediary, the Mediatrix of our salvation. May she shatter and strike off the multiple heads of the wicked hydra."[1]

There are, of course, many reasons why you should pray the rosary. It would be impossible to list them all. The four most important reasons are listed and explained in the pages that follow.

1) The rosary conquers the evil one

We live in a fallen world where fallen angels (demons) seek to destroy us. Such evil can only be overcome by having a greater weapon than the enemy possesses. Jesus Christ, having bound the dragon, has entrusted to his Church the weapons that enable his followers to be victorious over the evil one. These weapons are the Sacraments and the teachings of the one, holy, catholic, and apostolic Church. It is these mysteries and truths that are encapsulated in the weapon of the rosary.

As has been stated many times in this book, the rosary is a spiritual sword made by the Divine Craftsman. Popes and saints have repeatedly emphasized this reality. Pope Leo XIII stated very clearly: "The origin of this form of prayer [the rosary] is divine rather than human."[2] The genius of this spiritual sword is that it is easily memorized and can be prayed anywhere, anytime, and in almost all circumstances. It encapsulates the life-giving wonders of the Sacraments and the teachings of the Church, and brings them into your home and into every aspect of your life. The rosary is mobile, portable, and greatly feared by the enemy. Saint Louis de Montfort once said: "The devils have an overwhelming fear of the rosary. Saint Bernard says that the Angelic Salutation puts them to flight and makes all hell tremble."[3]

To pray the rosary is to pray the Word of God. What better devotional prayers could ever be said than the Our Father and the Hail Mary? The words of the Our Father came from the lips of Jesus Christ himself. The words of the Angelic Salutation were uttered on God's behalf by a holy angel (St. Gabriel). God has providentially arranged for the majority of the prayers recited in the rosary to be directed to Mary, because it is through her that the world received the instrument of our salvation, the flesh of the God-Man. Through Mary's cooperation with God, the sacred Flesh and holy mysteries of the God-Man were entrusted to the Church. Through Mary, the God-Man has conquered the darkness and vanquished the evil one forever. This mystery of salvation continues to be worked out in every generation until the end of time. It is especially through the sacred mysteries of the rosary-sword that Jesus continues to win victories over evil through his Mystical Body. Jesus himself said: "Do not think that I have come to bring peace on earth; I have not come to bring peace, but a sword" (Mt 10:34).

The rosary will make you an armed soldier, a sword-wielding knight on the battlefield of life. A rosary a day keeps the devil away!

2) The rosary preaches Jesus Christ and brings peace

The rosary is an evangelical tool that brings the light of Christ into all situations. It has the power to bring about world peace because the mysteries focus on the Truth, that is, on Jesus Christ. The original purpose of the rosary, as revealed to St. Dominic by Our Lady, was to combat heresy (false teachings). This clarification of truth was not just meant for the 13th century, but for all time, since Jesus is the same yesterday, today, and forever (see Heb 13:8). For this reason, Pope Leo XIII rightly stated, "Our need of divine help is as great today as when the great Dominic introduced the use of the rosary of Mary as a balm for the wounds of his contemporaries."[4]

In subsequent apparitions of Our Lady, as at Fatima, Mary reiterated that the rosary should be prayed every day in order to help people return to Jesus Christ and have peace. She even noted that the rosary has the power to stop wars. In light of that, it becomes plain that praying the rosary benefits individuals, families, and the entire world. Popes and saints have incessantly taught this reality. Pope Leo XIII emphasized the following in this regard: "The rosary, if devoutly used, is bound to benefit not only the individual but society at large."[5]

The rosary was born in an age of chivalry. The world is once again in need of knights who are willing to fight for truth and peace. Only truth will bring about world peace. Today's knight must use this spiritual weapon to win people back to the light of the Gospel. The ability of the rosary to change hearts and bring about the reign of Christ has been proven throughout history by causing countless miracles and victories. It has saved marriages, helped turn men into saints, overcome Islam, overthrown dictators, and is one of the most richly indulgenced prayers of the Church. It even has the ability to free souls from purgatory with its indulgences. The forces of darkness in the world today threaten the very foundations of human civilization, but they are no match for the power of the rosary. Historically, the rosary has been proven to overcome all falsehoods. A rosary crusade and a new Holy League are very much needed today to bring the light and peace of Christ back into souls.

3) The rosary teaches virtue

No one ever becomes holy without acquiring virtue. All the virtues that lead to sanctity are exemplified in the lives of Jesus Christ and his Immaculate Mother. The rosary-sword is *the* sacramental that disposes souls to sanctifying grace. It is a proven fact that the rosary draws hearts closer to the Sacraments and the teachings of the Church. By its very nature, the rosary leads a person into a more fervent participation in the life of the Church, especially faithful attendance at Holy Mass and the frequent reception of the Sacrament of Reconciliation (Confession).

In the acquisition of virtue, not only do we have fallen angels and a sinful world to overcome, but we also have the daily struggle to conquer our sinful inclinations and conform our lives to the pattern of all virtue found in Jesus and Mary. Just as children learn how to behave by looking at their parents and imitating them, so the Christian learns to become like Jesus and Mary by meditating on their virtues. The rosary is a tool to prayerfully bring those virtues to mind. Unlike the many New Age practices in the world today that are self-centered and anti-Christian, the rosary offers a form of meditation that leads the soul to true freedom, which can only be found in Jesus Christ. For this reason, the rosary is therapeutic and healing. It helps a person to conquer vice, stop sinning, and acquire virtue. The rosary is heavenly medicine, an antidote that draws the poison of sin and vice out of our hearts.

Perseverance in praying the rosary has proven to be a tremendous means of helping a person avoid sin and remain in a state of grace. Saint Louis de Montfort once wrote:

> It was because Our Lady wanted to help us in the great task of working out our salvation that she ordered St. Dominic to teach the faithful to meditate upon the sacred mysteries of the life of Jesus Christ. She did this, not only that they might adore and glorify him, but chiefly that they might pattern their lives and actions upon his virtues.[6]

This is one of the many reasons why the rosary is the favored prayer of the saints. The rosary will help you become holy.

4) The rosary is an expression of our love for Jesus and Mary

All people who are in love never tire of telling each other, "I love you." This is also true for parents and their children. Telling someone you love them can have the appearance of a merely repetitious statement, since the same words are repeated over and over again, but everyone knows that telling someone they are loved is never routine or boring. Every time the phrase is uttered, it is new and fresh. The Venerable Fulton Sheen understood this and shared the following insight: "When we say the rosary — we are saying to God, the Trinity, to the Incarnate Savior, to the Blessed Mother: 'I love you, I love you, I love you.'"[7] By praying the rosary, we express our gratitude to Jesus and Mary by "calling to mind" the tremendous sacrificial love that they have for us. This act moves the Sacred Heart of Jesus and the Immaculate Heart of Mary to pour out countless graces upon us. Expressions of love from us are reciprocated by gifts of love from heaven.

Saints and popes have often noted in their writings that no one is capable of loving Mary more than Jesus. Therefore, Jesus is not offended when we pray the rosary. On the contrary, he himself takes great delight in the praying of the rosary by his disciples because to pray the rosary is to lay spiritual roses at the feet of his mother. This practice would never offend him. All children would do well to bring flowers to their mother as an expression of love. Would Jesus not inspire others to perform the same loving acts toward his mother that he himself does? After all, he shared the gift of his mother with all of his disciples as he was hanging from the Cross. Thus, when we pray the rosary, we, too, are able to lay lovely garlands of roses at the feet of our beautiful mother. This practice brings joy to the heart of our spiritual mother and greatly pleases the heart of our Savior.

When we pray the rosary, we show that we are faithful to the Word of God, which explicitly states that *all* generations are to call Mary blessed (see Lk 1:48). As Bl. James Alberione succinctly put it, "The rosary is the easiest way to honor God and the Blessed Virgin. It is the surest way to triumph over spiritual enemies, the most suitable way to progress in virtue and sanctity."[8]

How to Pray the Rosary

The rosary is very easy to pray. It can be prayed on your own or with others. The most important thing to remember about praying the rosary is that it is a blending of vocal and mental (meditative) prayer. Saint Louis de Montfort once remarked: "I know of no better way of establishing the kingdom of God than to unite vocal and mental prayer by saying the rosary."[1] The combination of vocal and mental prayer makes the rosary a prayer of the body and also a prayer of the soul. Having stated this, it is important to remember that if you pray the rosary by yourself, you do not need to vocalize the prayers with your lips.

When praying the rosary, it is better to pray it on one's knees, since this is the most pious position for prayer. Not everyone is able to kneel due to health issues and/or age, and so it is perfectly acceptable to pray the rosary while sitting or, as has already been mentioned, while walking, exercising, driving, etc. For those who are unfamiliar with the structure of the rosary, a diagram will be presented at the end of this section that includes the prayers associated with the rosary, how it is to be prayed, and a list of the 20 mysteries, as well as which mysteries are prayed on different days of the week. What follows below is a brief description of the vocal and meditative aspects of the rosary.

1) Vocal Prayer

When the rosary is prayed on your own, it should take at least 15 to 20 minutes. It is possible to spend more than 20 minutes praying the rosary and taking more time to meditate on the mysteries. If a person prays the rosary in less than 15 minutes, they are praying it too fast because there really is no way a person can devoutly meditate on the mysteries and say the prayers reverently in less time than that. If a person prays the rosary with other people, the normal amount of time that should be allotted is 20 minutes — no less. There are several dangers to avoid when praying the rosary in a group, including praying the rosary too fast, too slow, too loudly, or emphasizing certain words over others.

Saint Louis de Montfort had the following to say about those who pray the rosary too fast:

> It is really pathetic to see how most people say the holy rosary —they say it astonishingly fast and mumble so that the words are not properly pronounced at all. We could not possibly expect anyone, even the most unimportant person, to think that a slipshod address of this kind was a compliment and yet we expect Jesus and Mary to be pleased with it![2]

These are strong words, but he is absolutely correct. If you have ever tried to pray the rosary with someone who speeds through it, it becomes an endurance test, a burden, and a barely-tolerated act of piety for everyone else. Such a rosary is hardly a meditative prayer at all. As the famous Dominican rosary priest Fr. Gabriel Harty once noted: "*Speed Kills* is what the road sign shouts. So too with the highway of the rosary. Speed destroys its rhythm and kills the spirit, and the principal victim is the holy name of Jesus."[3] In other words, when the rosary is prayed in common, everyone should pray it at the same pace, a pace that is not hurried or rushed. Saint Anthony Mary Claret used to instruct his seminarians that when they prayed the rosary, they were to remember that their words were addressed to the King of Kings and the Queen of Heaven and earth. In this regard, he noted the following: "The rosary should not be prayed hastily, but slowly and with devotion, pronouncing all of the words well, and not starting one part until the other has finished."[4]

Those who pray the rosary in common should also remember that the rosary is not to be prayed too slowly, either. If you have ever prayed the rosary with someone who drags out every word, their voice becomes a distraction and makes the others in attendance feel like they are pushing a heavy train up a mountain. When the rosary is prayed too slowly, the other participants cannot meditate because their focus is being drawn to the unnatural pace of the slow person. Forcing others to pray the rosary at that pace is neither charitable nor prayerful for the others in the group.

The rosary is being prayed perfectly when all the members pray it at the same natural and prayerful pace. This gives the rosary a beautiful rhythm, flow, and harmonious timing that match normal breathing patterns. On the other hand, if one member prays too loudly, allowing his voice and pace to dominate the others, everyone automatically begins to focus on his voice and is no longer able to meditate; the vocal aspect becomes a distraction for all the other members. Similarly, if a person places an emphasis on one particular word of the Hail Mary prayer, it breaks the flow and rhythm of the group's timing. All of the above aspects should be taken seriously, because a group's failure to pray the rosary well and harmoniously is often the reason why many people do not join in praying the rosary before or after Mass. Very few people are interested in praying a rosary that is chaotic and a verbal wrestling match. If you desire to hear a perfectly timed and well-prayed communal rosary, visit any chapel of the Missionaries of Charity and listen to how they pray the rosary in common.

2) Meditative Prayer

It is true that most people become easily distracted when praying the rosary. Almost everyone will find their mind wandering away from the mysteries at least once. Even saints struggled with this. God is well aware that we are neither angels nor robots, and do not have the ability to ponder one thing for long periods of time without other things coming to mind. Saint Thérèse of Lisieux expressed her struggles this way:

> I feel that I say the rosary so poorly! I make a concentrated effort
> to meditate on the mysteries of the rosary, but I am unable to focus

my concentration. For a long time I was disconsolate about my lack of devotion, which astonished me since I so much loved the Blessed Virgin that it ought to have been easy for me to recite the prayers in her honor that so much pleased her. But now I am less sad, for I think that the Queen of heaven, who is also my Mother, ought to see my good intentions and that she is pleased with them.[5]

Everyone who prays the rosary is going to lose their concentration and find their mind wandering from time to time. Do not let this discourage you. Praying the rosary is an act of the will because it is an act of love. Feelings will come and go. True love perseveres through difficulties, distractions, and no sensible consolation. When distractions come, simply re-focus your mind on the mystery at hand. This may occur many times throughout the rosary, but it is very pleasing to Jesus and Mary when a person turns their mind and heart back to the mysteries. Saint Louis de Montfort noted the following in this regard:

> Even if you have to fight distractions all through your whole rosary, be sure to fight well, arms in hand: that is to say, do not stop saying your rosary even if it is hard to say and you have absolutely no sensible devotion. It is a terrible battle, I know, but one that is profitable to the faithful soul.[6]

A person will learn many virtues by perseverance in praying the rosary and, over time, will acquire the ability to become less distracted and more focused on the mysteries. The Servant of God Dolindo Ruotolo offers these consoling and encouraging words for those who struggle in this area: "To know how to pray is a gift of God. It is part of the gift of piety, a gift of the Holy Spirit. With diligent practice every day, it is possible to succeed in reciting the holy rosary worthily."[7] Perseverance makes a champion!

How to pray the Rosary

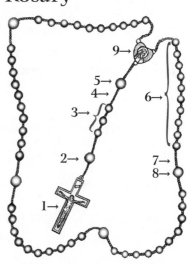

1. Make the Sign of the Cross and say the "Apostles' Creed."

2. Say the "Our Father."

3. Say three "Hail Marys."

4. Say the "Glory be to the Father."

5. Announce the First Mystery; then say the "Our Father."

6. Say ten "Hail Marys" while meditating on the Mystery.

7. Say the "Glory be to the Father." After each decade, say the following prayer requested by the Blessed Virgin Mary at Fatima: "O my Jesus, forgive us our sins, save us from the fires of hell, lead all souls to Heaven, especially those in most need of Thy mercy."

8. Announce the Second Mystery: then say the "Our Father." Repeat 6 and 7 and continue with the Third, Fourth, and Fifth Mysteries in the same manner.

9. Say the "Hail, Holy Queen" on the medal after the five decades are completed.

As a general rule, depending on the season, the Joyful Mysteries are said on Monday and Saturday; the Sorrowful Mysteries on Tuesday and Friday; the Glorious Mysteries on Wednesday and Sunday; and the Luminous Mysteries on Thursday.

Prayers of the Rosary

THE SIGN OF THE CROSS
In the name of the Father, and of the Son, and of the Holy Spirit. Amen.

THE APOSTLES' CREED
I believe in God, the Father almighty, Creator of heaven and earth, and in Jesus Christ, his only Son, our Lord, who was conceived by the Holy Spirit, born of the Virgin Mary, suffered under Pontius Pilate, was crucified, died, and was buried; he descended into hell; on the third day he rose again from the dead; he ascended into heaven, and is seated at the right hand of God the Father almighty; from there he will come to judge the living and the dead. I believe in the Holy Spirit, the holy catholic Church, the communion of saints, the forgiveness of sins, the resurrection of the body, and life everlasting. Amen.

OUR FATHER
Our Father, who art in heaven; hallowed be Thy name; Thy kingdom come; Thy will be done on earth as it is in heaven. Give us this day our daily bread; and forgive us our trespasses as we forgive those who trespass against us, and lead us not into temptation; but deliver us from evil. Amen.

HAIL MARY
Hail Mary, full of grace. The Lord is with thee. Blessed art thou among women, and blessed is the fruit of thy womb, Jesus. Holy Mary, Mother of God, pray for us sinners, now and at the hour of our death. Amen.

GLORY BE TO THE FATHER
Glory be to the Father, and to the Son, and to the Holy Spirit. As it was in the beginning, is now, and ever shall be, world without end. Amen.

HAIL, HOLY QUEEN

Hail, Holy Queen, Mother of Mercy, our life, our sweetness and our hope, to thee do we cry, poor banished children of Eve; to thee do we send up our sighs, mourning and weeping in this valley of tears; turn, then, most gracious Advocate, thine eyes of mercy towards us, and after this, our exile, show unto us the blessed fruit of thy womb, Jesus. O clement, O loving, O sweet Virgin Mary!

Pray for us, O holy Mother of God, that we may be made worthy of the promises of Christ.

The wording of the Apostles' Creed conforms with the Roman Missal.

Mysteries of the Rosary

JOYFUL MYSTERY

FIRST JOYFUL MYSTERY

THE ANNUNCIATION

And when the angel had come to her, he said, "Hail, full of grace, the Lord is with you" (Lk 1:28).

One Our Father, Ten Hail Marys, One Glory Be, etc.

FRUIT OF THE MYSTERY: *HUMILITY*

SECOND JOYFUL MYSTERY

THE VISITATION

Elizabeth, filled with the holy Spirit, cried out in a loud voice and said, "Most blessed are you among women, and blessed is the fruit of your womb" (Lk 1:41-42).

One Our Father, Ten Hail Marys, One Glory Be, etc.

FRUIT OF THE MYSTERY: *LOVE OF NEIGHBOR*

THIRD JOYFUL MYSTERY

THE BIRTH OF JESUS

She gave birth to her firstborn Son. She wrapped Him in swaddling clothes and laid Him in a manger, because there was no room for them in the inn (Lk 2:7).

One Our Father, Ten Hail Marys, One Glory Be, etc.

FRUIT OF THE MYSTERY: *POVERTY IN SPIRIT*

FOURTH JOYFUL MYSTERY

THE PRESENTATION

When the days were completed for their purification according to the law of Moses, they took Him up to Jerusalem to present Him to the Lord, just as it is written in the law of the Lord, "Every male that opens the womb shall be consecrated to the Lord" (Lk 2:22-23).

One Our Father, Ten Hail Marys, One Glory Be, etc.

FRUIT OF THE MYSTERY: *OBEDIENCE*

FIFTH JOYFUL MYSTERY

FINDING THE CHILD JESUS IN THE TEMPLE

After three days they found Him in the temple, sitting in the midst of the teachers, listening to them and asking them questions (Lk 2:46).

One Our Father, Ten Hail Marys, One Glory Be, etc.

FRUIT OF THE MYSTERY: *JOY IN FINDING JESUS.*

LUMINOUS MYSTERY

FIRST LUMINOUS MYSTERY

BAPTISM OF JESUS

After Jesus was baptized, ... the heavens were opened [for Him], and he saw the Spirit of God descending like a dove [and] coming upon Him. And a voice came from the heavens, saying, "This is My beloved Son, with whom I am well pleased" (Mt 3:16-17).

One Our Father, Ten Hail Marys, One Glory Be, etc.

FRUIT OF THE MYSTERY: *OPENNESS TO THE HOLY SPIRIT*

SECOND LUMINOUS MYSTERY

WEDDING AT CANA

His mother said to the servers, "Do whatever He tells you." ... Jesus told them, "Fill the jars with water." So they filled them to the brim (Jn 2:5-7).

One Our Father, Ten Hail Marys, One Glory Be, etc.

FRUIT OF THE MYSTERY: *TO JESUS THROUGH MARY*

THIRD LUMINOUS MYSTERY

PROCLAIMING THE KINGDOM

"As you go, make this proclamation: 'The kingdom of heaven is at hand.' Cure the sick, raise the dead, cleanse lepers, drive out demons. Without cost you have received; without cost you are to give" (Mt 10:7-8).

One Our Father, Ten Hail Marys, One Glory Be, etc.

FRUIT OF THE MYSTERY: *REPENTANCE AND TRUST IN GOD*

FOURTH LUMINOUS MYSTERY

TRANSFIGURATION

While He was praying His face changed in appearance and His clothing became dazzling white. Then from the cloud came a voice that said, "This is My chosen Son; listen to Him" (Lk 9:29, 35).

One Our Father, Ten Hail Marys, One Glory Be, etc.

FRUIT OF THE MYSTERY: *DESIRE FOR HOLINESS*

FIFTH LUMINOUS MYSTERY

INSTITUTION OF THE EUCHARIST

Then He took the bread, said the blessing, broke it, and gave it to them, saying, "This is My body, which will be given for you ..." And likewise the cup after they had eaten, saying, "This cup is the new covenant in My blood" (Lk 22:19-20).

One Our Father, Ten Hail Marys, One Glory Be, etc.

FRUIT OF THE MYSTERY: ADORATION

SORROWFUL MYSTERY

FIRST SORROWFUL MYSTERY

THE AGONY IN THE GARDEN

He was in such agony and He prayed so fervently that His sweat became like drops of blood falling on the ground. When He rose from prayer and returned to His disciples, He found them sleeping from grief (Lk 22:44-45).

One Our Father, Ten Hail Marys, One Glory Be, etc.

FRUIT OF THE MYSTERY: *SORROW FOR SIN*

SECOND SORROWFUL MYSTERY

THE SCOURGING AT THE PILLAR

Then Pilate took Jesus and had Him scourged (Jn 19:1).

One Our Father, Ten Hail Marys, One Glory Be, etc.

FRUIT OF THE MYSTERY: *PURITY*

THIRD SORROWFUL MYSTERY

CROWNING WITH THORNS

They stripped off His clothes and threw a scarlet military cloak about Him. Weaving a crown out of thorns, they placed it on His head, and a reed in His right hand (Mt 27:28-29).

One Our Father, Ten Hail Marys, One Glory Be, etc.

FRUIT OF THE MYSTERY: *COURAGE*

FOURTH SORROWFUL MYSTERY

CARRYING OF THE CROSS

And carrying the cross Himself, He went out to what is called the Place of the Skull, in Hebrew, Golgotha (Jn 19:17).

One Our Father, Ten Hail Marys, One Glory Be, etc.

FRUIT OF THE MYSTERY: *PATIENCE*

FIFTH SORROWFUL MYSTERY

THE CRUCIFIXION

Jesus cried out in a loud voice, "Father, into Your hands I commend My spirit"; and when He had said this He breathed His last (Lk 23:46).

One Our Father, Ten Hail Marys, One Glory Be, etc.

FRUIT OF THE MYSTERY: *PERSEVERANCE*

GLORIOUS MYSTERY

FIRST GLORIOUS MYSTERY

THE RESURRECTION

"Do not be amazed! You seek Jesus of Nazareth, the crucified. He has been raised; He is not here. Behold the place where they laid Him" (Mk16:6).

One Our Father, Ten Hail Marys, One Glory Be, etc.

FRUIT OF THE MYSTERY: *FAITH*

SECOND GLORIOUS MYSTERY

THE ASCENSION

So then the Lord Jesus, after He spoke to them, was taken up into heaven and took His seat at the right hand of God (Mk 16:19).

One Our Father, Ten Hail Marys, One Glory Be, etc.

FRUIT OF THE MYSTERY: *HOPE*

THIRD GLORIOUS MYSTERY

DESCENT OF THE HOLY SPIRIT

And they were all filled with the Holy Spirit and began to speak in different tongues, as the Spirit enabled them to proclaim (Acts 2:4).

One Our Father, Ten Hail Marys, One Glory Be, etc.

FRUIT OF THE MYSTERY: *LOVE OF GOD*

FOURTH GLORIOUS MYSTERY

THE ASSUMPTION

"You are the glory of Jerusalem! ... You are the great boast of our nation! ... You have done good things for Israel, and God is pleased with them. May the Almighty Lord bless you forever!" (Jud 15:9-10).

One Our Father, Ten Hail Marys, One Glory Be, etc.

FRUIT OF THE MYSTERY: *GRACE OF A HAPPY DEATH*

FIFTH GLORIOUS MYSTERY

THE CORONATION

A great sign appeared in the sky, a woman clothed with the sun, with the moon under her feet, and on her head a crown of twelve stars (Rev 12:1).

One Our Father, Ten Hail Marys, One Glory Be, etc.

FRUIT OF THE MYSTERY: *TRUST IN MARY'S INTERCESSION*

How to Become a Champion of the Rosary

To be a champion of the rosary, it is not necessary to write books on the rosary or give conferences about it. All that is needed is a heart docile to the Holy Spirit and a desire to make the rosary more known. Here are three simple methods that allow anyone to become a champion of the rosary:

1) Pray the rosary

During a papal visit to the Shrine of Our Lady of the Rosary of Pompeii, Pope Benedict XVI provided the following understanding of what is required in order to become a champion of the rosary. He stated:

> To be apostles of the rosary it is necessary to experience personally the beauty and depth of this prayer which is simple and accessible to everyone. It is first of all necessary to let the Blessed Virgin Mary take one by the hand to contemplate the Face of Christ: a joyful, luminous, sorrowful and glorious face.[1]

In other words, a person cannot give what a person does not have. Thus, it is first necessary for a person to pray the rosary himself; only then can he truly and effectively became an apostle and champion of the rosary. It is from personal experience and a love for the rosary that champions and apostles of the rosary are born.

In becoming a champion of the rosary, it is important to remember that praying the rosary is not about experiencing good feelings. Many times, as in any relationship, pleasant feelings come and go. What determines one's faithfulness in any relationship is perseverance through the difficult and dry times. Champions of the rosary are made when a soul perseveres in praying the rosary, no matter what. Love endures dryness and is consistent in all seasons of life, whether those seasons are joyful, luminous, sorrowful, or glorious. Saint Louis de Montfort knew this and noted the following about persevering in praying the rosary:

> Even if you suffer from dryness of soul, boredom and interior discouragement, never give up even the least little bit of your rosary. On the contrary, like a real champion of Jesus and Mary, you should say your Our Fathers and Hail Marys quite drily if you have to, without seeing, hearing or feeling any consolation whatsoever, and concentrating as best you can on the mysteries.[2]

True champions of the rosary never give up!

2) Encourage others to pray the rosary

It is only natural that after having experienced the power of the rosary to conquer evil, you would desire to hand on the great spiritual sword to another. Like St. Louis de Montfort, we should want to tell the whole world about the great secret of the rosary so that they, too, might tap into its power. A champion of the rosary will have at his disposal a plethora of means to spread the devotion of the rosary to others, such as praying for others to be lit on fire with the same burning love for Our Lady and her rosary as the great champions we've read about in this book, as well as sharing rosary beads and giving away good books on the rosary to family members, friends, godchildren, fellow parishioners, and co-workers. As you have read in this book, many saints followed this last method of spreading the rosary through sharing good books. Blessed James Alberione had these encouraging words to say about how to promote the rosary:

> Make Mary known and loved by others. Invite all to go to Mary. Where Mary enters, Jesus follows. *Through Mary to Jesus.* Foster the recitation of the rosary in every family. The fruits will be numberless, and we will be able to count them only in heaven. Diffuse books and pamphlets on the rosary; speak of this devotion; exhort its recitation on all good occasions which present themselves. Also give the example: the rosary witnesses to itself. One who sees the rosary beads in the hands of another will feel the desire to do the same, will receive a first grace, that is, will at least conceive a good thought.[3]

As a concrete way of passing on the knowledge of the rosary, it is recommended that a champion of the rosary seek to give away copies of the following three books on the rosary:

- *The Secret of the Rosary* by St. Louis de Montfort

- *Champions of the Rosary: The History and Heroes of a Spiritual Weapon* by Fr. Donald Calloway, MIC

- *Rosary Gems: Daily Wisdom on the Holy Rosary* by Fr. Donald Calloway, MIC

In addition to evangelizing others by giving them one of the three books above, if your parish does not have a rosary prayer group, try to start one. Always be sure to get the permission of the pastor of the parish first, however. Most times, pastors are very favorable to such practices, and will have no problem with people praying the rosary either before or after Mass. Most priests find that this practice fosters a greater sense of devotion in the hearts and souls of their parishioners and leads to a greater participation in the life of the Church.

Other ways to encourage the faithful to pray the rosary, as Bl. Alberione and so many other saints have noted, is to begin to pray it as a family and as spouses. It is also a highly praiseworthy practice for a family to initiate a weekly rosary prayer group in their home and invite other families and parishioners over to pray the rosary. Once this practice catches on, the families and parishioners can begin to alternate homes so that a community of faith is formed and relationships are built. This practice is certain to bring about devout Catholic communities and help build holy families and devout parishes. Whatever way you seek to encourage others to pray the rosary, remember the words of St. Louis de Montfort: "Our Lady blesses not only those who preach her rosary, but she highly rewards all those who get others to say it by their example."[4]

3) Join an official organization that promotes the rosary

Joining an official organization that promotes the rosary is an extraordinary way to champion the rosary and share in the spiritual benefits of the organization. Many of these organizations function as spiritual benefit societies and offer their members many blessings. Organizations such as the Association of Marian Helpers, the Thirteenth of the Month Club, the Legion of Mary, the Schoenstatt Rosary Campaign, the Militia Immaculatae, the World Apostolate of Fatima, and Holy Cross Family Ministries are some of the great organizations that you can join to help spread the rosary.

Two rosary organizations that I particularly recommend are the Thirteenth of the Month Club (see page 445) and the Confraternity of the Rosary. The Thirteenth of the Month Club, based out of Stockbridge, Massachusetts, is operated by the Marian Fathers of the Immaculate Conception, the religious congregation to which I belong. The Marian Fathers operate the National Shrine of The Divine Mercy in Stockbridge and are a zealous group of men promoting devotion to Our Lady (especially as the Immaculate Conception), the Divine Mercy message and devotion, Marian consecration, and the rosary. As the spiritual director for the Thirteenth of the Month Club, I can assure you that it is a very worthwhile group to join, a great way to champion the rosary, and a true means of offering support for a very orthodox Marian religious community. I strongly encourage you to find out more about the Thirteenth of the Month Club and become a member:

Thirteenth of the Month Club
Eden Hill
Stockbridge, MA 01263
1-800-462-7426
www.marian.org/13th

The other rosary organization that I most highly recommend is the Confraternity of the Rosary. This is the worldwide organization that was founded by St. Dominic, renewed by Bl. Alan de la Roche, and has been promoted by many popes. In the United States, contact the Confraternity at either of the following two locations:

Confraternity of the Rosary	**Confraternity of the Rosary**
PO Box 3617	280 North Grant Ave.
Portland, OR 97208	Columbus, OH 43215
1-503-236-8393	1-614-240-5929
www.rosary-center.org	www.rosaryconfraternity.org

In addition to the above rosary organizations, I also highly recommend that all Catholic men join the Holy League movement, founded in Wisconsin in 2014. This organization has its spiritual headquarters at the Shrine of Our Lady of Guadalupe in La Crosse, Wisconsin; Cardinal Raymond Burke is its spiritual head. The Holy League is a parish-based network of men dedicated to fighting against the evils of our day by means of a monthly Eucharistic Holy Hour, which includes making available the Sacrament of Confession and praying the rosary. It is done in an effort to help Catholic men remain strong in the power of grace.

Holy League
PO Box 1266
La Crosse, WI 54602
www.holyleague.com

THE 15 PROMISES OF OUR LADY TO THOSE WHO PRAY THE ROSARY

1) To all those who shall recite my rosary devoutly, I promise my special protection and very great graces.

2) Those who shall persevere in the recitation of my rosary shall receive signal graces.

3) The rosary shall be a very powerful armor against hell; it will destroy vice, deliver from sin, and dispel heresy.

4) The rosary will make virtue and good works flourish, and will obtain for souls the most abundant divine mercies; it will draw the hearts of men from the love of the world to the love of God, and will lift them to the desire of eternal things. How many souls shall sanctify themselves by this means!

5) Those who trust themselves to me through the rosary shall not perish.

6) Those who shall recite my rosary devoutly, meditating on its mysteries, shall not be overwhelmed by misfortune. The sinner shall be converted; the just shall grow in grace and become worthy of eternal life.

7) Those truly devoted to my rosary shall not die without the Sacraments of the Church.

8) Those who faithfully recite my rosary shall find during their life and at the hour of their death the light of God, the fullness of his graces, and shall share in the merits of the blessed.

9) I shall deliver very promptly from purgatory the souls devoted to my rosary.

10) The true children of my rosary shall enjoy great glory in heaven.

11) What you ask through my rosary, you shall obtain.

12) Those who propagate my rosary will be aided by me in all their necessities.

13) I have obtained from my Son that all the members of the Rosary Confraternity shall have as their intercessors, in life and in death, the entire celestial court.

14) Those who recite my rosary faithfully are all my beloved children, the brothers and sisters of Jesus Christ.

15) Devotion to my rosary is a great sign of predestination.

* The above list is taken from a book by the Servant of God Patrick Peyton.[1]

INDULGENCES OF THE ROSARY

People are often quite unaware of how rich the rosary is in indulgences. This is because many priests, when preaching on the rosary, hardly ever mention indulgences and give rather a flowery and popular sermon which excites admiration but scarcely teaches anything.[1]

~ St. Louis de Montfort

The words above serve as a reminder that, over the course of the centuries, there have been many indulgences given by the Church to those who pray the rosary. The Catholic Church is the storehouse of the graces of the redemption, and the Savior works through his Mystical Body to dispense many of these graces to souls in the form of pardons. These gifts are not magic, but rather graces and mercies that flow from the heart of a merciful God who loves his children. Our heavenly Father is more than willing to indulge us with his mercy and love.

On January 1, 1967, Bl. Pope Paul VI promulgated a revision of the sacred indulgences available to the Church in an apostolic constitution titled *Indulgentiarum Doctrina*. It was published on June 29, 1968 and has since undergone several editions. On July 5, 1999, in preparation for the Jubilee celebrations for the third Christian millennium, St. John Paul II approved a revised fourth edition. Then, on October 12, 2005, the Apostolic Penitentiary in Rome approved the English translation of the text, now known in English as the *Manual of Indulgences*.

Below are the selected and pertinent *Norms* from the *Manual of Indulgences* that the reader will find helpful for understanding what an indulgence is (plenary or partial), how often one may be obtained, and what conditions must be met to gain it. Presented at the end are the specific indulgenced Grants from the *Manual of Indulgences* that the Church offers to those who pray the rosary.

NORMS

n. 1 — An indulgence is a remission before God of the temporal punishment for sins, whose guilt is forgiven, which a properly disposed member of the Christian faithful obtains under certain and clearly defined conditions through the intervention of the Church, which, as the minister of Redemption, dispenses and applies authoritatively the treasury of the expiatory works of Christ and the saints.

n. 2 — An indulgence is partial or plenary according to whether it removes either part or all of the temporal punishment due sin.

n. 3 — The faithful can obtain partial or plenary indulgences for themselves, or they can apply them to the dead [souls in purgatory] by way of suffrage. [No one gaining an indulgence may apply it to other living persons].

n. 15 — The faithful can acquire an indulgence if they use devoutly one of the following properly blessed pious objects, namely, a crucifix or cross, rosary, scapular, or medal.

n. 17 — In order to be capable of gaining indulgences one must be baptized, not excommunicated, and in the state of grace at least at the completion of the prescribed works.

n. 18 — A plenary indulgence can be acquired only once in the course of a day; a partial indulgence can be acquired multiple times.

n. 20 — To gain a plenary indulgence, in addition to excluding all attachment to sin, even venial sin, it is necessary to perform the indulgenced work and fulfill the following three conditions: sacramental confession, Eucharistic Communion, and prayer for the intention of the Sovereign Pontiff.

- The three conditions may be fulfilled several days before or after the performance of the prescribed work; it is, however fitting that Communion be received and the prayer for the intention of the Holy Father be said on the same day the work is performed.

- The condition of praying for the intention of the Holy Father is fully satisfied by reciting one Our Father and one Hail Mary; nevertheless, one has the option of reciting any other prayer according to individual piety and devotion, if recited for this intention.

* Many numbers have not been presented because they are not pertinent to the topic at hand.

GRANTS

n. 17 — Prayers to the Blessed Virgin Mary

A plenary indulgence is granted to the faithful who

- devoutly recite the Marian rosary in a church or oratory, or in a family, a religious community, or an association of the faithful, and in general when several of the faithful gather for some honest purpose;

- devoutly join in the recitation of the rosary while it is being recited by the Supreme Pontiff and broadcast live by radio or television. In other circumstances, the indulgence will be *partial*.

NB: According to the *Manual of Indulgences*, the plenary indulgence is gained when only five decades of the rosary are recited. However, the five decades must be recited without interruption.[2]

APPENDIX A:
THE ROSARY IN ART

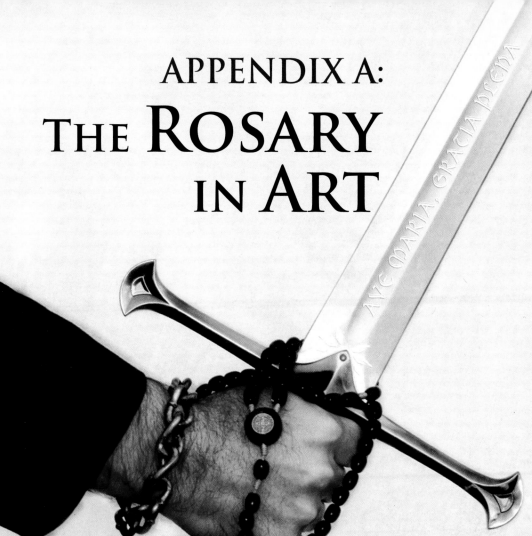

Ave Maria, gratia plena,
Dominus tecum.
Benedicta tu in mulieribus,
et benedictus fructus ventris tui, Iesus.

Sancta Maria, Mater Dei,
ora pro nobis peccatoribus,
nunc, et in hora mortis nostrae.
Amen.

St. Michael and the Scales (15ᵗʰ century). Alabaster. Sculptor unknown.
Pembroke College Chapel. Cambridge, England. Used with permission.

Altarpiece of the Virgin of the Rosary (c.1500). Ludovico Brea (1450-1523). Church of Biot, France/Bridgeman Images. Used with permission.

Madonna of the Rosary (1539). Lorenzo Lotto (1480-1557). Cingoli, Italy. Mondadori Portfolio/Electa/Antonio Quattrone/Bridgeman Images. Used with permission.

Madonna and Child (early 16ᵗʰ century). Bernard van Orley (1487-1542).
© Museo Nacional del Prado. Madrid, Spain. Used with permission.

Madonna of the Rosary (16th century). Bartolomeo Passerotti (1529-1592) Mondadori Portfolio/Electa/Vincenzo Negro/Bridgeman Images. Used with permission.

St. Dominic receiving the Rosary (16th century). Federico Fiori Barocci (1535-1612). Ashmolean Museum, University of Oxford, England/Bridgeman Image. Used with permission.

Madonna of the Rosary (c.1569). Jacopo Zucchi (1540-1596). Chiesa di San Ilario, Bibbona, Italy/Bridgeman Images. Used with permission.

Madonna of the Rosary (c. 1605). Caravaggio (1571-1610). Kunsthistorisches Museum. Vienna, Austria. Public Domain.

Madonna of the Rosary (c.1615). Giovanni Battista Paggi (1554-1627). Accademia Ligustica di Bella Arti. Florence, Italy/Bridgeman Images. Used with permission.

The Vision of St. Dominic (c.1640). Bernardo Cavallino (1616-1656). © The National Gallery of Canada, Ottawa. Used with permission.

Madonna of the Rosary with St. Dominic and St. Catherine of Siena (c.1642).
Giovanni Francesco Barbieri (Guercino) (1591-1666). Chiesa di San Marco. Osimo,
Italy. Courtesy of COMUNE di OSIMO. Used with permission.

The Virgin of the Rosary (c. 1650). Bartolomé Esteban Murillo (1617-1682).
© Museo Nacional del Prado. Madrid, Spain/Bridgeman Images. Used with permission.

La Remise du Rosaire (17th century). Guillaume Perrier (1600-1656). Musée des Ursulines de Mâcon, France. Public Domain.

Virgin of the Rosary (17th century). Francisco de Zurbarán (1598-1664). Museum of Fine Arts. Seville, Spain. Used with permission.

Our Lady of the Rosary (17th century). Giovanni Battista Salvi (Sassoferrato) (1609-1685). Chapel of St. Catherine of Siena (Basilica of Santa Sabina). Rome, Italy. De Agostini Picture Library/G. Nimatallah/Bridgeman Images. Used with permission.

The Virgin Offering the Rosary to St. Dominic (1641). Gaspard de Crayer (1584-1669). Musée des Beaux-Arts, Valenciennes, France/Bridgeman Images. Used with permission.

Our Lady of the Rosary (17th century). Carlo Ceresa (1609-1679). San Francesco al Dosso Church. Lombardy, Italy. Mondadori/Everett Collection. Used with permission.

Madonna of the Rosary (late 17th century). Bartolomé Esteban Murillo (1617-1682).
© Dulwich Picture Gallery. London, England/Bridgeman Images. Used with permission.

Virgin of the Rosary (late 17ᵗʰ century to early 18ᵗʰ century). Melchor Pérez de Holguín (1660-1732). Dallas Museum of Art. The Cleofas and Celia de la Garza Collection, gift of Mary de la Garza-Hanna and Virginia de la Garza and an Anonymous Donor. Used with permission.

St. Dominic Receiving the Rosary from the Virgin Mary (c.1700). Attributed to Pier Leone Ghezzi (1674-1755). The Fitzwilliam Museum. Cambridge, England/Bridgeman Images. Used with permission.

Madonna of the Rosary with St. Dominic, St. Catherine, St. Mary Magdalene, and St. Joseph (1732). Luigi Crespi (1709-1779). Monastero di San Niccolo Prato, Tuscany, Italy/Bridgeman Images. Used with permission.

Madonna of the Rosary with Sts. Dominic and Francis (early 18th century) Nicolo Grassi (1682-1748). Photographed by Bojan Salaj. © Narodna galerija, Ljubljana, Slovenia. Used with permission.

Our Lady of Las Lajas. (1754). Colombia, South America. Joana Toro/VIEWpress. Used with permission.

Madonna of the Rosary (18ᵗʰ century). Giovanni Battista Tiepolo (1696-1770). Private Collection/Bridgeman Images. Used with permission.

The Virgin of the Rosary in Glory with St. Dominic and St. Catherine of Siena (c.1800).
Vicente Lopez (1772-1850). Private Collection.

Our Lady of the Rosary of Pompeii (19ᵗʰ century). Artist Unknown. Basilica of Our Lady of the Rosary of Pompeii, Italy.

Champions of the Rosary by Vivian Imbruglia. (2016). Commissioned by Fr. Donald H. Calloway, MIC. www.sacredimageicons.com.

The 26 Champions of the Rosary by Maria Madonna Bouza Urbina. (2016). Commissioned by Fr. Donald H. Calloway, MIC. www.fathercalloway.com.

St. Dominic: Champion of the Holy Rosary by Nellie Edwards. (2016).
Commissioned by Fr. Donald H. Calloway, MIC. www.PaintedFaith.net.

Queen of the Rosary and St. Dominic by Vivian Imbruglia. (2016).
Commissioned by Fr. Donald H. Calloway, MIC. www.sacredimageicons.com.

APPENDIX B:

Our Lady's Words to
Blessed Alan de la Roche

*T*hrough *the rosary, hardened sinners of both sexes became converted and started to lead a holy life, bemoaning their past sins with genuine tears of contrition. Even children performed unbelievable penances: devotion to my Son and to me spread so thoroughly that it almost seemed as though angels were living on earth. The Faith was gaining, and many Catholics longed to shed their blood for it and fight against the heretics. Thus, through the sermons of my very dear Dominic and through the power of the rosary, the heretics' lands were all brought under the Church. People used to give munificent alms; hospitals and churches were built. People led moral and law-abiding lives and worked wonders for the glory of God. Holiness and unworldliness flourished; the clergy were exemplary, princes were just, people lived at peace with each other and justice and equity reigned in the guilds and in the homes.*

Here is an even more impressive thing: workmen did not take up their tools until they had said my Psalter [rosary] and they never went to sleep at night without having prayed to me on their knees. If they happened to remember that they had not paid me this tribute they would get up — even in the middle of the night — and then would salute me with great respect and remorse.

The rosary became so widespread and so well-known that people who were devoted to it were always considered by others as obviously being Confraternity members. If a man lived openly in sin, or blasphemed, it was quite the usual to say: "This man cannot be a brother of Saint Dominic."

I must not fail to mention the signs and wonders that I have wrought in different lands through the holy rosary: I have stopped pestilences and put an end to horrible wars as well as to bloody crimes, and through the rosary people have found the courage to flee temptation.

When you say your rosary the angels rejoice, the Blessed Trinity delights in it, my Son finds joy in it, too, and I myself am happier than you can possibly guess.[1]

APPENDIX C:

Endorsements from Cardinals and Bishops

Jesus loves his mother immensely and has given her to us to be our mother and a great intercessor. In our combat against evil, the Mother of God has given us the rosary as a powerful spiritual weapon. *Champions of the Rosary* is a book to be read and reflected upon by all. I highly recommend it!

His Eminence Malcolm Cardinal Ranjith, DD, SSL
Archbishop of Colombo, Sri Lanka

Myanmar Catholics' long, turbulent journey of faith has been sustained and fortified by their intense devotion to Mary and her rosary. I am very grateful that *Champions of the Rosary* has been written. It probes the creative contours of this inspiring devotion and illuminates the important role of the rosary in spreading the faith across cultures. This book is a pivotal contribution to our Catholic faith. I heartily endorse it and encourage every Catholic to draw countless blessings from this treasure house of Mariology.

His Eminence Charles M. Cardinal Bo, SDB, DD
Archbishop of Yangon, Myanmar

In Chinese culture, we have always shown a special love for our mother and consider this to be one of the greatest expressions of human love. For this reason, Chinese Catholics pray the rosary because we understand it to be one of the best ways of expressing our love for our spiritual mother, Mary. *Champions of the Rosary* will help us love our spiritual mother even more!

His Eminence John Cardinal Tong Hon, DD, STD
Bishop of Hong Kong, China

It is with great pleasure that I endorse *Champions of the Rosary*. In the Arab Christian world, the rosary is an essential part of our devotion to the Mother of God. I will encourage everyone to read this inspiring book and find in the rosary a protection against every evil.

Most Rev. Maroun E. N. Lahham, DD, STD
Archbishop of Tunis, Tunisia, and
Knight Commander of the Sacred Military Constantinian Order of St. George

Champions of the Rosary is an encyclopedic work by Fr. Calloway. It presents an extensive history of the rosary and details how it has served God's people as a spiritual lifeline through the centuries. It also reveals insights into the practical transformation that the rosary has had in forming and sustaining some of history's greatest saints, propelling them to the depths of holiness and the heights of humility. This book is a timely reminder of the great spiritual weapon in the arsenal of every Catholic, a weapon that each of us needs to sustain us in the spiritual life.

Most Rev. Gintaras L. Grušas, DD, JCD
Archbishop of Vilnius, Lithuania

The history of the Church is dotted with significant events where the Mother of God intervened in a powerful manner and changed the course of world history. Such is the story of the rosary. In this incredible theological treatise, Fr. Calloway offers us the most up-to-date account of these history-making events, as well as an urgent appeal to the Church in our day to once again turn to the rosary for heavenly aid. Everyone should read this book!

Most Rev. Ramón C. Argüelles, DD, STL
Archbishop of Lipa, Philippines

Catholics are known for their love of the rosary. For many, it is *the* Catholic prayer. A number of religious congregations even have the practice of wearing a large rosary from their belt. This practice is a sign that the rosary is integral to their spirituality and charism. In *Champions of the Rosary,* the Dominican link to the rosary is rightly highlighted and beautifully presented. I commend Fr. Calloway for this inspiring book.

Most Rev. Julian C. Porteous, DD
Archbishop of Hobart, Tasmania

Champions of the Rosary is a great resource for bringing about the renewal of the family rosary in our day. Though a simple prayer, the rosary of Our Lady has proven itself to be one of the best methods available for binding families together.

Most Rev. Bernard B. Moras, DD
Archbishop of Bangalore, India

In Spain, we have a great devotion to the rosary and are very honored that St. Dominic was born in our land. *Champions of the Rosary* is a very well-written book and offers a complete historical, theological, and spiritual overview of the origins of the rosary, as well as the saints and popes who have championed it. This book will do much to help spread devotion to the rosary.

Most Rev. Jesús Catalá Ibáñez, DD, STD
Bishop of Málaga, Spain

Champions of the Rosary is a unique work that draws its inspiration from the long litany of saints who have been devoted to the Blessed Virgin Mary. A good number of these saints have also been champions and heroes of the rosary. May we draw strength from these saints and attain a deeper union with the Triune God through our contemplation of the sacred mysteries of the rosary.

Most Rev. Mylo H. Vergara, DD, STD
Bishop of Pasig, Philippines

Champions of the Rosary is an epochal work and can genuinely stand alongside the miraculous beginnings of the rosary in the life of St. Dominic. It is refreshing that even our own Scottish martyr and champion of the rosary, St. John Ogilvie, is mentioned in this honorable tome. In authoring this book, Fr. Calloway has responded to a divine commission from the Holy Spirit and Mary, Co-Redemptrix, to bring the spiritual weapon of the rosary onto the spiritual battlefield of the 21st century.

Most Rev. John Keenan, DD
Bishop of Paisley, Scotland

Champions of the Rosary offers a solid foundation for appreciating in a deeper way the greatness of the rosary of St. Dominic. As a promoter of the Divine Mercy message and devotion in Nigeria, I was very inspired to learn of the profound connection between the rosary and the Chaplet of Divine Mercy as given to St. Faustina. A wonderful book!

Most Rev. Martin I. Uzoukwu, DD, JCD
Bishop of Minna, Nigeria

For as long as I can remember, Filipinos have been called a *"Pueblo amante de Maria"* ("a people in love with Mary"). An expression of this filial devotion to Mary has been our great love of the rosary. In *Champions of the Rosary*, the Philippines will find an inspiring and encouraging book that will strengthen our desire to always go to Jesus through Mary.

Most Rev. Jesse E. Mercado, DD
Bishop of Parañaque, Philippines

Champions of the Rosary is the greatest book written on the rosary in the last 300 years! It accomplishes exactly what Fr. Calloway intended, namely, it retells the story of the rosary and picks up where St. Louis de Montfort left off. I pray the whole world reads this book!

Most Rev. Francis Serrao, SJ, DD
Bishop of Shimoga, India

Champions of the Rosary is a rich treasure for the Church! Digging deep into history, Fr. Calloway presents those heroes of God who, at different times and in different places, emerged as champions of the rosary. This book reveals the rosary to be a spiritual sword that continues to be one of the most valuable means available for converting souls, transforming lives, and conquering evil. We in the present time are also called to become champions of the rosary by promoting this weapon throughout the world. This is a must-read book for everyone. I will treasure it for the rest of my life!

Most Rev. Oliver Dashe Doeme, DD
Bishop of Maiduguri, Nigeria

Beginning with St. Dominic, the founder and pioneering champion of the rosary, *Champions of the Rosary* wonderfully enumerates the most prominent heroes of the rosary throughout the centuries. I pray that Fr. Calloway's exhaustive research helps spread this devotion to every corner of the world.

Most Rev. Anthony Chirayath, DD
Bishop of Sagar, India

In *Champions of the Rosary*, Fr. Calloway gives us a most inspiring and thorough collection of references to the rosary by many saints and popes over the centuries. No one could read these pages without deepening their commitment to the daily rosary, renewing their commitment if it has lapsed or being inspired to begin the practice if it is not yet an integral part of their daily spiritual devotion. This book is also an excellent resource for fostering the practice of the family rosary!

Most Rev. Robert F. Vasa, DD
Bishop of Santa Rosa, California

As a bishop in the Philippines, I wholeheartedly endorse *Champions of the Rosary*! This book offers a clear and comprehensive knowledge of the rosary, and will greatly help the faithful in their love for this devotion.

Most Rev. Guillermo D. Afable, DD
Bishop of Digos, Philippines

In *Champions of the Rosary*, Fr. Calloway has written a book that is encyclopedic in nature. Many Christians consider the rosary to be an obsolete prayer, but this book shows that it is the perfect prayer for men and women of all time: clergy and laity, rich and poor, scholars and non-scholars. The rosary is our weapon! Why not use it today to combat the many atrocities occurring throughout the world?

Most Rev. William H. Shomali, DD, STD
Auxiliary Bishop of Jerusalem and
Patriarchal Vicar for Palestine

This is *the* book for our times. The answer to the moral crises in the world today is for people to turn back to the saving mysteries of Christ. The rosary encapsulates these mysteries and is a mini-catechism that has proven to be extremely effective in bringing divine light back into souls. *Champions of the Rosary* is simply one of the best books I have ever read!

Most Rev. Gilbert E. Chávez, DD
Auxiliary Bishop Emeritus of San Diego, California

REFERENCES

* Initial quotes at the beginning of the book:
~ Blessed Bartolo Longo, as quoted in Ann M. Brown, *Apostle of the Rosary: Blessed Bartolo Longo* (New Hope, KY: New Hope Publications, 2004), 27.
~ Pope Leo XIII, *Parta Humano Generi*, Apostolic Letter (September 8, 1901), in *The Rosary of Our Lady: Translations of the Encyclical and Apostolic Letters of Pope Leo XIII*, ed. William Raymond Lawler, OP (Paterson, NJ: St. Anthony Guild Press, 1944), 195-196.
~ St. Anthony Mary Claret, as quoted in Fr. Juan Echevarria, *The Miracles of St. Anthony Mary Claret*. trans. Sr. Mary Gonzaga. (Charlotte, NC: TAN Books, 1992), 61.

Introduction

[1] St. Louis de Montfort, *The Secret of the Rosary*. trans. Mary Barbour, TOP (Bay Shore, NY: Montfort Publications, 1988), 85.
[2] St. John Paul II, *Rosarium Virginis Mariae*, Apostolic Letter (October 16, 2002), 8.

Part I:
History of the Rosary

* Image on pg. 25: The picture of the sword with rosary and chain was taken at the Marian House of Studies in Steubenville, Ohio, in 2015 at the request of Fr. Donald Calloway, MIC. All rights reserved to the Marian Fathers of the Immaculate Conception.
* Image on pg. 26: *The Warrior's Rosary* by Thomas K. Sullivan. www.thewarrior-rosary.com

From the Angelic Salutation to the 12th Century:
The Antecedents of the Rosary

[1] St. Louis de Montfort, *The Secret of the Rosary*. trans. Mary Barbour, TOP (Bay Shore, NY: Montfort Publications, 1988), 46.
[2] Pope Leo XIII, *Iucunda Semper Expectatione*, Encyclical (September 8, 1894), in *The Rosary of Our Lady: Translations of the Encyclical and Apostolic Letters of Pope Leo XIII*, ed. William Raymond Lawler, OP (Paterson, NJ: St. Anthony Guild Press, 1944), 119.

The 13th Century:
St. Dominic and the Birth of the Rosary

[1] *"Our Lady's words to St. Dominic,"* as quoted in Augusta Theodosia Drane, OP, *The History of St. Dominic: Founder of the Friars Preachers* (London: Longmans, Green, and Co., 1891), 122.
[2] Pope Leo XIII, *Parta Humano Generi*, Apostolic Letter (September 8, 1901), as quoted in *The Rosary of Our Lady: Translations of the Encyclical and Apostolic Letters of Pope Leo XIII*, ed. William Raymond Lawler, OP (Paterson, NJ: St. Anthony Guild Press, 1944), 192-193.

[3] Reginald Garrigou-LaGrange, OP, *Mother of Our Savior and the Interior Life.* trans. Bernard Kelly, CSSp (Dublin: Golden Eagle Book, 1948), 297.

[4] Pope Leo XIII, *Supremi Apostolatus Officio,* Encyclial (September 1, 1883), as quoted in *The Rosary of Our Lady: Translations of the Encyclical and Apostolic Letters of Pope Leo XIII,* ed. William Raymond Lawler, OP, 4.

[5] St. Maximilian Kolbe, "1021 – Arcybractwo Rózanca Sw"[Grodno 1922-1925] in *Pisma Sw Maksymiliana Kolbego* (Niepokalanów, Poland), trans. Fr. Thaddaeus Lancton, MIC, from the original Polish. In the Italian *Scritti di Massimiliano Kolbe* (Roma, 1997), it is found in section 1257 with a different, and inaccurate, translation.

[6] Pope Leo XIII, *Parta Humano Generi* (September 8, 1901), in *The Rosary of Our Lady: Translations of the Encyclical and Apostolic Letters of Pope Leo XIII,* ed. William Raymond Lawler, OP, 193-194.

[7] See Wilfrid Lescher, OP, *St. Dominic and the Rosary* (London: R. & T. Washbourne, 1902), 92-93.

[8] Nicholas Trivet, OP, as quoted in Robert Feeney, *The Rosary: "The Little Summa,"* fourth edition (USA: Aquinas Press, 2003), 31.

[9] Pope Leo XIII, *Augustissimae Virginis Mariae,* Encyclical (September 12, 1897), 7.

[10] Pope Clement VIII, as quoted in Wilfrid Lescher, OP, *St. Dominic and the Rosary,* 9.

[11] Pope Sixtus V, as quoted in Wilfrid Lescher, OP, *St. Dominic and the Rosary,* 10.

[12] See Wilfrid Lescher, OP, *St. Dominic and the Rosary,* 31.

[13] See Msgr. George W. Shea, STD, "The Dominican Rosary," in *Mariology,* Vol. 3, ed. Juniper B. Carol, OFM (Milwaukee, WI: Bruce Publishing Company, 1961), 114.

[14] Ibid., 102.

[15] See Augusta Theodosia Drane, OP, *The History of St. Dominic: Founder of the Friars Preachers* (London: Longmans, Green, and Co., 1891), 130.

[16] Ibid., 301.

[17] Ibid., 130.

[18] St. Ignatius of Antioch, "Letter to the Ephesians," in *Early Christian Fathers,* ed. Cyril C. Richardson (New York: MacMillan Company, 1970), 113.

[19] See Andrew Skelly, OP, *"St. Dominic and the Rosary or Was He Its Founder?"* (Providence, RI: Providence College Digital Commons) *Historical Catholic and Dominican Documents, Book 1* (1915), pages 77-79.

[20] Pope Urban IV, as quoted in Pope Leo XIII, *Supremi Apostolatus Officio,* 5.

The 14th Century:
Plagues and Schism: The Rosary is Almost Forgotten

[1] Maisie Ward, *The Splendor of the Rosary* (New York: Sheed and Ward, 1945), 34.

[2] Venerable Fulton J. Sheen, *The World's First Love* (San Francisco, CA: Ignatius Press, 1996), 207.

[3] See Wilfrid Lescher, OP, *St. Dominic and the Rosary* (London: R. & T. Washbourne, 1902), 117-118.

[4] See Andrew Skelly, OP, *"St. Dominic and the Rosary or Was He Its Founder?"*

(Providence, RI: Providence College Digital Commons), *Historical Catholic and Dominican Documents, Book 1* (1915), page 76.

[5] See Raymond P. Devas, OP, "The Rosary Tradition Defined and Defended," in *American Catholic Quarterly Review* (Volume XLI, January 1916), 143.

The 15th Century:
Blessed Alan de la Roche and the Revival
of the Confraternity of the Rosary

[1] Pope Leo XIII, *Adiutricem,* Encyclical (September 5, 1895), 28.

[2] See André Duval, OP, "Rosaire," in *Dictionnaire de spiritualité ascétique et mystique: Doctrine et histoire*, XIII (Paris: Beauchesne, 1988), 949.

[3] For an example of the Carthusian rosary in the style of Dominic of Prussia, see Daniel Frattarelli, *The Life of Christ Rosary (also known as the Carthusian Rosary)* (Amazon Digital Services, Inc. 2012). NB: In the text, Dominic of Prussia is referred to as a saint, but he has never been canonized. Also see Fr. Edward Lee Looney, *A Rosary Litany: Renewing a Pious Custom* (Phoenix, AZ: Flores Mariae Publishing, 2016)

[4] "*Our Lord's words to Bl. Alan de la Roche*," as quoted in St. Louis de Montfort, *The Secret of the Rosary.* trans. Mary Barbour, TOP (Bay Shore, NY: Montfort Publications, 1988), 23.

[5] "*Our Lord's words to Bl. Alan de la Roche*," as quoted in "The Life and Times of B. Alain de la Roche in the Fifteenth Century: Restorer of the Confraternity of the Most Holy Rosary: Chap. II – The Trials of B. Alain," in *The Monthly Magazine of the Holy Rosary,* no. 2 (September 1872), 35.

[6] Antoninus de Monroy, as quoted in Augusta Theodosia Drane, OP, *The History of St. Dominic: Founder of the Friars Preachers* (London: Longmans, Green, and Co., 1891), 132.

[7] St. Louis de Montfort, *The Secret of the Rosary,* 23.

[8] Jacob Sprenger, as quoted in Anne Winston-Allen, *Stories of the Rose: The Making of the Rosary in the Middle Ages* (University Park, PA: Pennsylvania State University Press, 1997), 174.

[9] Unfortunately, as many historians attest, Jacob Sprenger is considered to be the co-author of the infamous *Malleus Maleficarum* ("The Hammer of the Witches"), a medieval treatise on the prosecution of witches. Although some recent historians believe that the book was primarily written by the Dominican Heinrich Kramer and that it was Kramer who attached Sprenger's name to it as co-author in order to lend as much authority to the book as possible, Sprenger himself may have willingly gotten mixed up in the publication of the witch-hunting manual. Whatever the case, this situation only goes to show that Our Lady used imperfect instruments to bring about the renewal of the rosary and its confraternity in the 15th century. See Hans Peter Broedel, *The* Malleus Maleficarum *and the Construction of Witchcraft: Theology and Popular Belief* (England: Manchester University Press, 2013)

[10] Alexander of Forli, as quoted in Andrew Skelly, OP. *St. Dominic and the Rosary or Was He Its Founder?* (Providence, RI: Providence College Digital Commons).

Historical Catholic and Dominican Documents. Book 1. (1915), page 21.

[11] Pope Innocent VIII, as quoted by Pope Leo XIII, *Augustissimae Virginis Mariae,* Encyclical (September 12, 1897), 11.

[12] Pope Alexander VI, *Illius qui,* Papal Bull, as quoted in William G. Most, *Mary in Our Life* (Garden City, NY: Image Books, 1954), 305.

The 16th Century:
The Rosary in Battle: Lepanto and Our Lady of Victory

[1] Pope Leo X, *Pastoris Aeterni,* as quoted in Juan Carlos Villa Larroudet, *El Rosario: Historia, Redescubrimiento y Propuestas* (Buenos Aires, Argentina: Agape Libros, 2013), 282-283. Trans. Miss Ileana E. Salazar, MA.

[2] Pope Adrian VI, as quoted in Donald H. Calloway, MIC, *Rosary Gems: Daily Wisdom on the Holy Rosary* (Stockbridge, MA: Marian Press, 2015), 105.

[3] Pope Julius III, as quoted in Pope Leo XIII, *Supremi Apostolatus Officio,* 5.

[4] St. Pope Pius V, as quoted in Pope Leo XIII, *Augustissimae Virginis Mariae,* 11.

[5] Anne Winston-Allen, *Stories of the Rose: The Making of the Rosary in the Middle Ages* (University Park, PA: Pennsylvania State University Press, 1997), 130.

[6] St. Louis Bertrand, as quoted in Garbriel Harty, OP, *The Riches of the Rosary* (Dublin, Ireland: Veritas, 1997), 75.

[7] St. Pope Pius V, *Consueverunt Romani Pontifices* (September 17, 1569), as quoted in Juan Carlos Villa Larroudet, *El Rosario: Historia, Redescubrimiento y Propuestas* (Buenos Aires, Argentina: Agape Libros, 2013), 269-270. Trans. Miss Ileana E. Salazar, MA.

[8] G.K. Chesterton, *Lepanto* (San Francisco, CA: Ignatius Press, 2004), 11.

[9] Don Juan of Austria, as quoted in ibid., 62.

[10] Miguel Cervantes, as quoted in Rev. J.A. Rooney, OP, "Rosary Sunday and Month: The Dominican Portiuncula," *The Rosary Magazine* (October, 1892), 449-450.

[11] See *The English-Latin Sacramentary for the United States of America* (New York: Catholic Book Publishing Co., 1966), 480.

The 17th Century: Witnesses of the Rosary

[1] Niccolò Ridolfi, OP, as quoted in "Confraternity of the Rosary," in *The Rosary Magazine,* vol. 26 (1905), 104.

[2] St. Francis de Sales, as quoted in Robert Feeney, *The Rosary: "The Little Summa,"* fourth edition, (USA: Aquinas Press, 2003), 82.

[3] See St. John Eudes, *The Admirable Heart of Mary.* trans. Charles di Targiani and Ruth Hauser (Buffalo, NY: Immaculate Heart Publications, 1947), 331.

[4] John ab Eckersdorff, as quoted in Daniel Conway, "The Story of a Scottish Martyr," in *The Month and Catholic Review,* vol. 32, no. 13 (March 1878), 356-357.

[5] Oliver Cromwell, as quoted in Bishop Brendan Kelly, "The Rosary: A Prayer for our times," in *Intercom: A Pastoral and Liturgical Resource* (May 2009), 24.

[6] Courtesy of the Lay Dominicans in Ireland

[7] King Jan Casimir II, as quoted in John Procter, OP, *The Rosary Guide for Priests and People* (London: Kegan and Trubner, 1901), 109.

[8] In addition to the heroic efforts of King Jan Sobieski, the holy Franciscan priest Blessed Marco Aviano (1631–1699) also played a key role in the Battle of Vienna. He was appointed by Bl. Pope Innocent XI to serve as the papal legate for the Holy League. He was a great preacher and often preached against the heresies of Protestantism and the falsehoods of Islam. On the morning of the decisive Battle of Vienna, Bl. Marco celebrated Mass and extended a blessing to the army of Sobieski. When Bl. Marco was beatified on Divine Mercy Sunday in 2003, St. John Paul II noted the following in his homily: "An unarmed prophet of Divine Mercy, he [Bl. Marco] was impelled by circumstances to be actively committed to defending the freedom and unity of Christian Europe."

[9] King Jan Sobieski, as quoted in Robert Debs Heinl, *Dictionary of Military and Naval Quotations* (Annapolis, MD: United States Naval Institute, 1966), 65.

[10] Pope Clement VIII, as quoted in Wilfrid Lescher, OP, *St. Dominic and the Rosary* (London: R. & T. Washbourne, 1902), 9.

[11] In an address given in Lourdes, France, in 1998, Fr. Timothy Radcliffe, OP, Master General of the Order of Preachers, referenced the 17th century depiction of the rosary in art and noted the following: "There is a long tradition of pictures of Our Lady giving the rosary to St. Dominic. But at one time, other religious orders grew jealous, and started commissioning paintings of Our Lady giving the rosary to other saints, to St. Francis and even St. Ignatius. But we [Dominicans] fought back, and, I think in the 17th century, persuaded the pope to ban the competition. Our Lady was only allowed to be shown giving the rosary to St. Dominic!" See "Address from the Master General of the Order at Lourdes" (October, 1998). www.op.org

The 18th Century:
St. Louis de Montfort and *The Secret of the Rosary*

[1] St. Louis de Montfort, *Jesus Living in Mary* (Bayshore, NY: Montfort Publications, 1994), 1213.

[2] Pope Leo XIII, *Supremi Apostolatus Officio*, 4.

[3] Pope Leo XIII, *Augustissimae Virginis Mariae*, 8.

[4] Cardinal Prospero Lambertini, as quoted in Robert Feeney, *The Rosary: "The Little Summa,"* fourth edition. (USA: Aquinas Press, 2003), 4.

[5] Ibid., 6.

[6] Rosary Sunday Reading, as quoted in William G. Most, *Mary in Our Life* (Garden City, NY: Image Books, 1954), 306.

[7] Rosary Sunday Reading, as quoted in Wilfrid Lescher, OP, *St. Dominic and the Rosary* (London: R. & T. Washbourne, 1902), 93.

[8] Rosary Sunday Reading, as quoted in John Procter, OP, *The Rosary Guide for Priests and People* (London: Kegan and Trubner, 1901), 24.

The 19th Century: Lourdes and The Pope of the Rosary

[1] Bl. Anne Catherine Emmerich, as quoted in Carl E. Schmöger, CSsR. *The Life of Anne Catherine Emmerich,* vol. 2 (Charlotte, NC: TAN Books, 1976), 333.

[2] Henri-Dominique Lacordaire, OP, as quoted in Gabriel Harty, OP, *The Riches of the Rosary* (Dublin, Ireland: Veritas, 1997), 8.

[3] Henri-Dominique Lacordaire, OP, *Thoughts and Teachings of Lacordaire* (New York: Benziger Bros., 1903), 30-31.

[4] Gabriel Garcia Moreno, as quoted in Reuben Parsons, DD, "Freemasonry in Latin America," in *The American Catholic Quarterly Review,* vol. XXIII (1898), 826.

[5] Bl. Hyacinth Cormier, OP, as quoted in Francis Lasance, *With God: A Book of Prayers and Reflections* (New York: Benziger Bros., 1911), 709.

The 20th Century: Marian Apparitions and Apostles of the Rosary

[1] Servant of God Joseph Kentenich, as quoted in Fr. Jonathan Niehaus, *New Vision and Life: The Founding of Schoenstatt (1912-1919)* (Waukesha, WI: Schoenstatt Fathers, 2004), 33.

[2] St. Pope Pius X, *Pascendi Dominici Gregis,* Encyclical (September 8, 1907), 43. It is highly recommended that the reader obtain a copy of this encyclical in order to better understand the intricacies of Modernism.

[3] Fr. Joseph Crehan, SJ, *Father Thurston: A Memoir with a Bibliography of his Writings* (London: Sheed & Ward, 1952), 104.

[4] Andrew Skelly, OP. *"St. Dominic and the Rosary or Was He Its Founder?"* (Providence, RI: Providence College Digital Commons), *Historical Catholic and Dominican Documents, Book 1* (1915), page 7.

[5] Ibid., 14.

[6] Fr. Joseph Crehan, SJ, *Father Thurston: A Memoir with a Bibliography of his Writings,* 105.

[7] Fr. Herbert Thurston, SJ, as quoted in Joseph Crehan, SJ, *Father Thurston: A Memoir with a Bibliography of his Writings,* 135.

[8] See Joseph Crehan, SJ, *Father Thurston: A Memoir with a Bibliography of his Writings,* 135.

[9] See Paul J. Gaunt, "A Surprising Jesuit," in *PsyPioneer,* vol. 2, no. 9 (September, 2006), 188-191.

[10] Ibid., 188.

[11] See Joseph Crehan, SJ, *Father Thurston: A Memoir with a Bibliography of his Writings,* 141.

[12] Ibid., 142.

[13] Ibid., 66.

[14] For examples of Fr. Thurston's ridicule of saints and holy mystics, see the following works: Herbert Thurston, "The Phenomena of Stigmatization," in *Proceedings of the Society for Psychical Research,* vol. 32 (1922), 179-208; *The Physical Phenomena of Mysticism* (London: Barnes & Oates, 1952); *Surprising Mystics* (Barnes & Oates, 1955).

[15] See Fr. Herbert Thurston, *Beauraing and Other Apparitions: An Account of Some Borderland Cases in the Psychology of Mysticism* (London: Oates & Washbourne, 1934).

[16] Pope Pius XI, *Ingravescentibus Malis,* Encyclical (September 29, 1937), 14.

[17] *Catechism of the Catholic Church,* Second Edition (Citta del Vaticano: Libreria Editrice Vaticana, 1994), entry 67.

[18] See Finbar Ryan, OP (Archbishop of Port of Spain), *Our Lady of Fatima* (Dublin: Richview Press, 1939), 77-99.

[19] See Teresita L. Castillo, *I am Mary, Mediatrix of All Grace* (Lipa, Philippines, 2008), 37. See also Rene C. de Jesus, *Mary, Mediatrix of All Grace: A Journey of Suffering and Holiness* (Mandaluyong City: LSA Printing Press Inc., 2015)

[20] See June Keithley, *Lipa (with the original account of the events of Lipa Carmel in 1948 by Mother Mary Cecilia of Jesus, OCD)* (Mandaluyong, Philippines: Cacho Publishing House, Inc., 1992), 125-126.

[21] See Dr. Courtenay Bartholomew, "The Eucharist and the Rosary: The Link between Fatima, Amsterdam, and Akita," in *Missio Immaculatae,* vol. 12. no.1 (January/February 2016), 25-29.

[22] Our Lady's message to Sr. Agnes Sasagawa, as quoted in Teiji Yasuda, OSV, *Akita: The Tears and Message of Mary* (Asbury, NJ: 101 Foundation, Inc., 1989), 77-78.

[23] Bernardo Martinez, as quoted in *Apparitions of Our Blessed Mother at Cuapa, Nicaragua: A Report of the Events in Cuapa* (Washington, NJ: The World Apostolate of Fatima, 1982), 11.

[24] "Father Dominic, the Carthusian, who was deeply devoted to the holy rosary, had this vision: Heaven was opened for him to see and the whole heavenly court was assembled in magnificent array. He heard them sing the rosary in an enchanting melody and each decade was in honor of a mystery of the life, passion or glory of our Lord Jesus Christ and of his Blessed Mother. Father Dominic noticed that whenever they said the sacred name of Mary they bowed their heads and at the name of Jesus they genuflected and gave thanks to God for the great good that he had wrought in heaven and on earth through the holy rosary, which the Confraternity members say here on earth." See St. Louis de Montfort, *The Secret of the Rosary,* trans. Mary Barbour, TOP (Bay Shore, NY: Montfort Publications, 1988), 70-71.

[25] Immaculée Ilibagiza, *Our Lady of Kibeho: Mary Speaks to the World from the Heart of Africa* (Carlsbad, CA: Hay House, 2008), 115.

[26] Gladys Quiroga de Motta, as quoted in *Messages of Our Lady of San Nicolás,* trans. Eleonora O'Farrell De Nagy-Pal and Marie-Helene Gall (Milford, OH: Faith Publishing Company, 1991), 8-9.

[27] *"Our Lady to Gladys Quiroga de Motta,"* as quoted in Fr. René Laurentin, *An Appeal from Mary in Argentina: The Apparitions of San Nicolás,* trans. Juan Gonzalez (Milford, OH: Faith Publishing Company, 1990), 83.

[28] Adrienne von Speyr, *The Book of All Saints: Part One.* ed. Hans Urs von Balthasar, trans. D.C. Schindler (San Francisco, CA: Ignatius Press, 2008), 361.

[29] It is also well known that in 1940, the former Soviet Union deported more than 22,000 Polish nationals (military leaders, academics, authors, and those in other professional roles) to the Katyn forest in western Russia. Once there, the prisoners were all executed and thrown into mass graves. When this atrocity was discovered years later, the bodies were exhumed and many rosaries were found among the corpses. Many of the dead still held a rosary in their hand, a sign that they were grasping the rosary in the final seconds of their life. This horrific event is known as the Katyn massacre.

[30] Pope Benedict XV, *Fausto Appetente Die,* Encyclical (June 29, 1921), 11. In the November 1, 1914 encyclical *Ad Beatissimi Apostolorum,* Pope Benedict XV condemned Modernism and its negative effects on private practices of piety, stating: "Infatuated and carried away by a lofty idea of the human intellect, by which God's good gift has certainly made incredible progress in the study of nature, confident in their own judgment, and contemptuous of the authority of the Church, they [Modernists] have reached such a degree of rashness as not to hesitate to measure by the standard of their own mind even the hidden things of God and all that God has revealed to men. Hence arose the monstrous errors of 'Modernism,' which our predecessor [St. Pope Pius X] rightly declared to be 'the synthesis of all heresies,' and solemnly condemned. We hereby renew that condemnation in all its fullness, Venerable Brethren, and as the plague is not yet entirely stamped out, but lurks here and there in hidden places, we exhort all to be on their guard against any contagion of the evil, to which we may apply the words Job used in other circumstances: 'It is a fire that devoureth even to destruction, and rooteth up all things that spring' (Job 31:12). Nor do we merely desire that Catholics should shrink from the errors of Modernism, but also from the tendencies or what is called the spirit of Modernism. Those who are infected by that spirit develop a keen dislike for all that savors of antiquity and become eager searchers after novelties in everything: in the way in which they carry out religious functions, in the ruling of Catholics institutions, and even in private practices of piety." See Pope Benedict XV, *Ad Beatissimi Apostolorum,* 25.

[31] Pope Pius XI, *Inclytam ac perillustrem,* Letter, (March 6, 1934).

[32] Pope Pius XI, *Ingravescentibus Malis,* 12.

[33] Venerable Pope Pius XII, *Letter to the Most Rev. Master General, Michael Browne, OP, concerning the Marian rosary* (July 11, 1957).

[34] Pope Pius XI, *Inclytam ac perillustrem,* as quoted in Gabriel Harty, OP, *The Riches of the Rosary* (Dublin, Ireland: Veritas, 1997), 22.

[35] Pope Pius XI, *Inclytam ac perillustrem,* as quoted in Finbar Ryan, OP (Archbishop of Port of Spain), *Our Lady of Fatima,* 97-99.

[36] Fr. Marie Étienne Vayssière, OP, as quoted in Gabriel Harty, OP, *Heaven Sent: My Life Through the Rosary,* 105.

[37] Reginald Garrigou-LaGrange, OP, *Mother of Our Savior and the Interior Life,* trans. Bernard Kelly, CSSp (Dublin: Golden Eagle Book, 1948), 297. In 1959, Fr. Jerome Wilms, OP, published a book on the life of St. Dominic, and noted the following: "According to a tradition mentioned in many papal encyclicals, it was during Dominic's missionary years in France that our Blessed Lady revealed to him a project forged from all eternity in God's mind ... [T]his assertion has been passed in review by many historians. Some say that the rosary antedates Dominic, others that it came after him. It is true that long before his time Our Fathers and Hail Marys were checked and numbered by a string of beads, but it is only since the thirteenth century that we find the division into decades or groups of ten, separated by larger beads called Our Fathers, and meditation on a particular scene of the life of Christ or Mary during each decade." See Jerome Wilms, OP, *As the Morning Star: The Life of St. Dominic* (Milwaukee, WI: Dominican Sisters of the Perpetual Rosary, 1956). Republished by Mediatrix Press (2014), 99.

[38] Fr. Anicetus Fernandez, OP, as quoted in Robert Feeney, *The Rosary: "The Little Summa,"* fourth edition (USA: Aquinas Press, 2003), 44.

[39] Cardinal Michael Browne, OP, as quoted in Robert Feeney, *The Rosary: "The Little Summa,"* 45.

[40] Fr. Vincent de Couesnongle, OP, as quoted in Robert Feeney, *The Rosary: "The Little Summa,"* 45. It should also be mentioned that in 1985, the Master General of the Order, Fr. Damian Byrne, OP, wrote an in-depth letter on the rosary that lauded the Dominican rosary tradition (even referencing the story of how Our Lady asked St. Dominic to preach her Psalter), praised Alan de la Roche, and reminded all Dominicans of their rosary heritage. Oddly, the French and English versions of the letter are radically different in content and no other versions of the letter are available. The French version makes no reference to the pious tradition, while the English version notes the following: "Whatever critical historians may have to say about the legend of the rosary [the pious tradition], it bears witness to the charismatic gift entrusted by the Church to the Order of Preachers, a gift which we must exercise by reason of profession, by our legislation, and by the constant exhortation of the See of Rome." See Damian Byrne, OP, *The Rosary: Letter from the Master of the Order* (September 1985). www.op.org

[41] Robert Feeney, *The Rosary: "The Little Summa,"* 1.

[42] St. Pope John XXIII, *Sacerdotti Nostri Primordia*, Encyclical (August 1, 1959), 42-43.

[43] Bl. Pope Paul VI, *Christi Matri*, Encyclical (September 15, 1966), 9.

[44] In 1968, the Redemptorist Fr. Joseph Manton presented a paper at the annual Mariological Society of America meeting that sought to defend the papacy and its promotion of the rosary by demonstrating that the downgrading of devotion to Our Lady and her rosary was not coming from the Vatican but from priests. He wrote: "On the parish level, people may hear about some curate standing in the pulpit on Sunday morning scornfully ripping a rosary to shreds and dramatically tossing it into the center aisle. I have met one young priest who tolerated the Pastor saying the beads with the people after Mass in October, but who stipulated, 'Please don't ask *me* to go through the agony of that monotonous repetition!' I remember another curate who looked down on me with Alpine condescension and wanted to know when I was going to get rid of 'that medieval ornament that some of you Orders drape round your cincture.'" Father Manton went on to note: "As a private devotion, all recent popes have canonized the beads. Did not Pope Paul VI say, 'We ardently desire that Mary be more fervently invoked during October by the pious rite of the rosary?' And he added that the recent Council, 'urges the Church's children to value highly the practices directed to Mary and approved over the centuries by the magisterium.' So, where do you go for your evaluation of the beads, to some curate in East Cupcake, West Virginia, who at the moment seems to be yearning more for publicity than for Paradise, or to the Supreme Pontiff? If parochial devotion to Mary, as exampled by the rosary, is hurting, it is certainly not the result of any official frown from the top. It is from the random shots of sophisticated snipers on the sidelines." See Joseph E. Manton, "Profile of Marian Devotion on the Parochial Level," *Marian Studies*, vol. 19 (1968), 43-44. For a presentation on the same theme from a Dominican

theologian, see the following article: Fr. Matthew F. Morry, OP, "Mary and the Contemporary Scene," *Marian Studies,* vol. 23 (1972), 133-153.

[45] *Behold Your Mother: Woman of Faith,* (Washington, DC: National Conference of Catholic Bishops, 1973), 92.

[46] Bl. Pope Paul VI, *Marialis Cultus,* Apostolic Exhortation (February 2, 1974), 43.

[47] Bl. Pope Paul VI, *Marialis Cultus,* 43.

[48] By the end of the 1970s, the crisis in devotion to Our Lady and her rosary had reached its apex. In 1978, Fr. John Hardon, SJ, lamenting the fact that many theologians were promoting heterodox ideas, gave a presentation at the annual Mariological Society of America meeting and noted the following regarding why Catholic youth were not being taught devotion to Mary and her rosary: "Those who know what is going on have no illusions. No mask of theological rhetoric can hide the fact that millions of our Catholic young are not being taught a deep and true love for the Mother of God. When a stout volume is being published under the guise of scholarship, casting doubt on the historicity of the Infancy Narratives in the Gospels; when priest-writers are telling the faithful that doctrines like the Assumption are not required to be a professed Catholic; when authors writing with an *Imprimatur* are claiming that Christ never identified himself with the Father, is it any wonder that the youth are not being taught a deep and true love for the Mother of God? Love for the Blessed Virgin must be based on sound doctrine about the Blessed Virgin. In the absence of true doctrine there cannot be true love; and without love there can be no devotion." See John A. Hardon, SJ, "The Blessed Virgin in Modern Catechetics," *Marian Studies,* vol. 29 (1978), 91-92.

[49] In 1973, on the Feast of the Rosary, then Cardinal Albino Luciani (the future Pope John Paul I) expressed his love for the rosary, and his concern for its abandonment by many Catholics, in an article in a diocesan paper in Venice. He wrote: "Windthorst, the German statesman, was invited one time by certain friends not practicing the faith to show them his beads; it was a joke; they had previously taken them from his left pocket. Windthorst, not having found them in his left pocket, put his hand in his right pocket and came out the victor. He always had an extra rosary! Christophe Willibald von Gluck, a great musician, during court receptions in Vienna, used to go aside for a few minutes to recite his rosary. Blessed Contardo Ferrini [1859-1902], professor at the University of Pavia, invited the friends in whose house he was a guest to recite it. Saint Bernadette affirmed that when Our Lady appeared to her, she had the rosary on her arms. She asked Bernadette if she had a rosary with her, inviting her to recite it. Why do I give all these examples of people reciting the rosary? Because the rosary is contested by some. They say: it is a prayer that is superstitious, infantile and not worthy of a Christian adult. Or else, it is a prayer that is automatic, reduced to a hasty repetition of *Ave Marias,* monotonous and boring. Or else, it is a relic of the past; today it is better to read the Bible, which is said to be to the rosary what fine flour is to chaff. Permit me to disagree by giving some impressions of a pastor of souls. First impression: The crisis of the rosary doesn't come first. What comes first is the crisis in prayer in general today. People are all taken up in material interests; they think little about the soul. Second impression: When people today speak of 'adult Christians' in prayer, sometimes they exaggerate. Personally, when I speak alone with

God and with Our Lady, more than as a grown-up, I prefer to feel myself a child; the mitre, the zucchetto, and the ring all disappear. I send the grown-up on vacation, and even the bishop along with all the grave dignity and ponderousness due to his rank! And I abandon myself to the spontaneous tenderness that a child has for his mamma and papa. The rosary, a simple and easy prayer, helps me to be a child again, and I am not ashamed of it at all." See Albino Cardinal Luciani, "My Rosary," as quoted in the Servant of God Patrick Peyton, *Marian Year: 1987-1988* (Albany, NY: The Family Rosary Inc., 1987), 52-53.

[50] *Code of Canon Law*, Latin-English Edition (Washington, DC: Canon Law Society of America, 1989), canon 246, no.3.

[51] *Catechism of the Catholic Church*, entry. 2678.

[52] Maisie Ward, *The Splendor of the Rosary* (New York: Sheed and Ward, 1945), 34.

[53] John S. Johnson, *The Rosary in Action* (Charlotte, NC: TAN Books, 1977), 26.

[54] William G. Most, *Mary in Our Life* (Garden City, NJ: Image Books, 1963), 308-309.

[55] See Anne Winston-Allen, *Stories of the Rose: The Making of the Rosary in the Middle Ages* (University Park, PA: Pennsylvania State University Press, 1997), 7-8; 17.

[56] See André Duval, OP, "Rosaire," in *Dictionnaire de spiritualité ascétique et mystique: Doctrine et histoire*, XIII (Paris: Beauchesne, 1988), 949.

[57] Gabriel Harty, OP, *Heaven Sent: My Life Through the Rosary*, 166.

The 21st Century: Luminous Mysteries in Dark Days

[1] St. Faustina Kowalska, *Diary: Divine Mercy in My Soul* (Stockbridge, MA: Marian Press, 1987), entry 745.

[2] St. John Paul II, *Beatification Homily of Blesseds Luigi and Maria Beltrame Quattrocchi* (October 21, 2001).

[3] St. John Paul II, *Rosarium Virginis Mariae*, Apostolic Letter (October 16, 2002), 1.

[4] Ibid., 2.

[5] Ibid., 17.

[6] Fr. Carlos A. Azpiroz Costa, OP., as quoted in Robert Feeney, *The Rosary: "The Little Summa,"* fourth edition (USA: Aquinas Press, 2003), 46. On January 1, 2016 the Master General of the Order of Preachers, Very Rev. Bruno Cadoré OP, issued a circular letter for the 800th Jubilee of the Order, titled "Letter for the Jubilee Year of the Order of Preachers." In the letter he stated: "It is well known that [St.] Dominic was not the 'creator' of the rosary." At first glance, the Master General's statement may appear to contradict the pious tradition and the circular letter of the previous Master General, Fr. Azpiroz. However, Fr. Cadoré is correct to observe that St. Dominic is not the "creator" of the rosary since neither the Church nor the Dominican tradition have ever stated that St. Dominic "created" the rosary. It has always been understood that because it was Our Lady who gave the rosary to St. Dominic, it is more accurate to refer to St. Dominic as the "founder" of the rosary, rather than its "creator." Also, during the colloquium on the rosary held at Lourdes from November 10-11, 2011, Fr. Cadoré affirmed that there are many possible interpretations of the rosary tradition within the Dominican Order. See Fr. Bruno Cadoré, OP, "Le Rosaire dans la tradition dominicaine," in *Le Rosaire: Historie*

et spiritualité. Les Actes du Colloque. (Français: NDL Éditions, 2012), 52-61. It is also worth noting that, after reading the manuscript for *Champions of the Rosary* in December 2015, Fr. Cadoré graciously offered his endorsement for the content of this book (see Endorsements from Dominicans).

[7] Pope Benedict XVI, *Angelus message,* October 7, 2008.

[8] Bishop Oliver Dashe Doeme, as quoted in Alan Holdren, "After vision of Christ, Nigerian bishop says rosary will bring down Boko Haram," *Catholic News Agency (CNA),* April 21, 2015. Online edition.

[9] Fr. Carlos A. Azpiroz Costa, OP, *Rosary Letter from the Master of the Order (January 1, 2008),* as quoted in *Newsletter,* No. 86 (May, 2008), the Dominican Nuns of the Perpetual Rosary Monastery of Pius XII in Fatima, Portugal.

[10] Ibid.

[11] Fr. Gabriel Harty, OP, *Heaven Sent: My Life Through the Rosary* (Dublin, Ireland: Veritas, 2012), 163.

Part II:
Champions of the Rosary

* *Initial quote:*

~ St. Faustina Kowalska, *Diary: Divine Mercy in My Soul,* third edition (Stockbridge, MA: Marian Press, 2002), entry 450.

(The references listed below are in the same order in which they appear for each Champion)

St. Dominic

* Image on pg. 191: *The Virgin Presenting the Rosary to St. Dominic* by Antonio Palomino (1655-1726). Seattle Art Museum. Used with permission.

~ *"Our Lady's words to St. Dominic,"* as quoted in Augusta Theodosia Drane, OP, *The History of St. Dominic: Founder of the Friars Preachers* (London: Longmans, Green, and Co., 1891), 122.

~ Pope Alexander VI, as quoted in William G. Most, *Mary in Our Life* (Garden City, NY: Image Books, 1963), 305.

~ St. Pope Pius V, *Consueverunt Romani Pontifices,* Papal Bull *(September 17, 1569).* Servant of God Pope Benedict XIII, as quoted in William G. Most, *Mary in Our Life.* (Garden City, NY: Image Books, 1963), 306.

~ St. Louis de Montfort, *The Secret of the Rosary.* Trans. Mary Barbour, TOP, (Bay Shore, NY: Montfort Publications, 1988), 18.

~ Ibid., 22.

~ Ibid., 27.

~ Ibid., 69.

~ Ibid., 74.

~ Ibid., 101.

~ Bl. Pope Pius IX, as quoted in Deacon Andrew J. Gerakas, *The Rosary and Devotion to Mary* (Boston, MA: St. Paul Books & Media, 1992), 20.

~ Bl. John Henry Newman, *Sayings of Cardinal Newman* (Dublin: Carraig Books,

1976), 44-46.

~ Pope Leo XIII, *Adiutricem,* Encyclical (September 5, 1895), 12.

~ Pope Leo XIII, *Supremi Apostolatus Officio,* 3.

~ Ibid., 8.

~ Pope Leo XIII, as quoted in Robert Feeney, *The Rosary: "The Little Summa,"* fourth edition (USA: Aquinas Press, 2003), 10.

~ Pope Benedict XV, *Fausto Appetente Die,* Encyclical (June 29, 1921), 11.

~ Servant of God Joseph Kentenich, as quoted in Fr. Jonathan Niehaus, *New Vision and Life: The Founding of Schoenstatt (1912-1919)* (Waukesha, WI: Schoenstatt Fathers, 2004), 32.

~ Bl. James Alberione, *Mary, Mother and Model: Feasts of Mary,* trans. Hilda Calabro, MA (Boston, MA: Daughters of St. Paul, 1958), 202.

~ Bl. James Alberione, *Lord, Teach Us to Pray* (Boston, MA: Daughters of St. Paul, 1982), 223.

~ Ibid., 225.

~ Ven. Fulton J. Sheen, *The World's First Love: Mary, Mother of God* (San Francisco: Ignatius Press, 1996), 206.

~ Servant of God Patrick J. Peyton, *The Ear of God* (Garden City, NY: Doubleday & Company, Inc., 1951), 113.

~ Pope Benedict XVI, *Angelus message* (October 7, 2007).

Recommended Reading on St. Dominic

~ St. Louis de Montfort, *The Secret of the Rosary,* trans. Mary Barbour, TOP (Bay Shore, NY: Montfort Publications, 1988).

~ Pope Benedict XV, *Fausto Appetente Die* (Encyclical Letter on St. Dominic). June 29, 1921.

~ J.M.P. Heaney, OP, *A Short Treatise on the Rosary* (New York: Dominicans, 1863). Augusta Theodosia Drane, OP, *The History of St. Dominic: Founder of the Friars Preachers* (London: Longmans, Green, and Co., 1891).

~ John Procter, OP, *The Rosary Guide for Priests and People* (London: Kegan and Trubner, 1901).

~ Wilfrid Lescher, OP, *St. Dominic and the Rosary* (London: R. & T. Washbourne, 1902).

~ Andrew Skelly, OP, *St. Dominic and the Rosary.* (Providence, RI: Providence College Digital Commons), *Historical Catholic and Dominican Documents. Book 1,* (1915).

~ Humbert Clerissac, OP, *The Spirit of St. Dominic* (Mercer Island, WA: Cluny Media LLC, 2015). Reprinted from the 1939 edition.

Blessed Alan de la Roche

* Image on pg. 198: Berlin/Kupferstichkabinett, Staatliche Museen, Berlin, Germany/Herbert Boswank/Art Resource, NY. Used with permission.

~ Bl. Alan de la Roche, as quoted in Rev. Charles G. Fehrenbach, CSsR, *Mary Day by Day* (New York: Catholic Book Publishing Co., 1987), 147.

~ Bl. Alan de la Roche, as quoted in St. Louis de Montfort, *The Secret of the Rosary,* trans. Mary Barbour, TOP (Bay Shore, NY: Montfort Publications, 1988), 21.

~ St. Louis de Montfort, *The Secret of the Rosary,* trans. Mary Barbour, TOP (Bay Shore, NY: Montfort Publications, 1988), 23.

~ Ibid., 23.

~ Ibid., 23-24.

~ Ibid., 84.

~ Ibid., 86.

~ Ibid., 68-69.

~ Ibid., 66.

~ Ibid., 67.

~ Ibid., 81.

~ St. Alphonsus Liguori, as quoted in Susan Tassone, *Day By Day for the Holy Souls in Purgatory: 365 Reflections* (Huntington, IN: Our Sunday Visitor, Inc., 2014), 298.

~ Bl. James Alberione, *Lest We Forget* (Boston, MA: Daughters of St. Paul, 1967), 143.

~ Bl. Gabriele Allegra, *Mary's Immaculate Heart: A Way to God* (Chicago, IL: Franciscan Herald Press, 1985), 72.

Recommended Reading on Bl. Alan de la Roche

~ St. Louis de Montfort, *The Secret of the Rosary,* trans. Mary Barbour, TOP (Bay Shore, NY: Montfort Publications, 1988).

~ Dominican Fathers, "The Life and Times of B. Alain de la Roche in the Fifteenth Century: Restorer of the Confraternity of the Most Holy Rosary," in *The Monthly Magazine of the Holy Rosary,* no. 1 (August, 1872), 13-16; no. 2 (September, 1872), 32-35.

~ Raymond P. Devas, OP, "The Rosary Tradition Defined and Defended," in *American Catholic Quarterly Review,* vol. XLI (January, 1916), 128-147.

~ William G. Most, *Mary in Our Life* (Garden City, NY: Image Books, 1963).

~ John S. Johnson, *The Rosary in Action* (Charlotte, NC: TAN Books, 1977).

~ Michael Müller, CSsR, *The Devotion of the Holy Rosary* (Fitzwilliam, NH: Loreto Publications, 2011).

~ Pepin Guglielmo, OP, *Il Salutate Mariam* (Firenze, Italia: 1950).

St. Pope Pius V

~ St. Pope Pius V, *Consueverunt Romani Pontifices,* Papal Bull (September 17, 1569).

~ Ibid.

~ St. Pope Pius V, as quoted in Deacon Andrew J. Gerakas, *The Rosary and Devotion to Mary* (Boston, MA: St. Paul Books & Media, 1992), 21.

~ St. Pope Pius V, as quoted in David Supple, *Virgin Wholly Marvelous* (Cambridge, MA: Ravengate, 1991), 131.

~ St. Pope Pius V, as quoted in Wilfrid Lescher, OP, *St. Dominic and the Rosary* (London: R. & T. Washbourne, 1902), 11.

~ St. Louis de Montfort, *The Secret of the Rosary,* trans. Mary Barbour, TOP (Bay Shore, NY: Montfort Publications, 1988), 64-65.

~ Pope Benedict XV, *Fausto Appetente Die,* Encyclical (June 29, 1921), 11.

~ Servant of God Joseph Kentenich, as quoted in Fr. Jonathan Neihaus, *New Vision and Life: The Founding of Schoenstatt (1912-1919)* (Waukesha, WI: Schoenstatt

Fathers, 2004), 35.

Recommended Reading on St. Pope Pius V

~ St. Pope Pius V, *Consueverunt Romani Pontifices* (September 17, 1569).
~ St. Pope Pius V, *Salvatoris Domini* (March 5, 1571).
~ Catherine M. Antony, *Saint Pius V: Pope of the Holy Rosary* (London: Longmans, Green and Co., 1911).
~ G.K. Chesterton, *Lepanto* (San Francisco, CA: Ignatius Press, 2003).
~ Robin Anderson, *St. Pius V: His Life, Times and Miracles* (Charlotte, NC: TAN Books, 2009).

St. Louis de Montfort

* Image on pg. 207: O.D.M. pinxit, Editions Magnificat, Mont-Tremblant, Québec. Used with permission.
~ St. Louis de Montfort, *God Alone: The Collected Writings of St. Louis de Montfort* (Bay Shore, NY: Montfort Publications, 1995), 421.
~ St. Louis de Montfort, *The Secret of the Rosary,* trans. Mary Barbour, TOP (Bay Shore, NY: Montfort Publications, 1988), 27.
~ Ibid., 9.
~ Ibid., 9.
~ Ibid., 16.
~ Ibid., 9.
~ Ibid., 17-18.
~ Ibid., 98.
~ Ibid., 26.
~ Ibid., 27.
~ Ibid., 29.
~ Ibid., 85.
~ Ibid., 62.
~ Ibid., 67.
~ Ibid., 71.
~ Ibid., 13.
~ Ibid., 97.
~ Ibid., 98.
~ Ibid., 12.
~ St. Louis de Montfort, as quoted in Rev. Charles G. Fehrenbach, CSsR, *Mary Day by Day* (New York: Catholic Book Publishing Co., 1987), 149.
~ St. Louis de Montfort, *God Alone: The Collected Writings of St. Louis de Montfort,* 403.

Recommended Reading on St. Louis de Montfort

~ St. Louis de Montfort, *The Secret of the Rosary,* trans. Mary Barbour, TOP (Bay Shore, NY: Montfort Publications, 1954).
~ St. Louis de Montfort, *True Devotion to the Blessed Virgin* (Bay Shore, NY: Montfort Publications, 1996).
~ St. Louis de Montfort, *God Alone: The Collected Writings of St. Louis de Montfort*

(Bay Shore, NY: Montfort Publications, 1995).

~ St. Louis de Montfort, *Jesus Living in Mary: Handbook on the Spirituality of St. Louis Marie de Montfort* (Bay Shore, NY: Montfort Publications, 1995).

St. Alphonsus Liguori

* Image on pg. 213: Courtesy of the Redemptorists. Used with permission.

~ St. Alphonsus Liguori, *Hail Holy Queen: An Explanation of the Salve Regina.* (Charlotte, NC: TAN Books, 1995), 225-226.

~ Ibid., 226.

~ Ibid., 226.

~ Ibid., 226.

~ St. Alphonsus Liguori, *The Glories of Mary* (Charlotte, NC: TAN Books, 2012), 545. Used with permission.

~ Ibid., 546.

~ Ibid., 546.

~ Ibid., 545.

~ St. Alphonsus Liguori, *Hail Holy Queen: An Explanation of the Salve Regina*, 35.

~ St. Alphonsus Liguori, as quoted in Catherine Moran, *Praying the Rosary with the Saints* [E-reader version], 2013.

~ St. Alphonsus Liguori, *Hail Holy Queen: An Explanation of the Salve Regina*, 226.

Recommended Reading on St. Alphonsus Liguori

~ St. Alphonsus Liguori, *Hail Holy Queen: An Explanation of the Salve Regina* (Charlotte, NC: TAN Books, 1995).

~ St. Alphonsus Liguori, *The Glories of Mary* (Charlotte, NC: TAN Books, 2012).

~ Fr. Donald H. Calloway, MIC, *Marian Gems: Daily Wisdom on Our Lady* (Stockbridge, MA: Marian Press, 2014).

~ Fr. Donald H. Calloway, MIC, *Rosary Gems: Daily Wisdom on the Holy Rosary* (Stockbridge, MA: Marian Press, 2015).

Blessed Pope Pius IX

~ Bl. Pope Pius IX, as quoted in *The Official Handbook of the Legion of Mary* (Dublin: Concilium Legionis Mariae, 2005), 146.

~ Bl. Pope Pius IX, as quoted in Msgr. Joseph A. Cirrincione and Thomas A. Nelson, *The Rosary and the Crisis of Faith* (Charlotte, NC: TAN Books, 1986), 35.

~ Bl. Pope Pius IX, as quoted in Don Sharkey, *The Woman Shall Conquer: The Story of the Blessed Virgin in the Modern World* (Milwaukee: Bruce Publishing Company, 1952), 246.

~ Bl. Pope Pius IX, as quoted in Patrick J. Peyton, *The Ear of God* (Garden City, NY: Doubleday, 1951), 107.

~ Bl. Pope Pius IX, as quoted in Wilfrid Lescher, OP, *St. Dominic and the Rosary.* (London: R. & T. Washbourne, 1902), 8.

~ Ibid., 8-9.

~ Bl. Pope Pius IX, as quoted in M. Josef Frings, *The Excellence of the Rosary: Conferences for Devotions in Honor of the Blessed Virgin* (New York: Wagner, 1912), 9.

~ Bl. Pope Pius IX, as quoted in Wilfrid Lescher, OP, *St. Dominic and the Rosary,* 8-9.

~ Bl. Pope Pius IX, *Ad Perpetuam rei memorium (Papal Bull granting indulgences to the Members of the Association of the Perpetual Rosary,* April 12, 1868), quoted in *The Monthly Magazine of the Rosary* (December, 1872), 130-131.

~ Bl. Pope Pius IX, as quoted in *Rosary* (Revised edition of the special rosary issue of *The Immaculate* magazine, 1970), 40. Originally published in vol. 16. no. 5 (October 1965).

Recommended Reading on Bl. Pope Pius IX

~ Bl. Pope Pius IX, *Eregus Sues,* Apostolic Letter (December 3, 1869).

~ Bl. Pope Pius IX, *C'est un Fait Eclant. To the Superior and Missonaries of the Sanctuary of Lourdes,* Apostolic Letter (February 8, 1875).

~ Bl. Pope Pius IX, *Ubi Primum,* Encyclical (February 2, 1849).

~ Bl. Pope Pius IX, *Ineffabilis Deus,* Apostolic Constitution (December 8, 1854).

~ Fr. Donald H. Calloway, MIC, ed., *The Immaculate Conception in the Life of the Church* (Stockbridge, MA: Marian Press, 2004).

St. Anthony Mary Claret

* Image on pg. 221: General Government, Claretian Missionaries, Rome, Italy. Used with permission

~ St. Anthony Mary Claret, *Autobiography.* ed., Jose Maria Vinas, CMF (Chicago, IL: Claretian Publications, 1976), 14-15.

~ Ibid., 38.

~ Ibid., 38.

~ Ibid., 17.

~ Ibid., 237.

~ St. Anthony Mary Claret, as quoted in Fr. Juan Echevarria, *The Miracles of St. Anthony Mary Claret,* trans. Sr. Mary Gonzaga (Charlotte, NC: TAN Books, 1992), 61.

~ St. Anthony Mary Claret, *El Colegial Ó Seminarista Teórica y Prácticamente Instruido: Tome II* (Barcelona, Spain: Librería Religiosa, 1861), 503. Trans. Miss Ileana E. Salazar, MA.

~ St. Anthony Mary Claret, *The Golden Key to Heaven* (Buffalo, NY: Immaculate Heart Publications, 1955), 358.

~ St. Anthony Mary Claret, *El Colegial Ó Seminarista Teórica y Prácticamente Instruido: Tome II* (Barcelona, Spain: Librería Religiosa, 1861), 503. Trans. Miss Ileana E. Salazar, MA.

~ St. Anthony Mary Claret, *Autobiography,* 241.

~ Ibid., 115.

~ St. Anthony Mary Claret, as quoted in Juan Maria Lozano, CMF, *Mystic and Man of Action: Saint Anthony Mary Claret,* trans. Joseph Daries, CMF (Chicago, IL: Claretian Publications, 1977), 141.

~ St. Anthony Mary Claret, *El Colegial Ó Seminarista Teórica y Prácticamente Instruido: Tome I.* (Barcelona, Spain: Librería Religiosa, 1861), 276. Trans. Miss Ileana E. Salazar, MA.

~ Ibid., 276.

~ Ibid., 277.

~ Ibid., 277.

~ Ibid., 277.

~ Ibid., 277.

~ Ibid., 277.

~ Ibid., 341.

~ Ibid., 279.

~ St. Anthony Mary Claret, *Autobiography,* 95.

Recommended Reading on St. Anthony Mary Claret

~ St. Anthony Mary Claret, *Autobiography.* (ed.) Jose Maria Vinas, CMF (Chicago, IL: Claretian Publications, 1976).

~ St. Anthony Mary Claret, *Devocion del Santísimo Rosario* (Barcelona, Spain: Libreria Religiosa, 1858).

~ St. Anthony Mary Claret, *El Santísimo Rosario Explicado* (Barcelona, Spain: Libreria Religiosa, 1864).

~ Gabriel Mary Mesina, FI, "Saint Anthony Mary Claret: Son of the Immaculate Heart of Mary," in *Missio Immaculatae,* vol. 11. no.1 (January/February, 2015), 17-23.

~ Juan Echevarria, *The Miracles of St. Anthony Mary Claret,* trans. Sr. Mary Gonzaga (Charlotte, NC: TAN Books, 1992).

~ Perrin, Joseph-Marie, "Le V. Antoine-Marie Claret, archeveque. Le Dominique de xix siècle." *Revue de Rosaire* 10 (1931): 296-302, 329-337.

Pope Leo XIII

~ Pope Leo XIII, *Adiutricem,* Encyclical (September 5, 1895), 4.

~ Pope Leo XIII, *Fidentem piumque animum,* Encyclical (September 20, 1896), 5.

~ Pope Leo XIII, as quoted in Rev. Charles G. Fehrenbach, CSsR, *Mary Day by Day* (New York: Catholic Book Publishing Co., 1987), 144.

~ Pope Leo XIII, *Adiutricem,* 24.

~ Pope Leo XIII, as quoted in Msgr. Joseph A. Cirrincione and Thomas A. Nelson, *The Rosary and the Crisis of Faith* (Charlotte, NC: TAN Books, 1986), 34-35.

~ Pope Leo XIII, *Adiutricem,* 25.

~ Ibid., 26.

~ Ibid., 27.

~ Pope Leo XIII, *Fidentem piumque animum,* 2.

~ Pope Leo XIII, *Iucunda Semper Expectatione,* Encyclical (September 8, 1894), 2.

~ Ibid., 7.

~ Pope Leo XIII, *Laetitiae Sanctae,* Encyclical (September 8, 1893), 18.

~ Pope Leo XIII, *Magnae Dei Matris,* Encyclical (September 8, 1892), 7.

~ Ibid., 18.

~ Ibid., 29.

~ Pope Leo XIII, as quoted in Rev. J.A. Rooney, OP, "Rosary Sunday and Month: The Dominican Portiuncula," *The Rosary Magazine* (October, 1892), p. 453.

~ Pope Leo XIII, *Diuturni Temporis,* Encyclical (September 5, 1898), 3.

~ Pope Leo XIII, *Laetitiae Sanctae,* 16.

~ Pope Leo XIII, *Octobri Mense,* Encyclical (September 22, 1891), 8.

~ Pope Leo XIII, *Diuturni Temporis,* as quoted in *The Rosary of Our Lady: Translations of the Encyclical and Apostolic Letters of Pope Leo XIII,* ed. William Raymond Lawler, OP (Paterson, NJ: St. Anthony Guild Press, 1944), 173-174.

~ Pope Leo XIII, *Letter to the Master General of the Order of Preachers* (September 15, 1883).

~ Bl. James Alberione, *Mary: Hope of the World,* trans. Hilda Calabro, MA (Boston, MA: Daughters of St. Paul, 1981), 156.

~ Bl. James Alberione, *Mary, Mother and Model: Feasts of Mary,* trans. Hilda Calabro, MA (Boston, MA: Daughters of St. Paul, 1958), 203.

~ St. Pope John XXIII, *Grata Recordatio,* Encyclical (September 26, 1959), 2.

Recommended Reading on Pope Leo XIII

~ William Raymond Lawler, OP, ed., *The Rosary of Our Lady: Translations of the Encyclical and Apostolic Letters of Pope Leo XIII* (Paterson, NJ: St. Anthony Guild Press, 1944).

~ *A Light in the Heavens: The Great Encyclical Letters of Pope Leo XIII* (Charlotte, NC: TAN Books, 1995).

~ All 11 Rosary encyclicals of Pope Leo XIII (www.vatican.va).

~ Charles R. Auth, OP, *Rosary Bibliography: English Language Works* (Washington, DC: Dominican House of Studies, 1960).

~ *The Rosary: Papal Teachings.* Texts from 1758-1978, selected and arranged by the Monks of Solesmes (Boston: St. Paul Editions, 1980).

~ Paul A. Böer, Sr., *Enchiridion Sanctissimi Rosarii: A Manual of the Most Holy Rosary* (Veritatis Splendor Publications, 2013).

Blessed Bartolo Longo

* Image on pg. 233: Reprinted with permission of Catholic Online www.catholic.org

~ Bl. Bartolo Longo, as quoted in Ann M. Brown, *Apostle of the Rosary: Blessed Bartolo Longo* (New Hope, KY: New Hope Publications, 2004), 43.

~ Ibid., 53.

~ Bl. Bartolo Longo, as quoted in St. John Paul II, *Rosarium Virginis Mariae,* 15.

~ Bl. Bartolo Longo, as quoted in Ann M. Brown, *Apostle of the Rosary: Blessed Bartolo Longo,* 53.

~ Bl. Bartolo Longo, as quoted in Rory Michael Fox, *Saints, Popes and Blesseds Speak on the Rosary* [E-reader version], 2012.

~ Bl. Bartolo Longo, as quoted in Ann M. Brown, *Apostle of the Rosary: Blessed Bartolo Longo,* 21.

~ Ibid., 51.

~ Bl. Bartolo Longo, as quoted in St. John Paul II, *Beatification Homily of Bl. Bartolo Longo* (October 26, 1980). Trans. Miss Ileana E. Salazar, MA.

~ Bl. Bartolo Longo, *Supplication to the Queen of the Holy Rosary,* as quoted in St. John Paul II, *Rosarium Virginis Mariae,* 43.

~ Bl. Bartolo Longo, as quoted in Barbara Calamari and Sandra DiPasqua, *Visions of*

Mary (New York, NY: Harry N. Abrams, Inc., 2004), 82.

~ Bl. Bartolo Longo, as quoted in Ann M. Brown, *Apostle of the Rosary: Blessed Bartolo Longo*, 27.

~ Ibid., 55.

~ Bl. Bartolo Longo, as quoted in Robert Feeney, *The Rosary: "The Little Summa,"* fourth edition (USA: Aquinas Press, 2003), 107.

~ St. John Paul II, *Beatification Homily of Bl. Bartolo Longo.*

~ St. John Paul II, as quoted in Ann M. Brown, *Apostle of the Rosary: Blessed Bartolo Longo*, 47.

~ Pope Benedict XVI, *Homily: Pastoral Visit to the Pontifical Shrine of Pompeii* (October 19, 2008).

~ Ibid.

Recommended Reading on Bl. Bartolo Longo

~ Bl. Bartolo Longo, History of the Sanctuary of Pompeii (Valle di Pompeii: Editing School of Typography of Bartolo Longo, 1895)

~ Bl. Bartolo Longo, *Supplication to the Queen of the Holy Rosary,* as quoted in St. John Paul II, *Rosarium Virginis Mariae*, 43.

~ Bl. Bartolo Longo, *Fifteen Saturdays of the Most Holy Rosary*, trans. Luigi Caturelli (Valle Pompeii, Italy, 1894).

~ Ann M. Brown, *Apostle of the Rosary: Blessed Bartolo Longo* (New Hope, KY: New Hope Publications, 2004).

~ Msgr. Charles M. Mangan, *Blessed Bartolo Longo: Apostle of the Rosary* (Goleta, CA: Queenship Publishing).

Servant of God Joseph Kentenich

~ Servant of God Joseph Kentenich, *Mary, Our Mother and Educator: An Applied Mariology,* trans. Jonathan Niehaus (Waukesha, WI: Schoenstatt Sisters, 1987), 11.

~ Servant of God Joseph Kententich, *The Marian Person,* trans. Jonathan Niehaus. (Waukesha, WI: Schoenstatt Fathers, 2007), 37.

~ Servant of God Joseph Kentenich, *Marian Instrument Piety* (Waukesha, WI: Schoenstatt Center, 1992), 116.

~ Servant of God Joseph Kentenich, *Mary, Our Mother and Educator: An Applied Mariology*, 11.

~ Servant of God Joseph Kentenich, *Talk by Fr. Joseph Kentenich in the Church at Ennabeuren, Germany* (May 3, 1945). Courtesy of Schoenstatt Sisters, Waukesha, WI.

~ Ibid.

~ Ibid.

~ Ibid.

~ Servant of God Joseph Kentenich, *Mary, Our Mother and Educator: An Applied Mariology*, 11.

~ Servant of God Joseph Kentenich, *Heavenwards: Prayers for the Use of the Schoenstatt Family* (Waukesha, WI: Schoenstatt Fathers, 1992), 91.

Recommended Reading on the Servant of God Joseph Kentenich

~ Servant of God Joseph Kentenich, *Mary, Our Mother and Educator: An Applied Mariology*, trans. Jonathan Niehaus (Waukesha, WI: Schoenstatt Sisters, 1987)

~ Servant of God Joseph Kentenich, *Talk by Fr. Joseph Kentenich in the Church at Ennabeuren, Germany* (May 3, 1945). Original Title: *Unsere Marianische Sendung: Ansprachen in Ennabeuren.* 2 Aufl ed. Horb a. N.: Geiger Druck, 1982.

~ Servant of God Joseph Kentenich, *Exchange of Hearts: The Transforming Power of Consecration to the Immaculate Heart of Mary.* ed., Jonathan Niehaus (Vallendar, Germany: Schoenstatt Fathers, 2012).

~ Fr. Donald H. Calloway, MIC, *The Virgin Mary and Theology of the Body* (Stockbridge, MA: Marian Press, 2005).

~ Fr. Donald H. Calloway, MIC, *Marian Gems: Daily Wisdom on Our Lady* (Stockbridge, MA: Marian Press, 2014).

Servant of God Lúcia Dos Santos

* Image on pg. 244: © Postulação de Francisco e Jacinta Marto.

~ Our Lady to Sr. Lúcia Dos Santos, as quoted in Fr. Robert J. Fox, *2,000 Year Chronology of Mary Through the Ages* (Redfield, SD: Fatima Family Apostolate, 2000), 136.

~ Servant of God Lúcia Dos Santos, *Fatima in Lucia's Own Words* (Fatima, Portugal: Secretariado Dos Pastorinhos, 2011), 50.

~ Servant of God Lúcia Dos Santos, *'Calls' from the Message of Fatima* (Fatima, Portugal: Secretariado dos Pastorinhos, 2000), 134.

~ Servant of God Lúcia Dos Santos, *Fatima in Lucia's Own Words: Volume II.* (Fátima, Portugal: Secretariado dos Pastorinhos, 2006), 106.

~ Servant of God Lúcia Dos Santos, *'Calls' from the Message of Fatima*, 271.

~ Servant of God Lúcia Dos Santos, as quoted in Fr. Robert Fox, *The Intimate Life of Sister Lucia* (USA: Fatima Family Apostolate, 2001), 315.

~ Servant of God Lúcia Dos Santos, as quoted in Rory Michael Fox, *Saints, Popes and Blesseds Speak on the Rosary* [E-reader version], 2012.

~ Servant of God Lúcia Dos Santos, as quoted in Robert Feeney, *The Rosary: "The Little Summa,"* fourth edition (USA: Aquinas Press, 2003), 112.

~ Ibid., 112.

~ Ibid., 114.

~ Servant of God Lúcia Dos Santos, *'Calls' from the Message of Fatima*, 271-272.

~ Servant of God Lúcia Dos Santos, as quoted in Fr. Robert Fox, *The Intimate Life of Sister Lucia*, 316.

~ Ibid., 316.

~ Ibid., 316.

~ Servant of God Lúcia Dos Santos, *A Pathway Under the Gaze of Mary: Biography of Sister Maria Lucia of Jesus and the Immaculate Heart*, trans. James A. Colson (Washington, NJ: World Apostolate of Fatima, 2015), 176.

~ Servant of God Lúcia Dos Santos, as quoted in *The Rosary with Sister Lucia*, trans. James A. Colson (Portugal: Edições Carmelo, 2010), 86.

~ Bl. Gabriele Allegra, *Mary's Immaculate Heart: A Way to God* (Chicago, IL: Franciscan Herald Press, 1985), 54.

Recommended Reading on the Servant of God Lúcia Dos Santos

~ *Fatima in Lucia's Own Words: Sister Lucia's Memoirs. Volume 1.* ed., Fr. Louis Kondor, SVD (Fatima, Portugal: Secretariado Dos Pastorinhos, 2007).

~ *Fatima in Lucia's Own Words: Sister Lucia's Memoirs. Volume 2.* ed., Fr. Louis Kondor, SVD (Fatima, Portugal: Secretariado Dos Pastorinhos, 2006).

~ Servant of God Lucia Dos Santos, *'Calls' from the Message of Fatima* (Fatima, Portugal: Coimbra Carmel, 2000).

~ Carmel of Coimbra, *A Pathway Under the Gaze of Mary: Biography of Sister Maria Lucia of Jesus and the Immaculate Heart,* trans. James A. Colson (Washington, NJ: World Apostolate of Fatima, 2015).

~ Carmel of Coimbra, *The Rosary with Sister Lucia,* trans. James A. Colson (Portugal: Edições Carmelo, 2010).

~ Msgr. Joseph A. Cirrincione and Thomas A. Nelson, *The Rosary and the Crisis of Faith* (Charlotte, NC: TAN Books, 1986).

~ Fr. Robert Fox, *The Intimate Life of Sister Lucia* (USA: Fatima Family Apostolate, 2001).

St. Maximilian Kolbe

* Image on pg. 250: Courtesy of Franciscan Archives, Niepokalanów, Poland. Used with permission.

~ St. Maximilian Kolbe, as quoted in Hilda Elfleda Brown, *She Shall Crush Thy Head: Selected Writings of St. Maximilian Kolbe* (Phoenix, AZ: Leonine Publishers, 2015), 40.

~ Ibid., 40-41.

~ Ibid., 39.

~ Ibid., 119.

~ Ibid., 141.

~ Ibid., 122-123.

~ St. Maximilian Kolbe, *The Writings of St. Maximilian Maria Kolbe.* Vol. II: Various Writings (Lugano, Swizerland: Nerbini International, 2016), no. 1267.

~ St. Maximilian Kolbe, *Scritti di Massimiliano Kolbe* (Roma, 1997), section 1171 [Il Rosario, 1933].

~ St. Maximilian Kolbe, *Scritti di Massimiliano Kolbe* (Roma, 1997), section 505.

~ St. Maximilian Kolbe, *The Writings of St. Maximilian Maria Kolbe.* Vol. II: Various Writings, no. 1088.

~ Ibid., no. 1127. ·

~ St. Maximilian Kolbe, as quoted in Hilda Elfleda Brown, *She Shall Crush Thy Head: Selected Writings of St. Maximilian Kolbe,* 186.

~ Ibid., 54.

~ Ibid., 42.

~ St. Maximilian Kolbe, *The Writings of St. Maximilian Maria Kolbe.* Vol. II: Various Writings, no.1171.

~ St. Maximilian Kolbe, *Aim Higher,* trans. Fr. Dominic Wisz, OFM Conv. (Libertyville, IL: Marytown Press, 2007), 97.

~ St. Maximilian Kolbe, *Scritti di Massimiliano Kolbe,* section 1171 [Il Rosario, 1933].

~ St. Maximilian Kolbe, *Scritti di Massimiliano Kolbe,* section 1117 [Rycerz Niepo-

kalanej, 1926].
~ St. Maximilian Kolbe, *Scritti di Massimiliano Kolbe,* section 1021[Grodno 1922-1925; The Archconfraternity of the Holy Rosary].

Recommended Reading on St. Maximilian Kolbe

~ St. Maximilian Kolbe, *The Writings of St. Maximilian Maria Kolbe.* Vol. I: Letters and Vol. II: Various Writings (Lugano, Switzerland: Nerbini International, 2016).
~ St. Maximilian Kolbe, *Aim Higher: Spiritual and Marian Reflections of St. Maximilian Kolbe* (Marytown Press, 1994).
~ Jerzy Domanski, *Maria Was His Middle Name* (Benziger Sisters Publication, 1979).
~ Francis Kalvelage, ed., *Kolbe: Saint of the Immaculata* (San Francisco, CA: Ignatius Press, 2002).
~ Hilda Elfleda Brown, *She Shall Crush Thy Head: Selected Writings of St. Maximilian Kolbe* (Phoenix, AZ: Leonine Publishers, 2015).

Servant of God Frank Duff

~ Servant of God Frank Duff, *Virgo Praedicanda* (Dublin: Mount Salus Press, 1986), 98.
~ Ibid., 101-102.
~ Ibid., 102.
~ Ibid., 101.
~ Ibid., 101.
~ Ibid., 95.
~ Ibid., 97.
~ Ibid., 94.
~ Ibid., 100.

Recommended Reading on the Servant of God Frank Duff

~ *Legio Mariae: The Official Handbook of the Legion of Mary* (Dublin, Ireland: Concilium Legionis Mariae, 1993).
~ Servant of God Frank Duff, *Virgo Praedicanda* (Dublin: Mount Salus Press, 1986). Servant of God Frank Duff, *Walking with Mary: The Spirit of the Legion of Mary* (Glasgow: J.S. Burns, 1956).
~ Servant of God Frank Duff, *The DeMontfort Way* (Montfort Fathers, 1947).
~ Fr. Donald H. Calloway, MIC, *Rosary Gems: Daily Wisdom on the Holy Rosary* (Stockbridge, MA: Marian Press, 2015).

Pope Pius XI

* Image on pg. 261: © AS400 DB/Corbis. Used with permission.
~ Pope Pius XI, *Inclytam ac perillustrem* (Letter to R.P. Gillet, Master General of the Dominicans, March 6, 1934)
~ Pope Pius XI, *Inclytam ac perillustrem,* as quoted in Finbar Ryan, OP (Archbishop of Port of Spain), *Our Lady of Fatima* (Dublin: Richview Press, 1939), 97-99.
~ Pope Pius XI, *Ingravescentibus Malis,* Encyclical (September 29, 1937), 29.
~ Pope Pius XI, as quoted in Rev. Charles G. Fehrenbach, CSsR, *Mary Day by Day*

(New York: Catholic Book Publishing Co., 1987), 148.

~ Pope Pius XI, *Ingravescentibus Malis,* 15.

~ Ibid., 9.

~ Pope Pius XI, as quoted in Rev. Charles G. Fehrenbach, CSSR, *Mary Day by Day,* 149.

~ Pope Pius XI, *Ingravescentibus Malis,* 28.

~ Ibid., 12.

~ Ibid., 16.

~ Ibid., 23.

~ Ibid., 22.

~ Pope Pius XI, as quoted in Msgr. Joseph A. Cirrincione and Thomas A. Nelson, *The Rosary and the Crisis of Faith,* 33.

Recommended Reading on Pope Pius XI

~ Pope Pius XI, *Ingravescentibus Malis,* Encyclical (September 29, 1937).

~ Pope Pius XI, *Inclytam ac perillustrem* (Letter to R.P. Gillet, Master General of the Dominicans, March 6, 1934).

~ Pope Pius XI, *Lux Veritatis* (December 25, 1931).

Blessed James Alberione

* Image on pg. 266: Courtesy of Daughters of St. Paul. Used with permission.

~ Bl. James Alberione, *Lord, Teach Us to Pray* (Boston, MA: Daughters of St. Paul, 1982), 222.

~ Ibid., 223.

~ Bl. James Alberione, *Mary, Queen of Apostles* (Boston, MA: Daughters of St. Paul, 1976), 169-170.

~ Ibid., 264.

~ Bl. James Alberione, *Glories and Virtues of Mary,* trans. Hilda Calabro, MA (Boston, MA: Daughters of St. Paul, 1978), 198.

~ Ibid., 200.

~ Bl. James Alberione, *Lord, Teach Us to Pray,* 226-227.

~ Bl. James Alberione, *Glories and Virtues of Mary,* 52.

~ Bl. James Alberione, *Mary, Queen of Apostles,* 180.

~ Ibid., 180.

~ Ibid., 235.

~ Bl. James Alberione, *Glories and Virtues of Mary,* 52.

~ Ibid., 52.

~ Ibid., 46.

~ Ibid., 37.

~ Bl. James Alberione, *Mary, Queen of Apostles,* 179.

~ Bl. James Alberione, *Glories and Virtues of Mary,* 37.

~ Bl. James Alberione, *Mary Leads Us to Jesus: The Marian Spirituality of Blessed James Alberione, SSP.* ed. Marianne Lorraine Trouvé, FSP (Boston, MA: Pauline Books & Media, 2004), 78.

~ Bl. James Alberione, *Mary, Mother and Model: Feasts of Mary,* trans. Hilda Calabro, MA (Boston, MA: Daughters of St. Paul, 1958), 200.

~ Ibid., 200.

~ Ibid., 201.

~ Bl. James Alberione, *Mary, Queen of Apostles,* 32.

~ Ibid., 104.

~ Bl. James Alberione, as quoted in Stephen Lamera, SSP, *James Alberione: A Marvel of Our Times* (Philippines: Daughters of St. Paul, 1977), 157-158.

~ Bl. James Alberione, *Mary: Hope of the World,* trans. Hilda Calabro, MA (Boston, MA: Daughters of St. Paul, 1981), 216.

~ Bl. James Alberione, as quoted in Stephen Lamera, SSP, *James Alberione: A Marvel of Our Times,* 158.

~ Bl. James Alberione, *Glories and Virtues of Mary,* 250.

~ Bl. James Alberione, *Blessed Are the Imitators of Mary Who Bring Jesus to the World,* trans. from his sermons by the Daughters of St. Paul of the USA Province, 24.

~ Ibid., 203.

~ Bl. James Alberione, *Lest We Forget* (Boston, MA: Daughters of St. Paul, 1967), 96.

~ Bl. James Alberione, *Lord, Teach Us to Pray,* 225.

~ Ibid., 226.

~ Ibid., 228.

~ Ibid., 228.

~ Bl. James Alberione (Primo Maestro), *Practices of Piety* (Boston, MA: Daughters of St. Paul), 190.

Recommended Reading on Bl. James Alberione

~ Bl. James Alberione, *Mary, Mother and Model: Feasts of Mary,* trans. Hilda Calabro, MA (Boston, MA: Daughters of St. Paul, 1958).

~ Bl. James Alberione, *Mary, Queen of Apostles* (Boston, MA: Daughters of St. Paul, 1976).

~ Bl. James Alberione, *Glories and Virtues of Mary,* trans. Hilda Calabro, MA (Boston, MA: Daughters of St. Paul, 1978).

~ Bl. James Alberione, *Mary: Hope of the World,* trans. Hilda Calabro, MA (Boston, MA: Daughters of St. Paul, 1981).

~ Bl. James Alberione, *Lord, Teach Us to Pray* (Boston, MA: Daughters of St. Paul, 1982).

Venerable Pope Pius XII

~ Ven. Pope Pius XII, as quoted in Deacon Andrew J. Gerakas, *The Rosary and Devotion to Mary* (Boston, MA: St. Paul Books & Media, 1992), 76.

~ Ven. Pope Pius XII, *Letter to the Most Rev. Master General, Michael Browne, OP, concerning the Marian rosary* (July 11, 1957).

~ Ven. Pope Pius XII, as quoted in Msgr. Joseph A. Cirrincione and Thomas A. Nelson, *The Rosary and the Crisis of Faith* (Charlotte, NC: TAN Books, 1986), 33.

~ Ibid., 33.

~ Ven. Pope Pius XII, *Ingruentium Malorum,* Encyclical (September 15, 1951), 15.

~ Ven. Pope Pius XII, as quoted in Bl. Gabriele Allegra, *Mary's Immaculate Heart: A Way to God* (Chicago, IL: Franciscan Herald Press, 1983), 105.

~ Ven. Pope Pius XII, *Mediator Dei,* Encyclical (November 20, 1947), 173-174.

~ Ven. Pope Pius XII, *Ingruentium Malorum,* 13.

~ Ibid., 14.

~ Ibid., 8.

~ Ven. Pope Pius XII, *Radio address delivered on the 25th anniversary of the apparitions of Our Lady of Fatima* (October 31, 1942).

~ Ven. Pope Pius XII, *Ad Caeli Reginam,* Encyclical (October 11, 1954).

~ Ven. Pope Pius XII, *Radio message to the Marian Congress of the Philippines* (December 5, 1954).

Recommended Readings on Ven. Pope Pius XII

~ Ven. Pope Pius XII, *Bis Saeculari,* Apostolic Constitution (September 27, 1948).

~ Ven. Pope Pius XII, *Ad Caeli Reginam,* Encyclical (October 11, 1954).

~ Ven. Pope Pius XII, *Ingruentium Malorum,* Encyclical (September 15, 1951).

~ Ven. Pope Pius XII, *Letter to Cardinal Griffin, Archbishop of Westminster* (July 14, 1952).

~ Ven. Pope Pius XII, *Fulgens Corona,* Encyclical (September 8, 1953).

~ Sr. M. Pascalina Lehnert, *His Humble Servant: Sister M. Pascalina Lehnert's Memoirs of Her Years of Service to Eugenio Pacelli, Pope Pius XII,* trans. Susan Johnson (South Bend, IN: St. Augustine's Press, 2014).

Servant of God Dolindo Ruotolo

* Image on pg. 279: © Casa Mariana Editrice-Apostolato Stampa. Used with permission.

~ Servant of God Dolindo Ruotolo, *Meditations on the Holy Rosary of Mary,* trans. Giovanna Invitti Ellis (Napoli, Italy, 2006), 36.

~ Ibid., 4.

~ Ibid., 35.

~ Ibid., 5.

~ Ibid., 36.

~ Ibid., 5.

~ Ibid., 41.

~ Ibid., 41.

~ Ibid., 3.

~ Ibid., 4

~ Ibid., 18-19.

~ Ibid., 35.

~ Ibid., 20.

Recommended Reading on the Servant of God Dolindo Ruotolo

~ Servant of God Dolindo Ruotolo, *Meditations on the Holy Rosary of Mary*, trans. Giovanna Invitti Ellis (Napoli, Italy, 2006).

~ Servant of God Dolindo Ruotolo, *A Month with Mary: Daily Meditations for a Profound Reform of Heart in the School of Mary*, trans. Msgr. Arthur B. Calkins (New Bedford, MA: Academy of the Immaculate, 2006).

~ Fr. Donald H. Calloway, MIC, *Rosary Gems: Daily Wisdom on the Holy Rosary* (Stockbridge, MA: Marian Press, 2015).

St. Pio of Pietrelcina

* Image on pg. 284: © Fondazione Voce di Padre Pio – Archivio Fotografico. Used with permission

~ St. Pio of Pietrelcina, as quoted in *Padre Pio: The Wonder Worker*, ed. Francis Mary Kalvelage, FI (New Bedford, MA: Franciscan Friars of the Immaculate, 2009), 67.

~ St. Pio of Pietrelcina, as quoted in Pietro Tartaglia, *The Mysteries of the Rosary and Padre Pio*, second edition (Our Lady of Grace Capuchin Friary: San Giovanni Rotondo, Italy, 1999), 106.

~ Ibid., 10.

~ St. Pio of Pietrelcina, as quoted in *Padre Pio: The Wonder Worker*, 68.

~ St. Pio of Pietrelcina, as quoted in Liz Kelly, *The Rosary: A Path to Prayer* (Chicago, IL: Loyola Press, 2004), 86.

~ St. Pio of Pietrelcina, as quoted in *Padre Pio: The Wonder Worker*, 68.

~ St. Pio of Pietrelcina, as quoted by Most Rev. Paola Carta (Bishop Emeritus of Foggia) in *From the Voice of Padre Pio* (July, 1997). Friary of Our Lady of Grace, San Giovanni Rotondo, Italy.

~ St. Pio of Pietrelcina, as quoted in Gabriel Harty, OP, *The Rosary: The History of my Heart* (Dundalk, Ireland: Dundalgan Press, 2015), 29.

~ St. John Paul II, *Rosarium Virginis Mariae*, 8.

Recommended Reading on St. Pio of Pietrelcina

~ St. Pio of Pietrelcina, as quoted by St. John Paul II in Fr. Robert J. Fox, *First Saturdays for the Triumph of the Immaculate Heart* (Minnesota: Fatima Family Apostolate, 2000).

~ St. Pio of Pietrelcina, *Padre Pio's Words of Hope*, ed. Eileen Dunn Bertanzetti (Huntington, IN: Our Sunday Visitor, Inc., 1999).

~ *Padre Pio: The Wonder Worker*, ed. Francis Mary Kalvelage, FI (New Bedford, MA: Franciscan Friars of the Immaculate, 2009).

St. Josemaría Escrivá

* Image on pg. 288: Courtesy of the Communications Office of Opus Dei. Used with permission.

~ St. Josemaría Escrivá, *Furrow* (New York: Scepter Press, 1986), 265.

~ St. Josemaría Escrivá, *Holy Rosary* (New York, NY: Scepter Press, 2003), 9.

~ St. Josemaría Escrivá, *The Way,* no. 558, p.117, as quoted in Jason Evert, *Purity 365: Daily Reflections on True Love* (Cincinnati, OH: Servant Books, 2009), 105.

~ St. Josemaría Escrivá, *Holy Rosary,* 11.

~ St. Josemaría Escrivá, *Furrow,* 186.

~ Ibid., 186-187.

~ St. Josemaría Escrivá, *Christ is Passing By* (Manila: Sinag-Tala, 1973), 325.

~ St. Josemaría Escrivá, *Friends of God* (New York: Scepter, 1981), 450.

~ St. Josemaría Escrivá, *Holy Rosary,* 12.

~ St. Josemaría Escrivá, *Furrow,* 186.

~ St. Josemaría Escrivá, *Holy Rosary,* 14.

~ St. Josemaría Escrivá, *Friends of God,* 461.

~ St. Josemaría Escrivá, *Holy Rosary,* 15.

Recommended Reading on St. Josemaría Escrivá

~ St. Josemaría Escrivá, *Holy Rosary* (Chicago, IL: Scepter, 1953).

~ St. Josemaría Escrivá, *Christ is Passing By* (Manila: Sinag-Tala, 1973).

~ St. Josemaría Escrivá, *Friends of God* (New York: Scepter Press, 1981).

~ St. Josemaría Escrivá, *The Way: Furrow: The Forge* (New York: Scepter, 2001).

St. Pope John XXIII

* Image on pg. 289: © Universal Images Group North America LLC / DeAgostini / Alamy Stock Photo. Used with permission.

~ St. Pope John XXIII, Letter to Clement Cardinal Micara (September 28, 1960), as quoted in Francis Beauchesne Thornton, *This is the Rosary* (New York: Hawthorn Books, 1961), 10.

~ St. Pope John XXIII, as quoted in Servant of God Patrick Peyton, *All For Her* (Hollywood, CA: Family Theater Productions, 1973), 189.

~ St. Pope John XXIII, as quoted in Jeanne Gosselin Arnold, *A Man of Faith: Father Patrick Peyton, CSC* (Hollywood, CA: Family Theater, Inc., 1983), 133.

~ St. Pope John XXIII, as quoted in Rev. Charles G. Fehrenbach, CSsR, *Mary Day by Day* (New York: Catholic Book Publishing Co., 1987), 148.

~ St. Pope John XXIII, *Grata Recordatio,* Encyclial (September 26, 1959), 2.

~ St. Pope John XXIII, as quoted in Andrew J. Gerakas, *The Rosary and Devotion to Mary* (Boston, MA: St. Paul Books & Media, 1992), 23.

~ St. Pope John XXIII, *"Radio Message for the Coronation of Our Lady of the Rosary of La Coruña, Spain,"* (September 11, 1960). Trans. Ileana E. Salazar, MA.

~ St. Pope John XXIII, as quoted in Msgr. Joseph A. Cirrincione and Thomas A. Nelson, *The Rosary and the Crisis of Faith* (Charlotte, NC: TAN Books, 1986), 32.

~ St. Pope John XXIII, Letter to Clement Cardinal Micara (September 28, 1960), as quoted in Francis Beauchesne Thornton, *This is the Rosary,* 10.

~ Servant of God Patrick Peyton, as quoted in Laetitia Rhatigan, STD, "The Marian Spirituality of the Servant of God Father Patrick Peyton, C.S.C (1902-1992)," in *Marian Studies,* vol. LXIII (2012), 41.

Recommended Reading on St. Pope John XXIII

~ St. Pope John XXIII, *Grata Recordatio,* Encyclical (September 26, 1959).

~ St. Pope John XXIII, "*Radio Message for the Coronation of Our Lady of the Rosary of La Coruña, Spain,*" (September 11, 1960).

~ St. Pope John XXIII, *Letter to Clemente Cardinal Micara* (September 28, 1960), as quoted in Francis Beauchesne Thornton, *This is the Rosary* (New York: Hawthorn Books, 1961), 9-10.

~ St. Pope John XXIII, *Allocution to the First Pilgrimage of the Living Rosary* (May 4, 1963).

Servant of God Patrick Peyton

* Image on pg. 297: Courtesy of Archives, Holy Cross Family Ministries. North Easton, MA. Used with permission.

~ Servant of God Patrick Peyton, in "Mary, the Pope, and the American Apostle of the Family Rosary," by Fr. Willy Raymond, CSC, in *Behold Your Mother: Priests Speak about Mary,* ed. Stephen J. Rossetti (Notre Dame, IN: Ave Maria Press, 2007), 52.

~ Servant of God Patrick Peyton, as quoted in Jeanne Gosselin Arnold, *A Man of Faith: Father Patrick Peyton, CSC* (Hollywood, CA: Family Theater, Inc., 1983), 250.

~ Ibid., 34.

~ Servant of God Patrick Peyton, in "Mary, the Pope, and the American Apostle of the Family Rosary," by Fr. Willy Raymond, CSC, in *Behold Your Mother: Priests Speak about Mary,* 53.

~ Servant of God Patrick Peyton, as quoted in Jeanne Gosselin Arnold, *A Man of Faith: Father Patrick Peyton, CSC,* 250.

~ Ibid., 48.

~ Ibid., 63.

~ Ibid., 250.

~ Ibid., 250.

~ Ibid., 268.

~ Servant of God Patrick Peyton, *All For Her* (Hollywood, CA: Family Theater Productions, 1973), 1.

~ Servant of God Patrick Peyton, *Family Prayer* (New York: Benziger Bros., Inc., 1964), 13.

~ Servant of God Patrick Peyton, as quoted in Jeanne Gosselin Arnold, *A Man of Faith: Father Patrick Peyton, CSC,* 27.

~ Ibid., 295.

~ Servant of God Patrick Peyton, as quoted in Laetitia Rhatigan, STD, "The Marian Spirituality of the Servant of God Father Patrick Peyton, CSC (1902-1992)," 31.

~ Servant of God Patrick Peyton, as quoted in *Rosary* [Revised edition of the special rosary issue of *The Immaculate* magazine, 1970], 40. Originally published in October 1965 (Vol. 16. No. 5).

~ Servant of God Patrick Peyton, *Marian Year: 1987-1988* (Albany, NY: The Family Rosary Inc., 1987), 75.

Recommended Reading on the Servant of God Patrick Peyton

~ Servant of God Patrick Peyton, *All For Her* (Hollywood, CA: Family Theater Productions, 1967).

~ Servant of God Patrick Peyton, *Family Prayer* (New York: Benziger Brothers, Inc., 1964).

~ Servant of God Patrick Peyton, *The Ear of God* (Garden City, NJ: Doubleday & Company, Inc., 1951).

~ Jeanne Gosselin Arnold, *A Man of Faith: Father Patrick Peyton, CSC* (Hollywood, CA: Family Theater, Inc., 1983).

Blessed Pope Paul VI

~ Bl. Pope Paul VI, *Marialis Cultus,* Apostolic Exhortation (February 2, 1974), 44.

~ Ibid., 47.

~ Ibid., 46.

~ Bl. Pope Paul VI, *Recurrens Mensis October,* Encyclical (October 7, 1969).

~ Bl. Pope Paul VI, *Marialis Cultus,* 48.

~ Bl. Pope Paul VI, *Mense Maio,* Encyclical (April 29, 1965), 14.

~ Bl. Pope Paul VI, *Marialis Cultus,* 54.

~ Bl. Pope Paul VI, *Christi Matri,* Encyclical (September 15, 1966), 9.

~ Bl. Pope Paul VI, as quoted in Rev. Charles G. Fehrenbach, CSsR, *Mary Day by Day* (New York: Catholic Book Publishing Co., 1987), 150.

~ Bl. Pope Paul VI, as quoted in St. John Paul II, *Rosarium Virginis Mariae,* 12.

~ Bl. Pope Paul VI, *Christi Matri,* 10.

~ Bl. Pope Paul VI, *Marialis Cultus,* 52.

~ Bl. Pope Paul VI, as quoted in Jeanne Gosselin Arnold, *A Man of Faith: Father Patrick Peyton, CSC* (Hollywood, CA: Family Theater, Inc., 1983), 202.

~ Bl. Pope Paul VI, as quoted in *Rosary* (Revised edition of the special rosary issue of *The Immaculate* magazine, 1970), 10. Originally published in October 1965 (Vol.16. No.5).

Recommended Reading on Bl. Pope Paul VI

~ Bl. Pope Paul VI, *Marialis Cultus,* Apostolic Exhortation (February 2, 1974).

~ Bl. Pope Paul VI, *Mense Maio,* Encyclical (April 29, 1965).

~ Bl. Pope Paul VI, *Christi Matri,* Encyclical (September 15, 1966).

~ Bl. Pope Paul VI, *Recurrens Mensis October,* Apostolic Exhortation (October 7, 1969).

~ Bl. Pope Paul VI, *Allocution to the Children of the Living Rosary* (May 10, 1964).

~ Bl. Pope Paul VI, *General Audience* (October 7, 1964).

Venerable Fulton J. Sheen

~ Ven. Fulton J. Sheen, *The World's First Love: Mary, Mother of God* (San Francisco, CA: Ignatius Press, 1996), 207-208.

~ Ibid., 209.

~ Ibid., 210.

~ Ibid., 211.
~ Ibid., 211.
~ Ibid., 215.
~ Ibid., 209.
~ Ibid., 213-214.
~ Ibid., 210.
~ Ibid., 214-215.
~ Ibid., 213.
~ Ibid., 213.
~ Ibid., 214.
~ Ibid., 208.
~ Ibid., 211.

Recommended Reading on Ven. Fulton J. Sheen

~ Ven. Fulton J. Sheen, *The World's First Love: Mary, Mother of God* (San Francisco, CA: Ignatius Press, 1996).
~ Ven. Fulton J. Sheen, *Three to Get Married* (Princeton, NJ: Scepter Publishers, 1951).
~ Peter J. Howard, *The Woman: The Mystery of Mary as Mediatrix in the Teaching of Fulton J. Sheen* (Phoenix, AZ: Leonine Publishers, 2014).
~ Fr. Donald H. Calloway, MIC, *Mary of Nazareth: The Life of Our Lady in Pictures* (San Francisco, CA: Ignatius Press, 2014).

St. Teresa of Calcutta

~ "Our *Lady's words to St. Teresa of Calcutta*," as quoted in Fr. Joseph Langford, MC, *Mother Teresa: In the Shadow of Our Lady* (Huntington, IN: OSV Press, 2007), 60.
~ St. Teresa of Calcutta, *Heart of Joy* (Ann Arbor, MI: Servant Books, 1987), 19.
~ St. Teresa of Calcutta, as quoted in *Rosary Meditations from Mother Teresa of Calcutta,* ed. V. Lucia (USA: Missionaries of the Blessed Sacrament, 1984).
~ St. Teresa of Calcutta, as quoted in Brian Kolodiejchuk, MC, (ed). *Mother Teresa: Come Be My Light: The Private Writings of the Saint of Calcutta.* (New York: Doubleday, 2007), 141.
~ St. Teresa of Calcutta, *From a Letter to Father Lawrence T. Picachy, S.J., February 13, 1963,* as quoted in Fr. Benedict J. Groeschel, CFR, *The Rosary: Chain of Hope* (San Francisco, CA: Ignatius Press, 2003), 16.
~ St. Teresa of Calcutta, as quoted in Susan Conroy, *Praying in the Presence of Our Lord with Mother Teresa* (Huntington, IN: OSV, Inc., 2005), 70.
~ St. Teresa of Calcutta, as quoted in Matthew Kelly, *Rediscover Catholicism* (USA: Beacon Publishing, 2010), 272.
~ St. Teresa of Calcutta, as quoted in Susan Conroy, *Mother Teresa's Lessons of Love & Secrets of Sanctity* (Huntington, IN: OSV Press, 2003), 129.

Recommended Reading on St. Teresa of Calcutta

~ Fr. Brian Kolodiejchuk, MC, ed. *Mother Teresa: Come Be My Light: The Private Writings of the Saint of Calcutta* (New York: Doubleday, 2007).

~ Fr. Joseph Langford, MC, *Mother Teresa: In the Shadow of Our Lady* (Huntington, IN: OSV Press, 2007).

~ Fr. Donald H. Calloway, MIC, *Rosary Gems: Daily Wisdom on the Holy Rosary* (Stockbridge, MA: Marian Press, 2015).

St. John Paul II

~ St. John Paul II, *Angelus Message* (October 29, 1978)

~ St. John Paul II, *Address in Rome* (October 8, 1980)

~ St. John Paul II, *Rosarium Virginis Mariae,* Apostolic Letter (October 16, 2002), 1.

~ Ibid., 40.

~ Ibid., 1.

~ St. John Paul II, *Address at Fatima (May 13, 1982),* as quoted in *John Paul II's Book of Mary,* ed. Margaret R. Bunson (Huntington, IN: OSV Publishing, 1996), 129.

~ St. John Paul II, *Rosarium Virginis Mariae,* 3.

~ St. John Paul II, *Address in Rome (October 8, 1980),* as quoted in *John Paul II's Book of Mary,* 131-132.

~ St. John Paul II, *Rosarium Virginis Mariae,* 3.

~ Ibid., 4.

~ Ibid., 33.

~ Ibid., 5.

~ St. John Paul II, *Angelus message* (October 1, 1995)

~ St. John Paul II, *Rosarium Virginis Mariae,* 41.

~ Ibid., 41.

~ Ibid., 25.

~ Ibid., 26.

~ Ibid., 38

~ Ibid., 39.

~ St. John Paul II, *Angelus message* (September 30, 2001)

~ St. John Paul II, *In Response to questions about the Third Secret whilst speaking in Fulda, Germany (1980),* as quoted in *Magnificat,* vol. 15, no.8 (October, 2013), 308.

~ St. John Paul II, *Message to the Bishop of Leiria-Fatima* (October 1, 1997)

~ St. John Paul II, *Rosarium Virginis Mariae,* 15.

~ Ibid., 17.

~ St. John Paul II, *Beatification Homily* (January 21, 1995)

~ St. John Paul II, *Message for the 18th World Youth Day* (April 13, 2003)

~ St. John Paul II, *Rosarium Virginis Mariae,* 43.

~ Pope Benedict XVI, *Angelus* (October 1, 2006)

Recommended Reading on St. John Paul II

~ St. John Paul II, *Rosarium Virginis Mariae,* Apostolic Letter (October 16, 2002).

~ St. John Paul II, *Theotokos: Woman, Mother, Disciple (A Catechesis on Mary, Mother of God)* (Boston, MA: Daughters of St. Paul, 2000).

~ St. John Paul II, *Familiaris Consortio,* Apostolic Exhortation (1981).

~ Margaret R. Bunson, ed., *John Paul II's Book of Mary* (Huntington, IN: OSV Publishing, 1996).

~ Fr. Donald H. Calloway, MIC, *Under the Mantle: Marian Thoughts from a 21ˢᵗ Century Priest* (Stockbridge, MA: Marian Press, 2013).

Pope Benedict XVI

* Image on pg. 324: © Stefano Spaziani. Used with permission.

~ Pope Benedict XVI, *Angelus message* (October 7, 2007).

~ Pope Benedict XVI, *Address at Shrine of Our Lady of Fatima* (May 12, 2010).

~ Pope Benedict XVI, *General Audience* (October 8, 2008).

~ Pope Benedict XVI, General Audience (May 1, 2006).

~ Pope Benedict XVI, *Papal Address* (May 3, 2008).

~ Pope Benedict XVI, *Angelus* (October 1, 2006).

~ Pope Benedict XVI, *Angelus message* (October 7, 2012).

~ Pope Benedict XVI, *Homily from Apostolic Journey to Lourdes* (September 14, 2008).

~ Pope Benedict XVI, *Canonization Homily* (October 23, 2005).

~ Pope Benedict XVI, *Papal Address* (June 11, 2011).

~ Pope Benedict XVI, *Angelus message* (October 3, 2010).

~ Pope Benedict XVI, *Homily: Pastoral Visit to the Pontifical Shrine of Pompeii.* (October 19, 2008).

~ Pope Benedict XVI, *General Audience* (October 26, 2005).

~ Pope Benedict XVI, *God and the World: A Conversation with Peter Seewald,* trans. Henry Taylor (San Francisco, CA: Ignatius Press, 2002), 318.

~ Pope Benedict XVI, *General Audience* (February 3, 2010).

Recommended Reading on Pope Benedict XVI

~ Pope Benedict XVI, *Mary* (Spiritual Thoughts Series) (Washington, DC: USCCB, 2008).

~ Pope Benedict XVI, *General Audience* (October 8, 2008).

~ Pope Benedict XVI, *Angelus* (Oct. 1, 2006; Oct. 7, 2008; Oct. 3, 2010; Oct. 7, 2012).

~ Pope Benedict XVI, *Meditation from the Pastoral Visit to Shrine of Pompeii* (October 19, 2008).

Part III:
Praying the Rosary

Why Pray the Rosary?

[1] Pope Leo XIII, *Parta Humano Generi,* Apostolic Letter (September 8, 1901), as quoted in *The Rosary of Our Lady: Translations of the Encyclical and Apostolic Letters of Pope Leo XIII,* ed. William Raymond Lawler, OP (Paterson, NJ: St. Anthony Guild Press, 1944), 195-196.

[2] Pope Leo XIII, *Diuturni Temporis,* Encyclical (September 5, 1898), 3.

[3] St. Louis de Montfort, *The Secret of the Rosary,* 80-81.

[4] Pope Leo XIII, *Supremi Apostolatus Officio,* 7.

[5] Pope Leo XIII, *Laetitiae Sanctae,* Encyclical (September 8, 1893), 3.

[6] St. Louis de Montfort, *The Secret of the Rosary,* 56.

[7] Ven. Fulton J. Sheen, *The World's First Love: Mary, Mother of God* (San Francisco: Ignatius Press, 1996), 208.

[8] Bl. James Alberione, *Mary, Mother and Model: Feasts of Mary,* trans. Hilda Calabro, MA (Boston, MA: Daughters of St. Paul, 1958), 201.

How to Pray the Rosary

[1] St. Louis de Montfort, *God Alone: The Collected Writings of St. Louis de Montfort.* (Bay Shore, NY: Montfort Publications, 1995), 104.

[2] St. Louis de Montfort, *The Secret of the Rosary,* trans. Mary Barbour, TOP (Bay Shore, NY: Montfort Publications, 1988), 93.

[3] Gabriel Harty, OP, *Heaven Sent: My Life Through the Rosary* (Dublin, Ireland: Veritas, 2012), 153.

[4] St. Anthony Mary Claret, *El Colegial Ó Seminarista Teórica y Prácticamente Instruido: Tome I.* (Barcelona, Spain: Librería Religiosa, 1861), 278. Trans. Miss Ileana E. Salazar, MA.

[5] St. Thérèse of Lisieux, as quoted in Romanus Cessario, OP, *Perpetual Angelus: As the Saints Pray the Rosary* (Staten Island, NY: Alba House, 1995), 136.

[6] St. Louis de Montfort, *The Secret of the Rosary,* 91.

[7] Servant of God Dolindo Ruotolo, *Meditations on the Holy Rosary of Mary,* trans. Giovanna Invitti Ellis (Napoli, Italy, 2006), 37.

How to Become a Champion of the Rosary

[1] Pope Benedict XVI, *Meditation from the Pastoral Visit to Shrine of Pompeii* (October 19, 2008).

[2] St. Louis de Montfort, *The Secret of the Rosary,* trans. Mary Barbour, TOP (Bay Shore, NY: Montfort Publications, 1988), 103.

[3] Bl. James Alberione, *Lord, Teach Us to Pray* (Boston, MA: Daughters of St. Paul, 1982), 231.

[4] St. Louis de Montfort, *The Secret of the Rosary,* 28.

The 15 Promises of Our Lady To Those Who Pray the Rosary

[1] Servant of God Patrick Peyton, *The Ear of God* (Garden City, NJ: Doubleday & Company, Inc., 1951), 114-115.

Indulgences of the Rosary

[1] St. Louis de Montfort, *The Secret of the Rosary,* trans. Mary Barbour, TOP (Bay Shore, NY: Montfort Publications, 1988), 86.

[2] *Manual of Indulgences: Norms and Grants.* United States Catholic Conference of Bishops Publishing (December 1, 2006).

Appendix B: Our Lady's words to Blessed Alan de la Roche

[1] "*Our Lady's words to Bl. Alan de la Roche*," as quoted in St. Louis de Montfort, *The Secret of the Rosary*, trans. Mary Barbour, TOP (Bay Shore, NY: Montfort Publications, 1988), 119.

Acknowledgments

* Permission to cite from the following works is gratefully acknowledged:

~ St. Alphonsus Liguori, *The Glories of Mary* (Charlotte, NC: TAN Books, 2012).

~ St. Alphonsus Liguori, *Hail Holy Queen: An Explanation of the Salve Regina*, (Charlotte, NC: TAN Books, 1995).

~ Deacon Andrew J. Gerakas, *The Rosary and Devotion to Mary* (Boston, MA: St. Paul Books & Media, 1992).

~ Ann M. Brown, *Apostle of the Rosary: Blessed Bartolo Longo* (New Hope, KY: New Hope Publications, 2004).

~ St. Anthony Mary Claret, *Autobiography*, ed. Jose Maria Vinas, CMF (Chicago, IL: Claretian Publications, 1976).

~ Rev. Charles G. Fehrenbach, CSsR, *Mary Day by Day* (New York: Catholic Book Publishing Co., 1987).

~ Ven. Fulton J. Sheen, *The World's First Love: Mary, Mother of God* (San Francisco, CA: Ignatius Press, 1996).

~ St. Faustina Kowalska, *Diary: Divine Mercy in My Soul* (Stockbridge, MA: Marian Press, 1987).

~ Hilda Elfleda Brown, *She Shall Crush Thy Head: Selected Writings of St. Maximilian Kolbe* (Phoenix, AZ: Leonine Publishers, 2015).

~ Bl. James Alberione, *Glories and Virtues of Mary*, trans. Hilda Calabro, MA (Boston, MA: Daughters of St. Paul, 1978).

~ Bl. James Alberione, *Lest We Forget* (Boston, MA: Daughters of St. Paul, 1967).

~ Bl. James Alberione, *Lord, Teach Us to Pray* (Boston, MA: Daughters of St. Paul, 1982).

~ Bl. James Alberione, *Mary, Mother and Model: Feasts of Mary*, trans. Hilda Calabro, MA (Boston, MA: Daughters of St. Paul, 1958).

~ Bl. James Alberione, *Mary, Queen of Apostles* (Boston, MA: Daughters of St. Paul, 1976).

~ Bl. James Alberione, *Mary: Hope of the World*, trans. Hilda Calabro, MA (Boston, MA: Daughters of St. Paul, 1981).

~ Jeanne Gosselin Arnold, *A Man of Faith: Father Patrick Peyton, CSC* (Hollywood, CA: Family Theater, Inc., 1983).

~ St. Josemaría Escrivá, *Furrow* (New York: Scepter Press, 1986).

~ St. Josemaría Escrivá, *Holy Rosary* (New York, NY: Scepter Press, 2003).

~ St. Josemaría Escrivá, *Friends of God* (New York: Scepter, 1981).

~ Msgr. Joseph A. Cirrincione and Thomas A. Nelson, *The Rosary and the Crisis of Faith* (Charlotte, NC: TAN Books, 1986).

~ Servant of God Joseph Kentenich, *Talk by Fr. Joseph Kentenich in the Church at*

Ennabeuren, Germany (May 3, 1945). Courtesy of Schoenstatt Sisters, Waukesha, WI.

~ Fr. Juan Echevarria, *The Miracles of St. Anthony Mary Claret,* trans. Sr. Mary Gonzaga (Charlotte, NC: TAN Books, 1992).

~ Juan Maria Lozano, CMF, *Mystic and Man of Action: Saint Anthony Mary Claret,* trans. Joseph Daries, CMF (Chicago, IL: Claretian Publications, 1977).

~ St. Louis de Montfort, *God Alone: The Collected Writings of St. Louis de Montfort* (Bay Shore, NY: Montfort Publications, 1995).

~ St. Louis de Montfort, *Jesus Living in Mary* (Bayshore, NY: Montfort Publications, 1994).

~ St. Louis de Montfort, *The Secret of the Rosary,* trans. Mary Barbour, TOP (Bay Shore, NY: Montfort Publications, 1988).

~ Fr. Robert J. Fox, *2,000 Year Chronology of Mary Through the Ages* (Redfield, SD: Fatima Family Apostolate, 2000).

~ Fr. Robert Fox, *The Intimate Life of Sister Lucia* (USA: Fatima Family Apostolate, 2001).

INDEX

About the Author

Father Donald Calloway, MIC, a convert to Catholicism, is a member of the Congregation of Marian Fathers of the Immaculate Conception. Before his conversion, he was a high school dropout who had been kicked out of a foreign country, institutionalized twice, and thrown in jail multiple times. After his radical conversion, he earned a BA in philosophy and theology from the Franciscan University of Steubenville, MDiv and STB degrees from the Dominican House of Studies in Washington, D.C., and an STL in Mariology from the International Marian Research Institute in Dayton, Ohio.

Father Calloway has written many academic articles and is the editor of two books: *The Immaculate Conception in the Life of the Church* (Marian Press, 2004) and *The Virgin Mary and Theology of the Body* (Marian Press, 2005). He is also the author of the following books: *Purest of All Lilies: The Virgin Mary in the Spirituality of St. Faustina* (Marian Press, 2008); *No Turning Back: A Witness to Mercy* (Marian Press, 2010); *Under the Mantle: Marian Thoughts from a 21st Century Priest* (Marian Press, 2013); *Marian Gems: Daily Wisdom on Our Lady* (Marian Press, 2014); *Mary of Nazareth: The Life of Our Lady in Pictures* (Ignatius Press, 2015); and *Rosary Gems: Daily Wisdom on the Holy Rosary* (Marian Press, 2015).

To learn more about Marian vocations, visit
Marian.org/vocations
or visit
Fr. Calloway's website,
www.fathercalloway.com.

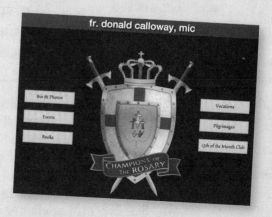

Under the Mantle:
Marian Thoughts from a 21st Century Priest

Father Donald Calloway, MIC, deftly shares his personal insights on topics including the Eucharist, the papacy, the Church, Confession, Divine Mercy, prayer, the Cross, masculinity, and femininity. The Blessed Virgin Mary is the central thread weaving a tapestry throughout with quotes about Our Lady from saints, blesseds, and popes. Paperback. 300 pages.
Y51-UTM   ebook: Y51-EBUTM

Mary of Nazareth:
The Life of Our Lady in Pictures

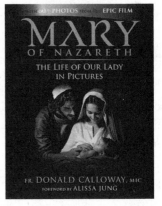

This illustrated companion to the movie *Mary of Nazareth* brings together iconic still photos from the recent film with Scripture passages and wonderful meditations selected by Fr. Donald Calloway, MIC, offering a unique way to deepen your knowledge and love of Our Lady. Perfect for the Marian devotee in your life. Hardcover, 128 pages. Y51-MNBK

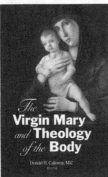

The Virgin Mary and Theology of the Body

In these brilliant essays, prominent experts explore how St. John Paul II's groundbreaking *Theology of the Body* applies to the Blessed Virgin Mary. Edited by Fr. Donald H. Calloway, MIC. Paperback. 285 pages. Y51-TVM

Marian Gems
Daily Wisdom on Our Lady

In *Marian Gems: Daily Wisdom on Our Lady*, Fr. Donald Calloway, MIC, shares gems or quotes on Mary. He includes a gem for each day of the year, drawn from the writings of the popes, saints, blesseds, and venerables. When these gems first appeared in his book *Under the Mantle*, many readers loved them and suggested he publish them in a separate book for daily prayer. He was delighted and took their advice. Paperback. 232 pages. Y51-MGEM

Call 1-800-462-7426 or visit www.fathercalloway.com

No Turning Back:
A Witness to Mercy

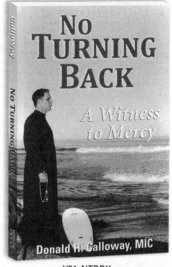

In this bestselling book, Fr. Donald H. Calloway, MIC, shares his own dramatic conversion story, told with a compelling immediacy and honesty that will touch your heart. Popular Catholic author and apologist Peter Kreeft writes: "Read this book and watch the same wave lift Donald Calloway that lifted Paul and Augustine, Francis and Ignatius, from 'incorrigible' and 'impossible' to 'radically converted.' It's the old, old story, and it's irresistibly new every time. Here, it's told with winsome candor and simplicity by an ex-druggie, ex-criminal, surfer-priest." 262 pages, includes color photo section.

Y51-NTBBK
Spanish: Y51-NTBBKS
E-Book: Y51-EBNTB

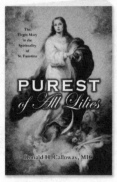

Purest of All Lilies:
The Virgin Mary in the Spirituality of St. Faustina
Paperback. 128 pages.

Y51-POAL

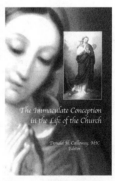

The Immaculate Conception in the Life of the Church
Paperback. 198 pages.

Y51-ICLC

Rosary Gems
Daily Wisdom on the Holy Rosary

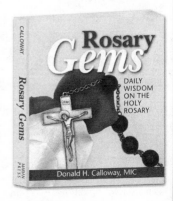

Inspired by his own love for the rosary and the saints, Fr. Donald Calloway, MIC, has gathered and arranged into one book the largest collection of quotes on the rosary to ever appear in print. The quotes have been selected from the writings of popes, saints, blesseds, and the many venerables of the Church. This is the perfect book to help you rediscover the power and wisdom of the holy rosary! Paperback, 245 pages. Y51-RGEM

Call 1-800-462-7426 or visit www.fathercalloway.com

Marian Inspiration from Fr. Calloway

Champions of the Rosary T-Shirt

Show your love of the Rosary with this t-shirt bearing the cover image of Fr. Donald Calloway's new book, *Champions of the Rosary* — the perfect gift for those who want to spread their love for this devotion! T-shirts are black cotton/polyester blend and come in a variety of sizes.

Product Codes for Women's Sizes:
Y51-FCRS (small)
Y51-FCRM (med)
Y51-FCRL (large)
Y51-FCRXL (x-large)
Y51-FCRXXL (xx-large)

Product Codes for Men's Sizes:
Y51-MCRS (small)
Y51-MCRM (med)
Y51-MCRL (large)
Y51-MCRXL (x-large)
Y51-MCRXXL (xx-large)

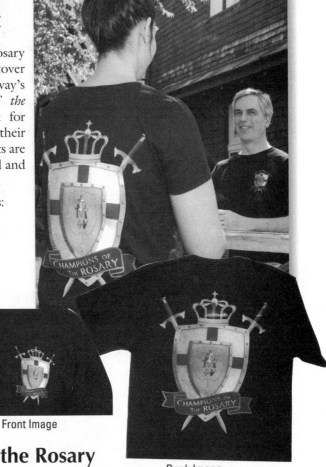

Front Image

Back Image

Champions of the Rosary in Canvas Art

Canvas image with Champions of the Rosary: Y51-RC10GW

Canvas image with names of 26 Champions of the Rosary: Y51-CR10GW

Commissioned by Fr. Donald Calloway, "The 26 Champions of the Rosary" image was painted by artist Maria Madonna Bouza Urbina in 2016. Now available on canvas, the image depicts the Blessed Mother holding the rosary and a sword, surrounded by 26 individuals who made the rosary central to their very being. Father Calloway tells the stories of how they lived out their love for this devotion in his book. Image size is 10"x 18".

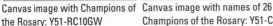

Call 1-800-462-7426 or visit www.fathercalloway.com

Teach others to pray the Rosary.
Leave extra copies at your doctor's office or in the back of your church.

Pray the Rosary Daily
Pamphlet
"Pray the Rosary Daily" is a beautifully illustrated guide to praying the Rosary. Over a million sold every year! "Pray the Rosary Daily" also includes St. John Paul II's reflections on all four sets of mysteries of the Rosary. Y51-PR2

The Holy Rosary
Booklet
You will treasure the meditations and colorful art accompanying every mystery of the Rosary in this booklet. Stephanie Wilcox-Hughes, 64 pages. Y51-THRB

A. **The Hail Mary**
Y51-HML

B. **Practice of the Three Hail Marys and Efficacious Novena**
Y51-POTE

C. **I Am the Lady of the Rosary**
Y51-ILR

D. **Novena to Our Lady of Guadalupe**
Y51-NOLG

E. **A Dream Come True**
Written by Fr. Donald H. Calloway, MIC.
Y51-MOGP

F. **Graces Offered by the Brown Scapular**
Y51-GOBS

G. **The Blue Scapular**
Y51-BLS

Call 1-800-462-7426 or visit ShopMercy.org

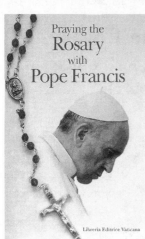

Libreria Editrice Vaticana

Praying the Rosary with Pope Francis

This is an easy-to-carry booklet of meditations by Pope Francis on the 20 mysteries of the Rosary covering the lives of Jesus and Mary. Immerse yourself in the Joyful, Luminous, Sorrowful, and Glorious mysteries of the Rosary with Scripture passages and easy-to-understand reflections from our Holy Father. Each mystery is accompanied by beautiful, full-page color illustrations. This convenient booklet fits into a pocket or purse and makes a perfect gift. Paperback. 40 pages.

Y51-PFPR

Marians of the Immaculate Conception Rosary Gift Sets

This rosary was designed exclusively for the Marian Fathers of the Immaculate Conception. It reflects our mission to spread devotion to Mary Immaculate. Each set comes enclosed in a matching gift box. **Y51-OMR3**

I Thirst

Satisfy Jesus' thirst for souls the way St. Faustina and Mother Teresa did. Their writings show how our prayers and sacrifices make an eternal difference for souls in need. Fr. George W. Kosicki, CSB. 73 pages. **Y51-ITH**

The World's First Love: Mary, Mother of God

With his characteristic eloquence and brilliance, Venerable Fulton J. Sheen presents a moving portrayal of the Blessed Virgin Mary that combines deep spirituality with history, philosophy, and theology. All the major aspects and events of Mary's life are lovingly portrayed in this word portrait that is a never failing source of information, consolation, and inspiration. Sheen also gives profound insights into all the Marian beliefs ranging from the Immaculate Conception to the Assumption. Paperback, 276 pages. Y51-TWFL

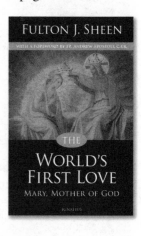

Call 1-800-462-7426 or visit ShopMercy.org

Guadalupe: The Miracle and the Message DVD

The most important event in the evangelization of the New World occurred in December 1531. Over the course of four days, the Virgin Mary appeared to an indigenous convert named Juan Diego. As a result of this encounter and the image miraculously imprinted on Juan Diego's tilma (cloak), nine million Native Americans embraced the Catholic faith. Our Lady of Guadalupe's message of love had replaced the institutionalized violence of the Aztec culture and built a bridge between two worlds.

Guadalupe: The Miracle and the Message traces the history of this transformative event from the 16th century to the present. Featuring interviews with leading theologians (such as Fr. Donald Calloway, MIC), historians, and experts on the scientific inquiries into the miraculous image, this gripping film explores both the inexplicable mysteries behind the image and the continued relevance of the Guadalupe apparition to the modern world. Also includes a special Rosary of Guadalupe prayer booklet. The DVD is in English and Spanish. Narrated in English by Jim Caviezel, and by Plácido Domingo in Spanish. Run time 58 minutes.   Y51-GMMDVD

Padre Pio's Spiritual Direction for Every Day

Saint Padre Pio was celebrated for his understanding of the spiritual life and the struggles we all face. The letters he wrote to his spiritual directors and to the many people who sought his advice are a profound source of direction and encouragement. This collection of 365 reflections, drawn from those letters, offers inspiration for every day of the year. Let Padre Pio share his wisdom with you and become your guide to holiness. Paperback, 286 pages.

Y51-PPSBK

True Devotion To Mary

This book is considered to be one of the greatest books on the Blessed Virgin Mary ever written. By St. Louis Marie Grignion De Montfort, translated by Fr. Frederick Faber. Paperback, 215 pages.

Y51-TDTM

Devotion to Mary

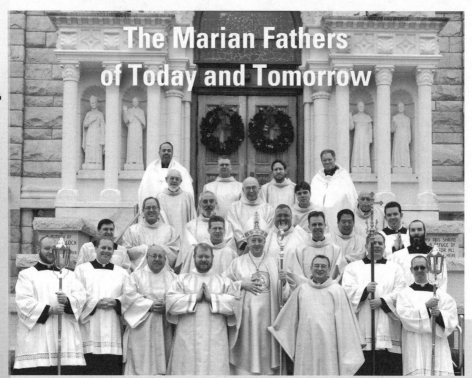

Father Donald Calloway, MIC, Marian Vocation Director, participates in a recurring feature in the Thirteenth of the Month Club newsletter.

I'm honored and delighted to do this for the club, since it's a good way for me to help people come to a better place in their relationship with Our Lady. I want to let people know that by being in the Thirteenth of the Month Club, they're part of the Marian family. They are praying for us [the Marian Fathers of the Immaculate Conception], and we are praying for them.

Thirteenth of the Month Club members are a group of special friends who help support the work of the Marian Fathers of the Immaculate Conception. On the thirteenth of each month, members pray the Rosary for the intentions of the Club. The Marians residing in Fatima offer a special Mass on the thirteenth of the month for members' intentions. All members pledge a monthly gift and receive the Club newsletter published by the Association of Marian Helpers, Stockbridge, MA 01263.

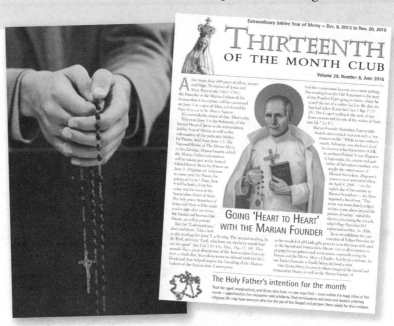

For more information, call: 1-413-298-1382
Online: Marian.org/13th   E-mail: thirteenth@marian.org

Give a
Consoling Gift:
Prayer

Request a Mass
to be offered by the Marian Fathers for your loved one

Marian Helpers

DATE DUE
